DATE DUE

DEMCO 38-296

THE FILMS OF CAROL REED

The Films of Carol Reed

Robert F. Moss

Columbia University Press
New York 1987

Bibliography: p.
Filmography: p.
Includes index.
1. Reed, Carol, 1906–   2. Moving-picture
producers and directors—Great Britain—Biography.
I. Title.
PN1998.A3R3755   1987   791.43'0233'0924 [B]   85–17512
ISBN 0–231–05984–1

To Robert and Joanna

Contents

List of Plates

1. *The Stars Look Down*   David Fenwick (Michael Redgrave) Jenny Sunley (Margaret Lockwood) and Joe Gowlan (Emlyn Williams) dine out in a restaurant in Tynecastle. Metro Goldwyn Mayer. Still by courtesy of Auerbach Film Enterprises Ltd.

2. *The Young Mr Pitt*   William Pitt (Robert Donat) and Eleanor Eden (Phyllis Calvert) share a romantic interlude. 20th Century-Fox. Still by courtesy of 20th Century-Fox.

3. *The Odd Man Out*   Rosie (Fay Compton) comforts wounded Irish Rebel Leader Johnny McQueen (James Mason). Universal Picture Corporation. Still from the film 'Odd Man Out' by courtesy of The Rank Organisation plc and Janus Films.

4. *The Fallen Idol*   Felipe (Bobby Henrey) Julie (Michèle Morgan) and Baines (Ralph Richardson) share tea and a pastry in a small café. 20th Century-Fox. Still by courtesy of THORN EMI Screen Entertainment and Janus Films.

5. *The Third Man*   Holly Martins (Joseph Cotten) roams Vienna in search of an explanation for his friend Harry Lime's mysterious death. 20th Century-Fox. Still by courtesy of THORN EMI Screen Entertainment and Janus Films.

6. *Our Man in Havana*   James Wormold (Alec Guinness) and Captain Segura (Ernie Kovaks) engage in a bizarre and dangerous form of chess. Columbia Pictures Corporation. Still by courtesy of Columbia Pictures Corporation.

7. *Oliver!*   Mayfair in the age of Dickens, abloom with splendid song and dance. Columbia Pictures Corporation. Still by courtesy of Columbia Pictures Corporation.

8. *The Last Warrior*   (Flap USA) Flapping Eagle (Anthony Quinn) cavorts with his girlfriend Dorothy Bluebell (Shelley Winters). Warner Bros. Inc.

1 British Films from 1895 to 1939: A Survey*

If the British cinema has failed to keep up with the headlong pace of its American and continental counterparts, it is not due to being last out of the stalls. The English were off and running at approximately the same time as the rest of the pioneering film cultures: the early to mid-nineteenth century. It was an Englishman, William George Horner, who invented the Zoetrope, a succession of pictures revolving rapidly within a drum, and another Englishman, Eadweard Muybridge, who, in 1877, first photographed a moving object, a galloping horse, in successive shots. In some circles, mostly American, Thomas Edison has been canonized as the progenitor of movies, but actually Robert Friese-Greene, an inventor from Bristol, patented a projector four years ahead of Edison in 1889. (However, Friese-Greene's own enshrinement as the father of kinematography, it should be noted, has been convincingly debunked.) Presumably no one would try to dislodge the Lumière brothers from their status as the organizers of the first commercial presentation of a projected film; the immortal event took place in Paris in December 1895. Yet it should also be recorded that an Englishman, R. W. Paul, made a similar presentation only three months later in London. Still another British innovator was Birt Acres, who invented both a camera and a projector and used them to offer the English public a film of the Oxford and Cambridge boat race of 1895, probably the earliest known record of a news event.

Acres dropped from sight after his initial successes, but Paul's ongoing contributions established him as the fountainhead of his country's cinema. An optician by training, Paul made the leap into film-making through an act of piracy, duplicating the Kinetoscope, an invention Edison had carelessly failed to take out a patent on in Great Britain. Paul then set about creating his own movies, beginning with *Rough Sea at Dover* (1896), thereby making himself the first English film producer. Most of his creations were topical occurrences such as political or sporting events, or 'simple actualities' (crowds promenading, oncoming trains, stormy seas), each occupying no more than a few minutes. Paul also coaxed many music hall performers of the period into appearing in his film strips. In 1896, he began a third and more promising genre when he produced *The Soldier's Courtship*, the first English film to tell a story. *Courtship* was a slapstick comedy with three characters which occupied only about a minute of screen time, but it was well received, and Paul followed it with a series of similarly constructed farces.

Another important source of early film activity was a group of Brighton photographers who decided they were more fascinated by pictures that moved than those that stood still. The principal figures in the 'school of Brighton' were G. A. Smith, Esme Collings and James Williamson. Collings, at one time Friese-Greene's partner, made a modest impact with an output of thirty short subjects in 1896 (each about a minute long). His *chef d'oeuvre* appears to have been derived from *The Broken Melody* (1896), a popular stage melodrama of the period. Collings's accomplishments were soon eclipsed by his neighbour, Williamson, a chemist as well as a photographer, who shot hundreds of films in every current mode: topical subjects (*Coronation*, 1902), actualities (*Bank Holiday at the Dyke*, 1899), comedies (*The Fraudulent Beggars*, (1899). Among his best-known works are *The Big Swallow* (1901), in which a man approaches the camera to take a bite of an unknown object, then retreats; *The Two Naughty Boys* (1898), a comedy series; and *Fire*, an experimental work in five scenes, with some rudimentary editing and frames tinted red to enhance the excitement.

The dominant figure in the Brighton school, however, was Smith. He began his career as a film-maker in 1897, contributing successful seascapes (*Waves and Spray*, 1898) and comedies (*The Miller and the Sweep*, 1897). But it was his ground-breaking use of trick photography, as in *The Corsican Brothers* (1898), that made him a premier director. He may have even preceded the far more celebrated Georges Méliès, the cinematic Merlin who is usually credited with originating such effects as double exposure, reverse action, the dissolve and the fade. Smith can also lay claim to the close-up, which he used as early as 1900 in *Grandma's Reading*

Glass. In that same year, he joined forces with Charles Urban, founder of the Warwick Trading Company, which, by 1903, was one of the largest film companies in England.

Aesthetically speaking, the dominant figure of the infant British film world was Cecil Hepworth. The son of a lantern lecturer, Hepworth was a precocious youth who entered the film business by selling several arc lamps to Paul. Later, he presented Urban with an improved version of Urban's own projector and won himself a job. Gathering his reflections on the new medium into a volume called *Animated Photography: The ABC of the Cinematograph* (1897), he gave the movies their first handbook. When Urban fired him not long afterwards, he self-confidently started his own firm, building an outdoor studio at his home in Walton-on-Thames. His first independent effort was *Express Train in a Railway Cutting* (1899). Like his contemporaries, he worked in all the popular genres and by 1900 his output had topped 100 films a year.

Hepworth explored the boundaries of the medium as restlessly as Smith or Paul, but with an orientation that made technique serve the cause of art rather than vice versa. When he used tracking shots in *John Gilpin's Ride* (1908), they enhanced the drama of a renowned English story and were integral to the tale. In the ambitious *Alice in Wonderland* (1903), an exceptionally lengthy work of sixteen scenes, each sequence dissolves skilfully into the next. Moreover, the pictorial quality is intensified by Hepworth's adherence to the Tenniel drawings. In *The Egg-Laying Man* (1900), he made brief (and perhaps inadvertent) use of the close-up, a novelty at this time. Hepworth, never a man to cloak his achievements in reticence, describes himself as the originator of these techniques in his autobiography, disputing the usual attribution of them to Griffith. Such assertions are hard to verify; what is certain is that Hepworth used these devices with adroitness.

A much heralded page in British film history was written in 1905 when Hepworth directed *Rescued by Rover*, easily the industry's best-known product prior to 1910. A seven-minute melodrama depicting the loss of a baby and the child's subsequent rescue by a collie, this landmark film might be described as the English *Great Train Robbery*. Not only does it tell a coherent narrative, it does so with a fluidity of movement that expanded the vocabulary of the medium. A clever low angle perspective puts the filmgoer at the eye level of the dog, and the expert cutting conveys the events at a headlong pace that is entirely appropriate to what is, in effect, a chase film. The smooth continuity thus achieved is a genuine breakthrough. That audiences appreciated Hepworth's innovations can be seen from the fact that some 395 prints of the picture were sold, though its 'production costs' barely exceeded £7.

Of the many men who helped to incubate their native cinema, Urban was the first to serve in a largely impresarial role; he was a prototype of the man with a cigar, an expansive personality, and a keen sense of what the public wants to see. An American and an employee of Edison's, Urban was sent to England to oversee Edison's interests. For the most part, he made his reputation by distributing the films of other men, among them Williamson and Smith. To this base, he added French and American imports, and within five years he was handling 500 to 600 pictures a year. He also broke new ground with scientific and educational films (they proved unexpectedly popular) and footage of warfare. During the Boer War and the Russo-Japanese War, he presented the work of cameramen like Joseph Rosenthal and Edgar M. Hyman, who thrilled audiences back home with newsreels that offered an immediacy which could not be equalled by even the ablest correspondents. In 1903, Urban left the WTC to found his own company, the Charles Urban Trading Company, leading an exodus of some of the WTC's major talents. One of the defectors was the ever-experimental Smith, whose Kinemacolor process, a two-colour system, was patented by Urban and introduced to the public with enormous success.

On Urban's departure from the WTC, managerial duties were assumed by W. G. Barker, whose experience certainly made him the right man for the job. He had set up the Autoscope Company in 1901, which concentrated on actualities, though it later released a highly compressed version of *Hamlet*, giving audiences their first taste of the photographed stage play, a genre which was soon to be a paramount feature – some would say plague – of British film-making. In 1908, he made history again, without knowing it, when the first of many studios at Ealing went up under his direction.

Another important pioneer was Walter Haggar (identified in some sources as William). Assisted by his wife and his four sons,

Haggar entered the movie business in the 1890s. Like a number of the early film-makers, he was a 'travelling showman', presenting his works at fairs throughout the land. When his creations had sufficient commercial appeal, a distributor could be found to produce prints and circulate them. In 1905, he scored an impressive success with *The Life of Charles Peace*, a biography of the famous nineteenth-century murderer which was remarkable for its length (about twelve minutes) and its realistic atmosphere. The same year, Haggar had his biggest hit with *The Salmon Poachers*, which provided an early example of the willingness of audiences to identify with outlaws. The poachers are the heroes, the police are the villains. This simple chemistry brought the public to the theatres in such large numbers that Haggar was able to sell some 480 prints of the movie.

In this primordial age of film-making, the contemporary trinity of producer, director and distributor did not exist. The first generation of English movie-makers were – indeed, had to be – protean figures who could write, direct, produce and photograph their own work. Often, family members formed the cast because professional actors were too expensive. In Haggar's *Charles Peace*, the film-maker's wife and sons all appeared. In Hepworth's classic *Rescued by Rover*, the dog and the baby both belong to Hepworth, while the nurse is Mrs Hepworth. Early studios were tiny enclosures, usually converted from small storehouses, sheds or greenhouses and refitted with glass roofs and sides to maximize the light. The films themselves, most of them no more than a minute or two, were exhibited most commonly at variety shows, where they were filler interpolated into live acts and presented as scientific curiosities. At the fairgrounds, booths were set up to exhibit the new invention. As movies displayed an independent appeal, small shops and stalls were transformed into cinemas. Their audience consisted primarily of working-class people who could not afford the London theatre or found the fare too highbrow for their taste. At the 'penny gaffs', as the makeshift movie houses were called, customers could enjoy knockabout comedies, newsreels or blood and thunder melodramas for three pence.

During the first decade or so of the cinema, films were more often than not sold outright to exhibitors, who were charged per foot. Soon, however, the inevitable middle man made his appearance and a separate sector of the business arose to rent, or distribute, the film-maker's work, which, in the days of flammable silver nitrate stock, was hard to store. Walturdaw, established in 1897 and destined for a long lineage, was probably the first of the major English film distributors. The earliest magnates of this new entertainment form set up shop on Cecil's Court, but soon the centre of gravity shifted to Wardour Street, which became the generic name for the British film industry.

But even in the energetic dawn of English movie-making, there was a foreign invasion. In 1898, Leon Gaumont, who had established a thriving film business in Paris, opened an office in London in order to distribute his work, and Colonel A. C. Bromhead was appointed director. Gradually Gaumont began to inch its way into film production, mostly newsreels. Within a few years, Pathé, another French giant-to-be, secured a foothold on English soil as well.

By 1910, England had slipped from the forefront in the rapid evolution of the cinema, which was proceeding at the pace of one of its own undercranked dramas. Nothing could better symbolize the shaky foundations on which the industry was built than the fact that its most seminal figure, Paul, left the field in 1910, unable to maintain a stable income. In the years that followed, the same vicissitudes continued to bedevil English moviemakers. While exhibitors thrived, film-makers themselves became a nomadic breed, wandering from studio to studio, never able to enjoy a sustained run of success. Film companies themselves were born and expired with the suddenness of fireflies. Simultaneously, the French and American movie businesses were growing hardier by the day. In 1910, the French, chiefly through Pathé's efforts, distributed between 36 and 40 per cent of the movies in England, and American firms accounted for 28 to 30 per cent. By the end of the First World War, the United States had taken the lead.

This American hegemony was hardly limited to England. By 1920, the US had established what was easily the most popular film culture in the world (though not necessarily the most artistically advanced). The explanations for this remarkable conquest are not hard to discern. Over the previous seventy-five years, Yankee ingenuity and an industrious citizenry had allowed America to outdistance her European rivals in material comfort and technological prowess. Under the circumstances, it wasn't surprising that this mastery of machines extended to cameras, projectors, film stock and the other accoutrements of movie-making. The enterprise and vitality of American merchandising skills were probably an equally important factor. Even more significant, no doubt, was the creative energy Americans were able to pour into their cinema. The artistic institutions of Europe – her legitimate theatres, museums and galleries, her symphonies and opera houses – had evolved to their present stature over several centuries. They were parthenons of cultural achievement with which America could not hope to compete. Other than a few writers and poets of international standing, the United States could claim no artists of major importance before the First World War; in fact, most American painters, composers and playwrights of this period were novices who followed European masters, sometimes slavishly so.

But the cinema was an entirely new form of creative expression, and the energetic Americans who entered it had no reason to be intimidated by models from abroad. Here was a medium in which there weren't any centuries-old traditions against which to be measured and in which a Yankee had the same chance of succeeding as an Englishman or a German. The country's populist heritage probably helped – also its philistinism. Popular entertainment was probably more widely accepted in the US than in Europe and drew a broader range of talent to its ranks. The American cultural establishment, if it could be so described, was small and had correspondingly less influence over its populace than its European counterparts. In addition, the relative innocence and optimism of the American spirit seems to have encouraged a capacity for pleasing, basically escapist creations, celluloid daydreams that captured huge audiences throughout the world.

Such speculations are subject to debate, of course, but there is little dispute about the more concrete discrepancies between American and British cinemas. Between 1912 and 1920, a lone genius, D. W. Griffith, virtually invented the basic language of the medium, and his accomplishment was reflected both in the reviews his movies received and in their box office receipts. In England, Griffith soon had imitators, but never a serious competitor. Similarly, the early British film comedians were hopelessly eclipsed by Charlie Chaplin, an Englishman who found the

American cinema more congenial to his talents. The Little Tramp, with his universally beloved, tragicomic persona, epitomized a crucial ingredient of film-making in the US – the star system. From Florence Lawrence to Rudolph Valentino to Mary Pickford, performers were carefully deified, converted into glittering icons of the popular sensibility, and audiences flocked to worship them at their flickering altars. The result of such shrewd American myth-making was that American distributors could commence soon-to-be-notorious practices like block booking and even blind booking without much resistance. Theatre owners in England were more than happy to commit their screens to American movies for months in advance, sometimes without having seen the merchandise at all, at the expense of the native product.

Though subverted by their own countrymen, British filmmakers did not yield the market without a fight. Meeting the challenge of longer, more elaborately structured narrative work from abroad, Barker filmed *Henry VIII* in 1911, starring Sir Herbert Beerbohm Tree in a recreation of his renowned stage role. As the earliest known two-reeler in England, the film can be said to have inaugurated a trend towards longer pictures. Moreover, it introduced England to the extravagances of the star system – Tree was paid £1000 for a day's work – and was a harbinger of the coming dependency on theatrical and literary adaptations. In a display of entrepreneurial cunning, Barker threatened to burn all prints of the film within six weeks, thus making it the most sought-after movie in the country.

Henry VIII confirmed Barker in his preference for grandiose historical pageantry, and when he teamed with the equally showmanlike G. B. Samuelson in 1913, their initial effort was *Sixty Years a Queen* (1913), a biography of Queen Victoria. This intensely patriotic, lavishly mounted production was a great popular triumph. Barker's style and choice of subject matter make him an obvious forerunner of Herbert Wilcox and Sir Alexander Korda, and, like Korda, he assembled a reliable stock company of performers and technicians and did his modest best to woo the public away from foreign stars with his own homegrown variety (e.g. Blanche Forsythe, Dora de Winton). Perhaps his most ambitious film after *Sixty Years* was *Jane Shore* (1915), an epic clearly inspired by Griffith's *Birth of a Nation*. The derivative, artistically unadventurous nature of the film is typical of Barker's approach, which revealed little understanding of the expressive possibilities of the cinema. For all his energy and resourcefulness, Barker could not survive the financial devastation of the First World War period, which smothered many film companies, and he disappeared from the scene in 1919.

Simultaneously, Barker's more illustrious competitor Hepworth retained his place in the vanguard of the industry. He too expanded his work to two reels and more, though he found plays and novels more congenial sources than historical subjects. Among the adaptations he produced in this period were *Oliver Twist* (1912; four reels), *The Vicar of Wakefield* (1913; three reels), and *David Copperfield* (1913; eight reels). He set much higher standards for himself than Barker, striving for a technical polish that was closer to Hollywood than Wardour Street. Like Barker, he assembled a cadre of co-workers who stayed with him for years, but in contrast to Barker's stable of lacklustre performers, his own little firmament – Alma Taylor, Chrissie White, Stewart Rome – at least captured the hearts of English audiences. Other important colleagues were the actor/director Henry Edwards and the scenarist Blanche MacIntosh. Although proud of his 'all-British' company, Hepworth also hired Larry Trimble, an American director, for a number of his productions.

After an hiatus of several years, during which he acted primarily as a distributor, Hepworth again began to direct in 1914 and moved a step closer to the fount of Griffith's glory when he bypassed literary classics for doleful popular novels of the day, such as Helen Mather's *Comin' Thro' the Rye*, which he produced and directed in 1916. Much of Griffith's best work, after all, derived from such material, tear-stained, moustache-twirling melodramas which aroused his deepest emotional commitment and his most remarkable cinematic innovations. Hepworth was, in this regard, a like-minded soul.

As pioneers like Barker and Hepworth toiled on industriously, new figures were crowding into the field. One of the most far-seeing of these was Dr Ralph Jupp, initially an exhibitor. His chain of ten cinemas, Provincial Cinematograph Theatres (PCT), was one of the earliest theatrical circuits and eventually grew into a major force in the business. In 1913, he expanded into film production, establishing the London Film Company (LFC) and arousing controversy at once through his reliance on the American producer/directors George Loane Tucker and Harold Shaw, as well as other American personnel. The bulk of the actors at LFC, however, were plucked from the West End stage; Henry Ainley, Mary Brough and Sir Cyril Maude were the headliners. With an exceptionally comfortable bankroll of £40 000, LFC could afford to refashion an estate as its studio, Twickenham (opened in 1913), thus becoming one of the initiators of the trend towards mansion-type facilities. The company made an impressive debut with the expensive and skilfully produced *The House of Temperley* (1913), Harold Shaw's adaptation of a Conan Doyle novel. After this encouraging start, though, Dr Jupp tried to play it safe with each new film, relying on tasteful, enervated screen versions of popular fiction (e.g. *The Prisoner of Zenda*, 1914). The public was bored and, in 1915, after a number of flops, production ceased at Twickenham.

In general, the smaller, feistier firms of this period compiled healthier profit and loss sheets than LFC because they assessed the desires of their audiences more precisely. Like most film companies in this era, they had started as renters and then decided to manufacture their own wares. Such was the origin of I. B. Davidson, which began producing pictures just prior to the First World War, with A. E. Colby as the presiding creative force. Often writing, producing and acting in his films, Colby stamped out adaptations of Marie Corelli tearjerkers (*The Treasure of Heaven*, 1916) and two-fisted adventure movies (*Kent, the Fighting Man*, 1916) with equal facility. Among Davidson's immediate competitors was Ideal, which opened its doors as a distributor in 1911 and began making films in 1915. In the first two years of its existence, Fred Paul was its most active director, turning out screen versions of *Lady Windermere's Fan* (1916) and *The Second Mrs Tanqueray* (1916) and overseeing the astonishingly star-encrusted *Masks and Faces* (1919), the cast of which included Johnston Forbes-Robertson, Irene Vanbrugh, Gladys Cooper and Matheson Lang.

Also making a name for itself at this time was British and Colonial (B & C), founded by A. H. Bloomfield and J. B. McDowell in 1909. It too began as a renting establishment, but within a few years it had commenced production and was a leading purveyor of fast-moving action films, the firm's proudest achievement being the 'Lieutenant Daring' series, starring Percy Moran. Although there was not much of distinction about B & C's body of work, it put down its own little milestone by sending a crew to Jamaica to film *Lt Daring and the Dancing Girl* (1913), the first English movie shot in a foreign locale. B & C may also have produced the earliest epic with a 'cast of thousands', the costly *Battle of Waterloo* (1913).

Leap-frogging amongst the foregoing companies, learning his craft as he went, was Maurice Elvey, an alumnus of the stage and a protégé of Harley Granville Barker. At this time, he was just embarking on a career that has record-breaking proportions to it: it began at Motograph, another of the junior firms, with *Maria Marten* (1913), included sojourns at B & C (*Black-Eyed Susan*, 1914), LFC (*When Knights Were Bold*, 1916) and Ideal (*The Man Who Saved the Empire*, 1918) and eventually encompassed hundreds of pictures over a span of forty-four years in the business.

In retrospect, however, the only film-maker of the teens who seems to stand a head taller than his contemporaries is George Pearson, a Scottish school-teacher who left the teaching profession at the age of thirty-seven to enter the film business. Serving a swift apprenticeship with Pathé, Pearson produced his first film, *The Fool* (1913), the same year. It was a cautionary tale about the perils of gambling, starring Godfrey Tearle. Pearson soon left Pathé to go to work for the peripatetic Samuelson, now owner of his own studio, a converted mansion in Isleworth called Worton Hall. There he and Samuelson filmed Conan Doyle's *A Study in Scarlet* (1914), a six-reeler and one of the earliest of Sherlock Holmes's countless screen appearances. A patriotic extravaganza, *The Great European War* (1914), which dealt with events leading up to the First World War, came next. It revealed Pearson's secure command of technique, telling its story in brisk, cinematic language.

But Pearson parted company with Samuelson as swiftly as Barker had, and in 1915 we find him working for Gaumont, where he and the chief of production, Thomas Welsh, struck up a fruitful partnership. Gaumont had remained largely a distributing arm for its parent company, though it had produced many newsreels and a two-reel *Romeo and Juliet* (1908), with Tearle. Now its owner, M. Gaumont, decided that it should commence production of feature films for the English market, and in 1915 he opened a studio at Shepherd's Bush. On his orders, Pearson conceived *Ultus, the Man from the Dead* (1915), a

British permutation of the current French hit, the *Fantômas* series of Louis Feuillade. Like Fantômas, Ultus was an avenger (true to the Latin origin of his name) and a daring escape artist who lived just beyond the reach of the law. His escapades excited audiences everywhere, and his return in several sequels was inevitable: *Ultus and the Grey Lady* (1916), *Ultus and the Secret of Night* (1916), and *Ultus and the Three Button Mystery* (1917).

By the end of the war, Pearson was not only one of the few British film-makers still working, he and Welsh had formed their own company, Welsh–Pearson. Curiously, their two most acclaimed creations both originated as widely popular comic strips, The *Better 'Ole* and *Kiddies in the Ruins* (both 1918). The former, which chronicled the comic misadventures of Cockney soldiers at the front, was an exceptionally big hit, returning some £40 000 in box office receipts on production costs of £5 600. In a stroke, Pearson and Welsh had achieved the highest trophy then available to an English producer: enough money for their own studio, built that same year at Craven Park, Harlesden.

Pearson's work in the teens reveals a man pushing at the narrow boundaries of the medium. He was impatient with the crude mercury vapour lighting used in studios at that time and yet natural lighting, which he used extensively, did not necessarily provide the best results either. He experimented with a fusion of the two. He also tried to accustom the rather convervative British moviegoer to shifts in point of view, then a novelty, and to a fluid editing technique, as opposed to the static camerawork which was far more commonly employed. Another fixture of these primordial days, the painted backdrop, became a *bête noir* to Pearson, who demanded realistically constructed sets. He was extremely exacting of his cast and crew, and they worked long hours for him.

Meanwhile, his one-time partner, Samuelson, maintained his position as one of the preeminent producers of the period. Although Worton Hall spawned occasional two-reel comedies like Reuben Gilmer's *Nursie! Nursie!* (1916), its main output consisted of the same four- to eight-reel adaptations and historical tales which other studios had found safe and at least minimally profitable. Among the major successes were *Milestones*, a family saga taken from a play by Arnold Bennett and Edward Knoblock and directed by Thomas Bentley, and *Hindle Wakes*

(1918), from Stanley Houghton's hoary Lancashire drama, a production directed by the already prolific Elvey.

This era also saw the establishment of the British Board of Film Censors (BBFC), an agency created by the industry itself to forestall government interference. The BBFC was able to require that all films shown in England bear its certificate, and it also devised a rating system ('A' for adult films, 'U' for those suitable for children, etc.) which purported to inform filmgoers about the content of each picture. Unlike the elaborately, even hilariously, detailed Hays Office code in America, the board's only explicit proscriptions fell on nudity and depictions of Christ, though the general ban on works that were 'subversive of public morality' was sufficiently broad to cover a multitude of cinema. The BBFC was to wield enormous power for decades to come, but to blame it for the fecklessness and conformity of so many English movies, as certain commentators have done, seems misguided. The relative paucity of serious discontent among movie-makers suggests that the inherent conservatism of the industry was a far more important factor in preventing bolder examinations of British society from reaching the screen. Most of the directors already subscribed to the values they were expected to uphold, so why should they feel rebellious?

The war years were turbulent for English producers and directors, but, as always, the theatre owners felt few of the jolts and tremors, for they had foreign markets to keep them well supplied. The transition from penny gaffs to full-fledged Bijous, with 200 to 300 seats and some attempt at decor, was well under way by the teens and, as in America, large blocks of theatres came under the control of individual owners. Long after Dr Jupp's career as a producer had faltered, his fleet of cinemas was still in full sail. In 1914 he founded a second chain, Associated Provincial Picture Houses, and later merged the two operations, building an empire of seventy theatres. Strenuously contesting his growing power as an exhibitor were the Electric Theatres, founded in 1908 with five cinemas, and the Albany Ward group, which began in 1912 with twenty-nine. The age of the theatre circuit was born.

Since America had suffered far less grievously than Europe in the war, her film industry had been able to strengthen its grip on the British market place, reducing the French to a subordinate role. Of the first generation of movie-makers, only Hepworth survived after 1918. Indeed, for a time he even flourished. With the advent of lengthier films, he grew dissatisfied with the embalmed look of photographed stage plays and literary classics. He decided it was more sensible to raid the current best-seller lists for film material. Oddly, his one runaway success was a comedy, *Alf's Button* (1920), from W. A. Darlington's novel about a soldier who discovers a magic button on his coat. Enlivened by trick photography, the film seems to have found a receptive mood in a nation emotionally ravaged by four years of sustained carnage on the battlefields of Europe. Unhappily, Hepworth, essentially a sober man, made little attempt to exploit the comic mode further. Instead, he retreated to the lachrymose women's fiction with which he was most comfortable; *Mist in the Valley* (1923) from the novel by Dorin Craig, and his 1923 remake of *Comin' Thro' the Rye* (both adoringly fashioned into vehicles for his favourite star, Alma Taylor). Evidently Hepworth made greater inroads with the big American audience than most of his countrymen, but the accomplishment was fleeting. Within a few years, his stories seemed out of date, as the more venturesome directors of the 1920s discovered – and cultivated – the filmgoer's taste for racy, sophisticated urban dramas dealing with the new postwar generation. His heart belonged to the English countryside, which he photographed with rapt devotion. More important, his approach to his subject matter was pictorial and static; forgetting his seminal contribution to cinematic story-telling in *Rescued by Rover*, he disdained the dynamic cutting techniques then being developed in different film cultures and stubbornly insisted on a monotonous, rigid, virtually pre-edited succession of scenes with dissolves instead of cuts, a relatively immobile camera, and no attempt to juxtapose or contrast shots for dramatic effect. In 1923, he embarked on an ill-advised scheme to raise capital and expand his studios; when it failed, he was forced into bankruptcy.

In fairness to Hepworth, it should be noted that some of his problems arose from the aggressive – many said ruthless – American business practices, which were now so pervasive that English producers had trouble finding space in the exhibitors' schedules, which were densely packed with the work of Fairbanks, Pickford, Chaplin and other idols from across the Atlantic. Hollywood moguls drove a tough bargain, and English theatre owners obviously found it to their advantage to accept these terms. As a consequence, the pulse of the native industry was always weak; even after a hit, revenues were seldom large and never steady. Frequent appeals to the patriotism of the English filmgoer and his neighbourhood theatre owners did little good. The two were in contented complicity with Hollywood.

Other figures from the prewar years staunchly fought the American tides. The resourceful Samuelson was off with a burst of energy in the period just after the war, producing more than twenty-five films by 1920. Fearlessly, he even took the battle directly to the 'enemy' when he descended on Universal Studios in Los Angeles with his staff and made six films there, among them *Love in the Wilderness* and *The Ugly Duckling* (both 1920). Behind the flurry of activity, however, was an eternally under-financed company, which passed through countless financial contortions in its efforts to avoid extinction. In contrast to Hepworth, Samuelson's story preferences were eclectic, a grab bag that included a controversial drama about venereal disease (*Damaged Goods*, 1919), a comedy for a then-popular midget (*Convict 99*, 1919), an old warhorse melodrama or two (*A Royal Divorce*, 1923), and, for prestige, an adaptation of a play by Pinero (*The Magistrate*, 1921). In most of these endeavours, Samuelson revealed a sensibility that was seriously behind the times and a budget that was too threadbare for the effects he sought. After 1923, only his buoyant, propulsive personality kept him going, and by the late 1920s, he had slipped into the back eddies of British movie-making.

Pearson, another veteran, showed better survival instincts than Samuelson and certainly more talent. He provided the creative leadership at Welsh–Pearson, directing most of the firm's features and cowriting a number of them, while Welsh looked after the business affairs. Pearson shared Hepworth's healthy mistrust of material borrowed from the theatre, but he leapt boldly beyond the security of popular novels to original stories written directly for the screen. This allowed him to custom-fit his narrative to the medium. Although he led off the postwar era with *Garryowen* (1920), a race track story based on a novel by Henry de Vere Stacpoole, he was soon at work on one of his own ideas, the bittersweet tale of an elderly musical hall performer. Released later in 1920, *Nothing Else Matters* was chiefly significant for introducing filmgoers to Betty Balfour, whose gift for uninhibited Cockney humour caught the fancy of the British public. Enthusiasm became adoration in *Squibs* (1921), the tale of an impish Piccadilly flower girl in which Pearson cemented the star's reputation; the film shot the actress up to a level of esteem rarely achieved by English film stars at this time. At the prompting of his distributor, William Jury, Pearson invented further adventures for his heroine, and the industry had its most successful series since Pearson's own *Ultus* saga: *Squibs Wins the Calcutta Sweep* (1922), *Squibs, M.P.* (1923), and *Squibs Honeymoon* (1923). The series was notable for its rapport with working-class life, here represented as a universe of sturdy values and simple loyalties, where emotional openness and relaxed, uncorsetted social behaviour are preferable to the well-starched snobberies of polite society. Considering the proletarian social backgrounds of early British movie audiences, it is not surprising that they found the Squibs pictures so endearing. The surprise is that more producers did not attempt to tailor their films to the values of the filmgoers; instead they doggedly clung to the mores and aesthetic principles of the upper stratum from which most of them came.

When Pearson felt that the public's love affair with Squibs was fading, he turned to a project he personally found more challenging, *Reveille* (1924). Also featuring Balfour, the movie dealt with ordinary citizens during and after the war and saturated its story in deeply felt patriotism. In keeping with Pearson's theory that films should strive for a more lifelike quality and should be governed by a theme not a plot, the picture was deliberately loose and episodic in construction. It succeeded both critically and commercially. But Pearson was not so fortunate with his next experiment, *The Little People* (1926), a very auspicious project coauthored with Thorold Dickinson, later an important director himself, and boasting imaginative sets by the youthful Alberto Cavalcanti, destined to be a major force in the British documentary movement. The story is gratifyingly far from the beaten track – an Italian girl who works in a puppet show is lured to London to become an exotic dancer and, after misery and failure, returns home – and the treatment is another illustration of Pearson's theory of elevating theme over plot. Significantly, it was publicized as 'just a bit of life caught by the camera', a case of art well concealed, for it is Pearson's dextrous and unobtrusive editing that provides the film's rhythmic contrast between simple Italian theatre and posh English cabarets, youth and age, cynicism and idealism. But even this rather mild departure from the norm was coldly received by reviewers and audiences alike.

The trials of Welsh–Pearson were certainly not the only hard luck story of the era. Hundreds of producers tried to gain a foothold during the 1920s, but the mortality rate on Wardour Street remained incredibly high. At LFC's Twickenham Studios, production revived in 1919, with many former executives like Harold Shaw at their posts again, but most of the films which emerged were of a prewar quality unacceptable to contemporary filmgoers. The strategy at B & C – studding its productions with American directors and stars – was much more up to date, but under the surface glitter, the work remained negligible, if only because of pinched budgets. Davidson fared better than either LFC or B & C because it preserved one of its time-tested formulas: headlong action stories about sports and crime. One of these pictures, *The Call of the Road* (1920), introduced Victor McLaglen. Even such marketable concoctions wore out their appeal, however, and by 1924, Davidson, along with LFC and B & C, was moribund.

The most determined and best-funded assault on the market place was made by Ideal, which expanded after the war, and Stoll, a new firm created by Sir Oswald Stoll in 1918. Dominated by an assembly-line mentality, each tried to match the productivity of Hollywood without Hollywood's abundant capital. The result was a cascade of mediocre, jerry-built films which found little favour with reviewers and still less with audiences. The favoured sources at Ideal – the novels of Dickens, Eliot, Thackeray and other eminent Victorians – further distanced the films from the sophisticated work then pouring into theatres from overseas, and, occasionally, from the more advanced outposts of the English cinema. If any of the directors at Ideal can be said to have stood out, it would probably be A. V. Bramble, who had a go at *Wuthering Heights* (1920) and Denison Clift, an American who mounted *A Woman of No Importance* (1921) and *The Loves of Mary Queen of Scots* (1923), one of the company's few generally admired efforts. Clift, who later went on to work for C. B. De Mille, and the young Clive Brook, a fairly regular leading man for Ideal, derived personal dividends from an operation that was too creatively feeble to survive beyond the mid-1920s.

Ambitious and determined, Stoll made his enterprise the largest movie company in England. As such, it was able to begin the postwar decade with two massive advantages over most of its competition: a brand new studio (at Cricklewood), with the most modern equipment, and £400 000 in its coffers. Yet these virtues could not compensate for lack of artistic vision in the company's leadership. Enthralled by the presumed cachet of celebrated authors and famous titles, Stoll laid in quite a supply of each in 1920. Among the writers scooped up under the general rubric of the Eminent British Authors Series were H. G. Wells, E. Phillips Oppenheim, Edgar Wallace, Conan Doyle, Marie Corelli and Sax Rohmer. Unfortunately, little thought was given to the appropriateness of the original material to the film medium, while the company's greater fiscal resources were used to guarantee more movies rather than better ones. From 1920 on, adaptation after adaptation lumbered forth from Cricklewood – ponderous, badly lit, poorly designed. Fittingly, much of the work was guided by the indefatigable Elvey, who ensured that no film would rise above a stolid proficiency. Nevertheless, his record at the box office exceeded that of any of Stoll's other directors, and he accounted for almost all of the first-year releases from Cricklewood. His most lucrative effort was *At the Villa Rose* (1920), taken from a novel by A. E. W. Mason. Subsequently, he showed his flair for short films in *The Adventures of Sherlock Holmes* (1921), fifteen two-reelers and, two years later, for feature-length treatments of the classics in *Don Quixote* (1923). Stoll also acquired the services of Harold Shaw, whose *Kipps* (1921), based on the Wells novel, was a popular success and had the added distinction of propelling George K. Arthur to stardom.

Few Stoll films could claim as much, however, and the general run of work at Cricklewood did not bring many customers into the cinemas. In 1923, the company suffered an especially crushing disappointment, the catastrophic reception of A. E. Colby's *The Prodigal Son*, a lumbering behemoth of a movie, some four hours long, from Hall Caine's novel. A smaller firm might have disintegrated immediately, but because of its size, Stoll was able to stagger on for several more years, finally abandoning production in 1928. Its overall losses during its seven-year lifespan were estimated at £200 000.

Another enterprise founded on the American model was Alliance, which appeared in 1919. It began with enormous financial backing and could afford to outfit its studio – Harrow Weald Park Estate – with the latest American-style facilities. To provide itself with a core of experienced professionals, the company absorbed a much smaller firm, British Actors Film Company, which is best remembered today for having given Leslie Howard, C. Aubrey Smith and Adrian Brunel their entrée to movies. In a serious error of judgement, the executives at Alliance then elected to sink £90 000 into a grandiose agenda of pictures before they were able to put a single movie into the theatres. The shareholders grew alarmed at such lavish spending and did not give the company time to produce and distribute enough of its films to recoup the investment. Its first major production, *Carnival* (1921), directed by Harley Knoles and starring the popular Ivor Novello, generated an impressive £43 000 in a few months. But by this time Alliance had already been done in by mutinous investors.

Famous Players was another company which ought to have prospered but didn't. It was a British cousin of the well-known American studio (the forefather of Paramount) and was financed by British capital, staffed by a mixture of English and American employees, and run according to American methods. A studio was erected at Islington and Hugh Ford, an American, directed the inaugural efforts, *The Call of Youth* and *The Great Day* (both 1920). The British-born actor–director Donald Crisp, who had long since proved his mettle in Hollywood, was given three features to direct, including *Beside the Bonnie Briar Bush* (1921). None of this work brought much in the way of honour or box office receipts to the company. George Fitzmaurice's *Three Live Ghosts* (1922), with Anna Q. Nillson, was a modest improvement, but evidently this was not enough. Despite paternalistic visits by both Jessie Lasky and Adolph Zukor to inspect the troops, Famous Players was not able to transplant its American success to English soil, and in 1924 the experiment was scrapped. Today the English branch of Famous Players is chiefly known as the studio through whose portals Alfred Hitchcock, hired to write and design titles, entered the film business in 1920.

Ironically, such ungainly leviathans as Ideal and Stoll were eclipsed by a tiny firm with which they were both associated,

British Instructional. The brainchild of Bruce Woolfe, British Instructional began in 1919 as a tenant at Ideal's Elstree studios and was purchased by Stoll in 1924. In the interim, Woolfe founded his own anomalous and highly idiosyncratic province of movie-making, the non-fiction film. His initial projects were painstaking reconstructions of great military encounters, featuring maps, animation and actual footage. *The Battle of Jutland* (1921), *Armageddon* (1923) – an account of General Allenby's activities in the Middle East – and *Zeebrugge* (1924) were impressive examples of Woolfe's method, and their shrewd, stirring brand of didacticism exhilarated British audiences. (It is said that George V became the first regent to patronize an English movie theatre when he attended a performance of *Zeebrugge*.) Even more unorthodox was the success Woolfe had with his next effort, the *Secrets of Nature* series, and a minor landmark in the British cinema. Inaugurated in 1922, these eight- to ten-minute essays in natural history were welcomed onto the bill with feature films for more than a decade. Drawing on the work of such expert cameramen as Charles Head, Walter Higham and Captain H. A. Gilbert, Woolfe created his own almanac of information on biological and botanical life.

Other important seeds were planted in this period as well. Gaumont became more and more important as a production house after the war, with Bromhead still in command. J. L. V. Leigh's *The First Men in the Moon* (1919) and Will Kellino's *The Fall of a Saint* (1920) were among Gaumont's earliest postwar offerings. In 1922, Colonel Bromhead and his brother R. C. Bromhead acquired complete control of the company from its Parisian founders and quickly expanded the scope of film-making at Shepherd's Bush, creating two separate units, British Screencraft and Westminster. The first supplied competent but pedestrian melodramas, usually with present-day settings, though its biggest hit proved to be a historical drama, *Bonnie Prince Charlie* (1923), with Novello. At Westminster, where Kellino was in charge, comedy was the basic commodity, and Kellino's own farce *The Fortune of Christina M'Nab* (1921) made an especially strong impression. Under one label or another, Gaumont achieved varying degrees of success with George A. Cooper's *The Eleventh Commandment* (1924) and Manning Haynes's *London Love* (1926) and with several films – e.g. Marcel l'Herbier's *Little Devil-May-Care* (1927) – featuring the beloved

Betty Balfour, pirated away from Pearson at no little expense. Bucking the deadly undertow that dragged down so many film houses year after year, Gaumont somehow stayed afloat and established the basis for its later durability in British cinema.

Also destined for a major role in the industry was Herbert Wilcox, who had begun his career as a distributor but switched to production in 1920. After a fairly inauspicious start with *The Breed of the Treshams* (1920), a stagebound screen version of a long-running theatrical success, transcribed almost gesture for gesture, Wilcox and Jack Graham Cutts, an exhibitor, formed a new company, Graham–Wilcox. Their first picture, which Wilcox produced and Cutts directed, was *The Wonderful Story* (1922), which drew enthusiastic notices but left the public cold. Wilcox and Cutts aroused far more popular elation with their second collaboration, *The Flames of Passion* (1922), a story as overheated as its name (it included a noblewoman with a guilty secret and a frenzied courtroom scene) and further accentuated by a full-colour ending. With the American star Mae Marsh in the lead, the film was not only a money-maker in Britain, it even cracked the normally impenetrable American market and was the first of many Wilcox productions that attained this distinction. After a subsequent success with the same creative team and star, *Paddy-the-Next-Best-Thing* (1923), Wilcox decided to direct his own films. His debut was another leaden transcription from the stage, *Chu Chin Chow* (1923), the famed Arabian Nights musical extravaganza, which he co-produced with Erich Pommer at the UFA studios in Germany. His leading lady was an American performer, Betty Blythe. Despite its turgidity, the picture showed a profit and, like so many producers, Wilcox followed the same recipe again, first in *Southern Love* (1924), a florid gypsy romance and then in *Decameron Nights* (1924), a distillation of one of Boccaccio's tales. Lionel Barrymore and Werner Krauss headed the large, formidable cast of *Decameron*, another co-production with Pommer, and the film hoisted Wilcox's reputation to a cloudy pinnacle. By now, he thought only on the grandest of scales, and, after allying himself with a new partner, A. E. Bundy, he brought out a massive film version of *The Only Way* (1925), Sir John Martin Harvey's stage adaptation of Dickens's *A Tale of Two Cities*, which was first performed in 1899. Again it was a 'super-production', the kind of mummified costume spectacle that had become Wilcox's stock in trade, but the public seems to have accepted it as a solemn cultural artefact, and it returned over £50 000 on production costs of £24 000.

Also ascending the greased pole of the British film industry in this era was Michael Balcon who, along with Victor Saville, entered the film rental business in 1920. By 1923 they had affiliated with John Freedman, and their firm had metamorphosed into Balcon–Saville–Freedman, a production company under the financial wing of C. M. Woolf and housed in the former Famous Players studio at Islington. Joined by Cutts, after his break with Wilcox, the company made *Woman to Woman* (1923), with Clive Brook and Betty Compson, imported from the US at the grandiose salary of £1000 a week. The story, filmed with considerable care, was a sentimental romance about an amnesiac First World War veteran which anticipated *Random Harvest* in some respects. It left audiences tearfully elated (and also helped make Brook a star). The Balcon–Saville–Cutts collaboration was not so fortunate with its next two releases, *The White Shadow* (1924) and *The Prude's Fall* (1924), both of which were rather haphazardly made and which were ignored by English filmgoers. Woolf withdrew his support, Saville departed, and Balcon and Cutts were compelled to reestablish themselves under a new aegis. Their new company was soon to become one of the very few royal families of the industry, Gainsborough. It got off to a soaring start with Cutts's *The Passionate Adventure* (1924), which costarred the American actress Alice Joyce and two of England's finest young silent screen stars, Brook and McLaglen. The tale of a well-bred young man who roams London in the guise of a tramp as a respite from an unhappy marriage was not very probable, but audiences embraced it rapturously.

In 1925, Cutts, whose sleek romantic dramas had dazzled the reviewers and the public alike, enjoyed his greatest triumph with *The Rat*, a steamy love triangle in which two women (Mae Marsh and Isabel Jeans) fought tigerishly for the attentions of a Parisian apache (Novello). This, like Cutts's other work, revealed an artful, increasingly assured hand; his mobile camerawork, sense of pacing and expert use of detail brought flair, almost distinction, to the pulpy subject-matter he worked with. He struck gold again with *Sea Urchin* (1926), which allowed Balfour to caper saucily through another gamine role. Next came the *The Triumph of the Rat* (1926), an encore for the director and his star which made Cutts's reputation glow still brighter. He was a prima donna, however, and the startling rise of his assistant, none other than Hitchcock himself, afflicted him with jealousy: he left Gaumont not long after *Triumph of the Rat*.

Still another figure of note in the 1920s was Adrian Brunel. An alumnus of the British Actors Film Company, he joined Leslie Howard in a brave experiment after British Actors was absorbed by Alliance. The two created Minerva Films, a spirited enterprise dedicated to distinctive English comedies and with a most promising board of directors: Howard, Brunel, C. Aubrey Smith and A. A. Milne. Minerva's abundance of talent was not, however, matched by an abundance of funds, and the studio could not afford anything longer than two reels, which imposed a ceiling on possible profits. Brunel drifted around the industry for several years, and it was not until 1923 that he found backing for *The Man Without Desire*, an intriguing romantic melodrama which benefitted from German and Venetian locales and the presence of Novello in the lead. The movie was not an overwhelming success, but Brunel's reputation was sufficiently enhanced for him to go on to several other features, among them *Lovers in Araby* (1924). He had not forsaken the comic muse either and turned out a number of humorous shorts – *So This Is Jolly-good, Cut It Out, Battling Bruisers*, etc. – all commissioned by Woolf and Balcon and made in 1925.

The vicissitudes of Brunel's career were all too representative of his peers. Even the most gifted of British film-makers seemed to have been unable to gain a solid footing in an industry characterized by eternally shifting sands. The elusiveness of that much sought after goal, the transatlantic success, accounted for much of the instability in the English film world. In 1922, 420 British features were peddled in the US, and only six found buyers. Production began to fall off sharply in the mid-1920s, as many companies disintegrated. Exact figures are impossible to obtain, but it seems unlikely that there were more than forty to fifty films being produced and distributed in 1926. Whereas in 1920, about 16 per cent of all pictures released in England were of native origin, six years later the percentage had dropped to 5 per cent; the overwhelming majority of the rest were American. For years, Hollywood had been denounced as the scourge of English movie-making, a den of unfair business practices and corporate ruthlessness. Yet it was English exhibitors, following the lead of their customers, who made American movies the prized commodities they were. Nevertheless, the cry for protectionism, which had been heard for a number of years, grew louder, and at last a reluctant Parliament took action in November 1927, passing the Cinematographic Act of 1927. Aimed at fostering the growth of a desperately stunted industry, this legislation set a timetable for gradually enlarging the share of screen time exhibitors devoted to English movies: 5 per cent the first year, 7½ per cent by 1929, and so on with an ultimate goal of 20 per cent by 1935, when the act expired.

In the beginning, the effect of the act appeared to be just exactly what had been intended, an enormous shot of adrenalin to a sinking patient. In fact, the medicine began to function even before it was officially administered. The knowledge that this remedy was on the way stimulated an infusion of energy and capital. In most cases, it was too late to save veteran companies like Pearson's and hopelessly retrogade firms like Stoll's, but the younger, more vigorous organizations – Gainsborough and Wilcox–Graham, for instance – profited significantly. Almost overnight the image of a much-tarnished industry took on a bright new sheen, and underwriters were soon busy offering public issues for hopeful new companies or old ones which wanted to expand. Firms like British Lion, British Screen Classics and Whitehall were set up through public subscription; shrewdly promoted when they were in their pinkest, most promising state, these infant enterprises attracted a queue of eager investors.

A graphic example of the impact of the quota on an established house was the massive reorganization of Gaumont, undertaken specifically in order to be able to take advantage of the coming increase in the demand for English pictures. The studio at Shepherd's Bush was modernized, several powerful financiers – C. M. Woolf, Isidore and Mark Ostrer – moved in, replacing the Bromheads, and Gaumont was rechristened Gaumont–British. Moreover, the consortium included Woolf's thriving rental business and his complex of theatres. In 1928, it added the PCT circuit and also purchased a substantial part of Gainsborough, which became Gainsborough Ltd. A three-tiered system of production, distribution and exhibition was thus unveiled, one of the first in England, and with such a vastly more efficient structure that the company was able to acquire a fiscal base of £2 500 000. One of the major beneficiaries of these developments

was Balcon, who was named head of production for both Gaumont–British and Gainsborough.

Suddenly jobs were plentiful. From directors to clapboard
operators, every position needed to be filled many times over,
and film companies swept up new employees like a vacuum
cleaner, indiscriminately employing all the native talent available
and also recruiting extensively from abroad. The more enterprising moguls also looked to other nations – especially Germany
– for cofinancing, coproduction and codistribution arrangements. This explosion of activity left the industry with a bulging
stockpile of new releases; in the waning months of 1927, some
160 films were in preparation or ready for distribution.

Yet while English producers rushed off ecstatically in all
directions, as if in search of Eldorado, the quota act soon began
to manifest deleterious side effects. Much of the film-making it
stimulated was careless and slapdash, the consequence being an
increase in the sort of feeble entertainment which exhibitors had
been turning their backs on for years. Now the quota comman-
deered space for these works in theatre schedules and put them
on display before a virtually conscript audience, one which was
forced to endure unwanted domestic fare along with the Hollywood variety it craved. Worse still, the American studios showed
that there was no market they would be willingly fenced out of.
Within a year of the quota, several American distributors were
handling English movies they would have shunned before, and
in 1929 there was an even darker omen: Warner Brothers began
to produce its own quota films through a British satellite.

No sooner was the quota system pumping its questionable
transfusions into the veins of the industry than another calamity
struck – the invention of sound pictures. Again English producers waffled and temporized while other film cultures made a
swifter transition to the new medium. In every country, of
course, there were scoffing, disbelieving voices decrying talkies
as 'just a fad', but in England these voices appear to have been
more pervasive and deafening. The pace of change need not have
been so glacial, for the same sound devices that had been under
experiment in other countries for several years had been tested in
Britain. As in the US, a struggle ensued between two alternative
techniques – sound-on-disc and sound-on-film. Dr Lee DeFor-
est, credited with the first workable sound-on-film system, Pho-

nofilm, registered his invention in Britain in 1923, and a public demonstration was held almost immediately. In 1926, the feasibility of sound was further established by such well-known directors as Thomas Bentley and G. A. Cooper in filmed comedy sketches, a Shakespearean scene and a reading by the Sitwells. Vitaphone, a sound-on-disc approach, appeared at approximately the same time, and since at this early stage, its auditory reproduction was superior to Phonofilm, Warners used it for *The Jazz Singer*. Yet the English were not far behind here either. Gaumont had its own variant, British Acoustic (patented in 1926), which put the sound on separate film strips and required a separate projector. This too was presented to the world; a public show in 1928 included Brunel's *In a Monastery*, another short.

These, then, were two of a number of systems being studied by British firms at the time, but inertia proved far greater in England than in America. Exhibitors matched or exceeded the producers in regressive thinking, and most theatres were not equipped with the new sound apparatus until the late 1920s. In 1929, American movies had become 'all-talking', while half the British features still hadn't spoken a word, and, commercially, many plummeted disastrously into the unbridged gap between the old and the new. Even such lively deviations from the norm as Walter Summers's *Bolibar* (1928), a drama about the Spanish campaign of the Napoleonic Wars, and Summers's *The Lost Patrol* (1929), a surprisingly realistic adventure story that would become a lesser classic in the American sound version a few years later, awakened scant interest in filmgoers.

A post mortem on the rest of Pearson's career is sadly informative in this context. With the chilly response to *The Little People*, the conservative elements in Pearson's company were confirmed in their mistrust of fresh thinking and, incredibly, this most prescient of English directors began to lose ground in his own firm. Two medium-range successes, *Huntingtower* (1927) and *Auld Lang Syne* (1929), both showcases for Sir Harry Lauder, did fairly well, but the antiquated work of other directors sponsored by Welsh–Pearson – e.g. Fred Paul's *The Broken Melody* and T. Hayes Hunter's *The Silver King* (both 1929) – brought the house to the brink of collapse. No one listened to Pearson when he argued passionately that the studio should adapt immediately to the production of sound films. Silents were still being made at

Welsh–Pearson well into the late 1920s, which left plenty of red ink on the books once this older product met head on with the new talking movies. Pearson had one last hit, the film version of R. C. Sherriff's renowned war drama, *Journey's End* (1930), but this was made in Hollywood, a coproduction with Gaumont, and Pearson was the producer, not the director. For the remaining twenty years of his professional life, he was relegated to a secondary role in the industry – not exactly a prophet without honour but certainly a prophet without opportunities. In the 1930s, he was relegated to quota films, and from 1937 until his retirement, he made documentaries for the government.

Nevertheless, the industry had its hours of tangible success – sometimes glory – just before and after the quota years and the advent of sound. In the mid-1920s, having made a considerable contribution to Stoll, Elvey moved on to another house, Astra, where he directed *The Flag Lieutenant* (1926), an extravagant, larger-than-life military adventure starring Henry Edwards, and scored one of the genuine smashes of the period. (As with so much of Elvey's work, the source was a prewar play.) Enhanced by well-executed battle scenes and a properly dashing performance by Edwards, the film achieved a direct hit on the box office, grossing £50 000, which was two or three times the amount most British films could expect at this time. His stature greatly augmented, Elvey was soon enthroned as the premier director at Gaumont. With Saville as his producer, he turned out a string of smoothly manufactured features, including two smash hits, *Mademoiselle from Armentiers* (1926), a by-product of the American classic *The Big Parade* (1925), and *Hindle Wakes* (1927), a remake of his own 1918 work. After *Hindle* came *Roses of Picardy*, *The Glad Eye* and *The Flight Commander* (all 1927), and though none was as profitable as *Hindle* or *The Flag Lieutenant*, the returns on each were more than sufficient to sustain Elvey's status as a director whose creative instincts were remarkably well synchronized with those of the common man and who knew how to transfer novels and plays to the screen gracefully. Still, to sophisticated eyes these were prosaic efforts, and the notices were frequently critical, sometimes scornful.

In a more quirky, inventive, individualistic vein, Cutts and Brunel marched on through the end of the decade. It is no accident that both men did much of their best work at Gainsborough, under the wise tutelage of Balcon. Given an opportunity to broaden his range, Brunel switched from comedy to drama, delivering *Blighty* (1927), a war film from an original scenario by Eliot Stannard which fused actual clips from the front with artificial-looking studio settings in a very odd amalgam, yet still managed to thrill a large sector of the public. The following year, Brunel had his closest encounter with permanent glory, directing three productions for Gaumont: *The Constant Nymph*, from the popular novel and stage work by Margaret Kennedy (the play coauthored by Basil Dean); *The Vortex*, a sanitized version of Noel Coward's controversial play; and *A Light Woman*, an original story by – of all people – Brunel's mother. Of the three, only *The Constant Nymph*, which starred Novello in the oft-told tale of a composer tormented by an ill-starred love, had wide appeal. The common assessment of the *The Vortex* was that Coward's dialogue did not survive the transition to silent film titles and of *A Light Woman* that Mrs Brunel's story and characters were irredeemably colourless. It was not long before Brunel had slipped into the category of directors whose promise had never been fulfilled, and the remainder of his career was devoted to quota work.

During the same brief, tumultuous transition period, Cutts's prestige reached its apex. In 1927, he travelled to Germany to direct *The Queen Was in the Parlor* (from the Noel Coward play), another well-received effort, then returned to England for *Confetti* (1927), a lavish drama set in Nice for First National-Pathé, with Jack Buchanan in the lead. The latter film's success was considerable and when Cutts rejoined his former associates at Gainsborough in 1929, there was every reason to be optimistic about the outcome. Disappointing these expectations, however, he tried further to exploit a worked-out vein with *The Return of the Rat* (1929), and as the sound era took hold, his muse seemed to desert him. He continued to direct for a decade or more, as if by reflex, and of the banal, uninspired results not even the titles turn up much in standard histories of the period.

A far greater talent than either Brunel or Cutts surfaced at Gainsborough during the mid-1920s; ironically, he came with the studio. Employed at Islington when it belonged to Famous Players, Hitchcock stayed on after Balcon took over in 1924 and soon acquired a mastery of practically every job on the lot. In 1926, he was entrusted with his first directorial assignment, *The Pleasure Garden*, an odd tale of passion in the Far East which was shot at the Emelka studios in Munich. It was a mundane work, but the severe Germanic lighting, stylized sets and gliding camera movements he learned in Germany were to leave their stamp on his movies for the rest of his career. After the inconsequential *The Mountain Eagle* (1926) he made his first major film, *The Lodger* (1926), a rendering of the Jack the Ripper story from a novel by Mrs Belloc Lowndes, featuring Novello, by now the leading screen idol in Britain. Here Hitchcock's affinity for the thriller was immediately apparent. Hitchcock archeologists have a field day digging out primeval examples of his mature motifs and devices. The hero, an enigmatic figure who emerges from the fog, is wrongfully suspected of a number of brutal murders (each of the victims is a lovely young blonde) and is almost lynched by an enraged mob. Like so many Hitchcock protagonists, his freedom is curtailed by handcuffs. Rather dishonestly, the plot is strewn with red herrings that suggest Novello's guilt, but there are also a number of fine visual strokes: cats jumping out of dustbins, a hand on a stair, a cleverly angled shot of Novello pacing in his room, a gloomy stairwell in which light and shadow war in stark Teutonic style.

Hitchcock did not, however, ascend to his destined greatness in anything like the unbroken trajectory we might expect. His experience provides yet another illustration of one of the intrinsic limitations of the British film industry, its inability to follow up a success, to maintain a continuity of achievement. Even under so sensitive a nurturer of talent as Balcon, Hitchcock was handed assignments that were too conventional for him, too devoid of the more sensational material on which his imagination thrived. Instead of mystery and intrigue, he was asked to deal with psychological and social deterioration (*Downhill*, 1927) and brittle drawing-room comedy (*Easy Virtue* 1927), neither of which showed him to best advantage.

During these same years, the far less gifted Wilcox was displaying a far more acute sense of his own aptitudes. Merging showmanship and business acumen, Wilcox hired Dorothy Gish at £1000 a week to play the lead in *Nell Gwyn* (1926), another handsome period piece swathed in sumptuous sets and costumes. He then sold distribution rights to the completed film, which had cost him £14 000, to British National, a new company set up with American backing, for £27 000. In England, virtually everyone seems to have been charmed by Gish's sprightly performance and Wilcox's narrative command, and the film was even accorded the honour of an American release. The director and star teamed up again in *London* (1926), the story of a poor girl's struggles in Limehouse, and *Madame Pompadour* (1927), with Gish as the royal favourite once more. Both movies appeared under the aegis of British International Pictures, which absorbed British National early in 1927. Expanding his scope still further, Wilcox created British and Dominion, with £55 000 in capital and, riding the giddy wave of quota euphoria for all it was worth, he went public the next year, acquiring £500 000 in support. Almost immediately, he justified his investors' faith with *Dawn* (1928), a restrained account of the life and death of Nurse Edith Cavell; it owed much to Sybil Thorndike's stunning performance in the lead. German protests made the film controversial, and Wilcox harvested a maximum of publicity value from the situation.

At British Instructional, a most unlikely name took its place on the roster, Anthony Asquith. As startled as the country was to see this offspring of the former prime minister, Sir Herbert Asquith, enter the movie business, it was even more surprised that he went on to make such an astounding success of it. No pampered scion, Asquith had made an energetic and far-flung study of film-making techniques and was steeped in the most *au courant* German, Russian and French theories. At twenty-six, he showed what he had learned with *Shooting Stars* (1928), a humorously ironic tale of life in a movie studio. One of the most celebrated debuts in English movie history, it was all the more remarkable for being based on Asquith's own screenplay. On his next assignment, *Underground* (1928), he felt venturesome enough to experiment with German lighting techniques and other continental touches. These methods were not applied to a credible story, unfortunately, and neither critics nor moviegoers were receptive to the film. After this setback, Asquith pulled in his horns temporarily, retreating to a more conservative vehicle, *The Runaway Princess* (1929), a German coproduction about the romantic dilemmas of rebellious young nobles. More successful than *Underground*, it nevertheless failed to confirm Asquith's status as a genius-in-the-making. He did better with *A Cottage on Dartmoor* (1929), a story of unrequited love and tragedy in the English countryside. Demonstrating a far deeper rapport with his material and his locale than in his two prior efforts, Asquith was able to suffuse the film with a deeply felt appreciation of rural life which redeemed a rather maudlin plot. *Dartmoor*, which contains a smattering of dialogue, was regarded as British Instructional's first talkie.

Another promethean figure stepped into the history of British cinema in 1927 when John Maxwell, a successful renter and theatre owner from Scotland, set up British International Pictures (BIP), taking over British National and setting up production facilities at Elstree. Through a number of acquisitions, including the absorption of several theatre chains, Maxwell was able to create distribution and exhibition outlets for himself, and thus lay down an unusually strong foundation for his company. As a producer, unhappily, he was closer to Stoll than Balcon or even Wilcox. The chief coordinates of his professional life seem to have been scale and volume of production, and with the vast financial resources he attracted through the public issue he offered, he was able to build the kind of factory system he wanted.

Like other British producers who could afford it, Maxwell launched a global talent search. His sprawling roster included German cameramen (Werner Brandes), American directors (Harry Lachman), Swedish leading men (Lars Hanson), and Eastern European actresses (the Czech Anny Ondra, the Hungarian Maria Corda). He also siphoned off all the talent he could from other English films. On a given project, the director might be a veteran like Thomas Bentley or Norman Walker, the cameraman an old hand such as John Cox, and the players renowned figures of the calibre of Jack Buchanan, Lillian Hall-Davis or the unfading Betty Balfour. Top-heavy with foreign contributors, even the most indigenous of Maxwell's productions had an international flavour, and critics searched in vain for a definably English character. The stories were largely escapist, slapstick comedies, mild dramas or innocuous romances, usually featuring a posh social ambiance; the leading men were cosmopolitan gents, smartly tuxedoed, and the women were chic, well-bred ladies of leisure in clinging gowns. In many cases, the titles say almost as much as a plot summary would: *A Little Bit of Fluff*, *Show Life*, *Weekend Wives*, and so forth. These were all released in 1928, a year of remarkable fecundity for BIP.

Yet few of the company's titles are memorable as anything more than historical curiosities or footnotes in somebody's career. One of the BIP standbys was the American comic Monty

Banks, who trained under Mack Sennett and appeared in a number of silent comedies for Warners. Emigrating to England when he was unable to adapt to talking pictures, he acted in or directed over forty British films prior to the Second World War. At BIP, he was seen in the disastrous disaster movie *Atlantic* (1929) and directed the long-forgotten *Cocktails* (1928). Saville, who made the leap from producing to directing at Gaumont with *The Arcadians* (1927), joined Maxwell the following year and directed *Tesha* (1928) and *Kitty* (1929), two maudlin romances, the former featuring Maria Corda, Alexander Korda's wife.

Maxwell got better results with foreign luminaries such as E. A. Dupont, whom he coaxed to England to make *Piccadilly* (1929). But even with such an unimpeachably English name and a story by no less native a literary giant than Arnold Bennett, the personality of the film was a blend of Oriental and Teutonic influences. A hothouse tale of seething passion set in the Limehouse district, it featured Anna May Wong as a Chinese dancer (and passion flower) and was most noteworthy for its brooding atmosphere, sharp contrasts of luxury and squalour, dramatic lighting and nimble camerawork.

From the contemporary vantage point, BIP seems less important for its non-stop ephemera and its arty continental work than for having provided a further crucible in the maturation of Hitchcock, who left Balcon after *Easy Virtue* for a lucrative contract with Maxwell. Dogged by the same absence of creative choice at Elstree, he found himself put to work on uncongenial projects such as *The Ring* (1928), a boxing story. Although Hitchcock coauthored the scenario and showed a flair for realistic detail in the movie's early sequences, it is unlikely that this mechanically plotted melodrama would have any place at all in film history were it not for its director's subsequent accomplishments. It was not to the public's liking, nor was *Champagne* (1928), an attempt to convert Balfour into a flapper, or *The Manxman* (1929), a static version of Hall Caine's novel.

These drab offerings were soon forgotten, however, in the wake of Hitchcock's next film, *Blackmail* (1929), which is generally regarded as having inaugurated the all-talking movie in England. First filmed as a silent work and later reshot with sound, it is one of the great landmarks of the British cinema. Based on a novel by Charles Bennett, it is a thriller about a girl who stabs a would-be rapist to death in self-defence and is blackmailed by an unscrupulous neighbour. The cast was headed by Anny Ondra (whose voice had to be dubbed by Joan Barry), Donald Calthrop and Cyril Ritchard. Despite sequences that seem stagy today, the movie is unmistakably the work of a masterful cinematic mind. Not only did Hitchcock create the industry's first talkie, he demonstrated, at the inception, how inventively sound could be used. Externalizing the heroine's morbid, terrorized state, he makes her (and the moviegoer) perceive the harmless clang of the doorbell as a deathly toll and isolate the word 'knife' in the otherwise barely audible babble of a minor character. His sense of pacing and rhythm, while far from flawless, are put in the service of adroit story construction, and a number of Hitchcockian traits are seen here in nascent form, among them the torment of a blonde heroine, the investing of simple objects with dire significance (e.g. the girl's glove, discovered near the body), the love of grandiose climaxes (the final chase through the British Museum, with its splendid trick photography).

The remarkable finesse with which Hitchcock used sound in *Blackmail* contrasted painfully with the fumbling efforts at speech in other British films of the period. The hybrid quality of *Dartmoor*, with its odd, jarring patch of sound in an otherwise wordless context, was all too typical of the technically backward work that English production houses were turning out. Hesitantly, timorously, they tested the waters of the new phenomenon, while American, German and French producers had already waded in waist-deep. As late as 1929, when the average Hollywood picture was being unabashedly marketed as 'all-talking', only a few English films could even boast 'synchronized sound', which merely meant that a reel or so of dialogue had been grafted onto a basically silent movie. Such was the case with Pearson's *Auld Lang Syne*, whose soundless story had been embellished by six Lauder songs, painstakingly recorded on RCA discs. Sound was not heard in a Gainsborough movie until the Anglo-French *The Wrecker* (1928), directed by Geza von Bolvary, which included only sound effects, and there was no talking until Cutts's *The Return of the Rat*, reedited with some dialogue after its initial release as a silent film. In the same year, at Gaumont–British, Elvey had the distinction of directing the first talkie, *High Treason*, a prophetic view of world tensions and foreign intrigue in 1940 which was derided by most reviewers. As for the musical, which had quickly become the dominant American genre as soon as movies could talk, England did not have one on the screen until BIP's *Elstree Calling* (1930), an inventory of contemporary music hall acts assembled by Brunel, Hitchcock and other British directors.

Once resolved to convert entirely to sound, British film-makers exhibited less technological facility than the pace-setting American and continental studios. British Instructional, one of the most advanced of the English companies, first installed an unworkable disc system, then had to switch to Germany's Klangfilm, a sound-on-film device. By 1930, an easy majority of the films shown in Britain were sound, but less than 15 per cent of them were English.

Viewed from a distance, the years 1930–7 have the look of a boom period in British movie-making. As in America, the cinema was now incontestably the preeminent form of popular entertainment. Some 40 per cent of the populace attended on a weekly basis, accounting for 20 000 000 tickets per year and an annual gross of £40 000 000. (The great unasked question of the decade, however, was what percentage of these riches did English productions account for?)

Under Maxwell's driving leadership, BIP pursued its attempted conquest of the industry, strengthening its distribution links wherever possible and gobbling up cinemas right and left. By 1933, it controlled a chain of 147, an increase of fifty-nine in four years. In 1937, it absorbed the old Union Circuit (136 theatres), and, with other acquisitions, rolled up a total of 431 theatres by the end of the year. Simultaneously, Woolf and the Ostrers were doing their best to match this fierce pace. In 1928, the Gaumont–British/Gainsborough total stood at 187, and, with the purchase of the PCT chain, it had climbed to 316 by 1929. Still more mergers boosted the figure to 345 by 1937.

Another man who made his presence felt in the British film world during these years was Oscar Deutsch, an exhibitor who had bought his first theatre in the mid-1920s. In 1930, he embarked on an empire-building campaign of his own, announcing the almost Napoleonic goal of constructing elaborate movie cathedrals all over England, each distinctly an Odeon. Happily Deutsch's business astuteness matched his grandiose vision, and within a few years he controlled the eighth largest circuit in the country. By 1937, it had swelled to the fourth largest, 142 theatres strong.

During this period, the industry was further galvanized by the arrival of two men who were to bestride it like twin colossuses. Brandishing a contract from Paramount, Alexander Korda landed on British shores in 1932, quickly appropriated the name of a defunct firm, the London Film Company, and went into business. He set out to prove that Hollywood-style flamboyance could flourish in an English setting. The mid-1930s brought still more new blood – and certainly new money – when the immensely wealthy Yorkshire industrialist J. Arthur Rank entered the movie business. Throughout the remainder of the decade, he would collect studios, theatres and the other components of a giant film conglomerate as effortlessly as a retired gentleman working on his favourite hobby. It was not until the war years that he entered film production and became the supreme potentate of the English cinema.

Yet as the industry seemed to be putting down durable roots at last, various forms of blight were at work to prevent it. Following Warners' lead, most of the American studios which did not already have production facilities in England soon established them and began churning forth 'quota quickies', as these works had become disparagingly known. The Americans had a double motive: seizing as large a share of the quota allotment as they could and guaranteeing themselves a market for their own vastly more alluring products. It was a one-way relationship, of course. While Hollywood retained ready access to English screens, the British were only rarely able to wedge themselves into American theatres.

Understandably, the 1930s are usually depicted as an era in which British films were a satrapy of Hollywood. Nevertheless, a few men successfully retained their independence. Wilcox showed that he had not lost his touch for crowd-pleasing entertainment, effectively promoted, in the sound era. Lacking a strong musical comedy tradition, British movie-makers had not been able to rush 'all-singing, all-dancing, all-talking' spectacles onto the screen with the velocity of American producers; hence, they looked abroad for their sources, shooting English versions of popular German operettas. Wilcox speedily exploited this fad with *Goodnight Vienna* (1932), a typically frothy confection about a Viennese secretary's love life, with pleasant songs and a performance by Jack Buchanan that was sufficiently dapper and debonair to make him a major film star after many attempts. The picture was a hit, though it was far less representative of Wilcox's career than *Nell Gwyn* (1934), which confirmed his commitment to big-scale historical subjects treated in an unassailably patriotic tone and featuring a star of luminous appeal. 'Luminous' was certainly the word for Anna Neagle, the ex-chorus girl whose performance perfectly captured the earthy, animated quality of one of history's most famous courtesans. The film made Neagle as big a celebrity as Nell had been in her day (though an expurgated American version failed, perhaps because of the expurgations), and Wilcox deftly capitalized on her popularity for years to come, most notably in *Victoria the Great* (1937) and its sequel *Sixty Glorious Years* (1938). Although Wilcox did not expand the scope of the English cinema in any way and was overshadowed by Alexander Korda, he did manage to gauge popular tastes pretty consistently. Adept at tilling his own small patch of cinematic ground, he limited his production to only four or five films per year and patiently imbued each with the proper blend of production values and craftsmanship. It is no surprise that *Victoria the Great* was the industry's most profitable film in 1937 and that it, like so many Wilcox pictures since the silent days, had a very respectable American distribution.

Quite a different approach prevailed at BIP, where Maxwell's imperial policy called for an appropriately grandiose production schedule. Renamed Associated British in 1931, the company became widely identified with its studio, Elstree, and in the remainder of the decade some 200 features were produced there. Like most of his fellow English moguls, Maxwell did his share of inconsequential quota work, though even the more ambitious films at Elstree seem negligible today or are chiefly remembered for historical reasons. *How He Lied to Her Husband* (1931), directed by Cecil Lewis, was ostensibly a great coup for BIP, since it was the first film adaptation George Bernard Shaw had permitted, but it emerged as a languid, hopelessly prolix rendering of the play. Predictably, musical comedies sprouted all over the studio, most of them left in the hands of foreign talent. Marcel Varnel, a Frenchman who had come to England via Hollywood, directed *Dance Band* (1935), with Buddy Rogers, while the Viennese Paul Stein sought to interest the British filmgoer in operetta with *Blossom Time* (1934) and *Heart's Desire* (1935), both starring the great lyric tenor Richard Tauber. English directors had their opportunity too: Arthur Woods made *Radio Parade of 1935* (1934), and Brian Desmond Hurst tried to bring the glossy charm of Novello's stage musicals to the screen in *Glorious Night* (1937).

Weightier work at Elstree was scarcely more memorable. Saville, who worked there briefly at the beginning of the decade, made *The 'W' Plan* (1930), a drab spy story about saboteurs. Thomas Bentley, who had become known as a Dickens adaptor in the 1920s, tried his hand at a talking version of *The Old Curiosity Shop* (1934), with results that were praiseworthy, dutifully revered and quickly forgotten. Especially high hopes rested on Dupont's *Atlantic*, an all-dialogue film about the Titanic catastrophe, but the fate of the picture almost duplicated that of the ship: launched with ceremonial awe, it soon collided with savage critical disapproval and sank immediately; much of the criticism focused on the movie's declamatory acting, stilted language and poor special effects.

As in the previous decade, any BIP work of permanent creative importance was supplied by one man alone – Hitchcock. Yet the prodigy's journey upwards remained erratic, interrupted by nosedives and regressions. After *Blackmail*, he allowed himself to become involved in another theatrical adaptation, Sean O'Casey's *Juno and the Paycock* (1929), which he reproduced with solemn, plodding accuracy and none of the tragic, folkloric fire of the original (though O'Casey was pleased). Hitchcock moved much closer to his true element with the subsequent *Murder* (1930), reconstructed from the Clemence Dane/Helen Simpson play, *Enter Sir John*, by Hitchcock, his wife Alma Reville and Charles Bennett. A whodunnit, the story concerns a famous man of the theatre (Herbert Marshall) who sets out to prove the innocence of a girl condemned for murder by exposing the actual killer. Here, away from the influence of a venerable playwright's lines, Hitchcock could experiment with sound again, as in the jury sequence when the voices of the misguided jurors climb to an unintelligible babble or the interweaving of the hero's thoughts of love, presented audibly, with the prelude from *Tristan and Isolde*, which is playing on the radio. The killing itself is handled in the highly elliptical, cinematic manner Hitchcock had already shown such an aptitude for, while the climax, set at a circus performance, presages the many films which end with a dramatic resolution at a public event. *Murder* also introduces the figure of the perverted villain (in this case a homosexual trapeze artist), a Hitchcockian obsession.

Although *Murder* was received as a superior thriller, Hitchcock detoured again into inappropriate material, a film of Galsworthy's play *The Skin Game* (1931), an astonishingly inept work and an embarrassment to the Hitchcockian canon. He was in much better form in *Rich and Strange* (1932), a rather cynical and partially autobiographical dissection of marriage, if not of humanity in general, dealing with a couple (Joan Barry and Henry Kendall) who, acquiring wealth through an inheritance, take a trip around the world and encounter a wild variety of ups and downs before regaining their original state of respectable but bickering domesticity. The film's slight, amusing misanthropy went unappreciated at the time, though it has since been hailed by most Hitchcock scholars. Hitchcock's stock sank considerably lower with the two movies that followed, *Number Seventeen* (1932), a spoof of thrillers, and *Waltzes from Vienna* (1934), a Jessie Matthews musical which he unaccountably and imprudently undertook for Tom Arnold, an independent producer.

Another survivor of the 1920s, Asquith, displayed a less certain eye for box office values than Wilcox or Maxwell but ultimately secured a more substantial place in British film history. After *Dartmoor*, he tried his hand at a military subject, *Tell England* (1931), an account of the disastrous Gallipoli campaign. Despite a rather standardized, Etonian view of the famous débâcle and a conventional story of well-bred officers and their Cockney subordinates, the film impressed almost everyone with the exciting verisimilitude of its battle scenes; the more discriminating observers also took pleasure in the undertones of futility, which helped lift the picture out of its stiffly patriotic mould. It remains one of the best-known films of the period. Unfortunately, Asquith's career went off the rails after *Tell England*, for his next effort, *Dance Pretty Lady* (1932), the adventures of a working-class girl in aristocratic circles, did little to enhance his name (though in retrospect it did anticipate some of the features of his masterpiece, *Pygmalion*, made six years later). After this came several years of frustration and disappointment, as he went from producer to producer trying to improve his fortunes. For Balcon, he directed *The Lucky Number* (1933), a cheerful but hopelessly hackneyed musical about a football player trying to find a winning lottery ticket. In 1934, his circumstances at Gaumont–British grew still more demeaning, as he was assigned solely screenwriting duties on *Marry Me*, directed by William Thiele, and second unit work on *Forever England* (1935), a Walter Forde film. Offering his services to Alexander Korda, he was saddled with *Moscow Nights* (1935), a remake of a French picture, and could find no way to freshen up what was essentially stale material. Asquith also lost considerable time dallying on doomed projects with the undependable German impresario Max Schach. It was not until 1938 that he regained his stride with *Pygmalion*, produced by Gabriel Pascal. Codirected by and starring Leslie Howard, the picture is everyone's favourite screen adaptation of Shaw, an ensemble of gifted editing (David Lean), acting (Howard, Wendy Hiller, Stanley Holloway), and music (Paul Honegger) in which it is hard to locate a blemish, let alone a flaw. Asquith illuminates the entire production with gentle, lambent nostalgia for Edwardian times, an elegiac mood he had begun to cultivate in *Dance Pretty Lady* and which was soon to be one of his trademarks.

It is odd that Asquith's gifts did not flower at Shepherd's Bush, since Balcon had such a Medicean influence on almost everyone else who came under his sway. Bestriding both Gaumont–British and Gainsborough, Balcon remained the country's primary nurturer of cinematic talent in the 1930s, gathering an astonishingly eclectic group about him. Initially, he accepted the conventional wisdom that a shopping expedition to Hollywood would yield valuable personnel, and on various trips he collected numerous directors (Chuck Riesner, Raoul Walsh) and stars (Edmund Lowe, Sylvia Sidney, Richard Dix). Most of these figures were able to command contracts laden with immense salaries and costly perquisites, and Balcon soon discovered that the financial burden he had accepted was not commensurate with the revenues of the films the Americans made. He got more for his money, creatively as well as monetarily, with home-bred talent such as Robert Stevenson, whose *Tudor Rose* (1936), a biography of Lady Jane Grey, was admired as an intelligent, finely textured costume drama and who went on to a glamorous Hollywood career that included *Mary Poppins*. Another productive member of the Balcon stable was Walter Forde, a prominent comedian of the 1920s (*Would You Believe It!*, 1929). When Forde's performing career was cut short by talkies, he was reborn a few years later as a director. His greatest success was *Rome Express* (1932), starring Conrad Veidt, masterful as usual, in an espionage tale which Forde guided smoothly up and down the rocking corridors of the Blue Train. A remake of the apparently deathless *Chu Chin Chow* (1934) proved Forde's adeptness with a musical, and *Forever England*, which launched John Mills film career, showed the director could handle a conventional patriotic/military tale as well. But, with his extensive comic background, it was perhaps inevitable that the bulk of his work for Balcon should be in comedy. His most popular creations were the farces he made with Jack Hulbert; *Jack's the Boy* (1932) and *Jack Ahoy!* (1934) are typical of the series.

An even more important mainstay of the Gaumont – British/ Gainsborough operation in these years was Saville, who was well on his way to becoming one of the most ubiquitous figures in British film history. As much a factotum as any other English director, he concocted histories, musicals, comedies with the same reliable proficiency. In keeping with the vogue for Germanic musicals, he translated *Die Privatsekretarin* into *Sunshine Susie* (1931), which turned a handsome profit for Gainsborough and was, in general, favourably reviewed. Saville's subsequent, highly prolific output encompassed the historical drama *The Iron Duke* (1935), starring George Arliss (brought over from America at the exorbitant fee of £40 000); the slapstick comedy *Love on Wheels* (1932), with Hulbert; and the espionage story *I Was a Spy* (1933), with Veidt.

Saville's biggest successes, however, came when he began directing vehicles for Jessie Matthews. Under Saville's supervision, the winsome, gifted musical star, with her toothy smile and shapely legs, made an effortless transition from stage to screen in *The Good Companions* (1933), which Saville (along with screenwriter W. P. Lipscomb) skilfully condensed from J. B. Priestley's rather bulky best-seller. Saville went on to fashion the movies that consolidated Matthews's success – *Friday the Thirteenth* (1933), *Evergreen* (1934), *First a Girl* (1935), and *It's Love Again* (1936) – all of them fast-moving backstage stories which gave their star plenty of opportunity to go into her dance. (Later, Matthews's husband, Sonnie Hale, took over the direction of her films, with less satisfactory results.)

The popularity of Matthews, one of the bright spots of English movie-making in this decade, indirectly highlights another of the industry's problems. By and large, it was not glossy, Hollywood-style action movies or high-minded, blue-ribbon dramas which audiences found enticing but rather the broad-gestured comedies whose formulas had been tested in the crucible of the music hall. The smart West End public might prefer something sleek and continental, or even passionate and Russian, but in less educated lower-middle-class neighbourhoods, which still accounted for the majority of moviegoers, low comedy remained the most desired fare. If English cinema continued to lurch from crisis to crisis, it was in part because success came so sporadically, without much opportunity to develop genres and performing styles that would have ongoing appeal. It was only the specialized, parochial humour of the music hall, with its local jokes and regional accents, that brought audiences back time after time to see a familiar actor doing patented routines.

The experience of Basil Dean, a man of the theatre who entered films in 1927, is an especially good case in point. After an apprenticeship with Brunel and others, Dean created Associated Talking Pictures, whose name itself announced its confidence that movies had found their voice for good. Regrettably, Dean's creative imagination never adapted from the small, enclosed world of the stage to the greater fluidity of the new medium. Instead, the aesthetic division that typified British films in general widened into a particularly stark dichotomy at ATP. The company had only occasional sputters of success with its 'quality' pictures. Affiliated with RKO, Dean recoiled when he discovered that he was expected to make ignoble quota films rather than the prestige movies he envisioned. But when he was able to obtain the backing and distribution for the movies to which he aspired, the consequence was a lifeless wax museum of famous stage works, current fiction and occasional classics. Among the fifteen movies he himself directed are *Escape* (1930) and *Loyalties* (1933) – stiffly reverential adaptations of two Galsworthy plays – a remake of *The Constant Nymph* (1933), and *Lorna Doone* (1935). Nor did the itinerant senior directors who alighted at ATP have much more to contribute than their boss, as Cutts's *Love on the Spot* (1932) would seem to indicate. Nevertheless, Dean can certainly not be written off as a judge of cinematic gifts since it was he who gave Carol Reed his introduction to the film business. Once Reed had demonstrated his exceptional promise with *Midshipman Easy* (1935), Dean was quick to give him as many assignments as he could handle. Unfortunately, most of this work was cut to the quota pattern, which, reluctantly, Dean had to adopt to avoid financial disaster.

In spite of the lofty goals he had set for ATP, Dean found that there was a bigger audience for some of his rough-hewn, modestly scaled productions than the prestigious works with which he hoped to elevate the status of English films. His most prodigious money-makers were consistently the comedies of George Formby, the grinning, ukelele-playing bumpkin whose national appeal was so enormous it didn't matter that the rest of the world remained unaware of him. Trained in the music hall traditions of Northern England, Formby delighted his working-class audience year after year with predictable slapstick adventures such as *No Limit* (1935), *Keep Your Seats Please* (1936), *Keep Fit* (1937), and *Come on George* (1939). The first two were directed by Monty Banks, who was hired away from Maxwell specifically to launch Formby as a film star. Anthony Kimmins took over the series thereafter.

Even more beloved than Formby was Gracie Fields, another Northerner, who had a spunky, wide-eyed charm and a spirited way with a song that made her the biggest draw in English films. Elvey directed her debut, *Sally in Our Alley* (1931), a run-of-the-mill comedy illuminated by Fields's radiance. Dean himself took charge for *Sing As We Go* (1934) and *Look Up and Laugh* (1935), and Banks replaced him in *Queen of Hearts* (1936), *Keep Smiling, We're Going to Be Rich* (both 1938) and *Shipyard Sally* (1939). As formulaic as the movies were, two Dean directed were enriched by original stories from the pen of Lancashire-bred J. B. Priestley and earned some carefully measured praise from Graham Greene. But even a friendly notice from the normally astringent Greene and £40 000 a picture was not enough to keep Fields in England, and she left for the more glamorous latitudes of Southern California at the end of the decade.

Despite all the best efforts of Balcon, Dean, Maxwell and Wilcox, only two members of the English film community succeeded in making their impact felt beyond England: Sir Alexander Korda and Alfred Hitchcock. Much has been made of Korda's non-English background, but it should be recalled that Hollywood too was shaped by men who wore their *Mitteleuropa* heritages in their speech and manner. Seemingly born to be an entrepreneur, Korda nevertheless had to earn his rank over a period of many years, studying the art of film-making first in his native Hungary, then in France, Austria and Germany. After a *Wanderjahre* of almost a decade, he arrived in Hollywood and found that his sensibility was not at home in the land of sunshine and palm trees. Of the ten films he made for First National and Fox, only one was an unqualified hit, *The Private Life of Helen of Troy* (1928), but it was a harbinger of the next phase of Korda's career. Eschewing the usual rhetoric-heavy posturing of historical epics, this *Helen* transformed the Trojan War into an irreverent domestic comedy, much in the manner of Lubitsch. In this 'keyhole' approach to the majestic past lay the embryo of the work for which Korda was to become famous. Contracting with Paramount to make quota films in Europe, he went to Paris and directed *Marius* (1931), from Marcel Pagnol's play. The film, which has since become a minor classic, made a strong enough impression on the magnates at Paramount that Korda was despatched to England to take over the studio's production unit there. He completed only one picture, the debonair comedy *Service for Ladies* (1932), with Leslie Howard, before it became clear to everyone that what Korda wanted was not to serve film czars but to *be* one. Slipping out of his contract to Paramount with Houdini-like panache, Korda set up London Films with his brothers Zoltàn and Vincent and even persuaded his former employer to finance his first five or six features, all quota films. He quickly exploited his knack for minor cosmopolitan satire, as in *Wedding Rehearsal* (1932), but he had long since set his sights much higher, and once the proper subject suggested itself, he plunged boldly forward.

How the Kordas' collective gamble, *The Private Life of Henry VIII* (1933), teetered on a perilously underfunded tightrope until the last reel was shot is only a little less legendary a tale than the movie's huge international success. Featuring Charles Laughton in his most archetypal performance, the film carved its image of Henry into the public consciousness so effectively that generations of carping historians, disparaging the film's inaccuracies, could not efface it. Laughton bellowing at his courtiers, Laughton clumsily wooing Anne of Cleves (Elsa Lanchester) over cards, and of course Laughton feasting at the banquet table – these are images that have passed into the memory of audi-

ences everywhere. True to its title, the picture ignores the
political issues of Elizabethan England, for Korda knew history
lectures would put filmgoers in a doze, while romance, humour,
robust and sentimental vignettes and opulent period decor
would keep them entranced. He followed the leads of Lubitsch
and Wilcox, far outstripping his countryman in the overall
artistry of his work.

That this hearty English feast was served up by foreigners did
not go overlooked at the time: Vincent Korda designed the sets,
Georges Perinal shot the film, another Hungarian, Lajos Biro,
coauthored the script and the American Harold Young edited it.
The sole British influence was Arthur Wimperis, the other
scenarist. Still, no one could accuse the film of forcing an alien
vision onto native subject-matter, as in *Piccadilly*. The atmosphere and dialogue were impeccably English, as were the
principal players, all of whom were superbly directed. Korda
also showed considerable rapport with his audience when he cast
two of his discoveries – Merle Oberon and Robert Donat – in key
roles.

The triumph of *Henry* gave Korda an Olympian aura. With a
wave of his sceptre he seemed to have delivered British films
from their ignominy. He had been hard-pressed to find £60 000
for *Henry* (not an exceptionally large amount for an English
feature at this time), but the film's handsome returns (some
£500 000 on its first release alone) gave Korda credentials in
Hollywood which no other British producer possessed. The
success of *Henry VIII* made it possible for its creator to enter the
privileged realms of Hollywood moguldum on equal terms with
the Zanucks and Mayers and Warners. Striking a deal with
United Artists (UA), he joined its board of directors and Douglas Fairbanks accepted a seat at London Films. The most
coveted prize, an American distribution outlet, was his, and in
England his power was expanded when UA bought up
Deutsch's Odeon theatre chain to ensure easy distribution of
Korda's films. He was proclaimed the 'saviour' of his country's
cinema, and the industry was intoxicated with dreams of duplicating his success. The Prudential Insurance Company, which
normally kept a wary distance between itself and any movie
company, opened its vaults to Korda, and he dipped into them
for millions of pounds. Naturally a new studio was a prerequisite
for any self-respecting mogul, and Korda spent £600 000 of the

Prudential's money erecting the well-equipped Denham studios in 1936, which provided the latest, the largest and the best of everything.

As it happened, while other producers exhausted themselves trying to draw the bow of Ulysses, the master himself could not manage the deed very often. Retaining his stable of collaborators through film after film, he demonstrated the limitations of his creative vision and the apparently intractable obstacles of large-scale film-making in England. Because of the scope of Korda's operations (which, even allowing for his celebrated extravagance, was probably necessary if he was to rival Hollywood's merchandise), he was cursed with the same handicaps as every other English producer: an erratic record at the box office and a chronic shortage of capital.

In his recruiting policies, Korda was no less dedicated an internationalist than his contemporaries. He combed the world as diligently as Maxwell, but with loftier standards and a bigger cheque-book. Hence, he was able to attract men like Jacques Feyder, Paul Czinner, Robert Flaherty and René Clair, all of whom worked for him in the mid to late 1930s. Yet however disparate the nationalities and artistic temperaments at London Films, they all circled in Korda's orbit. It was ultimately his imprint that was to be found on the work of even the most individualistic of the directors he employed.

The unity of creative vision Korda imposed on his films accounted for their strengths and their weaknesses. Given the gigantic sums he invested in each picture, and the degree of control he exercised, it was inevitable that the company's fortunes rose and fell with the reception of each new effort. For a time, he attempted to follow the recipe of *Henry VIII*. In *The Private Life of Don Juan* (1934), he had the right idea – a wry philosophical treatment of the Don Juan legend – but the wrong actor. The ageing Douglas Fairbanks Sr, making his farewell screen appearance, had a reedy, most unvirile speaking voice and proved more adept with a foil than with the Shavian quips Wimperis wrote for him. His son, Douglas Jr, was more effective as Grand Duke Peter in *The Rise of Catherine the Great* (1934), directed by Czinner, yet audiences did not take to Korda's choice as the fabled Russian queen, Elizabeth Bergner, and the failure of this £100 000 production rocked London Films badly.

By the end of the year Korda rebounded from these defeats

with *The Scarlet Pimpernel* (1934), directed by Harold Young, who gave the film just the right, Kordaesque blend of dashing heroics, patriotism, romance and dandaical comedy. Robert E. Sherwood helped concoct the amusing script, based on Baroness Orczy's tales, and Leslie Howard enjoyed one of his most ingratiating triumphs as the 'demned elusive Pimpernel', the fop-adventurer whose snuff box and velvet jacket concealed a fearless swordsman. Korda scored two more successes in quick order – Zoltàn Korda's *Sanders of the River*, with Paul Robeson, and Clair's delightful *The Ghost Goes West* (both 1935), with Robert Donat – before suffering another setback with his own *Rembrandt* (1936). Here Korda tried to accommodate his infatuation with decorative historical epics to a serious subject, the last, sombre years of a great artist's life. He had an actor more than equal to the challenge, Laughton again, but, despite flattering notices, the public was unresponsive. Sadly, Korda retreated to the more restrictive versions of his formula. Immensity defined H. G. Wells's *Things to Come* (1936) – the size of the sets and the presumed marquee-value of its author's name (Wells adapted his own novel, *The Shape of Things to Come*). Directed by William Cameron Menzies, the film was enterprising in many ways; it offered a bold forecast of military Armageddon in 1940; a picture of barbaric, post-holocaust society; and spectacular, futuristic sets. On the other hand, it sagged under the weight of Wells's cumbersome didacticism about the glories of the scientific mind and the villainousness of the artist. The reviews were respectful, if not enthusiastic, but the icy popular reception made the film one of Korda's bigger monetary disasters.

As a screenwriter, Wells the comic entertainer fared better than Wells the science fiction wizard and prophet. The next year he adapted a whimsical fantasy he had published in 1898, *The Man Who Could Work Miracles*. Lothar Mendes (another Hungarian!), working a small miracle of his own, expanded the work into a lively minuet of English village life. The peerless cast, including Leo G. Carroll, brought a glow to every character.

Still, even Korda's successes were far from blockbusters, and they were nullified by profligate exercises in cardboard epic-making such as *Knight Without Armor* (1937). Here was a project which must have sounded as if it had the components of an irresistible smash: a screenplay by Frances Marion (with Biro and Wimperis) based on a novel by James Hilton; an acclaimed

director, Feyder; the dark and exotic excitement of the Russian
Revolution; a love story in the foreground; two stars at the peak
of their fame, Donat and Marlene Dietrich. All that was missing,
it developed, was conviction and inspiration, and although the
film drew comparatively favourable reviews, audience response
was lukewarm, and it has long since been deserted by its critical
advocates.

To offset the losses of his cherished 'spectaculars', Korda had
to slip many inconsequential, small-scale efforts into his production schedule, and often rent out his studio and his name to other
producers. In the period after *Knight*, three of these *divertissement*
were quickly manufactured: *The Squeaker* (1937), an arthritic
Edgar Wallace mystery directed by the American William K.
Howard; *Storm in a Teacup* (1937), a comedy of misunderstand-
ings among the leisure class, adapted by Biro from his own play,
produced and directed by Saville and thoroughly squandering
the talents of Rex Harrison and Merle Oberon; and *The Divorce of
Lady X* (1938), which paired Oberon with Laurence Olivier in a
laboured comedy of manners based, astonishingly, on an earlier
quota quickie (*Counsel's Opinion*, 1933) and directed by another
American, Tim Whelan. Judged even as light entertainment,
these were films whose charms evaporated like soap bubbles.

More nourishing drama was emerging from Denham too. In
the year of *The Squeaker* and *Storm in a Teacup*, Erich Pommer was
also in residence, producing *Fire Over England* (1937), a fictionalized chronicle of England's victory over the Spanish armada.
Directed by Howard, it featured regal, commanding performances by Flora Robson as Elizabeth and Raymond Massey as
Philip of Spain, remarkably callow work by Olivier and Vivien
Leigh as young Elizabethan lovebirds, and excellent action
sequences. Almost concurrently, under the same roof, Saville's
most ambitious and most heralded film, *South Riding* (1938),
which he both produced and directed, was made. The stalwart
cast was headed by Ralph Richardson, Edna Best and Edmund
Gwenn, and despite being nearly choked to death by its contrived narrative, the film still managed to investigate a fresh and
thoroughly contemporary subject – social injustice and corruption in the supposedly edenic English countryside. Although
Korda seems to have regarded realistic subjects as slightly
subversive and certainly uncommercial, it is to his credit that he
allowed *South Riding* to be made under his aegis. The same

breadth of sensibility permitted him to appreciate the raw, youthful talent of Michael Powell, whose independently produced *The Edge of the World* (1937) was a Flahertyesque study of the pinched, wind-lashed, stubbornly heroic lives of islanders in the Outer Hebrides. On the basis of this film, Korda gave Powell a much-needed job, though one wishes he had found more challenges for his latest protégé than *The Spy in Black* (1939), a conventional espionage drama whose only asset was yet another strong performance by Veidt, and *The Lion Has Wings* (1939), a ludicrous propaganda film (codirected by Brunel and Hurst) touting the invincibility of the RAF; it was jeered at throughout the land even at the time of its release. Yet there was a hidden momentousness to Korda's actions, for it was he who paired Powell with another Hungarian he had taken under his wing, Emeric Pressburger. Assigned screenwriting duties on *The Spy in Black*, Pressburger forged a partnership with Powell that was to become world famous in the 1940s.

Still, all of Korda's multitudinous gifts were not sufficient ballast for his floundering enterprise. By 1938, the situation at London Films had reached such a low ebb that he was compelled to sell Denham to none other than J. Arthur Rank, who was to become his major rival for domination of the English cinema after the war. Ever resourceful, Korda withdrew to the United States, where he finally completed a film he had been toiling on in England, *The Thief of Bagdad* (1940) and found backing for *Lady Hamilton* (1941), an expertly timed retelling of one of England's great love affairs. The movie restored Korda's standing back home, and he returned to London to much adulation and a knighthood.

In comparison to other British producers of the 1930s, Korda travelled in seven-league boots. Where he led, others followed – or tried to. Yet the altitudes he sought were beyond even his capacities. Although he succeeded in joining the brotherhood of Hollywood tycoons, he was never able to approximate the diverse, world-conquering tide of pictures which they sent forth each year. The Caesar-like cohesiveness which he brought to his reign at London Films was as much a liability as an asset, since it harnessed all the creative energy on the lot to one man's personality. Some talent, like Clair's, might have burned brighter if left on its own. As it was, Korda, who had knighted himself long before King George did, used his movies as an impassioned display of allegiance to his adopted country, to affirm that, indeed, there would always be an England, and it would remain a nation governed by ruling-class mores. The realities of contemporary England, with its strikes and unemployment, appear to have held little interest for Korda, probably because it was so remote from his storybook image of the 'sceptred isle' and its 'happy breed of men'. He preferred to immerse himself in the heroic past (*Henry VIII*), where hearty monarchs banqueted and wenched. In contemporary or near-contemporary settings, an idealized colonialism prevailed; there even the most primitive of His Majesty's subjects appreciated the paternal firmness of the District Commissioner (*Sanders*) and were horrified by those natives who broke the king's law, while the gentleman–adventurer could be counted on to rescue imperilled members of his own class (*Pimpernel*). The setting might be foreign (*Catherine the Great*), but it was only an exotic veil through which the characteristic English virtues of tact, good breeding, self-sacrifice and devotion to duty shone through radiantly. Embodying these qualities were men and women of impeccable South Kensington speech (Ralph Richardson, Donat, Oberon); working-class accents were restricted to the supporting cast, who were expected to provide comic turns and, when necessary, die nobly for the Empire. Socialism, nationalism, poverty, class conflict, the trade union movement – these were all messy, volatile forces which did not even rattle the shutters of Korda's timelessly Victorian world.

By American standards, these were narrow artistic boundaries, and they ensured that London Films would ignore a number of lively and lucrative genres, particularly those with a fundamentally proletarian caste of mind, such as gangster films and dramas of social protest. In Hollywood, producers knew that the volume of their business depended in part on the diversity of their wares.

And yet somehow, all the intrinsic shortcomings of Korda's operation did not keep his best work from achieving a most durable appeal. His taste and intelligence, the rigorous professionalism of the staffs he assembled and the fine performances of his handpicked casts enabled him to make more films of enduring entertainment value – as opposed to archival interest – than any other English producer or director of the period, including Hitchcock. Other than *The Thirty-Nine Steps* and *The Lady Vanishes*, Hitchcock is brilliant only by flashes, with much dead weight and mediocre acting between the undeniably dazzling sequences. In his work one sees a quirky, original sorcerer emerging in slow, painful stages and in Korda's a graceful magician with a bag of tricks which, however old, are more consistently and adroitly deployed.

If many of Korda's imperial spectacles seem obviously Kiplingesque in inspiration, they can be praised for this quality as readily as condemned. Just as readers can reject Kipling's frequently shallow and propagandistic ideas yet appreciate the eternally fresh vigour of his artistry, so filmgoers can enjoy *The Drum, Sanders* and *Four Feathers* for their rousing renditions of classic adventure tales. In this connection, it is hardly surprising that one of Korda's best works was *The Jungle Book* (1942), in which not only the Indians but the animals themselves bow down in fealty to the crown! On approximately the same aesthetic plane, *Henry VIII* remains a pungent historical excursion, *The Scarlet Pimpernel* a pleasing romantic adventure and *The Ghost Goes West* an ingratiating satirical comedy. Moreover, after the war had battered and traumatized the British public into a more widespread acceptance of the realistic mode, it was Korda who led the way in producing much of the best work, often in collaboration with the man who, after Hitchcock's departure for the US, became England's foremost director: Carol Reed.

In terms of critical reputation, Hitchcock remains the transcendent figure of the British film world, almost certainly the most highly regarded English movie-maker of all time. In 1933, however, he was still a man who had not quite found his creative bearings. After the lacklustre reception of *Number Seventeen* and *Waltzes from Vienna*, Maxwell and Hitchcock seemed disenchanted with one another. Returning to Gaumont with a script by Bennett that excited him, *The Man Who Knew Too Much* (there was to be additional work by D. B. Wyndham-Lewis, A. R. Rawlinson and Edwin Greenwood), Hitchcock found his old mentor, Balcon, as supportive as ever. The completed film was released in 1934, and though far from a seamless creation, it shows a steadily evolving command of the thriller form coupled with an unflagging search for imaginative technical effects.

The igniting point of the story is an English couple's discovery, while on holiday, of a plot to assassinate a leading political figure during a concert at the Albert Hall. As the protagonists try frantically to thwart the murder, Hitchcock marshals his growing repertoire of cinematic devices: the sudden intrusion of lurid details in a peaceful setting, the exploitation of everyday items for sinister effect, and the attempt to propel the plot forward to a crowded, eye-filling finale. The penultimate scene at the concert shows the director's flair for virtuoso editing. New elements added to the Hitchcock calculus are the ominous secret society, the Tabernacle of the Sun, in whose midst the hero is trapped; the widened geographical panorama, including the Swiss Alps, the Albert Hall and the bleak, seedy Wapping section of London; and the choice of foreign intrigue as a framework for the story. Hitchcock's ingenuity and daring paid off beautifully, for *The Man Who Knew Too Much* was immensely popular with reviewers and moviegoers alike, though today it is remembered as little more than an artefact in a great director's career and a primitive ur-version of the far superior 1955 remake with James Stewart and Doris Day.

Full of confidence, and backed to the hilt by Balcon, Hitchcock adapted John Buchan's novel *The Thirty-nine Steps*, collaborating with Reville, Bennett and Ian Hay, The film, generally considered his best in England, brought him international laurels that no English film-maker other than Korda had yet attained and is probably the most acclaimed British spy story prior to the coming of James Bond. Here, the figures on Hitchcock's canvas finally fall into perfect harmony with one another. Espionage is again the genre (*The Man Who Knew Too Much*), while the dual characters of a wrongfully accused heroine and her detective-defender (*Blackmail, Murder*) were collapsed into a single protagonist, a man suspected of a crime he did not commit and fleeing from the authorities. Delightedly compounding the ironies wherever he can, Hitchcock makes his hero, Hannay (Donat), both quarry and hunter (since he can only prove his innocence by tracking down the leader of the spy syndicate); handcuffs him to a beautiful blonde (Madeleine Carroll) in a wicked parody of marriage (*Rich and Strange*); and locks up the explanation to the mystery in the last place Hannay would think of looking for it, the simple music hall tune he has been whistling throughout the film. For the first time, we see Hitchcock's spiny sense of humour in a full display of bristles. For example, a political rally becomes an audacious satire of political rhetoric when the hero has to make an impromptu speech. Yet Hitchcock adds another layer, as Hannay makes his own problems the secret text of his oration and becomes so impassioned that he transcends the mouldy platitudes he is uttering and brings the throng to its feet with tumultuous cheers. The setpiece is barely over when the humming machinery of the plot, in the person of two agents impersonating detectives, unobtrusively wisks Hannay off in a new direction.

Throughout its taut, economical eighty-one minutes, the film submerges most of its improbabilities in amusing and unexpected plot twists. It is virtually an inventory of the strategies and gimmicks Hitchcock had been developing since *The Lodger*: the ordinary possession (Hannay's pipe) used as a weapon, the blonde thrust into a dangerous predicament, a silent scream employed as a transitional device, the intrusion of the grotesque (Professor Jordan's mutilated finger), the big, full-dress climax in the music hall. Also of interest is the introduction of an authentic sexual tension between the hero and heroine, whose spirited duet of initial antagonism and eventual romance adds much to the picture and prefigures such wonderful pairings as Cary Grant and Ingrid Bergman in *Notorious*.

If Hitchcock's next two films fell short of the irridescent achievement of *The Thirty-nine Steps*, it was not for want of ambition – more likely because of it. Upgrading his sources to accord with his own newly elevated standing, he chose a few of the stories from W. Somerset Maugham's *Ashenden*, which he, Reville, Bennett and Jesse Lasky Jr wove into a script called *Secret Agent* (1936) that suited Hitchcock's temperament. This time the hero is a member of British intelligence (John Gielgud), the innocent man a suspected traitor (Percy Marmont), the heroine a British contact posing as Ashenden's wife (Carroll). The setting is again Switzerland, and it is behind that nation's most commonplace enterprise (a chocolate factory) that Hitchcock plants his most malevolent forces (a spy organization). The most complex and effective character is the actual traitor (Robert Young), a deceptively personable, well-mannered young man who is a forefather of some of Hitchcock's ambiguously attractive later heroes, such as those portrayed by Joseph Cotten in *Shadow of a Doubt* and Cary Grant in *Suspicion*, figures whose alluring surface may conceal a profound evil.

Overall, however, *Secret Agent* fails to take wing because the screenplay is devoid of the playful *brio* of *The Thirty-nine Steps* and the crucial romantic chemistry provided by Donat and Carroll is missing; the lifeless Gielgud lacks Donat's warm, engaging personality and displays no more passion for his leading lady than he would for a hatrack. The world-weary scepticism and probing eye which sustain Maugham's stories are reproduced only fleetingly; while Maugham holds the world of espionage at an ironic distance, Hitchcock embraces it for its surface excitement. Nor does the director show much more than a passing interest in Maugham's character development. His real forte, here unachieved, was for an odd but gripping amalgam of romantic melodrama, perverse wit, technical inventiveness and masterfully contrived shock effects.

In *Sabotage* (1936), Hitchcock moved still further from the dynamics which typified his most satisfying work. Since the source is Joseph Conrad's *The Secret Agent*, most commentators feel obliged to note that the film should not be confused with Hitchcock's previous effort or his subsequent American movie *Saboteur* (1942), starring Robert Cummings. What they fail to note is that it also should not be confused with the novel on which it is based, a harrowing study of human futility. This adaptation is much admired, particularly by people who do not have the disadvantage of having read the book. Conrad's story of a gloomy marriage and a band of inept but fanatic anarchists who plot to blow up the Greenwich Observatory is transformed into a failed hybrid – one part serious drama, the other glossy melodrama. The joyless union of M. Verloc and his wife (Oscar Homolka and Sylvia Sidney) occupies the centre of the story, but without Conrad's minute accretions of psychological detail, it smothers the picture in its ponderous weight. As usual, Conrad's dominant theme is the lethal but inescapable effect of human illusions, which Hitchcock toys with but betrays utterly. In the original, Mrs Verloc experiences a final, tragic disenchantment with her husband when he inadvertently sacrifices her retarded younger brother to the cause. Murdering her husband in reprisal, she quickly yokes herself to a new set of self-deceptions, involving another member of the radical cell, and is subsequently abandoned by him in her time of greatest need. In the film, all this is jetissoned in favour of a conventional detective–herc who comes to Mrs Verloc's rescue and preserves a happy ending. Also lost or diluted are Conrad's superb portraits of the individual conspirators. The justly praised performances of Homolka and Sidney and some good Hitchcockian effects (the suspense generated when Mrs Verloc's brother sits on a crowded bus, unaware that he carries a time bomb) are among the film's redeeming merits.

Sabotage received all the accolades Hitchcock could have hoped for, and he can be said to have rested – or slumped – on his laurels with *Young and Innocent* (1937), a film which shows the director at his slackest. In spite of the efforts of four screenwriters (Bennett, Reville, Anthony Armstrong and Edwin Greenwood), the screenplay, loosely based on Josephine Tey's novel *A Shilling for Candles*, is little more than a feeble reprise of *The Thirty-nine Steps*, with the Donat and Carroll parts assumed by two exceedingly bland juveniles (Derrick de Marney and Nova Pilbeam). The boy is suspected of murder, and as he and his companion follow the tiresome skein of clues that leads to the actual killer, a drummer in a black-faced orchestra at a tea dance, Hitchcock tries to interpolate some diversion – a children's party with a menacing aspect, the ground collapsing under a car the heroine is seated in – but none of it has much impact. The sets look artificial and studiobound, which is astonishing after the convincing *mise-en-scène* of *The Thirty-nine Steps*. The only effect worth noting in this lame offering is the frequently lauded tracking shot, near the end, in which the camera glides smoothly, almost langorously, from the doorway of a ballroom where the orchestra is performing through a progressively narrowing perspective of musicians until at last the convulsive eye of the drummer, our sole clue as to the murderer's identity, is isolated. Apart from this touch, if the film hadn't been signed by Hitchcock, it would be hard to distinguish from a quota quickie or an American B movie.

By now Hitchcock was really just marking time before he went to Hollywood. Still, he did not want such a meagre work as *Young and Innocent* to be his swansong in England, and his powers revived when he set to work on his next film, *The Lady Vanishes* (1938). As with most of his best movies, the source was not a serious, or even a quasi-serious, literary work but Ethel Lina White's *The Wheel Spins*, a second-rank thriller. The relative plasticity of a minor work allowed Hitchcock and his writing team to mould the story into something the master was comfortable with. An overly strong authorial personality, even a Raymond Chandler or an Agatha Christie, would constrict Hitchcock's own inspiration. Working with Sidney Gilliat and Frank Launder, active in the industry for about ten years and soon to become the best-known writing partnership in British films, Hitchcock converted the White novel into a thoroughly agreeable pastiche of his most carefully honed effects.

Yet again we begin on foreign soil with an assemblage of characters on a confined stage, this time a transcontinental train heading west from the Balkans. Once more the unusual masquerades as the ordinary: a chattering old lady (Dame May Whitty) is revealed as a British agent. Once more excitement and humour are neatly juxtaposed: a mysterious disappearance on the train is counterpointed by the droll dialogues of two cricket-obsessed Colonel Blimps (Basil Radford and Naunton Wayne), who remain unflappably oblivious to the cloak-and-dagger activities around them because all they are concerned with are the scores from home. Hitchcock pays no more obeisance to credibility than in his other films, but the razor-sharp pacing, richness of incident and well-timed surprises keep one's senses stimulated and one's rational faculty subdued. The secondary players all turn in finely modulated performances and the romantic leads, Michael Redgrave and Margaret Lockwood, are a big improvement on de Marney and Pilbeam.

In 1939, Hitchcock signed a lucrative contract with David O. Selznick, though as it happened he directed one more film in England, *Jamaica Inn* (1939), a misbegotten work (from Daphne du Maurier's novel) that even the exertions of Charles Laughton in the lead could not save. By now, Hitchcock was long overdue for a Hollywood career. He had exhausted the possibilities of film-making in Britain and the greater financial and technical resources available to him in America, as well as the larger pool of major stars, presented a chance to spread his wings even further than he already had. For all the solemn poppycock that has been written about the Catholic underpinnings of his work, his sense of human depravity and his ironic view of the world, he was essentially a gifted showman reaching out to the widest possible audience he could. In his breast beat a thoroughly commercial heart, more so than Asquith, Reed, Lean and other of his eminent countrymen. One can never imagine Hitchcock taking the risks Reed took in *Odd Man Out* or Lean did in

Lawrence of Arabia. Hitchcock's destiny lay in the swank, gold-plated fairy land of Hollywood, where he could hire the slickest writers (Ernest Lehman, Ben Hecht), employ the most glamorous stars (Grant, Stewart, Bergman) and build the most expensive sets (*Spellbound*). For over thirty years his insignia on a film guaranteed moviegoers an exhilarating brew of suspense, excitement and laughter. No wonder his name sold tickets. Out in the dream factory, he manufactured the most creative nightmares.

While the public was frequently dissatisfied with British movies because they weren't entertaining enough, a small group of film-makers was unhappy because the national cinema was all too entertaining. Indeed, it was purely escapist, only occasionally looking reality in the eye and then but glancingly. These men advocated factual narrative as an antidote to the gleaming artificiality of commercial motion pictures, and their leader, John Grierson, may have coined the word 'documentary' to describe their work. To many observers, this movement was the only truly indigenous school of film-making in England during the 1930s, which are normally summed up as an era of 'Hollywood colonization'.

A Scotsman educated at the University of Glasgow, Grierson went to the US for some informal additional schooling among American film-makers. Although he encountered a number of successful Hollywood directors and had a good deal of exposure to the inner workings of the studio system, he evinced no interest in movies as an entertainment form. Instead, he fell under the spell of Robert Flaherty, whose *Nanook of the North* (1922) had virtually established a unique genre of films, interpretive reportage. When Grierson returned to England, he had become a man with a mission: to establish an alternate cinema which found its subjects in the social and professional realities of the day and recorded them with complete fidelity, shunning the artifice of the commercial cinema. This new form would combine the first-hand excitement of the newsreel, one of the earliest types of film-making, with a point of view. The goal would be to educate audiences to the life which Wardour Street ignored.

Grierson found a sympathetic sponsor in Sir Stephen Tallants, head of the Empire Marketing Board who authorized the creation of a film unit at the Board. With EMB backing, Grierson directed *Drifters* (1929), a 50-minute documentary about the lives of Scottish fishermen in pursuit of herring. His treatment is microcosmic: the inquiring camera eye follows the crew of a trawler on a typical voyage to sea and back again, capturing every facet of their arduous lives. The tone of the film is one of muted celebration, with the stoic, plainspoken virtues of the fishermen set forth in *bas-relief*. Yet although they are shown wringing their livelihood from an uncharitable nature, there is no attention paid to the economic system within which they function or the class structure to which they belong.

Drifters made an enormous impression on that portion of the British populace which was receptive to a journalistic use of the film medium. It was hailed as a masterpiece, a native *Potemkin*, and though its reputation has inevitably dimmed over the years, it is still looked on as the seminal work of the British documentary movement. Grierson went on to train a whole generation of earnest and enthusiastic young film-makers who believed that directors, like writers and dramatists, could achieve greatness by holding a mirror up to life. Less comfortable as a director than as a supervisor of other directors, Grierson set himself up in a quasi-impresarial role at the EMB and later at the General Post Office, to which the film unit was transferred when Tallant became head of the GPO. Of the many young followers whom Grierson gathered about him, the most notable were Arthur Elton, Henry Legge and Basil Wright, a trio who had an almost eerie commonality of background: all three were from well-to-do families, had been born within a year or so of one another and had been educated at public school and at Cambridge.

Excitement ran high on Grierson's staff when an invitation to Flaherty to collaborate on a work about English craftsmen was accepted. Here was the *eminence grise* of the movement, the pioneer documentarian himself. Nevertheless, his English admirers found themselves uneasy about turning their own high priest loose on the proposed film, since the poetic style he had become famous for was somewhat at odds with the more sober, realistic credo of the English school. Flaherty, too, was entranced by the struggles of hard-working 'everymen' but he sought to transmute his subjects into Keatsian paragons of timeless beauty, figures on a Grecian urn. As a result, although most of the footage on the project was Flaherty's, Grierson, Elton and Harry Watt interpolated material of their own, and the editing was done by Grierson and Edward Anstey, another disciple. Released as *Industrial Britain* (1933), the film provided an inclusive compilation of skilled labour in England, always laudatory, its visual content embroidered with a lofty commentary by Grierson about the glories of craftsmanship. The film even attracted an illustrious distributor, Gaumont–British, which appended a musical score, and *Industrial Britain* became the benchmark of Grierson's years at the EMB, though it is now looked on as a musty antique, more interesting for its place in Flaherty's career than anything else.

After the move to the GPO, Grierson and his group embarked on a period of far greater productivity and creative ferment than they had known at the EMB. While Grierson remained the undisputed leader of the documentarians, a figure of almost equally commanding influence entered the unit, Alberto Cavalcanti, a Brazilian who had already won his share of laurels in France with experimental films during the preceding decade. The principal responsibility of the documentarians was to dispense information about the varied activities of the post office, presenting it in crisp, lucid forms suitable for a mass audience, and this they accomplished commendably in films such as *Telephone Workers* (1933), *Under the City* (1934), *Weather Forecast* (1934) and *Introducing the Dial* (1935). Since the basic format was usually a lecture illustrated by visuals and the subject-matter did not touch on many areas of vital human concern, the filmmakers had little motivation for enlarging the artistic scope of their work. There were exceptions, however. Some of Grierson's protégés adopted more experimental techniques, such as the animated creations of Len Lye, who used striking abstract patterns, some of them enlivened by hand-painted colour frames, to spread the word about postal matters (e.g. *Colour Box*, 1935). Later, in *Rainbow Dance* (1936) and *Trade Tatoo* (1937), he counterbalanced his drawings of lines and dots with live sequences.

An entirely different brand of exploration went on in Watt's *The Saving of the North Sea* (1938), an account of a fishing boat struggling back to port during a storm, partially due to the aid of the post office's ship-to-shore radio system. The film's novelty lies in its inclusion of narrative materials shot in a studio and merged with documentary footage, thus, according to Watt, giving the picture a stronger emotional grip on its audience. He demonstrated the possibilities of his method most compellingly in *Night Mail* (1936), one of the acknowledged classics of the movement. Seldom has such a starry assemblage of talent worked on a single, non-commercial film: Watt's codirector was Wright and his editor Cavalcanti; the commentary was written by W. H. Auden and the music composed by Benjamin Britten. Structurally, *Night Mail* reflected the simple synecdoche of *Drifters*, a single night flight from London to Scotland which symbolizes all the countless trips undertaken by the dogged servants of the post office to get the mail to its destination. The results are truly eclectic, a merger not only of different methods (strictly documentary components and studio-created segments) but also different temperaments, featuring the character-oriented drama of Watt as well as the poetic impulses of Cavalcanti and Wright.

In general, however, the most substantial accomplishments of the British documentary resulted from assignments outside the GPO. Wright's *Song of Ceylon* (1934), produced by Grierson but commissioned by the Ceylon Tea Production Board, captured a major spot in the history of British documentaries and was one of the few pre-Second World War efforts to be distributed and reviewed in the US. The film is a mosaic of Ceylonese life, encompassing the island's natural beauty, the primitive but contented lives of the populace, Buddhist ceremonies, and the planting, harvesting and refinement of tea. The mercantile aspect of the movie is, of course, its *raison d'être* and the complacent presentation of Britain's economic relationship with Ceylon makes the work an easy target for anticolonialist reproach. Nevertheless, the film remains a minor landmark in the English cinema due to Wright's lyrical vocation of his subject, the abundance of anthropological data on Ceylon, and the unusual soundtrack devised by Cavalcanti.

Those who wanted England's economic institutions subjected to a more incisive political critique were happier with Cavalcanti's own *Coalface* (1935). Although it begins and ends with a fairly bland, schoolmasterish dissertation on how critical coal is to the English way of life, Cavalcanti interpolates some alarming facts and figures on mining disasters. He also had the considerable assets of verse by Auden and music by Britten.

While the GPO unit was by far the most revered documentary group in England, the documentary impulse was also felt elsewhere. Some of the unit's alumnae went on to work for other

government bodies or in private industry, which was not slow to
see the propaganda potential of non-narrative film-making. The
Ministry of Labour underwrote Elton's *Men and Jobs* (1935), a
treatise on the utility of labour exchanges. Meanwhile, Elton's
colleague, Anstey, was setting up a film-making corps at Shell to
sway public opinion on issues vital to the company. The goal of
private enterprise was always to promote the capitalist philosophy, of course, but some of the new productions proved that
propaganda and artistry could coexist.

Of the many corporate patrons, it is generally felt that the gas
company had the most to be proud of, commissioning (or should
we say 'permitting'?) social documents of such trenchant honesty as Anstey's *Housing Problems* (1935), in which working-class
people tell their own stories against a background of urban
squalor; Wright's *Children at School*, which is in part an ode to
childhood joys, yet also uses its subject as a pertinent gloss on
the menacing international situation, for which, it argues, only
good schooling is proper preparation; and John Taylor's *The
Smoke Menace*, a cautionary work on the threat of pollution which
looks both backward to Blake's 'Satanic mills' and forward to
one of the most urgent contemporary issues.

The movement even produced an independent production
company, the brainchild of Donald Taylor. For Taylor, Paul
Rotha produced *Today We Live*, directed by Ruby Grierson and
Ralph Bond, a film which used photogenic rural settings to
advocate state support for community projects.

In the midst of all this activity, the giant who had inspired it,
Flaherty, toiled on not far away. Bizarrely enough, he had gone
to Wardour Street men for financing just as his progeny –
Grierson *et al.* – were looking in entirely different directions for
their money. After *Industrial Britain*, a gap opened between
Flaherty and his English followers, and he turned to Balcon for
support on his next endeavour, *Man of Aran* (1934). Three years
of work went into this movie, for which Flaherty shot enough
material to make ten pictures. Compressed into one, it presents a
rhapsodic chronicle of life among the fishermen of Aran. No one
who had seen the director's other work should have been surprised to encounter an essay in idealized primitivism, with heavy
emphasis on scenic and pictorial effects, a very romantic view of
simple labour and an exaltation of the eternal verities of family
life (as reflected through one household). In spite of the obvious

similarities between Flaherty's artistic posture and that of his English counterparts, *Man of Aran* was greeted with vociferous disapproval in England, both by native documentarians and film critics. Badly wounded, Flaherty was a long time in commencing a new film, and when he did, it was a venture that was obviously doomed from the start: an Indian story for Korda, a man whose sensibility couldn't have been further from Flaherty's. As usual, he went on location and shot to his heart's content, but in the end all the cannisters of film were merely trimmed down to a splendid backdrop for some cut-rate Kipling – the Gunga Din-style, sahib-infatuated *Elephant Boy* (1937), codirected by Zoltán Korda and starring Sabu. Following this fiasco, Flaherty returned dejectedly to America.

With the outbreak of war in 1939, the documentary movement entered a new and more prescriptive pattern. Quite understandably, after September 1939 every film was expected to cry God for Harry, England and St George and some, like Harry Watt's, did it superbly. Yet even before the documentarians were conscripted into the momentous struggle against Hitler, their work was assailed for its uncritical endorsement of the industries, social groups and institutions they studied. Grierson preached that the camera was always honest, its images of fishermen and schoolchildren and peasants ripe with truth; audiences were to be enriched by the cinematic lessons he and his disciples offered on their flickering spools of fact. But the camera's eye is rarely any more objective than the man behind it, and a movie is shot, cut, shaped and ordered to accord with a point of view, though it might be unconscious. The work done for the GPO was no exception. In this case, the films frequently exalted England's proletariat and its colonial subjects but never questioned their role in the existing socioeconomic system nor allowed anyone else to. Indeed, since most of the funding of documentary films came from governmental and corporate sources, such probes would seem to have been automatically precluded. Even the day-to-day operations of the film unit itself reinforced the status quo, since the directors all sprang from privileged backgrounds and thereby earned the right to command, while the cameramen they commanded did not.

Having conceded all this, however, it is hard to deny that the documentary movement exerted a highly salutary influence on the British film industry. When the commercial cinema fed its audiences escapist comedies and melodramas, films like *Drifters*, *Housing Problems* and *Today We Live* gave them the raw drama of real life; in place of smooth show-business artificiality, these works provided rough-grained immediacy; for the elegant speech and grooming of actors, they substituted the awkward, homely, inarticulate presence of ordinary citizens. The influence was to be felt far and wide in the work of the best English directors, Reed among them.

Throughout the 1930s, the British film world might have looked robust, at a cursory glance, since it kept a torrent of films pouring into the cinemas, but actually it bore a clear resemblance to one of its sets: a stately exterior fronting a lot of rickety, quickly eroding scaffolding. Propped up by the quota and invigorated by Korda's occasional transatlantic hits, the industry remained active, but it was still not getting sufficient distribution for its films, at home or abroad, to achieve fiscal stability. Economic realities were throttling the business, while self-deceived industry chieftains tried to pretend otherwise. At Gaumont–British, the balance sheets were so dire by 1936 that Balcon was forced to resign. Over 200 feature films were announced in 1937, but by the spring only a handful were in production. That same year, Gainsborough posted a loss of £98 000 and went into receivership, and Korda had to withdraw to Hollywood to recoup his losses.

Dismayed, Parliament reexamined its handiwork, the quota act, and succumbed to the delusion that a few more adjustments could make it function properly. What it wrought was the Film Act of 1938, which aimed at lifting the calibre of English productions. The index in measuring 'calibre', however, was largely the amount of money spent on a film. Although the staggering dislocations of the war which engulfed England the following year make it hard to guage the effect the act might have had, it is doubtful that such legislation could have accomplished its objectives.

And yet, independent of the efforts of cabinet ministers and MPs, the English cinema blossomed remarkably in the 1940s. Paradoxically, it was in a decade of war and rubble-strewn postwar deprivation that British movies finally came of age. With the country's former glory irretrievably lost, her filmmakers were finally able to achieve what her novelists, poets and playwrights had been doing for centuries: finding the universal-

ity of great art in the particulars of their own national experience. At last English directors managed to escape the slavishly
accepted patterns of foreign models and discover the unique
music of their own culture, with all its varied tonalities, inflections and rhythms.

Much of the best work of the period was done through modest
companies set up by individual directors, such as Powell and
Pressburger's The Archers. Most commonly these tiny entities
crouched under the financial and distributional canopy of either
Korda or Rank, though some found other means of support. In
1948, the government created a third source of capital when it
set up the National Film Finance Corporation, which was to
underwrite some 700 movies over the next two decades.

With these catalysts at work, the British made outstanding
pictures in many different modes. Lean showed his versatility by
moving from war films (*In Which We Serve*, 1942; codirected with
Noel Coward) to romance (*Brief Encounter*, 1945) to literary
adaptations (*Great Expectations*, 1946) and eventually to epics
(*Lawrence of Arabia*, 1962). Reed, whose career paralleled Lean's
in many ways, was just as protean, distinguishing himself in
documentary work (*The True Glory*, 1945), tragedy (*Odd Man Out*,
1947), detective stories (*The Fallen Idol*, 1948), international
thrillers (*The Third Man*, 1949), South Seas romances (*Outcast of
the Islands*, 1952) and suave parody (*Our Man in Havana*, 1960).
From Asquith came exceptionally well carpentered and handsomely varnished moral dramas, sometimes by Terence Rattigan (*The Winslow Boy*, 1948) and from Olivier some of the
cinema's most masterful exercises in filmed Shakespeare (*Henry
V*, 1945 and *Hamlet*, 1948). On a less rarified, more pungent level
were Leslie Arliss's cape-swirling melodramas of Regency England (*The Man in Grey*, 1943) and Compton Bennett's contemporary *The Seventh Veil* (1945), in which James Mason made
romantic tyranny so attractive that even the vast American
audience swooned. The idiosyncratic, fearlessly experimental
Powell and Pressburger tried their hand at social criticism (*The
Life and Death of Colonel Blimp*, 1943), comic fantasy (*A Matter of
Life and Death*, 1946), and opulent ballet and opera films (*The Red
Shoes*, 1948 and *Tales of Hoffman*, 1951). At Ealing, Balcon, who
became head of production in 1938, served up successful police
melodramas (Basil Deardon's *The Blue Lamp*, 1950) and one
classic horror film (*Dead of Night*, 1945; codirected by Robert

Hamer, Charles Crichton, Cavalcanti and Deardon), but the studio's most popular export proved to be its comedies, which were invariably wry, humane, whimsical and consummately English. Henry Cornelius's *Hue and Cry* (1947) was the first in a long parade of triumphs, including Alexander Mackendrick's *Whisky Galore!* (1949), Hamer's *Kind Hearts and Coronets* (1949), and Crichton's *The Lavender Hill Mob* (1951).

In the late 1950s and 1960s, the most sacrosanct British values and institutions came under attack, usually from a working-class perspective, by the Free Cinema movement and Woodfall Films, which made, or inspired, films such as Jack Clayton's *Room at the Top*, Tony Richardson's *Look Back in Anger* (both 1959), Karel Reisz's *Saturday Night and Sunday Morning* (1960), and Lindsay Anderson's *This Sporting Life* (1963). (Unexpectedly, however, Woodfall's splashiest success came when it reached back to the eighteenth century for its ebulliently bawdy romp *Tom Jones* (1963), from the Fielding novel.) A few years later, the Beatles expressed their own more antic revolutionary spirit on the screen in *A Hard Day's Night* (1964), directed by the American expatriate Richard Lester, while James Bond, in a series beginning with Terence Young's *Dr No* (1962), demonstrated that defending the establishment could be far more lucrative than attacking it. At the same time, foreign directors like Lester, Joseph Losey (*Accident*, 1967), Roman Polanski (*Repulsion*, 1965), Michelangelo Antonioni (*Blow-up*, 1967), and Stanley Kubrick (*2001: A Space Odyssey*, 1968) enriched the British movie world. In addition, a BBC-trained generation of directors, such as Ken Russell (*Women in Love*, 1969), made the transition from TV to features.

Nevertheless, beneath this ferment, the movie business in Britain still lacked a dependable infrastructure and a sufficiently devoted home audience to support more than throwaway comedies. In the postwar period, Rank had begun the latest and most ardent pursuit of that elusive grail, a meaningful share of the American market. Initially confident of victory, he failed in the end, done in by bad luck, the connivance of American producers and the absence of enough high-quality English films. By the late 1940s, his company was losing millions of pounds. This opened the way, or created the need, for even more American investment, and English movie-makers found themselves resting on the twin crutches of overseas capital and government funding (through the NFFC). The British cinema could not really

achieve self-sufficiency even when it had won aesthetic independence and, creatively, was in full bloom. Unhappily, in the years
1969–71, both of the industry's lifelines were cut off.

Suffering losses of their own, the American studios dramatically reduced their spending in England, while simultaneously
the new Conservative administration of Edward Heath decided
to terminate the NFFC. Except for isolated spurts of activity –
e.g. the off-beat work of Nicholas Roeg (*The Man Who Fell to
Earth*, 1976) – film-making in England has remained stagnant
since the 1970s. In accordance with the dreary pattern of the
past, English directors have been denied the opportunity to
develop their gifts on native soil with indigenous subject-matter.
Instead, those who don't want to retreat into TV or low-budget
films have joined the eternal migration to Hollywood, where
they are quickly swallowed up in the glossy, depersonalized
machine of American movie-making. The most recent candidate
for Hollywood-style tycoonhood, Lord Grade, seems to have
relived the failures of previous English impresarios without their
infrequent works of excellence. A man of immense dedication
and ability such as David Puttnam may arise, but it is unlikely
that other producers and directors will be able to overcome the
inherent vicissitudes of a business that has never stood on solid
ground. In the foreseeable future, a true English national cinema
– films of a distinctly British character comparable in worth to
those of France, Italy and the United States – seems an all but
unreachable goal.

2 A Biography of Reed

When Sir Carol Reed died in April 1976 his artistic and commercial reputation had long since preceded him, buried by increasingly disenchanted critics and an indifferent public. Still, as one of the preeminent ironists of English-speaking films, he might well have found a bleak amusement in his own obituaries, most of them relegated to the obituary page itself and tossed off in obvious haste and carelessness. In short, reports of his death were greatly understated, and although understatement was one of the outstanding features of his work, there is no indication that the parallel was intentional.

As far as biographical details are concerned, the superficiality of the newsmen is quite forgivable, since existing accounts of Reed's life are hardly rich in detail. He was born 30 December 1906 in Putney, London, and while standard biographical references give the impression of a conventional upper-middle-class upbringing in thoroughly respectable surroundings, they omit any direct reference to Reed's parentage. Apparently only Michael Korda, the nephew of Sir Alexander Korda and a friend of Reed's, and Madeleine Bingham, a biographer of Sir Herbert Beerbohm Tree, the great actor and stage manager, reveal the truth: that the director was actually the illegitimate son of Tree. Tree, who was married to Maud Holt, rather openly maintained a second household, with a 'wife' and children. The practice was common among the nobility in late Victorian and Edwardian England, and though these liaisons were frequently a matter of general knowledge, unspoken standards of decorum prevented any public allusions to them until an era of greater biographical candour arrived. Any last vestige of tactful silence ended emphatically with the airing of *The Duchess of Duke Street*, *Edward and Mrs Simpson*, and other British television series that took price in throwing open the bedroom doors of a previous generation of aristocrats.

Tree seems to have carried on this illicit tradition with considerable vigour. His relationship with Carol Reed's mother, May Pinney, was lengthy, and he appears to have bolstered it with as much financial and emotional support as was possible. This was no meagre effort, since his mistress bore him five children other than Carol. Most accounts portray Tree as a generous and affectionate man, but of course it would be naive to imagine that either his wife or his mistress accepted his brand of *droit du seigneur* without some measure of mortification and anger. Frances Donaldson, one of Tree's biographers, has recorded Lady Tree's fury over her husband's extramarital affairs and observes that 'Tree was as incapable of fidelity as his wife was of condoning infidelity.'[2] Of May's feelings on the matter we have no testimony, but if *Duchess of Duke Street* is any barometer of a woman's emotional state in these circumstances, she simply lived out the sad mummery Tree designed for her: she was cast as the wife of an eternally absent and quite fictitious 'Mr Reed', though all conjugal functions were performed by Tree. Since he could never give her his name, they made one up, and even this was a poignant reminder of her status as a shadowy appendage of her lover's grandiose, strutting existence. As Max Reed, Carol's son, explains it, 'Reed' was a 'semi-anagram of Tree'.[3]

Yet one wonders if Tree was flattered or embarrassed by the small offshoot of himself with which he was soon confronted in Carol Reed. The physical similarity was startling, and naturally it only increased with the passage of time. Moreover, the boy embraced his father's life still more closely by determining that he too would be an actor. These aspirations were not encouraged, however. Raised in bourgeois comfort, Reed was given a traditional public school education at King's School, Canterbury, one of the oldest boarding schools in England. His years there were most unhappy, a 'savage' experience, according to Max. Tree's sudden death in 1917 must have accentuated his sense of isolation, since now he didn't even have a semblance of a father.

Ignoring his theatrical hopes, his mother sent him to the United States in 1922, in the company of an older brother, to learn chicken farming, evidently as an apprenticeship for an agricultural career in England. Young Reed did not warm to the barnyard, however, and he was sent back home in less than a year. Seeing that further opposition was futile, Reed's mother permitted him to turn to acting, and he was subsequently able to join a company headed by Dame Sybil Thorndike. He made his London debut in 1924 at the age of eighteen, appearing in a play called *Heraclius*. Shortly afterwards he was accepted into a troupe founded by Edgar Wallace, the mystery writer, who was seeking to transfer his phenomenal popularity from the bookstalls to the footlights. Reed appeared in three Wallace productions in the West End; among them was *The Terror*, in which he played a detective. Offstage, he doubled as stage manager. Gradually his role in the company shifted to the production end, and in 1930 he was sent to New York to produce Wallace's *On the Spot*. While there, he saw Spencer Tracy in *The Last Mile* and subsequently produced the play in London.

Wallace also provided Reed's entrée to the movies. The youthful factotum was selected to oversee the numerous screen adaptations of Wallace's works that began to appear at this time. These activities brought him into contact with Basil Dean, the founder of Associated Talking Pictures, who had contracted to produce film versions of several of Wallace's stories. After Wallace's death in 1932, Reed moved onto Dean's staff, working first as dialogue director on the countless films that Associated was grinding out. Reed soon rose to second-unit director on *Autumn Crocus* (1934) and assistant director on *Java Head* and *Sing As We Go* (both 1934). The following year he codirected *It Happened in Paris*, with Robert Wyler. The film was an insignificant *jeu d'ésprit* from a French play about a rich man in disguise and did nothing in particular for Reed's reputation, but a few months later he was directing his first real film, *Midshipman Easy*. A rip-roaring naval adventure, it was moderately successful both with the reviewers and the public. Reed was immediately assigned a spot on the studio conveyor belt, where he turned out a number of the standard-issue melodramas and comedies favoured by British studios in this period. On a three-week visit to Hollywood in 1937, he had the opportunity to observe the glamour, affluence and technical supremacy of the 'film capital' at first hand; in later years, he implied that he would have preferred to stay but was not invited to do so. He was, after all, still only a minor director in a minor film culture.

By 1939 Reed had directed seven more movies. Although some of these were exported to America and received approximately the same plaudits they had in England, Reed's career up

to this point was primarily a British phenomenon. All this began
to change in the period 1939–41 when Reed directed *The Stars
Look Down* and *Night Train*, each a quantum leap in cinematic
mastery for its young director. The critical enthusiasm that the
films aroused in Britain was echoed on the other side of the
Atlantic, and, in addition, *Night Train* was a modest hit in the
US. For the next decade and a half, Reed was one of the most
acclaimed directors in England, and his reputation in America
did not lag far behind.

With the outbreak of the Second World War, Reed joined the
British film unit of the War Office, the Army Kinematograph
Service, where he managed to fuse professional activity and
patriotism. Under the sponsorship of the Department of Army
Psychology, he produced and directed *The New Lot*, a training
film for inductees. The film was deemed so effective by the War
Office that Reed was encouraged to expand the basic material
into a feature film and given a sizeable staff and generous
financial support. The completed film, *The Way Ahead*, was a
semi-documentary account of the initiation – through rigour and
discipline, flame and hail – of a company of raw recruits. The
picture was a huge hit with everyone – John Bull and Tommy
Atkins, the War Office and the newspaper critics. Reed followed
this with a traditional documentary, *The True Glory*, a superb
account of the Normandy invasion, codirected with the American writer/director Garson Kanin.

The war over, Reed was hired by J. Arthur Rank, by then the
single most powerful figure in British films, and set to work on
his first 'civilian' movie since 1941. His immense prestige, combined with a good commercial record, allowed him to select a
decidedly downbeat subject and to lavish more time and money
on it than most directors would be allowed. The result was *Odd
Man Out*, hailed as a masterpiece by many critics and a box office
hit – at least in Europe, where Reed had gauged the mood of
postwar despondency with a caliper-like accuracy.

Financial conflicts between Reed and the Rank organization
seem to have eliminated any possibility of further work under its
aegis, so Reed took his next project to Rank's chief rival, Sir
Alexander Korda. His next two films were both produced by
Korda and each added new lustre to the director's fame, while
simultaneously expanding the size of his audience. *The Fallen
Idol*, his first collaboration with Graham Greene, was a brilliant

piece of dramatic legerdemain in which little tricks of perception, flashed to us through the eyes of a small boy, created a dissertation on illusion and reality. *The Third Man*, another thinking man's melodrama by Greene, was even more remarkable. It featured a mesmerizing account of black market activity in postwar Vienna with an ingenious plot, an unforgettable mood of decay, a perfect mesh of mood and character and a famous score, performed entirely on a zither, that reinforced everything. An unmistakable crowd-pleaser, *The Third Man* eclipsed all other Reed films in popularity up to this point.

During this period, Reed's fame had reached its summit and bouquets were being flung from every direction. *The Fallen Idol* and *Odd Man Out* each received the British Film of the Year Award (the British equivalent of the Academy Award), and *The Third Man* took the grand prize at Cannes in 1949. The *New York Times Magazine* honoured Reed with a full spread. Back home, in October of 1952, England provided the ultimate accolade: Reed was knighted. To celebrate his achievements, a festival of his work was held at the British Film Institute.

Even after Reed had been hailed as the laureate of his country's cinema, the spotlights never captured much of his private life. Between 1941, the year of *Young Mr Pitt* and 1950, which saw *The Third Man* take the cinema world by storm, there were only a half dozen profiles of Reed in the press. Doubtless his reserved temperament, notably devoid of the riding-crop-and-beret flamboyance of other directors, helps explain much of this apparent neglect. In any event, it is a matter of public record that in 1943 Reed took time out from his film work to marry Diana Wynyard. A leading British actress of the 1930s and 1940s, Wynyard had starred in Noel Coward's famous *Cavalcade* (1933) and later in Reed's *Kipps* (1941), one of her better films. Of the marriage itself, the record shows nothing except that it produced no children and ended in divorce in 1947. A year later, Reed married Penelope Dudley Ward, an actress and the daughter of the prominent Liberal MP William Dudley Ward and his wife Frieda (who achieved minor immortality as Wallis Simpson's immediate predecessor in the affections of the Prince of Wales). In 1948, 'Pempy', as she was known, gave birth to Max, who was named for Carol's uncle, Sir Max Beerbohm. The boy was Reed's only child, though the marriage also brought him a step-daughter, Tracy, Pempy's child from her previous marriage to Tony Pelissier.

In appearance, Reed ought to have been less unmistakably English than he was. His grandfather, Julius Beerbohm, was a German immigrant, after all. Yet Reed was an impeccably Anglo-Saxon figure. The fullest physical description of him appears in C. A. Lejeune's 1941 interview with the director in *The New York Times*: 'Carol Reed is a tall, pale, serious young man. He has a long, oval face, light brown hair brushed straight back from his forehead, light blue-gray eyes close-set on a slightly curved nose, strong white teeth and a sensitive mouth. He wears light suits with broad, loose ties, and a signet ring . . . ,'[1]

In later years, Reed's large-boned frame accumulated girth, and his size was an essential feature of the vivid physical impression he made on people. Michael Korda, who was fourteen when he met Reed in 1947, has no difficulty summoning up images of him: 'He was enormous, very tall . . . bulky towards the end of his life but not fat. He had a huge face with noble, fleshy, larger than life features. His hands were very beautiful, I remember, very expressive.' In his dress, Reed somehow united the contradictory impulses of the disorderly artist and the man about town. Korda compares him to a 'dishevelled British lawyer – Rumpole of the Old Bailey' and explains the odd chemistry by which he achieved this look: 'He had a taste for expensive clothing but it was uncared for, unlike my Uncle Alex, who had a taste for expensive clothing beautifully cared for. Carol had the same tailor as Alex, his clothes were cut from the same cloth as Alex's. But the suits always looked different on Carol than on Alex for some reason. They didn't work on Carol. But it didn't matter.'

If we trusted the journalistic portraits of Reed, we would have to regard him as self-effacing to the point of invisibility. Interviewers seem to have been totally unable to locate an identifiable personality in him. He was generally willing to speak at length about his work but so earnestly as to seem almost colourless and without a tinge of egotism. Again and again he attributed his success to hard work and the ability to surround himself with excellent coworkers. The sheer frustration of trying to describe

Reed the man is a common theme in the secondary source material on him.

Nevertheless, when he is repeatedly depicted as polite, soft-spoken and enormously considerate, even these few jots give us the picture of a certain English type, a well-bred, intensely civil individual, the 'best of a breed', with an equable temperament and an effortless urbanity. In the profile in the *Times Magazine*, the author, Harvey Breit, quotes an unnamed critic who commented that even 'the people who have worked with him and know him best find it hard to describe him as a personality. To all intents and purposes he is not a man at all.' That Reed had a sense of humour off the set as well as on can be seen from his response: 'I realize what an unusual advantage this is going to give me in the future. After this, how can I any longer be blamed for anything I am supposed to have done wrong? I am not a man at all: it's in print.'[5]

But it seems that this courteous cipher, devoid of traits, is only the public persona Reed donned for the press. Those who were acquainted with him take emphatic exception to the notion that he was reticent or bland. If anything, they recall him as a welter of joyous idiosyncracies, a dignified merry andrew with his own brand of droll tricks and slightly outlandish behaviour. Although he had only one real hobby, for instance, collecting pets, he undertook it with a cockeyed passion that no one has ever forgotten. 'One wall of the Reeds' drawing room', writes Korda, 'was built in the form of a gigantic aviary in which dozens of birds of different kinds fought, screeched and defecated . . . Alex was particularly apprehensive about Carol's "zoo." He disliked going to other people's houses – even houses without tortoises in the bathrooms and guinea pigs on the stairs.'[6] Max gently disputes the menagerie-like scope of Korda's recollection ('Korda makes more of it than it was – he was terribly young'), but agrees with the essence of Korda's observation. It should also be noted that Pempy showed great cunning in combatting her husband's zoological obsession. 'She had a deal with the pet shop', says Max, 'that anything could be returned in twenty-four hours. So when my father would appear with some mad animal, my mother would send it back the next day.'

Reed's considerable physical presence was augmented by a powerful set of vocal chords. Troubled by hearing problems for years, he compensated, unconsciously, by allowing the volume of his speech to rise to a thunderous level. 'He had a great booming voice', says Korda, who takes obvious pleasure in his gift for mimicry and embroiders his reminiscences with amusing imitations. His 'Carol Reed' is spirited: ' "Pempy! Pempy! Come here! You must see what the bird is doing." '

Reed's Savile Row wardrobe was only one of a number of acquisitions by which the director celebrated his success. He and his wife occupied a large, attractive home on King's Road in Chelsea, and he was able to indulge a fondness for luxurious cars, first a Jaguar and then a Bentley. On at least one occasion, his eccentricity had fairly tragicomic results. Enamored of the ivy that clung to his house, he let it grow in untrammelled fashion, with the consequence that one day it pulled an entire wall down.

At the same time, Reed was a man of many dimensions, and the part of him that desired elegant suits was far less dominant than the part which mussed them up. Materialism and acquisitiveness never got much of a hold on him. 'He cared nothing for money', says Max. 'He certainly wasn't extravagant. In addition, he was always mucking up his tax matters. There's a law here which allows you to spend a year away and you don't pay all your tax on the year before when you were in England. You pay your tax when it's due, then you spend a year out of the country. You declare yourself non-resident, and then you get all the money back when you return. After *Oliver!*, my father was living in France and Italy, and he suddenly came back after ten and a half months because he was so bored. So he had to pay the whole lot.' Max chuckles and adds, 'Well, after all, it was his money.'

Nor did Reed ever seriously contemplate fleeing to some cosy tax haven, like so many of his fellow Englishmen. 'He felt he was English', says Max, 'and this was his country. In his own way he was terribly proud of being knighted.' Asked if leaving the country to escape the tax man might have seemed unpatriotic to Reed, Max replies, 'Yes, but he never would have used that word to describe his feelings.' In a characteristically British way, it was those values that were dearest to him about which he was most oblique and off-hand and those gestures that showed the greatest kindness about which he was most nonchalant. Andrew Birkin, Reed's nephew and a successful screenwriter, reports a telling incident from his lean and hungry days in Hollywood:

I was over there trying to break into the film business, and
Carol was making *Agony and the Ecstasy*. I had very little money
but quite a lot of pride. I remember going along to see him and
Pempy, and he asked, 'How's it going? Are you short of
money? I said, 'No, no – everything's fine.' It wasn't until I'd
gotten home that I found he'd put eighty or a hundred dollars
into my jacket. He didn't give it to me; he just tucked it into
the pocket, knowing that I'd find it later. When I rang him up
to thank him, he almost pretended that he didn't know what I
was talking about.

While Reed was failing to build up his bank account, he was
accumulating a resource that was far more important to him: an
abundant personal life. In the commerce of human relationships,
he was a true tycoon. Doubtless it wasn't a very difficult accomplishment for someone who, in Korda's words, was 'a wonderful,
funny, kind, perceptive, gentle man'. 'He adored his family',
Max declares, and there seems to be no one among the Reeds or
their various in-laws who did not reciprocate his feelings. His
second marriage flourished and he was an exceptionally devoted
father. Since his own childhood had been emotionally under-
nourished, he was determined that Max should be raised in a
loving and protective atmosphere. The boy was sent to excellent
preparatory and public schools (Selwyn House in Broadstairs
and Stowe in Buckinghamshire, respectively), yet he was spared
much of the Stalky-like unpleasantness Reed had evidently
endured under similar circumstances. 'He had had such a terrible time at school himself', says Max, 'that it was rather good for
me. If I happened to be in trouble, he was sure it was the
school's fault.' In 1968, his father made it possible for him to
enter the film business himself by hiring him to work on *Oliver!*
On one occasion, his loving treatment of his son had such
humorous repercussions that the episode has become a favourite
family vignette. Strolling along the London streets one day when
Max was a small boy, idling in front of shop windows, Reed was
so demonstrative in his affection for his son that he attracted the
attention of a policeman, who followed the two of them home.
Apparently thinking he might be on to a kidnapping, he knocked
on the door and demanded an explanation for Reed's 'suspi-
cious' behaviour.

Reed's personal life was rendered still fuller by his large assortment of friends. Despite the public appearance of diffidence and reserve, he was an intensely sociable man, at least among people of compatible backgrounds and interests. 'The house was always filled with people', Korda reports. Occasionally one of these visitors was Peter Ustinov, the Reeds' next-door neighbour and a close friend of theirs. Although on a given night almost any other member of the British theatrical and cinematic establishment might be on hand, the most frequent guests were, of course, the Kordas: Zoltán, a director of world renown; Vincent, a distinguished set designer (and father of Michael); and Alex, head of London Films and the acknowledged laird of the clan.

Little in Reed's life seems odder than his professional and personal links to this family of mercurial Anglo-Hungarians, with their cultured, Semitic origins, their canny sense of self-promotion, their volatile temperaments and their comedic accents. Who could have seemed more out of place in their midst than a genial, even-tempered, towering Englishman like Reed? Yet the affinity he discovered for them and they for him was as profound as a blood tie and as unchanging.

Among Reed's friends, there seems to have been general agreement that he was never more endearing than when his taste for whimsy and playfulness emerged. Evidently he saw nothing wrong with exercising his inventive powers on his own biography. 'He loved to make up stories about himself', says Max.

He told wonderful stories; then you'd find out they weren't true. He always told me Sir Henry Irving, his father's great friend and competitor, got him his first acting job, and his mother came to see him. He was playing the fourth swordsman in something or other and got so carried away that Irving pulled him into the limelight and left him standing there so his mother could see what a wonderful actor she'd raised.

The story is so charming it hardly seems to matter that Irving died a year before Reed was born. A fanciful quality also clings to Reed's version of how he came to be employed by Wallace. 'He was assistant stage manager', says Max.

You know those banks of switches backstage, about 500 switches? They turn on every light you could ever want, but you only use about eight of them if it's a small play. My father spent all his time turning the switches back and forth. And Edgar Wallace thought his command of the equipment was so wonderful, the way he kept the whole show going, that he engaged him.

Reed's playful streak can be traced back to a more primary characteristic, a sort of perpetual boyhood that survived alongside the ardent loyalty and decency, informed compassion, well-tempered irony and other traits that made up his mature personality. To Alex, the most surprising aspect of the collaboration of Reed and Greene was that it revealed not only two gifted artists but 'two English schoolboys', bantering back and forth in endless exchanges of public school wit. In fact, Alex was quite dismayed that Reed and Greene would not take the movie business more seriously!

'It sounds so trite', Birkin observes apologetically, 'but he had a Peter Pan quality. He was the ultimate kind of godfather. He was marvellous with children.' Reed's rapport with young people should not be much of a revelation to anyone who has seen his films, since children are often integral to his plots and his sensitive handling of child actors has been almost uniformly praised. It is startling, however, to learn how many boyhood impulses remained alive in the adult Reed. Throughout his life, he retained the capacity to transform himself into a kind of outsized Puck. 'He loved teasing and practical jokes', says Birkin. 'He absolutely adored Pempy, but he also loved teasing people. He used to tease her unmercifully with this parrot he had, until she was almost ready to throw him out on the street. He would say, "Pemp dear, what do you mean it's ruining the furniture? Of course it's not."'

Reed must have been especially delighted when he had the opportunity to unleash his prankishness among a group of children. One of Birkin's cherished memories of adolescence is a boat ride on the Thames for the children of the family – 'it was me and my sisters and Max' – which Reed organized one Christmas. It was raining heavily and a tarpaulin was set in place overhead to protect the passengers. Reed had had several drinks and was clearly intoxicated, but 'he was one of those people who got wonderful when he drank'. Mischievously, he began to tug at the ropes which secured the tarpaulin, releasing the pools of water which had collected on the canvas roof and drenching the passengers within. The impromptu performance delighted his audience of juveniles. 'I never laughed so hard in my life', says Birkin. 'Like all of Carol's practical jokes, it was done with an actor's sense of style, with real panache.'

Again and again one hears of this propensity for ingenuous mirth; whenever life provided the opportunity for simple, direct fun, Reed helped himself to it like party cake. According to Korda, the enjoyment Reed derived from his possessions was properly classified as childlike rather than materialistic: 'He was very proud of the Jaguar, but the Bentley! You couldn't go to the house without Carol taking you out to the garage to show it to you. He was like a child with a toy.' Another permutation of this irrepressibly youthful quality was his desire for immediate gratification. 'My father loved to see people', says Max, 'but he hated to make plans and arrange things. Often someone would have rung up to ask us out to dinner, and he'd say, "Oh good, let's go now." You'd say, "But we haven't been asked for now; we've been asked for next week", and he'd say, "But do we know we'll want to go next week? Or how do we know they'll want us to go next week?" He loved everything to be as spontaneous as possible.' Judy Campbell, Birkin's mother and a noted stage actress, remembers Reed's sudden fascination with a doll of hers after she mentioned in passing that it had a toy heart. Forgetting a social engagement which he and Pempy had, he became totally absorbed in the doll, seeking a way to detect the tiny heart buried under the rubber chest. 'Carol dear, we're going to be late', Pempy chided. 'Let's put it under the tap, and perhaps we can see the heart that way', said Reed.

If there was a boyish Reed, there was a sober one too – a man whom life had tested, challenged, rewarded and punished. Denied a real father, he was only eleven when he lost even the stand-in he had had. That his illegitimate parentage left a wound can be deduced from the fact that any direct mention of it was taboo. 'He just didn't talk about it', says Birkin. 'I was told off the record.' Korda views Reed as a man in search of a father and asserts that he found a substitute in Alex. Max regards this as an overly Freudian conception of a relationship in which business factors, not psychological hunger, created a certain dependency. Yet the two men are in complete accord on one matter: that Reed and Korda had an unusually productive symbiosis and that Alex's premature death in 1956 created a vacuum in Reed's professional life that was never filled. 'My father was in no sense a financier', Max remarks. 'He was not one to put packages together. Alex took care of that. The success of the relationship was the fact that Korda would say, "Here we are: you make the movie and leave the rest to me."' Although Reed was sometimes credited with producing as well as directing his films, the former was a purely nominal designation. It was Alex's invisible hand, moving with accustomed skill in the background, that set all the financial and administrative elements in place.

Liberated from external pressures, free to make the best films he was capable of, Reed rose brilliantly to the challenge, tapping his creative reources to the fullest and exacting the most from those around him. With Alex as his bulwark, Reed could adopt the working methods through which he achieved the most impressive results: a slow, methodical pace and an attentiveness to every detail and nuance of the film-making process. 'My father always worked terribly hard on each movie', says Max. 'I worked with him on *Oliver!*, so I saw it all first hand. He lived for his work.'

Professional harmony was another asset Reed could count on during his association with Alex. No one was assigned to a Reed film unless he was suitable for it, and that meant enjoying an artistic and temperamental rapport with its director. Like many successful film-makers, Reed accumulated a band of kindred spirits, and they became the frequent, if not permanent, personnel of his movies. Above all, at London Films he had the Kordas to sustain and strengthen his every endeavour. Vincent designed outstanding sets, Zoli was a fountain of shrewd suggestions and thoughtful tips, and Alex was the embodiment of a great producer. 'Alex was a producer in the old sense', Korda notes. 'He saw rushes every day. He would say to Carol, "Take my advice, my boy. This does not work. This should be changed." Carol was not an *auteur* director. His reaction would be, "God, you're right, Alex. Oh, Pempy, this is wonderful. Listen to what Alex just said. Get Graham on the phone. We'll write a couple of lines into the script to cover it."'

Working for Alex had other compensations. England's most

flamboyant entrepreneur could put as much energy into his after-hours revelry as he could into his work, and he saw to it that everyone around him had the opportunity to relieve the rigours of film-making with plenty of elegant soirées. Because of the constant interchange of ideas among the film-makers at these affairs, Korda views them as an intrinsic part of the creative process:

> These people saw each other socially. When they were making a movie, Carol and my father saw each other every night. Graham was often there. And at least twice a week the dinners would be held at Alex's, where they were much more elaborate dinners because they would include Winston Churchill, Max Beaverbrook, Larry Olivier and a cast of thirty. Which, in my uncle's opinion, was a modest dinner party. And so you can't really separate these elements from the films. There was an on-going collaborative effort.

Unlike Alex, whose command of languages and literate background impressed even Greene, Reed was culturally one-dimensional. Film was the only art he was interested in, and even narrative fiction did not have much influence on his creative make-up. 'He did not read books or even newspapers', Korda says flatly, an evaluation Birkin agrees with. (Ironically, after several years in the film business, Max became a rare book dealer.) Reed's imagination was largely visual. By contrast, Pempy was the intellectual in the household; she read extensively and made many recommendations to her husband (most of which the Kordas regarded as ill-considered, though they found her entrancing). Another woman to whom Reed looked for literary guidance, and one of the most colourful figures who orbited through the Korda universe, was Baroness Moura Budberg, a Russian émigré and the former mistress of several prominent authors. Alex kept her on his staff as a reader, and Korda thinks it likely that she had a hand in the preparations for *Outcast of the Islands*, Reed's film of the Joseph Conrad novel. He believes that Reed probably never read the book, relying instead on Budberg's precis, from which he developed his blueprint for the movie, visualizing each sequence as she read it to him. Working with Budberg had its unnerving aspects, however. 'She had been the mistress of Maxim Gorky', says Korda, 'and then the mistress of H.G. Wells, both of whom died in her arms. Carol was deathly afraid that he would die in her arms too. She was not his mistress, you understand, but he was still frightened that he might go the way of Gorky and Wells.'

Despite the support system Alex was able to provide, Reed's last few movies for London Films were far from blockbusters. After *The Third Man*, Alex's judgement began to betray him, a deterioration that was nowhere more evident than in his having cajoled Reed into adapting *Outcast*, one of Conrad's most commercially unsound novels. A book without a conventional hero or heroine and whose only sympathetic character is an elderly sea captain was bound to be unenticing to a mass audience. Reed's film was superb, as it turned out, but the public did not take to it. He tried to regain his footing with his next venture, *The Man Between* (1953), a recycling of *The Third Man*, but the movie failed to excite the critics or the public. The same was true of *A Kid For Two Farthings* (1955), Reed's first colour film, in which he essayed a new form – the comic fantasy. Regardless of its novelty, the movie had only a mild success in England and was hardly seen in America, where the critical response was tepid, and the audiences were indifferent.

In spite of these failures, Reed was contented with the Kordas and the Kordas with him. Indeed, considering how secure and settled Reed came to feel in this little polyglot world of expatriates, with their deep devotion to the English way of life and to uniquely English artists like Reed, the dislocation that he suffered when it all came to an end in 1956 must have been excruciating. Thrust out into a cheerless, indifferent void, he felt he had nowhere to go but Hollywood if he was to continue practising his craft. The people he encountered there were painfully far removed from the Kordas. 'After all those wonderful years with Alex', says Korda, 'Carol was suddenly flung out into the jungle with monsters like Martin Ransohoff, Marty Ritt, and Marlon Brando. He was a gentle man dealing with all these horrible creatures. A sensitive director forced to do awful films for big studios with horrible executives snapping at him.'

Of Reed's work during this period, Max only remarks that his father 'did films when he was asked to'. Korda is much blunter. While he expresses genuine sorrow over what he sees as the steady decline of an artist in Babylon, he also relishes the opportunity to show off his Hungarian accent, which is, quite understandably, the jewel of his repertoire: 'Alex would have said, "Carol, vat you vant to do this for? Carol, dear boy, is money the problem? Ve find it for you – 100 000, 200 000. Vatever you need. But don't go back there."'

Korda's interpretation of the close bond between Reed and Alex and what it meant to Reed's career has an undeniable core of truth. It would be exceedingly naive, however, to ignore the fact that Korda's perceptions are strongly coloured by family loyalties. In his view, Reed's only sustained stretch of memorable work came during his eight-year association with Alex. Unquestionably, these were happy and productive times for Reed. But by any reasonable artistic estimate, he created admirable movies before and after his affiliation with the Kordas and his greatest film, *Odd Man Out*, owed nothing whatsoever to them.

Reed's American films are especially in need of reappraisal. His first, *Trapeze*, was shot in Cinemascope and was very much a big budget Hollywood effort. It is always dangerous to ascribe specific motivations to a director who was both highly introverted and very complex, but it is hard to resist the hypothesis that Reed was retreating into the safest project he could find. In any event, the results were much better than has generally been admitted. A great popular success, *Trapeze* revitalized Reed's career. For whatever reason, he chose to exercise his new credibility in American or American-financed projects for the remainder of his career.

The Key (1958), written and produced by the American screenwriter Carl Foreman and shot in England, followed *Trapeze* – and in some respects imitated it as well. Although Reed was again working on British soil, and in conjunction with Trevor Howard, one of his favourite actors, the film was a disappointment. The reviews were respectful, but the movie didn't find much of an audience in the United States and was only able to show a small profit because of healthy grosses from overseas. Today *The Key* has few adherents.

Reed was back in 1960 with *Our Man in Havana*, shot in Cuba and written by Graham Greene, by far the best scenarist Reed had ever worked with. Together they managed to exact nimble performances from a 'star-studded' cast – presumably imposed by the studio – which might have been heavy baggage in a traditional Hollywood vehicle. The film was a critical but not a popular success, yet on the basis of this mixed record, 20th Century-Fox hired Reed for the perilous job of directing Marlon Brando in *Mutiny on the Bounty* (1962). But even Reed's famous tact was not enough to woo Brando into compliance and professionalism. After many quarrels with the star, Reed quit and was replaced by Lewis Milestone. Quickly Reed backtracked to the thriller form for his next work, *The Running Man* (1963), a minor but appealing film.

Perhaps the faultiest decision in Reed's career came when he agreed to direct *The Agony and the Ecstasy* (1965), Fox's adaptation of the Irving Stone best-seller about Michelangelo. There is probably no director who could have brought much life to the inert material, especially with the added encumbrance of Charleton Heston. In any case, Reed was not even able to lift it to the level of decent popular entertainment, let alone art. The critics were disparaging, and the public stayed far away.

At the age of sixty-two, Reed was still resilient, however, and three years later he returned triumphantly with *Oliver!*, a big, glossy screen version of the Lionel Bart musical that catapulted the director back into good favour at the studios. The reviews were mostly laudatory, but what Reed really needed at this juncture in his career was a box office smash, an accomplishment he had not really had since *Trapeze* in 1956. As it happened, *Oliver!* proved to be one of the major successes of the year – this in an era when most musicals were sinking like the Titanic. In addition to abundant revenues, *Oliver!* carried off two major Academy Awards: best film and best director.

Sadly enough, however, Reed's last two films – *Flap* (1970) and *The Public Eye* (1972) – were well below the standards of even his better Hollywood efforts. *Flap*, a misguided civil rights gesture on behalf of the Indians, starred Anthony Quinn and was shot in New Mexico, a locale which put Reed about as far out of his element as one could imagine. It would have been a miracle if the director had been able to demonstrate any rapport with his story. In an unimaginative interview on the set, Kevin Thomas of the *Los Angeles Times* stressed Reed's equipoise and made him seem even more nondescript than usual by summing him up, punningly, as 'unflappable'.[7] However temperate Reed's disposition, however, it was no help to him with material as disastrous as *Flap*, nor even with *The Public Eye*, a limp Peter Shaffer comedy set in London which a younger, more energetic Reed might have been able to salvage. Instead, the film was even drearier than the original one-act play and was coldly received by reviewers and filmgoers alike.

No doubt Reed's poor commercial showing in these last years pushed him to the sidelines of the industry, yet even in the crass dens of Hollywood, where a director's worth is almost always reckoned on a calculator, no one seems to have borne Reed any animosity. There is no reason to doubt Birkin's simple statement that 'everybody loved him – everybody'. On the other hand, Korda, a man of two cultures, offers an intriguing perspective on the 'Englishness' which permeated Reed's soul, and the way it bonded him to other men of his age and class:

If you want to know what Carol was like, think of Ralph Richardson. That kind of baffled Englishman, full of shy charm, behind which there lurks a certain maliciousness, a wariness, something held in reserve. Richardson, Oliver, Carol, even to a degree Graham Greene – all of them have a passionate need to be English gentlemen in the most theatrical sense of the word, which implies a certain lifestyle but also a kind of shy, baffled charm. There is a malicious spirit, a cleverness, an intelligence, a certain spiky hostility behind the blandest, the most engaging, even the most fatuous of English charm. I don't mean that these people are like that all the time. But it's crucial part of them, and Carol had that essence.

Korda's dissection of the species of Englishman represented by Reed and his friends is uttered with gusto and conviction, but with respect and admiration – even envy – as well. No matter how provocative his commentary becomes, it always exudes a sense of distant kinship, the cousinhood of an American who will always be partially English (and partial *to* the English). As such, he feels empowered to share his most pungent thoughts about the ethos Reed lived in and exemplified:

Carol was not good with women because like a lot of Englishmen of a certain age, I don't think Carol much liked or understood women. He was not a romantic figure, anymore than Ralph is. Or to be honest, Olivier is. Not that I'm

imputing homosexuality to them. It's just that women do not
enter very largely into their lives. Carol was devoted to Pempy.
And for good reason. Pempy was a wonderful woman. But
women as such – I can't imagine Carol playing around. Not
just because he was devoted to his wife but because women
did not interest him that much. He liked to be with Graham
and Vincent and Alex . . . And that shows in Carol's films. He
didn't make very many movies with good women characters.

Trevor Howard is another example. He'd rather drink with
his cronies than go home. They're all heavy drinkers, but that
is an English tradition too – a lot of heavy drinking without
getting drunk because they drink so much that they're anaes-
thetized to it. And the element of homosexuality is there, but
it's suppressed. I think Reed was entirely heterosexual and
had a baffled incomprehension of the whole idea of homosexuality. But there was an ambiguity there which is very English.

Whatever the merits of Korda's critique of the 'English gentleman', it remains true that Reed's closest associates were invariably men and that in his work it is the interaction of the male
characters that contains the most potent dramatic charge. From
The Stars Look Down, Reed's first major film, through *Oliver!*, his
last work of note, there are very few instances in which women
receive the same detailed, thoughtful, incisive treatment as the
men.

One enormous gap in the available biographical material on
Reed – including the interviews conducted for this study – is any
sense of his own perspective on his work. Self-appraisal would
appear to have run counter to his constitutional modesty. He
discussed *how* he made his films in a number of interviews, but
we have little idea what he thought about their relative merits,
what satisfaction or disappointment they brought him, what
facets of the film-making process he found easiest or most
difficult, whether he felt as mistreated by American studios as
Korda says he did, how he regarded individual colleagues,
American or British, and their contributions to his movies, what
went wrong (or right, for that matter) on a given project and
why. The most delicate subject is, of course, how he reacted to
the widespread notion of his irreversible creative decline after
Alex's death. 'I didn't really talk to him about the success or

failure of his films', says Max, 'because it would be like saying, why did you get it wrong on that one? I do remember that he was enormously hurt if he got bad reviews. He cared passionately about the English press in particular because he lived in England. If he got good reviews here but terrible ones in the rest of the world it would have been better than vice versa.'

To anyone who cared about Reed or who admires his work, the last years of his life have a terribly melancholy caste. From 1972, the year of his final film, to his death in 1976, his professional stature plummeted, dragging his morale and his ego along behind it. Darkness seems to have closed over him, with only an occasional flash of humour and hopefulness. To Max and to Andrew Birkin, Reed's biggest problem was his own inability to find a suitable story. 'He was very much aware that it was a certain type of story he did best', says Birkin. Korda gives a gloomier account of Reed's circumstances, a portrait edged in black:

> I saw him the year he died and he was not well. He missed his friends terribly. Alex was dead, Zoli was dead, and Graham had moved to the south of France. He was no longer a major force in motion pictures or even a minor one, and therefore all that life that had been built up around who he was and what he did no longer existed. He was drinking quite heavily and just sat in his house much of the time. My father came to see him, but perhaps that was no consolation since he was even older and more forgotten than Carol.

Yet up to the end, Reed seems to have remained anxious to work again and explored whatever possibilities came his way. John Woolf, who had produced *Oliver!*, sounded him out about taking on the film version of *Conduct Unbecoming*, Barry England's colonial courtroom drama which had been a hit on the stage, but Reed was not comfortable with the property. As Max puts it, 'He saw the work as a whodunnit where first you have all the action, then everyone sits down around the table to discuss it for twenty minutes. Then the culprit turns out to be mad, so my father felt it was cheating.' A far more promising project began to gestate when, by chance, Reed encountered Greene on a visit to the Riviera, and the two considered the prospect of collaborating again. Greene had a story that excited him, a period piece set in Spain during the Napoleonic War, with the Wandering Jew as the focal point. Max remembers that his father was enthusiastic about the idea but that, due to his sense of equity towards Greene, it never got near finished form:

> He approached a couple of studios about it. Maybe it was Columbia which said they'd do it in stages. But this is where my father wasn't a great putter together. He didn't feel that he could ask Greene to work on that basis; if he was going to work, he should know that the thing was going to be done. As opposed to saying, 'Well, Graham, they've got to see if they like it.' He'd feel that that was insulting to Greene.

In early 1976, Reed suffered a heart attack, but it was so mild that no one was alarmed. He appeared to be on the mend, said his brother Peter, when he succumbed to a second, more massive attack on 25 April. The funeral could not have been more bizarrely Reedian if he had concocted it himself. Anton Karas, composer of the famous zither music for *The Third Man*, flew over from Vienna to participate in the services, and, according to Birkin, gave his greatest performance, aided by an unexpected sound effect:

> The funeral was held in Chelsea Old Church, which is by the river. Nobody was really aware that Karas was there because he was up in the gallery. They had the ordinary choir and the ordinary organist through the ordinary funeral service and when they came to pick up the coffin an eerie sound, the twang of the theme from *The Third Man*, was heard, played very slowly. Six men carried the coffin down the aisle to that slow beat. Karas had turned the piece into funeral march. Then, as the pallbearers were coming down the embankment outside, we all heard the sound of a police siren, as if on cue!

One can't help wondering if the constabulary were worried that Harry Lime might be returning from the grave yet again.

As it turned out, the director's last creative gesture had nothing to do with movies but rather his own life, or rather death. With a recognizable exhibition of his wry sense of humour, he directed that his body be buried not in a quiet English churchyard but in a noisy cemetary along the M4, a highway leading to London's Heathrow airport. 'That way', says Birkin, 'Carol felt that people could remember him vaguely as they sped past on their way to the airport or on their way back. It's very noisy, with cars thundering overhead and he liked that.'

But 'vaguely' will never be a sufficient description for people's deeply felt memories of Reed, and, as for his inconspicuous resting place, the marvellous films he left behind are a far more imposing monument than the most majestic engraved marble. To be sure, one would have liked an artist of Reed's stature to have ended his career with a more praiseworthy achievement than *Flap* or *The Public Eye*, yet we must bear in mind that he belonged to a profession that is innately insecure, built as it is on the shifting sands of high finance and popular appeal and left to the whim of moguls and bankers. Under the best of circumstances, it is still dependent on the uncertain, fluctuating powers of the creative mind. Perhaps we should merely be grateful for the masterpieces that Reed did give us rather than regretting those he did not.

3 A Film-maker's Education

Reed's career at Associated Talking Pictures had been streaking rapidly forward when Basil Dean, head of the studio, decided to entrust him with his first directorial assignment, *It Happened in Paris* (1935), codirected by Robert Wyler. The film is one of a number of early Reed works which have largely disappeared from view. Michael Voigt, who has helpfully assembled thumbnail sketches of even the most obscure of these movies, summarizes the plot as a 'romantic drama in which a millionaire's son goes to Paris to study art and finds romance'.[1] The same year Dean gave his young apprentice complete possession of *Midshipman Easy* (US title: *Men of the Sea*). An adaptation of Captain Frederick Marryat's famous adventure story, *Mr Midshipman Easy*, the film had the advantage of retelling a yarn that thousands of Englishmen had thrilled to as adolescents. The film's budget was as limited as other British movies of the period, and most of it was shot in the Ealing Studios in London. English press coverage was affectionate and quite tolerant of the movie's limitations. The notice in *The Times* was typical. Noting the film's mood of harmlessly juvenile escapism, the anonymous reviewer remarked that 'it would be no surprise if at any moment Captain Hook and his crocodile were to heave into sight over the gunwale'. He allowed, however, that the movie was 'very seasonable fare', adding that *Midshipman Easy* was clearly most suitable for 'younger members of the audience'.[2] In the *Spectator*, Graham Greene welcomed Reed's arrival, attributing to him 'more sense of the cinema than most veteran British directors . . .'[3] In the United States, the film never had an official commercial release so there are no American reviews.

A minor financial and critical success in England, *Midshipman Easy* did not even strike the British themselves as more than a spirited bit of ephemera and there is very little about the picture to change anyone's mind today. The plot is true to its source, giving us as much of Captain Marryat's romance of a midshipman's initiation into life on the cruel sea as would fit into seventy-six minutes of screen time. As Voigt comments, 'It is very much a schoolboy adventure yarn containing all the traditional elements of the genre . . .'[4]

A great work of popular entertainment in its own era, Captain Marryat's novel was a logical subject for the mass audience that attends films. Marryat, usually classified as one of the middle-range authors of the early Victorian period, had enjoyed a successful career in the British navy – including distinguished service in the Napoleonic Wars – before retiring to his study to become a man of letters. His series of sea adventures, based on his own experience, looked back to Smollett and forward to Conrad, on whom he exerted a degree of influence. As a caricaturist and a lover of human eccentricity, he forms a bridge between the eighteenth-century masters and Dickens. *Mr Midshipman Easy* (1836), probably his best-known work, is episodic and digressive, shepherding its frolicksome, precocious young hero through a series of exploits, some dashing and some comic to the point of slapstick.

Fecundity of incident was one of Marryat's strengths; integration of plot elements was one of his shortcomings. Reed and his screenwriter, Anthony Kimmins, retain about as much of the novel as they can while also imparting to the story a significantly more organic shape than Marryat. Sacrificed in the process are the novelist's more outlandish episodes and the undercurrents of grim realism about nineteenth-century nautical life that enrich the plot. In Reed's rendering, the episodes are essentially colourful adolescent fantasies, the brand of swaggering boyhood tales that had been filtered profitably through the imagination of R. L. Stevenson, Rudyard Kipling, Raphael Sabatini and Christopher Wren, among others.

In the course of his first tour of duty on the HMS *Harpy*, Jack Easy (Hughie Green) subdues a bullying midshipman; saves his craft during a storm; seizes a Spanish merchantman choked with gold; engages in an idyllic flirtation with the nubile Donna Agnes Ribiera (Margaret Lockwood); fights a duel; and captures the notorious brigand Don Silvio (Dennis Wyndham). Seen today, these heroic and amatory exploits seem neither stirring nor dramatic, though they have the exotic charm of stories from another place and another time. Alongside such American rivals as the 1934 version of *Treasure Island* and *Gunga Din*, *Midshipman*

Easy strikes one as only adequate. Compared to other English films of the period, however, it was a cut above average in technique and narrative flair. Reed had made a noteworthy debut. It should also be borne in mind that, other than a number of rather gentlemanly war tales, the English have never excelled in action films. As late as 1962 they were turning out movies like Lewis Gilbert's nineteenth-century naval adventure, *Damn the Defiant*, a film so badly caulked, so unscreenworthy, it looked as if it might have been made in the 1930s.

Reed retained the strains of nineteenth-century liberalism which Marryat both satirized and endorsed in his tale. During the first third of the century in England, the Romantic movement had injected warm and generous impulses of humanism into the national consciousness. In their more widely accepted permutations, these impulses fuelled the anti-slavery movement; more esoterically, they accounted for such idiosyncratic schools of thought as the radical egalitarianism of William Godwin. *Mr Midshipman Easy* puts Godwinian idealism in the mouth of its teenage hero, while mocking its doctrines at every turn. 'Equality and trust are the basis of cooperation', Easy keeps saying, but the rigid hierarchy intrinsic to any military organization refutes him continually. This stratification is intensified by the inevitable British class divisions. As a midshipman, a rank open only to the sons of the gentry. Easy outranks the rest of the crew, apart from the ship's officers, and effortlessly barks out commands to men who are years older than he and vastly more experienced. In the famous three-way duelling sequence, he tyrannizes two middle-aged men, one of them the boatswain Mr Biggs (Harry Tate) and the other the pursar's steward, Mr Easthupp (Frederick Burtwell). It must be borne in mind, of course, that the hero of any adventure story has to be dynamic, even if he is an adolescent, and it is a convention of such stories that a juvenile protagonist can assume a dominant role with servants (*Kidnapped*), slaves (*Huckleberry Finn*), lesser breeds without the law (*Kim*). Still, the firmness with which Easy establishes dominion over Biggs and the other sailors aboard the HMS *Harpy* has a particularly English flavour to it. Naturally, as in most British films the accents demarcate class boundaries. The officers and midshipmen speak strictly 'U', while the rest of the crew speaks Cockney. As in so many English authors, from Shakespeare onward, Marryat's story depicts the major aptitudes of the lower classes as skullduggery and comic antics, never heroism or poetry. At one point, Briggs's upper torso is revealed as a dense map of tattoos, a parody of a sailor's chest. During a major battle he is used to inject more buffoonery when a dog tears off his pants.

Primitive though it is, *Midshipman Easy* does contain some foreshadowings of Reed's subsequent career. Despite being confined to a studio set for the most part, Reed was able to bootleg some location shooting into his film. The latter third of the story is set in Palermo, where Easy's battles with Don Silvio, who becomes his archenemy, take place. Reed displays a keen eye for scenic decor, setting a good deal of the action along a rugged coastline, though of course this particular coastline is actually English, not Sicilian. The spaciousness of these passages in the film help open up a movie whose meagre funding gives it a cramped, round-shouldered look. After the Second World War, location shooting was to become one of the hallmarks of Reed's work.

Another embryonic aspect of *Midshipman Easy* from the standpoint of Reed's career is its boy-hero. Anyone who has even a passing familiarity with Reed's work is probably aware of his career-long interest in children, both as narrative focuses and as subjects of psychological scrutiny. While it is true that most of the young people in Reed's films are pre-adolescents, not juveniles like Easy, the similarities are manifest none the less. Reed's profile of Jack seems to prefigure, in a very rudimentary fashion, the more sophisticated use of children he was to undertake in *The Fallen Idol* and *A Kid For Two Farthings*. Dim but quite discernible in the film's pedestrian plot development is the outline for a more complex treatment of Easy that would have given him an additional dimension. A rambunctious boy, thrust into a world of adults, Jack exhibits many traits of the hobbledehoy as he strives to fulfil the image of the masterful young officer who is born to command. In the first scene on board ship, we encounter him in the grips of *mal de mer*. Later, his bumptious somewhat pampered ideas of what shipboard life will be like for a gentleman of his class evoke disdain from Captain Wilson (Roger Livesey). We are led to expect a story of maturation in which we watch a raw youth come of age, and indeed Reed seems to toy with this idea. Easy's pontifications about equality and the right to disputation [in Her Majesty's Navy] ('I should like to argue that point', he keeps saying) sound callow when we first hear them and we anticipate scenes in which Easy is rudely disabused of his assumptions, in the manner of Kipling's *Captains Courageous*. Instead, as in Marryat's novel, these ideas are only lightly parodied and are rarely allowed to diminish the audience's affirmative view of Easy. The book pummels its hero with unpleasant truths somewhat more than the movie, but he still makes a remarkably simple transition from pampered scion to robust leader of men. As in the novel, Easy's notions of the inherent justice of the British naval system are vindicated when the black cook, Mesty (Robert Adams) is promoted to corporal in reward for his courage during the storm. Here Marryat is at his most liberal, echoing the Romantic fascination with the 'noble savage' and merging it, logically enough, with a denunciation of slavery. Under the beneficent star of the British navy everyone is treated equitably. As for the evolution of Easy's character, his initial immaturity vanishes with the first real crisis the *Harpy* encounters. Reed lets it metamorphose quickly into heroism, following the novelist faithfully ('in the course of one fortnight he [Easy] had at once from a boy sprung up into a man').[5] Nevertheless, *Midshipman Easy* does show the director experimenting with ideas that were later to be crucial attributes of his cinematic achievement.

Technically, the movie is a fairly impressive debut, revealing a young film-maker with a feeling for his medium. Unlike many directors who made the transition from the theatre to the cinema, Reed does not betray his origins. Remarkably enough, there is scarcely a scene in the film that is numbed by a stationary camera, by stagy acting or by garrulousness. The movie has an abundance of energy and hurtles along at just the right velocity. The editing is sometimes nervous and uncertain, but at other points surprisingly fluid, as in the battle between Easy's band and the Don Silvio outlaw horde at the Ribiera mansion. Earlier, there is a striking shot of these same brigands trapped in the galley of a ship that has run aground and is sinking rapidly. Reed works up considerable visual excitement and even moral and dramatic tension in this sequence, since Easy and his crew are compelled to rescue drowning men who are likely to turn on them afterwards. Under Don Silvio's savage prompting, the convicts rush off to assault the Ribieras' home. The editing in *Midshipman Easy* is complemented by several graceful tracking shots, the most remarkable of which occurs as the midshipmen rush to warn Don Ribiera (Arnold Lucy) and his family of an impending attack. Using his camera as a magic carpet, Reed wafts us into the tranquil, luxurious, aristocratic splendour of the grandee's home. The picturesqueness is completely synthetic, the stuff of which picture postcards are made, but the collage of details – servants in attendance, Dona Agnes in a swing playing a guitar, her parents relaxing nearby – communicates the placid mood of Latin patricians as succinctly and vividly as any director could have hoped for.

Midshipman Easy should also be rewarding to any student of racial characterization in English language films of the 1930s. The film follows the novel in portraying Mesty's bravery and greatness of soul as so consistent and overwhelming that Jack offers his hand in brotherhood. 'Mesty took the hand offered by Jack', writes Marryat. 'It was the first peace offering ever extended to him, since he had been torn away from his native land . . , the first acknowledgement . . that he was not an inferior being . . .'[6] But the temper of the times, or the medium he was working in, did not allow Reed to go quite this far. For two-thirds of the movie, Mesty is an eye-rolling, grinning stereotype, a junior edition of Paul Robeson in his less fortunate roles, such as Bosambo in *Sanders of the River* (and oddly enough, Adams played a character called Bosambo in Marcel Varnel's burlesque of *Sanders, Old Bones of the River*, (1937). His close association with the midshipmen makes him seem like a boy himself, even though he is a grown man. Midway through the film, however, he begins to demonstrate unexpected courage, foresight and presence of mind. He provides crucial assistance to Easy during the storm and later steadies the momentarily hysterical hero during the life-and-death struggle with the convicts. He also saves Gascoigne (Tom Gill), another midshipman, from immolation and rescues Easy from Don Silvio, whom he then defeats in a fistfight, hurling the bandit over a cliff. That a black man should be allowed to eclipse a white hero, albeit temporarily, in a movie of this era is certainly unusual. At the same time, we must remember that racial attitudes during the 1930s were a good deal more progressive in England than in America, if only because British films did not automatically depend on pleasing audiences in Alabama and Mississippi. In the well-known 1933 film of O'Neill's *The Emperor Jones*, a shot of the star, Robeson, knocking down a white man had to be excised from the film, whereas in *Midshipman Easy* the climactic contest is a prolonged fight in which a black man batters a white into submission and then kills him. No wonder Robeson seems to have preferred making movies in England!

Reed's second film for ATP, *Laburnum Grove*, bore only as much resemblance to his first as he could impose on it. Adapted from J. B. Priestley's play (by Kimmins and Gordon Wellesley), it came to the screen after a prodigious run in London and a much less substantial one in New York. It was released in England in 1936, but was not imported to the United States until 1941. With no prints available, we can only assess the movie second hand. Greene indicated continued appreciation of Reed's work: 'Here at last is an English film one can unreservedly praise'.[7] Andrew Sarris, writing many years after the film's release, praises it for 'photographing the vestigial manor pretensions of its suburban characters through over-stuffed gardens encroaching on cluttered interiors', but several of the reviews at the time of its release criticized the film for theatrical stiffness and loquacity.[8] In the main, though, *Laburnum Grove* was treated kindly by the American press, which looked on it as a slight but winsome effort, enlivened by British wit and a certain musty charm.

Reed was clearly comfortable with Priestley's whimsical story about an upper-middle-class businessman, starched with respectability, who stuns his family by casually informing them that he is not a 'paper merchant', as they believe, but a counterfeiter. The play is a post-Shavian mockery of the maddeningly smug British bourgeoisie, quite winningly executed, with a sketch of a parasitic, loud-mouthed brother-in-law done in broad, funny strokes. In the movie, Edmund Gwenn, already a veteran film actor, recreated the role of the businessman that he had first performed on the stage. Evidently Sir Cedric Hardwicke stole the show, however, abandoning his usual screen persona, the urbane man-about-town, and bringing the bounder of a brother-in-law uproariously to life. One yearns to see what Reed was able to do with this appealing material.

Like many English directors of the 1930s, Reed was forced to freelance, roaming Wardour Street in search of work. In 1937, Reed contracted with Herbert Wilcox's company, British & Dominions, to make *Talk of the Devil*. Whether there was not enough work at ATP to keep him busy or he saw an assignment from B&D as a step up professionally we do not know. Whatever Reed's motivations in leaving Dean, however, *Talk of the Devil* did nothing to improve his standing in the field, and it has since disappeared from circulation completely. Based on an original story by Reed himself and scripted by him, Kimmins and George Barraud, the film was a melodrama set at a seaside resort and starring Ricardo Cortez and Sally Eilers. Sarris observes that the coastal setting, with its seablown naturalism, was atypical for the studio-bound English movie industry of this period and presages the passion for shooting on location that marks Reed's later career. Basil Wright is more emphatic on this point: '*Talk of the Devil* . . . indicated Reed's preference for stories with roots in the actualities of life, on genuine locations with definite regional characteristics, and on recognizably human people, rather than on the cosmopolitan no-man's-land usually favoured by the makers of thrillers.'[9] On the other hand, a contemporary reviewer, Frank S. Nugent in the *New York Times*, was far less enchanted. 'We resent this intrusion into our class C market', he huffed.[10]

In terms of prolificacy, the late 1930s were the highpoint of Reed's career, but most of these pictures did nothing to enhance his reputation. It is true that there is a production line quality to his work in this period. Still, within the narrow parameters of the quota system, he was also able to experiment with different forms – melodrama, farce, musical comedy – most of which were to recur in his major work. After *Talk of the Devil*, Reed returned to comedy in *Who's Your Lady Friend?*, though the vehicle does not appear to have had the organic British attributes that made *Laburnum Grove* beguiling. Rather it was a story about a Viennese plastic surgeon, a reworking of a German play, *Der Herr Ohne Wohnung*, which had been filmed in Germany a few years before. From the available plot summaries, it sounds quite synthetic, even for a British production during this era, and it was never shown in the US.

At about the same time, Reed tried his hand at conceiving original material again, concocting a farce about jewel thieves, *No Parking* (1938), for Wilcox. The film was directed by Jack Raymond and quickly slipped into oblivion. Later that year, Reed was back at ATP to direct yet another frothy, perishable comedy, *Penny Paradise*, the story of a tugboat captain who

believes that he's won a football pool. Dean supplied the plot
and Thomas Thompson, W. L. Meade and Thomas Browne
wrote the script for what is, today, a totally forgotten venture. Its
only noteworthy aspects, apparently, are that it featured the
reliable Edmund Gwenn and was photographed by Ronald
Neame, later a prominent director in his own right.

In what was a very busy period for Reed, he was finally able to
climb a full level above the inconsequential work he had been
doing thus far when he was hired to direct *Bank Holiday* (US title:
Three on a Weekend) for Gainsborough. It was, by design, a fairly
ambitious project in that it mixed several modes – comedy,
sentimentality and naturalism. The story (by Rodney Ackland
and Hans Wilhelm) was original, and, as was usually the case
when Reed did a film, written directly for the screen; the script
(by Ackland and Roger Burford) was inferior. The core of the
film is a weepy, three-handkerchief tale of bereavement, temporarily thwarted love and near suicide. Far more interesting,
however, is the array of smaller stories with which Reed adorns
and enlivens his plot, which is set at a seaside resort over a long
holiday weekend in August. The source of the film is unquestionably *Grand Hotel* and indeed the principal hotel at the resort is
called 'the Grand'. Still, the English locales and flavour in *Bank
Holiday* give it a distinctive atmosphere.

Contemporary American reviews were exceptionally sensible
in appraising the merits and deficiencies of Reed's film. *Variety*
could find little to admire in the movie's love story, but by virtue
of the subplots was able to term the picture 'good entertainment'
with 'many rich characters'.[11] Otis Ferguson of the *New Republic*
liked these same secondary episodes because of 'their hold on the
familiar, on the intricate, unimportant sweet ways of life'.[12]
Similar sentiments were expressed by the major New York and
Los Angeles reviewers. The only dissenter was one 'T.M.P.' in
the *New York Times* who, astonishingly, preferred the cloying tale
of love and regretted that 'Mr. Reed did not edit out the long and
extraneous stretches contemplating the activities of the holiday
throngs at the beach.'[13]

The lugubrious foundation of the movie requires that Catherine (Margaret Lockwood), a nurse, become deeply attached to
Stephen (John Lodge), a handsome, kindly and unspeakably
dull gentleman whose wife dies in childbirth just as Catherine is

about to set off on a bank holiday with her boyfriend Geoffrey (Hugh Williams). The remainder of the film records Catherine's growing realization that she loves Stephen and her fearful intimations that he may attempt suicide before she returns to London (he does). Fortunately, this weepy woman's magazine narrative is relieved by a number of sprightly vignettes of different holiday-makers who surround Catherine and Geoffrey over the weekend.

The people we meet in *Bank Holiday* are almost all working class and Reed uses the opportunity to cultivate his eye for social nuances. Among the *dramatis personae* are Arthur and May (Wally Patch and Kathleen Harrison), a Cockney couple with a large, squalling family; Doreen (Renee Rey) and Milly (Merle Tottenham), two unsophisticated young shop girls, one of whom – Doreen – has entered a beauty contest; 'Miss Mayfair' (Jeanne Stuart), the favoured contender in the beauty contest. The visual economy in the segments of the movie devoted to these characters has a locomotive quality compared to the tortoise-paced sections in which Catherine moons over Stephen and, back in London, Stephen moons over Catherine. In contrast to the love story in *Bank Holiday*, these characters are rendered in brisk sketches that consist of closely observed social notation. Arthur and May are treated as objects of amusement. Arthur is dressed in what might be called a uniform of his social class – striped jersey, ill-fitting black jacket, black derby. With a cigar jutting out of the side of his mouth, Arthur needs only a coating of dust to pass for Alfred P. Doolittle. In what seems to be the tradition of poor people everywhere, the Cockneys' impecuniousness has not retarded their child-bearing impulses and they have kids at their heels constantly, usually crying for things like 'sugar pops'. One parent or the other is always lugging a baby and a child's toy. Overall, the atmosphere emanating from the Cockneys is one of tremendous encumbrance.

Although the Cockney family is the most extreme example of how tightly people's lives can be laced up by poverty, virtually everyone else in the movie leads a pinched existence as well. Indeed, if there is a major social theme developed in *Bank Holiday*, it is the pathetically constrained lives of blue-collar Britons. A holiday of this magnitude (two and a half days) is clearly a rare event, and the constant references to the monetary pressures tell us as much as any economist could about the plight of the holiday starved proletarians. Geoff, described as an office worker, has saved for months to be able to enjoy a long weekend with his fiancée Catherine. He, along with thousands of others, is seen streaming like an insect into Victoria Station and fighting for space on the dozens of resort-bound trains. At the seashore itself, the population density is just as great and either through lack of funds or lack of advance planning thousands of people have to sleep on the beach. The scenes on the beach, though principally used for humorous effect, also convey an intense mood of claustrophobia, which Reed views as the common lot of poor Londoners, whether they're at work or on holiday. The only beauty available to them is natural: a lyrical seascape of moonlight on the water. It is through a multitude of such keenly noted social particulars that, in Wright's words, Reed 'triumphed over the artifice of the story', using detail to 'build up an intimacy of experience between the screen and the audience'.[14]

The characters in *Bank Holiday* are mostly cardboard cutouts, but here and there one encounters an extra psychological layer of the sort that was to distinguish Reed's later work. Doreen, the aspiring 'Miss England' contestant, is satirized as vulgar and shallow, a cut-rate beauty who ironically has just been jilted by her fiancé. But when Geoff is similarly rejected by Catherine and the contrivances of the screenplay throw Doreen and Geoff together, Reed allows her a sobbing, drunken speech in which the depth of her grief emerges, altering our perception of her. Geoff is also depicted with surprising acuteness and psychological realism; a steady accretion of specifics about his deficiency of character and intelligence – most of them quite credible and unforced – make it easy for us to accept Catherine's decision to break off with him. At the station, his sexual aggression towards Catherine, while not really exaggerated, is unseemly, and he is selfish towards the other people who want to ride in his coach. At the resort, we learn that he has foolishly not booked in advance (thus leaving him and Catherine without a room for the night), that he is overly concerned with appearances and that he is just a shade or so too lecherous towards Catherine, even allowing for her decision as a 'modern woman' to engage in premarital sex. There is little in the slow unfolding of Geoff's character that is unusually imaginative, but its very gradualism, and the attention paid to detail, are a credit to the solidity of Reed's artistic instincts at this early phase in his career.

The film's dcnouement alternates between the cheerfully lightweight and the grossly sentimental. Back in London, Catherine saves Stephen from a suicide attempt which he has undertaken after reading too much Keats. Meanwhile, Reed delivers facile but amusing parthian shots, as the 'holiday trippers' alight at the train station: the dowdy cockney wife strikes back at her overbearing husband; 'Miss Mayfair', winner of the contest, steps off the train with the judge; and so forth.

In addition to its other assets, *Bank Holiday* demonstrates Reed's continuing mastery of cinematic language, even where his script was inferior. The witty opening shots summarize the ant colony aspect of London's working world with admirably spare strokes. Workers of every type and description are seen toiling away fiercely until the sound of Big Ben at noon liberates them for the rest of the day. The stampede to Victoria Station is dramatized as efficiently as one could imagine. In these early scenes, and later at the resort, the vagaries of the weather buffet the holiday-makers, a comedy summarized for us crisply through sharp cuts from newspaper headlines to sheets of rain and people scurrying this way and that. These sequences have far more vitality and sureness of touch than one would expect from a young British director working on his sixth movie. Reed already had his own creative ideas, which he would refine and amplify in future films. Among the more noticeable prefigurements is the black cat in Stephen's apartment playing gently with the tassle on the window shade. The pet, which reminds us of Reed's own fondness for animals, was destined to reappear in *The Girl in the News* and, most effectively, in *The Third Man*.

The origins of *Climbing High* (1938), which Reed directed for Gaumout-British, are obscure, but someone at the studio must have had the idea that Jessie Matthews, one of England's premier musical comedy stars, could be just as effective without songs, and the studio could save the money it would have invested in production numbers. Moreover, Matthews was no doubt attracted by the idea of expanding her range. She was familiar to American audiences, and in *Climbing High* she was seconded by a group of players who, like her, had a reasonable degree of exposure in the United States – Michael Rcdgrave, Basil Radford, Alistair Sim. The plot was pure confection, as

insubstantial as candyfloss, and ought to have looked quite
familiar to an American audience: it was a screwball comedy
that was obviously prepared from American recipes.

But when *Climbing High* arrived on American shores in the
summer of 1939, the reviewers were none too kind. An initialled
review in the *New York Times* declared that the misuse of Jessie
Matthews had become traditional with the British, citing the
'long, laborious' *Climbing High* as a case in point.[15] *Variety* felt
that the film lacked 'zest and sparkle'[16] and Archer Winston of
the *New York Post* dismissed it as 'neither very good nor very
bad.'[17] Wanda Hale in the *Daily News* was virtually alone in
admiring the film as 'good hot weather entertainment'.[18]

Seen today, *Climbing High* is an inoffensive trifle, retaining
some interest as an historical curiosity and as the apprentice-
work of a major director. The script (by Lesser Samuel, Stephen
Clarkson and Marian Dix) scoops up a number of devices from
the screwball genre and inserts them into English settings. As in
films like *Easy Living* and *You Can't Take It With You*, the hero,
Nicky Brooke (Redgrave) is a rich man wooing a working-class
heroine, Diana Castle (Matthews). Brooke steals a trick from the
Ray Milland character in *Easy Living* by posing as a poor man in
order to court his sweetheart. The other *dramatis personae* include
a predictable, American-inspired assortment of scheming golddiggers, comical servants, hefty matrons from the *beau monde* and
so forth. Much of the comedy consists of rapid-fire badinage, but
knockabout humour is by no means overlooked. *Climbing High* is
no more a comedy of manners than *Bringing Up Baby*, *Theodora
Goes Wild* or *The Awful Truth*. The chemistry of these films
required a tension between sophisticated characters in a posh
milieu and the rather rough, physical jokes to which they were
subjected. *Climbing High* adheres to formula. In a scene at a
photographer's studio, for instance, a wind machine runs amok,
setting every moveable object in motion and harrying the performers with – among other things – custard pies. The mistaken
identities and tortuous complications that make up the story
take place in creamy-looking, satin-covered drawing rooms, on
the streets of London, in a Swiss resort. Despite the contrasting
poles of wealth and poverty mandated by the story line, Reed
keeps his film securely located in the never-never land of farce.
The realities of the Depression scarcely intrude, not even to the
degree permitted in the Warners 'Golddiggers' series. Reed had

scant opportunity for the scrupulous chronicling of English
mores for which he had demonstrated so much talent in *Bank
Holiday*. With material as hackneyed as *Climbing High*, his paramount task was to maintain the breakneck tempo that was
essential to this type of comedy and to coax crisp, stylish performances from the cast. To the extent that he succeeded in each of
these objectives, he was able to conceal the hackneyed material
he had been given. Very few scenes sag at all, and it is surprising
that the *New York Times* should chastise the film for laboriousness. It is hard to disagree with the common verdict on tooth-
some Jessie Matthews, however. Not all of Reed's intelligent
guidance could provide her with any satisfactory comic resources.
Without her dancing shoes and a batch of songs, the usually
estimable Matthews was ineffectual. Fortunately, the other performers were better able to follow Reed's baton. Redgrave is
likeable as the dashing playboy hero, Radford confers a welcome
British dryness on the part of the photographer, and tubby
Francis L. Sullivan has an enjoyable turn as an escaped lunatic
who warbles operatic arias.

English audiences saw Reed's next film, *A Girl Must Live*
(made for Gainsborough) the year it was filmed, 1939, but
America had to wait until 1942. As far as the New York critics
were concerned, the film might just as well have been withheld
forever. It was immediately spotted as a British quota film and
punished accordingly. The New York *Morning Telegraph* labelled
it 'so much frou-frou',[19] and Bosley Crowther, recently, appointed film critic for the *New York Times*, declared the movie an
'obviously inferior and skimpy romance'.[20] In most of the notices, Reed was excused from serious condemnation because *The
Stars Look Down*, distributed in America the year before, had left
such a strong impression. Archer Winston in the *New York Post*
rated the movie 'the sort of film which lesser men can do much
better',[21] while *Variety*, though praising other Reed films, found
his direction in *A Girl Must Live* 'flighty'.[22]

Curiously enough, amidst all this disparagement, the reviewers
failed to note the unmistakably American models for the movie.
Its story is attributed to a novel by Emery Bonnet, as adapted
by Frank Launder and Austin Melford, but it appears to
have been cheerfully burglarized from several native sources –
42nd Street, the 'Golddiggers' series and *Stage Door*. The plot wisks
a well-bred young lady (Margaret Lockwood) from a fashion-

able girls' school in Switzerland to the chorus line of a London nightclub, and into the arms of Lord Pangborough (Hugh Sinclair), a fairy-tale nobleman who rescues her from even the minimal contact with reality she has been forced to endure. Plot complications compel the heroine to assume the identity of a classmate, Leslie James: to avoid confusion, she will be referred to as Leslie in this discussion. Her chief companions in the chorus are two squabbling adventuresses, Clytie Devine (Lilli Palmer) and Gloria Lind (Renee Houston), who are continually jostling one another aside in their pursuit of rich husbands or sugar daddies. Alternately, they receive assistance from Hugo Smythe Parkinson (Naunton Wayne), a suave con man who locates prospective victims for hard-working houris. The pleasantly seedy boarding house in which Leslie, Clytie and Gloria reside is an English variant of the establishment that MGM built for Lucille Ball, Ginger Rogers, Katherine Hepburn, *et al.* during the very same year. The musical review in which the girls appear is directed by tyrannical, wisecracking Joe Gold (David Burns), a close relation of the Warner Baxter character in *42nd Street*.

Servilely imitative though it is, *A Girl Must Live* does not commit the one aesthetic crime for which there is no extenuating circumstance; it does not fail to entertain. When European film-makers copy American originals, the constituent they most often overlook is pacing. Reed, however, keeps his frivolous bauble hurtling forward at all times. The speed of *A Girl Must Live* is no slower than its famous antecedents, though its style and subject-matter are as agreeably gamey and its sequences as spirited.

The first scene, at the girls' dormitory in Switzerland, is appropriately sportive and high-spirited. Their stays loosened and their rebelliousness spilling forth, the corps of proper young ladies plots a successful escape for the beleaguered heroine, whose plummeting family fortunes have left her unable to pay her tuition. The strategy of Leslie's escape is an adroit variation on the familiar device – a ladder of bedsheets. The long white rope is the first thing the camera shows us, conveying an impression of a hopelessly mechanical story. But it is typical of the story Reed does tell that the dangling ladder is not as standardized a device as it first appears. Rather the girls have cleverly anticipated the flight in advance, deliberately alerting the headmistress and her assistant (Muriel Aked and Martita Hunt).

The two doyennes of the school – deftly caricatured as black-clad shrews – bicycle away to find the fugitive. With the coast clear, Leslie, who has been hiding, emerges and makes her getaway down the rope ladder.

In the first moments before Lockwood's departure, the film's slender but sufficient premise is quickly established – that she will gain an entrée to the London theatre world by masquerading as a fellow student, the daughter of a famous actress of the previous generation, Leslie James. From this ingratiating start, *A Girl Must Live* speeds along in much the same brisk, unassuming fashion. In the boarding house at which Leslie stays in London, the landlady, an Eve Arden clone (Mary Clare), presides over an unruly, colourful roster of entertainers with tart-tongued authority. Nevertheless, the potential staleness of the subject-matter is redeemed by a number of factors, not the least of which are the unconventional changes that Reed is occasionally able to work on conventional situations and characters. He is not uniformly successful by any means – a washed-up Shakespearean actor orotundly proclaiming his greatness and calling for a national theatre is strictly a stiff, theatrical mummy.

But other members of the household are enjoyable, quirkily so, especially a dotty old lady (Drusilla Wills), whose speciality is sound effects ('I was the scream in East Lynne') and animal noises. Although her brief appearance in the movie is largely comedic, Reed gives her a slightly grotesque veneer. Simultaneously, the eternal conflict between the artist and the burgher is symbolized, however superficially, by the contrast between the show business folk and Mr Joliffe (Wilson Coleman), a sanitation engineer, architect of a 'porcelain palace' in Brighton, who sneeringly informs the perpetually struggling artistes that his livelihood is easily obtained because he 'builds things people need'.

Much of the screen time is devoted to the ceaseless rivalry between Clytie and Gloria. The dialogue they fling back and forth at each other is not as memorably pungent as their American models, but still the volleys of wisecracks have an agreeably antique flavour and are quite consistently entertaining. As the two feuding friends top one another in outrageous ploys and reprisals, they seem evenly matched, like Joan Blondell and Ginger Rogers in their gold-digging days. Here Reed has chosen antagonists who are a nice mixture of contrast, complement and identity. Even their accents, so aggresively on display, make them stand out from their fellow chorus girls – and apart from one another. With her curious brogue, which might even stump Professor Higgins, Houston is the perfect adversary for 'Viennese' Lilli Palmer (usually identified as a Viennese, Palmer was actually raised in Berlin and, at the time the movie was made, had never set foot in Vienna). A battle royal between the two, glimpsed in part through a keyhole, is exceptionally well staged, with the girls converting every conceivable item into a weapon.

The film has other points of interest as well. References to the difficulty of launching native theatrical properties remind us of Hollywood's success in colonizing the British film industry in this period. As the hard-driving, fiercely manipulative producer Joe Gold, David Burns, though American, strives to give his part a recognizable British flavour and the script has him complain about 'foreign fellows' moving in on the British entertainment industry. The schoolgirls refer to American screen idols like Robert Taylor but never to English players and in the scene at Pangborough's ancestral castle, the chorines remark that the august mansion is 'better than Hollywood', although ironically they reduce it to a Hollywood set by rehearsing in one of its enormous rooms.

Even in a mild divertissement like *A Girl Must Live*, Reed's inherent taste and intelligence show through. When Mrs Blount (Kathleen Boutall), the wife of the tycoon who is financing Gold's show, confronts Clytie, whom the businessman has been pursuing, she is not kidded nearly as broadly as her counterparts in American films. Clytie haughtily informs her, 'I wouldn't be caught dead with your husband', and the wife is permitted a surprisingly snappy reply, 'Well, I would and I hope to when the time comes.' The movie's comic climax has Hugo, who is trying to execute a blackmail scheme against Pangborough after drinking too much, stumbling into room after room, attempting to catch the nobleman in a compromising situation. Conceptually the sequence is dusty, but Reed's understated direction and Naunton Wayne's nimble acting give it some sheen.

For a young film director, working in England in the 1930s was precarious and demanding. Regardless of the so-called 'boom' on Wardour Street, most directors found the pressures enormous, the compensation meagre and the future uncertain. It was in this daunting atmosphere that Reed earned his stripes as a film-maker. He was a transient, ever on the move from one film company that had no more work for him to another that did need his services. For him, the experiences of the period combined a cram course in movie-making, a form of survival training and a baptism by fire. Inevitably, the lesson he learned most assiduously was how to squeeze the best possible results from the smallest, most constricted budget. This economy of means was nowhere more evident than in the editing procedures Reed acquired at Ealing and the other studios where he mastered his craft. In contrast to the Hollywood method of shooting vast quantities of film and then cutting the picture to the proper length and proportions afterwards, the English system required that directors edit each picture as they filmed it. Movies were shot in two to three months, at which point the director turned in his rough cut and took up his next project. He was not involved in the editing process, and hence it was imperative that he deliver a work which could only be cut according to his creative design, his blueprint for narrative structure, theme and character development. The strategy would seem to have given the director more aesthetic self-protection, and perhaps this is why we hear so little grumbling from British film-makers about 'studio interference' and so few tales of pictures 'butchered' by the 'front office'.

The virtues of this edit-as-you-go approach impressed themselves on Reed deeply, and he remained an adherent of it for the remainder of his working days. A third of a century later, Max could see the same *modus operandi* being applied to *Oliver!*:

> He'd get up in the morning and do the morning's shoot and then he'd go to the cutting room during lunchtime and cut the last two days or so of rushes. He would never have lunch. Then he would work through the end of the day, and come home and work on the next day's shoot. But by doing the cutting in the cutting room each day he could deliver a rough cut only a couple of days after shooting.

The movies discussed in this chapter were all five finger exercises in comparison to Reed's later work, yet one can certainly perceive in them some of the qualities which give his mature films their special character – for instance, his superb sense of pacing (evident even from an atypical effort such as *A*

Girl Must Live), his instinctive rapport with stories about children, and his addiction to realistic *mise-en-scène*. At the same time, in surveying Reed's apprentice years, nothing seems more important than the fact that he was denied the opportunity simply to put down his own creative roots wherever he chose. As a neophyte director, Reed was in no position to follow up the modest success of *Midshipman Easy* with a similar offering, even if he had wanted to. Instead of finding his way into a proficient and profitable groove, he faced the exigencies of finding work at one studio or another, and his search propelled him into a kaleidoscopic variety of films over the next five years – comedies, melodramas, musicals, love stories, etc. While few of these films have more than fragile charms for us today – and some appear to have vanished entirely – they suggest a questing sensibility, a restless imagination meeting each new creative challenge with energy and intelligence. Although Reed ultimately made his reputation in certain genres rather than others and developed recognizable stylistic and intellectual traits, he seems to have been driven to renew his powers through fresh departures. Perhaps this tendency is in part the heritage of his hectic apprenticeship, during which period he was forced to try his hand at whatever stories came his way.

4 The Emergence of an Artist

Writing in 1968, Pauline Kael observed that Carol Reed was only thirty-three when he made *The Stars Look Down*, and 'he had not yet acquired the technical virtuosity of his later style, but this straightforward film may just possibly be his best'.[1] Whether or not we can agree with this bold assessment, *The Stars Look Down* is certainly Reed's first major film and an important cornerstone of his career. Appearing at the end of a decade of social protest, it succeeded in applying the technique and social concerns of the documentary to the feature film, which, in England, had not been much of a receptacle for political themes in the past. Reed, who was soon to make some outstanding documentaries himself, appears to have learned much from works like Grierson's *Industrial Britain* (1933), Alberto Cavalcanti's *Coalface* (1936) and Paul Rotha's *The Face of Britain* (1939), and the lessons are reflected in *Stars*. An adaptation of A. J. Cronin's 1935 novel of the same name, *Stars* required an expensive production that, apart from Korda's opuses, was uncommon in England at the time. Isidore Goldsmith, an independent producer, was able to raise the then-enormous sum of £100 000, and the project went forward under the aegis of Grafton, a small production company. The financing was sufficient to permit six days of shooting at a real coal mine, St Helens Siddick Colliery at Workington in Cumberland, a coal-rich section of northeastern England. Then came seven weeks of shooting at Twickenham Studios in London, where an elaborate mine-head was simulated. Later the set was moved, *in toto*, to Shepperton Studios for an additional week of shooting. Richard Whitehall has unearthed some informative details on this, as well as other, aspects of the production:

the original set of the mine-head was used . . . to make up a huge composite set of 40 000 square yards – claimed to be the largest exterior set constructed for a British film until that time – consisting of an exact replica of the Workington mine where the location work had been done; a pit-head complete with cage, ramp, outer buildings, and rows of miners' cottages. Using three camera crews, shooting on this set lasted for a week.[2]

To guarantee verisimilitude, pit ponies from the Cumberland mines were used and the miners' costumes were clothes purchased from colliery workers.

Though the staff which Reed had at his command on *Stars* was not as impressive as the ones he assembled after the war, it was thoroughly professional, and the director got excellent contributions from cinematographers Mutz Greenbaum and Henry Harris, art director James Carter and editor Reginald Beck. If J. B. Williams's screenplay had deficiencies, Reed – who usually co-authored his films – must share the censure. His acumen also failed him when he persuaded the refined Margaret Lockwood to play the vulgar, lower middle-class Jenny, against the actress's better judgement. Every other performance is skilfully executed, however.

The critical reaction to *Stars* must have been deeply gratifying to the hard-working, ambitious director, who had at least been given the opportunity of making a film 'his way'. When the film premiered in England early in 1940, *The Times* lauded the authenticity of the movie's mining sequences, which 'all provide scenes of remarkable force and intensity'.[3] Aubrey Flanagan, in the *Motion Picture Herald*, pronounced the climax 'one of the most stirring passages yet to have been woven into a British film'.[4] In his last review of a Reed film for the *Spectator*, Greene, who had been acutely aware of Reed's potential from the beginning, exulted over the fact that the director 'at last had his chance and has magnificently taken it'. The notice begins: 'Dr. Cronin's mining novel has made a very good film – I doubt whether in England we have ever produced a better.'[5] Here and there a harsher voice was raised, such as Rotha's; the eminent British film historian, as well as a movie-maker himself, annihilated the picture, characterizing it as a shallow treatment of Cronin's themes, with underdeveloped characters and (incredible charge!) a lack of realism. 'Nor, to anyone familiar with the Northumberland coal fields, does the film get anywhere near the real people', Rotha wrote.[6]

In the United States, *Variety* was dubious about the film's chances as a mass market item,[7] but the *New York Times* critic was only concerned with the aesthetic merits of the movie, which he summed up as 'a film to be remembered in this or any other season'.[8] *Newsweek*, in its first review of a Reed movie, called the film a 'superior job of movie craftsmanship' and termed it 'grimly honest'.[9] Archer Winston in the *New York Post* recommended *Stars* as 'surely one of the greatest pictures England has ever sent us'.[10] *Variety* proved to be the *vox populi*, however, and Reed's movie did not reach an American theatre until 1941. *Variety* speculates that this was because of the distributor's anxiety over its 'artiness', but it was also held up by pressure from 20th Century-Fox, which wanted to be sure that its own Welsh coal-mining saga, *How Green Was My Valley*, had raked in all the receipts it could. By the time American filmgoers were permitted to see Reed's film, their interest in its subject matter may have been temporarily exhausted. In addition, Kael points out that the 'more sentimental American treatment was much easier for audiences to take . . . Nor does *Stars* indulge in those glorifications of unions and working men which literate film audiences seem to think necessary . . .'[11] Courageously, Reed chose to show the potential recalcitrance and pig-headedness of union leaders, who turn a deaf ear to the hero's warnings about the possibility of a mining cave-in and refuse to authorize a strike. Thus the picture made some enemies among union people who might otherwise have been friendly to it.

Cronin's novel is divided into three parts and covers a broad expanse of time and subject-matter: the idealistic young David Fenwick's rise from his lowly beginnings in the Sleescale colliery to a university education and a career in public life; his election to Parliament; the parallel rise of unscrupulous Joe Gowlan, who eventually replaces Fenwick in office; the problems of mine-owner Barras, one of the more progressive captains of industry, whose son becomes a conscientious objector in the First World War; the machinations of union officials and the Labour government, which ultimately betrays the miners; the love triangle of Fenwick, Jenny and Joe.

The novelist obviously knew his subject at first hand and the strongest portions of his book are the detailed, intensely lifelike renderings of an English coal-mining community. The verisimilitude is only as deep as coaldust, however; underneath it lies the palpitating heart of a 'best-seller', with its overripe style, tiresome plot contrivances and tableaux of waxen characters. The working-class hero who tries to use his education to help the miners; the shallow, unfaithful wife who temporarily deflects the hero from his goals; the ruthless bounder whose rise coincides with the hero's – it is largely a cast of caricatures.

Cronin himself claimed to be utterly delighted with the screen version of his saga, but to others Reed's efforts produced decidedly mixed results. In a move that was aesthetically destructive (though perhaps commercially sound), the director and scenarist chose to devote a large segment of the plot to Cronin's romantic drama, the tritest and least artistically challenging element in the novel. The narrative also loses something through contraction; the scope of the original, which encompasses the periods before and after the First World War as well as the war itself, is collapsed into a few years.

Still, the film has enough virtues partially to triumph over its soggy story. Clearly the chief appeal of the Cronin work for Reed was its naturalism, a tendency which he had been carefully nurturing in his own work. *Stars* is most impressive when it concentrates on the lives of the poor mining folk. The opening sequence, a deftly edited montage of Sleescale, a typical mining town, is practically a miniature treatise in itself and is all the more eloquent for being uncoercive. A few judiciously selected shots tell all – the look of the colliery; the dirty 'residential' streets of the community; the grim monotony of the miners' homes, as grey and regular and joyless as a collection of tiny blockhouses. A brief confrontation between Burras, the mine-owner (Allan Jeayes) and Robert Fenwick (Edwin Rigby), the unofficial leader of the miners and father of the movie's hero, establishes the film's basic conflict with true cinematic economy. The workers refuse to work without adequate safeguards in the potentially rich section of the mine known as Scupper Flats, which Fenwick knows to be vulnerable to flooding. During the strike that follows, Reed enhances our understanding of the inhabitants of Sleescale by focusing on the Fenwick family. In a necessary simplification of the novel, the siblings are reduced from three to two, David (Michael Redgrave), the young scholar and idealist, and Hughie (Demston Tester), the buoyant, good-natured football star. Under Reed's hand, the two are as sharply and unmistakably distinguished as this description would suggest. The parents, Robert and Martha (Nancy Price), are set off in subtler opposition. Each values his dignity, but measures it by a different yardstick. For Fenwick the greatest degradation is being shamed before his coworkers or bowing to the yoke of the bosses. For Martha, it is being unable to feed her family and seeing her credit rudely rejected by the local merchants. The expression on her proud, weather-beaten face when Ramage, the butcher (Edmund Willard), brusquely dismisses her is a wonderful portrait of sublimated pain.

The character of Martha is made to symbolize the indomitable spirit of the miners, struggling forward against all adversity; others, including one of her sons and her husband, are dead at the end of the film, but she goes on. Her years of deprivation have eroded any capacity for hope or optimism or for envisioning an alternative to vassalage in the mines. Hence, she discourages David's dreams of a better life through education and a post in the world that will allow him to fight for the miners; she even opposes the strike. It is left to Robert to help his son keep his aspirations alive and to provide leadership for the discontented workers.

It is the authenticity of these early scenes, with their perfect balance of sociology and psychology, that gives *Stars* its hold on us. When Reed jumps suddenly from the individual miseries of the Fenwick family to the collective suffering of the town, sending his characters forth in an angry assault on the callous, uncharitable Ramage, we are with them heart and soul. As they pillage the shop hungrily, the proletarians' upsurge against the bourgeoisie is far more effective than any Marxist propaganda because the participants have been fully humanized for us in the quick camerawork that preceded the outbreak of violence. Similar praise can be directed at David's departure for the university at Tynecastle. Maintaining consistency of character, Reed does not allow either David or Martha any egregious display of emotion. The young man fumbles ineffectually for a suitable leave-taking, while his mother remains stoical, betraying her agitation only slightly when she calls him back to give him some food she has wrapped up. In the last shot in the scene, we see her through the window, with the reflection of the all-important and all-dominating pit shaft towering in the background.

After David, in a remarkable coincidence, meets his old boy-hood friend Joe Gowlan (Emlyn Williams) and his unwanted mistress Jenny Sunley (Margaret Lockwood) in Tynecastle, there is nothing for the audience to do but watch the story run through its well-worn grooves; Joe's abandonment of Jenny; her subsequent seduction of David; their hasty marriage and un-happy life together back in Sleescale, where David must accept a demeaning teaching job to support his frivolous, self-indulgent bride. When Joe also returns to Sleescale, it is only a matter of time before David's domestic woes are compounded by his wife's infidelity.

Even the most ardent admirers of *Stars*, apart from Kael, have been troubled by the weakness of these episodes, which, after all, occupy a considerable portion of the film. In between his bursts of praise, the *New York Times* reviewer expressed the worry that 'Mr. Reed has sacrificed . . . a little in the unity of the film by deviating too long into the domestic contretemps of the miners' younger spokesman . . .'[12] Sixteen years later, Sarris, who found much to extol in *Stars*, had the same complaint: 'There is a lack of unity between the personal plot and the central theme.'[13] Actually, the lack of unity is less disturbing than the mechanical quality of the scenes, the absence of conviction. From David's *naïveté* to Joe's unscrupulousness to Jenny's insensitivity, the behaviour of Cronin's characters seems to be fatally predeter-mined by the artificiality of Cronin's quasi-Victorian story. There is something numbing about the prescriptive plot, with its seducers and innocents, its social consciousness and its 'fallen' hero whose role would have gone to Tess or Fanny Robin in one of Hardy's novels. Indeed, the shadow of Hardy becomes almost palpable during the climactic mine disaster when the critical rescue plan falls from the hand of the dying mine-owner into a stream.

Yet it is this final calamity, which Reed sensibly shifted from the early portion of Cronin's story to the end, that redeems the movie, restoring it to the sharp-eyed realism of the first scenes. Although the catastrophe is far too inevitable for its own good, Reed stages it splendidly. The onrushing tides invade every passageway and corridor, savagely devouring men and machines alike. The melding of excitement and terror as the men rush frantically for safety is cinematic action at its best. It may be true, as many critics have suggested, that the underground calamity in G. B. Pabst's mining film *Kameradschaft* is superior to Reed's, but if so, it is not by much. Moreover, the desperate rescue attempts, intercut with bits of dialogue among the doomed miners, are handled with a delicacy and restraint that has no parallel in the rather histrionic Pabst film. The miners' morale, fairly high at first, droops little by little each time the camera rediscovers them. The death of a small boy who was making his first trip into the mine is followed by an impromptu funeral chant ('I am the light of the world . . .'). Knowing he is missing the football game that might have changed his life, Hughie feverishly beats a rescue signal against the wall with a rock, as scenes of the game are superimposed. Up above, the rescue teams descend into the mine and emerge, while tense wives and children wait silently for news. Reed's editing and direction invest the disaster with the sad glow of real tragedy.

Reed's rapport with his actors (and his ability to shape their performances for maximum effect – as in the film's last few scenes) had continued to produce fruitful results. There is hardly a performance in *Stars* which can be faulted, though in some cases the *dramatis personae* that the actors are forced to squeeze into are narrow and false. Redgrave, the star of the film, has paid tribute to this facet of Reed's genius: 'he is able . . . to give the actor the feeling that everything is up to him and that all the director is doing is to make sure that he is being seen to his best advantage'.[14] One hopes that self-approval was the outcome when he finally did examine his work. He strikes a nice balance between the intimate scenes with Jenny and the family, and the big oratorical displays. Whether advocating nationalization of the mines or urging the union leaders to order a strike, he invests his rhetorical outbursts with such passion and sincerity that they almost achieve the eloquence that was intended.

Reed's evolving technique was also very much on display in *Stars*. The documentary influence he had absorbed from Grierson, Flaherty and others was put to good use in the newsreel-like authenticity of the mining sequences. Both visual and aural materials are often treated obliquely – lines are understated to the point of being subliminal and dramatic incidents are presented indirectly. The two devices are employed in the confrontation between David and Jenny, just after her assignation with Joe. David's accusing remarks are deliberately muted, and we see only his lowering shadow. The camera is fixed on Jenny's horrified face. The profusion of shadows in this and the preceding sequences has been criticized by Voigt as a misapplication of Expressionistic techniques,[15] but it is nevertheless a healthy, laudable sign of Reed's restive search for new cinematic methods. The slightly distorted angles from which the raging floodwaters are shot could be castigated as inappropriately Expressionistic too, though virtually everyone agrees that they contribute substantially to the desired sense of panic and terror. A smaller, less dramatic example of Reed's visual excellence occurs in the beautifully composed shot that reintroduces us to Sleescale after David and Jenny have returned to live there. In a vertical movement, the camera moves slowly upwards from a lake filled with swans to lovely attractive foliage and other animals surrounding them and then to the behemoth of the colliery that broods over this fragile loveliness as oppressively as over the miners' lives. The combination of dextrous irony, lyricism and acute social comment is typical of the mature Reed.

In addition to its strictly cinematic features, *Stars* affords us another illustration of the relationship between movies and literature. Anyone with the perseverance to examine Cronin's bulky, unrewarding novel will find most of the assets that have been lauded in this discussion of Reed's film – sincere outrage at the miserable lot of the miners, a deeply knowing account of their lives and working conditions, etc. That the novel cannot be praised along with the film is an indication of the staggering gap in sophistication, depth and intelligence between literature and the cinema. Cronin's fiction was a wilted imitation of certain Victorian and naturalistic originals, whereas its movie equivalent, appearing after years of sterile escapism and directed by a first-rate talent, had the bloom of youth on it.

In his autobiography, *Something of Myself*, Rudyard Kipling recalls that one of the principal dictums of his professional life was 'never to repeat a success'.[16] It is a credo to which Kipling's countryman, Carol Reed, seems to have aspired as well. Having established himself as an exponent of social realism in *The Stars Look Down* – and one with the technique to back up his humanism – Reed doggedly refused to entrench himself in this area, or even to explore it further. Instead, he shot off mercurially in another direction with *Night Train to Munich* (1940), a Hitchcockian foray into political intrigue which was made at the 20th Century-Fox studios in England. (Released in the United States as *Night Train*, the film will be referred to by its shorter American title in this discussion.)

Two years earlier, Launder and Gilliat had provided the scenario for one of the year's biggest hits, Hitchcock's *The Lady Vanishes*. The mixture of wit and excitement, threaded into a relentlessly underplayed spy melodrama, had struck audiences and reviewers of the time as inimitably smooth and self-assured, the sort of civilized entertainment that the British had long since patented. Now Launder and Gilliat sought to duplicate their achievement with a script that incorporated many of the same ingredients and a director who was not too proud or individualistic to follow in the footsteps of an illustrious predecessor. (At the time, Hitchcock was the only English director to have made any sustained impact outside Britain.) Perhaps the moment seemed quintessentially right for a successor, since Hitchcock had just vacated his throne in the British film world to try his luck in Hollywood.

Night Train was released in England in the spring of 1940. Though it was immediately identified as an imitation of *The Lady Vanishes*, there was general agreement that it was quite a good imitation. It was praised as an outstanding thriller, a good genre film, and no one plumbed it for hidden political significance. In America, Reed experienced the same frustration that he had with *Stars*: the release of *Night Train* was delayed until its freshness threatened to wither. Finally permitted into American theatres in late 1940, the film nevertheless attracted a comparatively large audience. American reviewers appraised the movie approximately as their British counterparts had, as superior entertainment. *Time*, which had never before reviewed a Reed film, lauded *Night Train* for its 'agonizing excitement'.[17] To 'TS' of the *New York Times*, *Night Train* was the 'year's most perilous ride, but we wouldn't exchange it for a season's commutation ticket on most of the similar vehicles running out of Hollywood'.[18] Otis Ferguson, writing in the *New Republic* was pleased by the 'fast and furious action' but also by the 'attention to character'.[19]

The film begins inauspiciously, with an opening that one is tempted to call pseudo- rather than semi-documentary. In his inner chambers, amidst bootlicking subordinates, Hitler rants (in German) over a map of Europe, pounding his fists on the areas he plans to annex – the Sudatenland, the Polish corridor and so forth. The actor is not identified in the credits, perhaps because he is so strangely unconvincing as the Führer ('strange' in that it is not difficult to make an actor up to look like Hitler). His German is so extravagantly, gutturally Teutonic as to suggest Sid Caesar rather than the intended source. The only word that emerges from the blur of sound is *Lebensraum*, the symbol of Hitlerian expansionism. Interspersed with these monologues are stock shots of goose-stepping Nazis, obviously borrowed from a film vault.

The next sequence is only a little more acceptable. A group of high government officials in Czechoslovakia, closeted with one of their top scientists, Axel Bomasch (James Harcourt), stand around like corpses, delivering a hasty exposition: a revolutionary form of armour plating must not fall into Nazi hands; arrangements have been made for Bomasch and his daughter Anna (Margaret Lockwood) to flee to England; and so on. These urgent promptings are underscored by the opportune arrival of a swarm of German war planes. Then, in two short and poorly executed sequences, Anna is arrested while Bomasch makes a narrow escape.

Once this plot machinery is set in motion, however, *Night Train* quickly becomes exactly what Reed aimed for, a stylish melodrama. Within the framework of the competent Gilliat–Launder screenplay, Reed rings numerous enjoyable changes on the basic flight-and-pursuit motif. The first flight takes Bomasch, and later Anna, to England; the second is a kidnapping in which they are spirited to Germany; later, yet another escape is engineered for them by a British agent, Gus Bennett (Rex Harrison), who infiltrates the German high command. As trains, boats and cars hurtle back and forth across Europe, Reed takes on the aura of a master dispatcher, presiding expertly over an exciting series of arrivals and departure.

'Always avoid the expected', Hitchcock has said again and again, and in his best work there is usually a surprise around every other corner – a harmless-looking crop duster that becomes a lethal weapon, a camera that conceals a gun, a catchy musical hall tune that yields the key to an espionage mystery. Similarly, Reed strives to upset our expectations as craftily as he can. When Anna is imprisoned in a concentration camp, she is befriended by a fellow prisoner, an apparently heroic Czech patriot named Karl Marsen (Paul von Hernreid, soon to de-Germanicize himself and reappear as Paul Heinreid). Reed maintains the counterfeit sincerity of the Marsen character so expertly that we root him on as he denounces his Nazi captors and plots an escape for him and Anna (another getaway!). Thus, it is a nastily effective shock when, shortly after the successful prison break, he and a friend, another refugee, greet each other with 'Heil Hitler!'

There is a more agreeable shock in a scene at an English resort where Anna has been sent to find Bennett, who is supposed to guide her to her father. Bennett is abruptly revealed as a small-time sidewalk entertainer, singing and hoofing for the crowd. Looking like a man without a cloak and dagger to his name, he feigns complete bafflement at Anna's insistence that he must know the whereabouts of her father. 'Is this a gag?', he inquires jauntily. Later, when he has the girl totally offguard, he casually points out that her father is standing nearby. Little tricks like this pour out of Reed's bag for the remainder of the film, culminating in an 'impossible' escape in a cable car high in the Swiss Alps.

Few commentators on *Night Train* have failed to celebrate the contributions of Basil Radford and Naunton Wayne, who portray the two unflappably British types that Gilliat and Launder had borrowed from their own *The Lady Vanishes*. Dry as bitters, the aroma of P. G. Wodehouse hovers about these two – Charters and Caldicott they are called, but the names might just as easily have been Wooster and Psmith. Members in good standing of the old boy network, staunch public school alumnae, Charters and Caldicott are amusing parodies of British stolidity. Their uninflected conversation never deviates from the inconsequential, and they remain serenely unperturbed by the momentous events around them. The dialogue Gilliat and Launder have given them is by no means imperishable, but it is pleasingly flecked with bits and pieces of the British temperament and the impeccable delivery makes it thoroughly droll. References to *Punch*, *The Mikado* and sundry public school practices add a modest patina of naturalism to these sequences. Confronted by the fact that an old schoolmate, Bennett, might be a criminal, one of them stubbornly insists, 'Crooks don't generally play for the Gentlemen.' The other responds, 'Raffles did.' The familiar

English reticence about sex is lightly chaffed when Charters speculates dimly that *Mein Kampf* may be the work that is often given to German brides on their wedding nights. 'Oh, I don't think it's that sort of book, old man', says Caldicott with slight alarm.

Their most overtly comical moment comes when they learn that England and Germany are at war, and their immediate concern is whether or not they will be able to retrieve a set of irreplaceable golf clubs they left with a friend in Berlin. In addition to its value as comedy relief, the episode creates an interesting link with the mainstream of the narrative. The clubs are valuable because they have a 'special plating'.

As a technician, Reed cannot be said to have advanced much in *Night Train*. The seaside milieu has less depth and variety than its counterpart in *Bank Holiday*, and the sequences in Prague and Switzerland look studio-bound, with little or no pictorial value to embellish the action. Indeed, the sense of an indigenous environment that Reed had communicated so well in *Stars* and *Bank Holiday* is missing here. *Night Train* rushes us all over the globe, but makes its glamorous locales – Czechoslovakia, Switzerland, England and Germany – seem indistinguishable.

The actors are uniformly able to meet the demands that Reed makes of them, but unfortunately he doesn't ask very much. Unblemished competence, the hallmark of the English thriller, is deemed sufficient. The only performer whose efforts reach higher levels is Harrison, who achieves a finely-tuned blend of breezy charm and deadly serious professionalism. His tall frame and matinee-idol face are offset by bad teeth, a slightly receding hairline and a slouch. Somehow these human deficiencies work in his favour, bringing an element of likeable imperfection to the inhuman paragonhood of the movie star.

Although virtually everyone who has troubled to write about *Night Train* finds more merits than shortcomings in it, there is little dissent from the view that the work is only a proficient copy of a masterwork. In fact, Wright, who finds much to like about the film, tries to halt any comparisons at all between Reed's movie and *The Lady Vanishes* by simply observing that *Night Train* 'could not really stand up to the inevitable comparison'.[20] But freed from the grip of Hitchcock's staggering – and intimidating – reputation, is it not possible to argue that Reed surpassed his model? The debts are clear enough: the Charters–Caldicott characters, the kidnapping for political reasons, the train setting, the revelation that an ostensibly admirable or harmless character is actually villainous. At the same time, *The Lady Vanishes* (hardly Hitchcock's best film anyway) is fairly static in comparison to *Night Train*. For example, the climactic battle at the Swiss railway station is much more dramatic than the lacklustre gunfight in *The Lady Vanishes*, as Sarris concedes.[21] The identity of the secret agent in *The Lady Vanishes*, while certainly unexpected, is less plausible than in *Night Train*.

Nor are these the only respects in which credibility is a useful tool for comparative study of the two films. With their inherent contrivances and coincidences, melodramas are usually strengthened by the inclusion of a realistic dimension of some kind. The absence of specific references to the Nazis in *The Lady Vanishes*, the logical culprits in 1938, gives the movie a forced, unnatural air. Voigt seems quite wrongheaded in asserting that 'Hitchcock was wiser than Reed in keeping the enemy anonymous.'[22] People are simply not this vague about their enemies, particularly when the conflicts involved are of national and international scope. *Night Train* not only puts swastikas out in plain view, it even supplies a rudimentary primer on the background of the Second World War, encapsulating the major events and telegraphing a few code words of the day at its audience. When Bennett asks permission to undertake the rescue mission, he stresses that he spent three years in Germany. 'Drinking lager', says one of his colleagues in the Secret Service. 'Vodka, isn't it?', says another, an unmistakable allusion to the German–Soviet non-aggression pact. At another point, sardonically topical, Bennett parrots Nazi propaganda, muttering to Anna, 'Those sweet, mysterious eyes . . . as the poet has it and I hope he was Aryan.'

It's easy enough to argue that Hitchcock disguised his Nazis because England was still seeking a peaceful coexistence with Germany in 1938 when *The Lady Vanishes* was released, whereas war had been raging for months when Reed's film appeared. This may be true, but Hitchcock's well-known indifference to politics probably has as much to do with the omissions in his movie as any fears of censorship. In this connection, it might be as instructive to study *Foreign Correspondent* alongside *Night Train* as *The Lady Vanishes*. Hitchcock's second American film, *Foreign Correspondent*, dealt with an American reporter who is sent abroad

to sniff out the political atmosphere of the day and make a
definitive forecast on the likelihood of war. In no time at all, the
unimaginatively named hero (Johnny Jones) blunders into a
ring of spies that has kidnapped a Dutch statesman and seeks to
extract a 'secret clause' from him that will, we are told, permit
them to foment a world war. Why they want to do this is never
explained, nor is the remarkable explosiveness of the passage in
the treaty. Who this gang is comprised of, except stock movie
villains, is pretty dim too. Their leader, an Englishman, pro-
fesses to be working for his country in his own unorthodox
fashion, but never elaborates on the subject. The audience gets no
assistance from the hero, who has been picked for the job
because he is too ignorant and simple-minded to have collected
any information about international politics. Presumably the
Dutchman, as one of the best informed men in Europe – privy to
secret clauses and all – could answer some of these questions or
at least offer an aside that might be pertinent to the European
situation of 1940. But no, his political wisdom is summed up by
the hope that someday the world will be safe for little birds! In
contrast to this prolonged display of intellectual fatuity, those
moments of political specificity in *Night Train*, however meagre,
are to be savoured and appreciated. The crumbs we get from
Reed about Hitler's geopolitics and his pacts with other nations
are more nourishing than anything in the two Hitchcock films.

Night Train also eclipses both its rivals in sexual sophistication.
The puritanism of the Hitchcock movies reduces the love interest
to banality and prudishness. A major plot device in *Foreign
Correspondent*, propelling the heroine into a perilous situation, is
her erroneous assumption that the reporter, with whom she is in
love, has the ungentlemanly inclination to spend the night with
her. She is so shocked she flees immediately. If we were meant to
see the girl as a prig or a study in arrested development, this
sequence would be wholly acceptable; but Hitchcock gives no
sign that he views his heroine as anything but a mature, well-
bred young lady. Even allowing for the different mores of 1940,
the girl's reaction is absurdly extreme.

Reed had shown his ability to handle sexuality in an adult
manner in *Stars*. Jenny's seduction of David, communicated to us
by their off-camera voices and two raindrops flowing together on
the pane, had an intimacy that was not diminished by Reed's
natural reticence. The treatment of erotic themes in *Night Train*

is much more superficial than in the earlier film, but it is still far more sophisticated than the prim, sexless romance of *Foreign Correspondent*. There are a number of sexual innuendoes in *Night Train*, as Bennett tries to dupe the Nazis by convincing them that he has seduced Anna in the past and can do it again to acquire the information they need. 'Do you really believe that you can influence the girl in a matter of hours?', asks one of the Germans disbelievingly. 'Shall we say – over night', is Bennett's self-confident reply. Subsequently, when he explains to Anna the deception he hopes to succeed in, he tells her, 'I shall indicate that once again you have succumbed to my charms.'

After *Night Train*, Reed turned to a more conventional property, Roy Vickers's murder melodrama *The Girl in the News* (1941), also for Fox. The story deals with a nurse who is brought to trial on a murder charge, acquitted, and then framed by her new employers for a second death. In transferring Vickers's novel to the screen, Reed once again had the expert assistance of Frank Launder. His cast included actors he had worked with before and found dependable: Margaret Lockwood, as the female lead; Emlyn Williams, the villain again; Basil Radford, once more on hand for comic relief. Judging by the contemporary reviews and other commentary on the movie, it was no more than an adequate tale of murder most foul and false accusation, with two big trial sequences surrounding the vile doings. The notices were largely complimentary. The *New York Times'* view was reasonably representative: 'Its tension increases like the tightening of a steel spring and it snaps only at the last moment.'[23] Sarris and others who have examined Reed's work in retrospect are impressed by his use of the cat as a tracking device during one of the critical scenes.[24] As an invalid lady who is bent on suicide totters toward the medicine cabinet, Reed keeps us at one remove by trailing the cat as the animal treads along beside its owner. A decade later Reed expanded this feline strategy in *The Third Man*, making Anna's cat symbolically and narratively noteworthy. Another component of *News* which was almost universally admired was Emlyn Williams's performance as the butler who frames Lockwood. Williams had refined and perfected his villainy in *Stars* and his own play *Night Must Fall*, in which he had starred on stage. His portrait of the machinating butler in *News* was ardently hailed, especially with respect to his final courtroom speech, with its unanticipated rush of emotions.

Reed and Fox were sufficiently pleased with one another that the director stayed on to make a third film, *Kipps*, also in 1941. Adapted from H. G. Wells's 1904 novel, the movie was the seventh of Reed's films to originate in a literary or theatrical medium and can be seen as a harbinger of his life-long preference for stories that someone had already told in a novel or a play. His refusal to depart substantially from the plot line and spirit of the Wells novel is also typical of his movies. While undergoing a necessary compression, *Kipps* remains remarkably close to Wells's sociological tale of a draper's assistant who rises above his social station by a miraculous bequest. Reed had demonstrated his aptitude as a social observer in several films, turning his camera into a delicate instrument for registering the myriad nuances and refinements of class-constricted British culture. No doubt the opportunities for social satire in *Kipps* were alluring to a director of Reed's temperament, while at the same time, the project offered him – and his countrymen – a chance to escape from their life and death struggle against Nazism into the late Victorian era, when life was quaint and secure, and the sun had not yet begun to set on the British Empire.

With *Stars* and *Night Train*, Reed had created a place for himself in international film culture and become one of the few English directors with ready access to the all-important American marketplace. In the case of some of Reed's early films, there was a considerable lag between the time they were released in England and the time they were distributed in America. *Kipps*, on the other hand, opened in London in the summer of 1941 and had its American premier only a few months later. The film was rechristened *The Remarkable Mr Kipps* – a ludicrous and misleading change, given Kipp's personality – but for most part American reviewers were not impressed and bestowed only modest laurels on the movie. Although no one could deny its finesse, it lacked the excitement of *Night Train* and the contemporaneousness and passion for social justice of *Stars*. *Variety* praised the film's authenticity and high calibre of acting, but thought *Kipps* did not have enough red blood in its veins: 'Impression sneaks through that Carol Reed wasn't exactly comfortable in the director chore on this type of limp yarn.'[25] The *New York Journal American* thought the film was 'old hat now' but a 'quaint period piece' all the same.[26] The *New York Post* effused over the 'scenic charm of the English provinces, and the picturesque costumes and customs of the turn of the century'.[27] 'TS', standing in for Crowther at the *New York Times* (and doing a better job) was able to enjoy the fragile beauty of *Kipps*, which he saw as a 'gently satirical portrait of Victorian caste and snobbery . . . Although it has the innocent and old-fashioned charm of a bouquet of wax roses under a glass bell it conceals a few thorns.'[28] The *Daily Worker* found enough socialist realism in the movie to applaud Reed for his 'beautifully etched portraits of lower middle class life'.[29]

By the turn of the century, Wells had grown weary of his 'scientific romances' – *The War of the Worlds*, *The Time Machine*, etc. – and began to turn his hand to novels of comic realism. Published in 1905, *Kipps* was the second work (after *Love and Mr Windham*) in this new phase of Wells's career. It was a book that reminded almost everyone of Dickens: written to entertain as well as to instruct, with a well-made plot which was based, unapologetically, on extreme contrivances, it included a mixture of humour, naturalism and social criticism. Like *David Copperfield*, *Kipps* was autobiographical, the tale of a poor boy who made good, yet in Wells's novel the gaps between the creator and his protagonist are more intriguing than the correspondences. Wells's escape route from the dungeon of working-class life was education – he won a scholarship to study with T. H. Huxley – and his literary talents fully liberated him. Kipps seeks improvement at the Folkestone Institute, but wood-carving is as far as he gets. Like Wells, he rises above his background, but the helium that lifts him is a mystifying legacy not the exertions of his brain.

The autobiographical roots of *Kipps* make it one of the more palatable of Well's sociological novels, guaranteeing it an abundance and precision of detail in its recreation of working-class life, as well as a special emotional charge. Still, even with such 'personal' subject-matter and a privileged perspective, Wells was not able to produce a work of major achievement. Laboriousness and mechanical plotting undermine *Kipps*, and it is a fatiguing work to read today, despite the humour and gusto of some of its episodes. Whether he is exposing the mistreatment of the poor or satirizing the pretensions of the rich, Wells's scenes are so overextended and repetitious that the narrative slows to a crawl without any compensating insights or character development. As Kipps's life describes its wild fluctuations between bleak poverty and unexpected wealth, accumulating costly social education along the way, the reader longs for it all to be over.

Under Reed's touch, however *Kipps* was transformed into a small joy of a movie. All the fatty tissue of the narrative was trimmed away and the flat, planed surfaces of most of Wells's characters rounded significantly by the fine performances of Michael Redgrave as Kipps; Phyllis Calvert as Ann Pornick, Kipps's childhood sweetheart; Diana Wynyard as Helen Walshingham, Kipps's fiancée; and the rest of the uniformly excellent cast. No one could do much with Wells's plot and Reed does not try. He faithfully recapitulates the story of Kipp's early deprived years as a draper's apprentice in Folkestone, his spectacular, Dickensian bequest, his painful initiation into genteel society at the hands of grasping Helen Walshingham, his bankruptcy, his rescue through yet another financial miracle and his happy reunion with Ann. The only unpredictable features of Wells's plot are its two *deus ex machinas*. Yet Reed transforms the clumsy architecture of *Kipps*, lightening its tone and streamlining it. Where Wells's satire often seems bison-footed, as he tramples the objects of his anger, Reed is far nimbler, an elegant miniaturist. Not even Shalford (Lloyd Pearson), Kipps's tyrranical, rule-obsessed employer in the drapery shop, suffers the same satirical perforations as in Wells's novel.

Despite its Victorian plot devices, there is relatively little action in *Kipps*, which uses its hero's growth as its focus. The harshness of life among the lower classes is economically and entertainingly portrayed in the sequences at Shalford's, where the clerks toil in abject servitude, with long hours and low pay, forever under their boss's lash. The hopelessness of their predicament is obliquely expressed in the beautifully staged farewell dinner for Kipps in the basement of the establishment. The undercurrents of sadness beneath the boisterous festivities tell us not only that the drapers will miss their colleague, but that they know an incredible stroke of fortune like Kipps's is the only possible deliverance from their melancholy, hole-in-the-corner lives. Before Kipps's departure, we are introduced to a chubby young apprentice (another Dickensian echo, this time the immortal 'fat boy' from *The Pickwick Papers*), who will presumably become the new Kipps, maintaining the dismal continuity of the profession.

After claiming his inheritance, Kipps's newly prosperous standing renders him acceptable to genteel (or at least *shabby* genteel) society in Folkestone. The tutorship which was cruelly and self-servingly performed by Shalford is now assumed by Helen, who snares Kipps as a fiancé, and the emblematically named Chester Coote (Max Adrian), a cultivated and unctuous gentleman of limited means who specializes in supplying cultural edification for the benighted. Coote's hypocrisy – his main goal is to help the Walshingham family separate Kipps from his money – is clear from the beginning, yet Reed never over-dramatizes it. Nor are the social and intellectual pretensions of the Coote–Walshingham circle punctured with more than efficient pinpricks. 'I'm afraid we're without a servant at the moment', Helen apologizes with hauteur when Kipps comes to visit. She longs for the wider society of London as an outlet for her creative instincts. In addition to her wood-carving, she writes poetry, which Coote describes as 'like Swinburne in his quieter moments'. An exquisitely drawn dilettante, he delivers such verdicts with an effortless intellectual self-confidence that is quite funny. Paderewski, he observes, is 'too free with his rubato', and at other times he makes glancing references to 'Omar' and *Sartor Resartus*. In a marvellous touch, his nasal tones can be heard in the background of an ensemble of 'Waiting at the Church'. The focus of cultural life in Folkestone, according to Coote, is the bandstand in the park, where kitsch-like opera duets and other upper middle-brow music can be heard. The dilettantism of Coote and the Walshinghams reaches its amusing, frustrating pinnacle at Mrs Bindon Botting's 'anagram party', in which Kipps shows his lack of aptitude for foolish literary games. The sequence brings Kipps face to face with Ann, his old sweetheart, who is working for Mrs Bindon Botting as a domestic, and, at last seeing the folly of his engagement to Helen, he flees with Ann.

'Education is the great leveller', says Coote, but *Kipps* refutes this point of view completely. Indeed, while the hero is being hauled uncomfortably through Coote's pseudo-pedagogy and fraudulent self-improvement course, trying in vain to absorb the corona of knowledge and refinement that he thinks he sees radiating from Coote, Kipps is undergoing a different education, a slow, inward elucidation that helps him to see that the promptings of the heart are more important than the injunctions

of fashionable society and that the values of his class are immensely more nourishing to him than the corrupt values of the
Cootes and the Walshinghams of the world. The story isn't so
shallow as to allow Kipps an instant awakening to bourgeois
phoniness. Instead, he and Ann embark on an unsatisfactory
experience with the grandeur of upper-middle-class life when
they attempt to build a house suitable to Kipps's new station in
life. Ultimately, the two finds happiness running a simple to-
bacco shop. Yet Reed never patronizes his 'little people'. Sarris
is correct in commenting, 'A sensibility is at work here, an
objective sensibility that looks at people from the outside and yet
treats them with dignity and compassion'.[30]

The moral superiority of the working class is demonstrated
most dramatically in the contrast between Helen, who views
Kipps as a rough but valuable commodity, like unrefined ore,
with which to purchase her escape from stultifying Folkestone;
and Ann, who sees and appreciates the old 'Artie', the simple
soul of her youth beneath the well-lacquered, smartly-suited
Arthur Kipps. Ann's unpretentiousness is typical of the other
common folk in *Kipps*, whose capacity for relaxed camaraderie is
the antithesis of the cold, formal relations of the gentry. To be
sure, the same contrasts can be found in Wells's novel, but in a
more belaboured form. Reed, who is seldom overly insistent,
never tugging at our sleeve, allows Helen to preserve her dignity
throughout and even permits her a final, dolorous meeting with
Kipps in which she has to inform him that her brother Ronnie
(Michael Rennie), a solicitor with whom Kipps has been persuaded to entrust his money, has lost every farthing. As Reed
directs the scene, Helen appears convincingly sorry about the
calamity and about having misused Kipps's affections in general.

The only character in *Kipps* who seems to exist outside the
British caste system is Chitterlow (Arthur Riscoe), the actor who
befriends Kipps and is his benefactor on two occasions – once
when he informs Kipps of the newspaper advertisement that
leads the hero to his legacy and again when a play which he has
cajoled Kipps into backing becomes a surprise success. Boisterous, exuberant, garishly dressed, Chitterlow leaps straight out of
the cupboard of literary types: demonstrative, irresistibly colourful theatricals. He may also have been Wells's projection,
conscious or unconscious, of the artist. Unlike James, Hawthorne,

Kipling and other writers who produced allegories of the creative spirit, Wells envisioned artists as people who descended into the market place to make a living (his own experience) and who amused and educated their public rather than bringing exaltation. In none of Wells's fiction, neither his scientific romances nor his realistic work, is there anything like the Jamesian ideal of art as elevation, a notion of the sublimity of the creative process of art. At least at this point in his career, Wells was content to display the artist as a drunken actor–playwright, entertaining the masses with his deflations of high society (apparently the effect of Chitterlow's farce 'The Pestered Butterfly'). Later, he was to engage in a celebrated feud with James over aesthetic issues and to ridicule artists in his novel *The Shape of Things to Come* and the film he adapted from it, *Things to Come*.

Reed gets a robust performance from Riscoe as the high-spirited actor; it's just broad enough to be engaging but not so extravagant as to poke through the realistic fabric of the story. As Riscoe plays him, Chitterlow is egoistic in such a childlike, unassuming way that it is quite as lovable as intended. His performance is matched by everyone in the cast. As a director of actors, Reed was near the top of his form in *Kipps*. Redgrave finds the halting, insecure yet good-hearted key in which Kipps must be played and never varies from it. Wynyard modulates from muted snobbery to insincerity to saddened resignation exactly on cue, and, as her accomplice, Adrian stuffs Coote with just the right amount of sanctimoniousness. Calvert, lit up with the unspoiled charm of Ann, is no less satisfying. For the first time in his career, Reed seemed in complete control of his story and characters. The cinematic qualities are kept at an unobtrusive level, and other than an unusual shot of Kipps in his night shirt seen through the letter slot in the front door, we are seldom aware of the camera's eye or the cutting-room scissors. *Kipps* is a film in which nothing very great or profound is attempted, but what *is* undertaken – a pleasing comedy of manners – is executed flawlessly. The movie cannot be called a jewel, but it is certainly a semiprecious stone.

In 1938, Reed had been unknown outside of England and not terribly celebrated at home either. But over the next four years his career went into high gear. In Britain, his work was a resounding success with the reviewers as well as the British filmgoers, and in America, though the jubilation was far less thunderous, he definitely wedged himself into the world's most competitive and glamorous film culture like no Englishman since Hitchcock. With *Stars* and *Kipps*, Reed had the opportunity to refine his aptitude for social observation, and though protest films were not destined to be his *métier* (indeed, of his subsequent *corpus*, only *Odd Man Out* comes anywhere near this genre), the skilful use of sociological detail did become one of his principal artistic tools. *Stars* also reveals Reed's increasingly venturesome approach to the technical vocabulary of the film medium, from which he sought to exact the maximum in visual expressiveness. Ultimately, however, the social critique of *Stars* was probably a less significant precursor of Reed's lasting achievements than the melodrama of *Night Train*, in which humour and suspense were counterpointed effectively and a very adroit hand stirred the plot. From *Odd Man Out* to *The Running Man*, much of the director's best work was in the thriller mode.

5   The War Years

During the war, Reed expressed his patriotism through his camera, first as a civilian, using military themes, then as a member of the Army Kinematographic Service, where he made official training films. *A Letter from Home*, a seventeen-minute salute to the courage of Londoners who had endured the Nazi blitz, was produced under the auspices of the Ministry of Education for foreign consumption. The film opened in New York in December 1941 on the same bill with *Laburnum Grove*, which had been imported five years after its original British release. The short documentary juxtaposes a cursory letter from an English mother (Celia Johnson, in her first screen appearance) to her children – who have been evacuated to the United States for greater safety – with the details of her life. Existence in London at this time is shown as a daily drama of loyalty, dedication and self-sacrifice. Through a catalogue of Johnson's daily activities, including her work as an air-raid warden, the film creates a tight-lipped drama of courage, loyalty and self-sacrifice among the wives of London that, as propaganda films go, remains quite stirring.

Discussions of Reed's wartime films usually proceed from *A Letter* to *The New Lot*, but it might be more apt to turn to *The Young Mr Pitt*, a nationalistic allegory in which England's struggle against the French during the Napoleonic Wars is implicitly compared to her lonely, heroic stand against the Nazis prior to the American entry into the war. Launder and Gilliat were enlisted to write the screenplay, with assistance from Viscount Castlerosse.

In England, *Pitt* was received as a welcome investigation of the country's glorious past, but the American critics – those who chose to review the movie at all – were not so gentle. Winston of the *Post* predicted that the picture would 'produce brain, eye and ear fatigue in the audience'.[1] At the *Daily News*, Kate Cameron dismissed *Pitt* as a 'talky, pictorial study'.[2] *Variety* was more indulgent, finding much to acclaim in the movie but judging it 'too leisurely in its unfoldment' for American audiences.[3] At *Commonweal*, evidently the only well-known magazine to review the film, Philip Hartung was thoroughly derisive: 'considering the exciting things that were going on, the picture is incredibly dull'.[4] Crowther of the *New York Times* wrote admiringly of Donat's 'smooth and dignified' acting style, but also felt that 'the nature of the historical period in which the film is set and the evident fidelity of the authors to the facets of Mr Pitt's life conspire to prevent this picture from having a sharp dramatic impact'.[5]

In the first two scenes of the film, Reed gets as solid a grip on his audience as a director could hope for. Pitt the Elder (an artificially aged Robert Donat) eloquently pleads the cause of the American colonists and implores the House of Commons to set them free without bloodshed. His young son (Geoffrey Atkins) watches raptly from the visitors' gallery. Later at home, celebrating the boy's birthday, Pitt permits his son to drink wine. As Pitt Jr sips port, Pitt Sr lays down guidelines for the boy's future political career, which is already deemed a certainty. Although it is a bit too self-consciously principled to ring wholly true ('Do not seek fame through war', etc.), it is delivered with just enough affection and pomposity to offset its excessive nobility. Another tonic for this pontification is Pitt's gouty leg, which he keeps propped up on a chair. The contrast between his Ciceronian utterances and his oddities of manner and appearance creates a salutary tension; it is the stuff drama is made of. Pitt Jr adds to the credibility of the scene by imperfectly comprehending his father's advice and by growing tipsy.

But the movie that follows this hopeful prologue disappoints more often than it satisfies. In the next scene, Pitt is a brilliant twenty-four-year-old who has just been named Prime Minister. Appealing to his arch-rival Charles Fox (Robert Morley) for support, in the national interest, he is stingingly rebuffed. Fox is greedy for power, the exercise of which he wishes to alternate with his dissolute pleasures. Having revealed its biases, the movie proceeds to sort out all the complex issues of life in eighteenth- and nineteenth-century England into a morality play in which there is no doubt as to who is virtue and who is vice. The glorification of Pitt is supposed to be, by historical transference, a glorification of Churchill, who, like Pitt, was the 'pilot that weathered the storm', the leader who rallied the country's spirits in the dark days of war and fought on against a dangerous continental foe. Meanwhile, Fox plays the Neville Chamberlain role, supinely appealing for a peaceful resolution to England's conflict with France. Wright finds in this aspect of *Pitt* a solution to the 'problem of historical perspective' and praises the movie as a 'remarkably compelling film'.[6] He is virtually alone in this view.

The structure of *Pitt* is provided by the historical events it chronicles, and little effort is made to dramatize the inner lives of the characters. Instead, Reed's camera rather passively records the script's progress through the momentous events of the age – the reforms of the Pitt administration, the increase of French power during the rise of Napoleon, the ebb and flow of Pitt's fortunes as he seeks to unite the English nation and revive her power and influence. History gave Reed two splendid climaxes for Pitt's biography – Nelson's destruction of the French fleet at Aboukir Bay in the Battle of the Nile (1798) and later in the Battle of Gibraltar (1804). As recreated on the screen, each follows a prolonged period of public dissatisfaction with Pitt, with the short-sighted populace, their bread and circuses severely rationed, subjecting him to intense obloquy. The Prime Minister's noble crusade is rendered all the more heroic by its loneliness and by the obtuse, selfish opposition he faces. As portrayed in the film, Pitt is a prophet who is only infrequently honoured in his own country. Except for his staunch ally Wilberforce (John Mills), Pitt must contend with a largely frivolous Parliament; the MPs, brocaded and periwigged to their ankles, are an effete bunch who are either openly corrupt and purblind or too distracted by aristocratic dissipations to attend to the national interests. It is only by the sheer force of Pitt's personality and oratory that he is able to impose his sensible and far-seeing policies on these recalcitrant parliamentarians.

On the oscilloscope of popular support, the needle swings wildly from warm affirmation to virulent condemnation, usually depending on how sharp the pinch of economic deprivation is during times of stress. The English people are depicted, not quite intentionally, as a changeable, superficial mass of whims, incapable of comprehending the larger issues of state. In the early scenes, they are dissatisfied with the graft-ridden, self-indulgent coalition government of Charles Fox and Lord North (Felix

Aylmer) and transfer their support to young Pitt, who seems likely to carry on the inspiring, high-minded traditions of his father, the 'Great Commoner'. When the king dissolves Parliament and calls for a general election, Pitt sweeps to victory. As the moral and economic health of England is quickly reestablished under his leadership, Pitt's popularity soars. Later, when the first phase of the Napoleonic War results in a defeat and a painful attrition of men and material goods, the people are unable to perceive the necessity of smashing Napoleon; howling mobs follow Pitt's carriage and throw rocks through his window. After his hand-picked admiral, Horatio Nelson (Stephen Haggard), crushes the French fleet in Egypt, the pendulum swings back resoundingly in Pitt's favour. Another period of public scorn follows, however, when the English are defeated on land, and Pitt feels compelled to submit his resignation. Only in the hour of greatest national crisis, with the French massing across the channel for invasion, is the unimpeachable wisdom of Pitt's statecraft appreciated. Then the people rally behind him, his political enemies are converted, and his protégé Nelson demolishes the French once more. An exultant nation celebrates the greatness of its selfless leader.

As indicated earlier, very little of the drama in *The Young Mr Pitt* arises from Pitt's private life, which is largely non-existent, or even his psychic life, which is simply a continuum of self-denying dedication to the state. A less marmoreal side of Pitt is revealed in his abortive romance with Eleanor Eden (Phyllis Calvert), an ambassador's daughter, and to a lesser extent, in his bantering relationship with his protective old nanny (Jean Cady). Although Pitt and Eleanor fall in love, the self-sacrificing Prime Minister renounces his beloved because the duties of the state are so all-consuming. The scolding, protective familiarity of the nanny recurs throughout Pitt's life, but the episodes are hackneyed and do nothing to round out the portrait of Pitt.

Raymond Durgnat reviles *Pitt* for its political inaccuracies,[7] but even an historically ignorant observer can see that the movie is tendentious and oversimplified. It is a rare epoch indeed in which the momentous dilemmas of the day can be so confidently and unqualifiedly reduced to black and white. Similarly, men are seldom as easy to tag and label as this film would suggest. Except for Wilberforce, the men who surround Pitt are either knaves, like Fox, or fools, like Addington (Henry Hewitt). This

oppressive hagiography cripples the drama, diluting its conflict
and denying Pitt the human frailties that would make him
believable. His incompetence in financial affairs is touched on
briefly, but dismissed as another example of his indifference to
anything other than England. Morally as well as politically, he
would be more credible if he were less perfect.

An epic hero like Pitt needs a monster to slay, and this role is
tailored to Napoleon, whose Hitlerian appetite for power is the
only explanation that is put forward for his aggressions. Sarris
pungently characterizes this aspect of *Pitt* as a 'topical allegory
in which the arch-demon is transferred from Nürnberg to
Corsica'.[8] The first episode in the allegory deals with the birth of
the French emperor in Corsica, where his birth certificate is
made to look as if it were written in blood. A few segments of his
life are intercut with Pitt's, so that we are prepared in advance
for the coming struggle between good and evil. Later, in early
manhood, the coldly brilliant Frenchman instructs his elders on
military strategy. By the time he assumes the leadership of the
French state, he is a ruthless monomaniac bent on global conquest. Not content with making Napoleon a hydrophobic dicta-
tor, Reed rather obviously embellishes the contemporary
overtones by giving Talleyrand (Albert Lieven) a slight German
accent. As Napoleon himself, the Czech Herbert Lom is even
less Gallic than Lieven. (He was to repeat his brooding Eastern
European version of Bonaparte – far more memorably – in Dino
De Laurentiis's *War and Peace* in 1956.) Reed even denies the
French their elegant language!

By far the best sequences in *Pitt* are the parliamentary de-
bates. Despite the unhappily partisan point of view, these scenes
are vigorously staged, with a reconstructed House of Commons
serving as the forum. Some of the exciting parry and thrust of
British parliamentary debate is conveyed, as the MPs rise to try
their rhetorical steel on one another. Many of the speeches are
taken directly from the records and in the mouths of Donat,
Morley and Mills they occasionally reach the level of great
oratory.

In terms of *mise-en-scène*, Pitt strengthens the impression left by
The Stars Look Down that Reed was an artist with a rich visual
imagination. The stately homes and townhouses of Georgian
England frame the action like a lovely succession of Constables
and Turners. Their relaxed yet dignified atmosphere is re-

inforced by yawning fireplaces and vast corridors, graceful car-
riages and intricately carved balconies, lap dogs and children's
ponies, lush arbors and serene lily ponds. The costumes are by
Cecil Beaton, who, ostentatiously enough, signed his name in the
credits; yet he has dressed the performers in Pitt handsomely.
The waistcoats and cravats, the crinolined gowns and petticoats
are exquisite. The actors move around in them as easily as if they
had never worn anything else. As always, Reed's sense of taste is
unfailing. The sets and costumes have a refined beauty that
avoids the vulgar, overripe quality of similar Hollywood productions. Freddie Young's black and white photography stresses the
order and classical patterns of English life at this time.

Reed's gift for miniaturism flourished in *Pitt*. The use of wine
to reflect and symbolize different aspects of the story shows a
high degree of cinematic sophistication. As Pitt the Elder in the
second scene, Donat is able to toast himself and his successor at
the same time. The wine is port, as simple and unaffected a
creation as the old earl himself, and, defying his doctor's orders,
he lifts a glass to his lips and smiles at Wilberforce.

There are other fine touches in *Pitt*. Less intricately developed
but equally memorable is the housekeeper's intrusion into one of
Pitt's late-night labours over the affairs of state with a veal pie
that she insists he eat. In an American film of this era, the food
would be nondescript. Reed defines it specifically, choosing a
typically English dish, a homely but endearing contrast to the
sautéed and puréed meals of the pretentious cuisine across the
channel.

The technical excellence which Reed had been nurturing also
adds a layer of artistry to the film. There is an especially striking
shot of Eleanor's younger brother through the window of Pitt's
carriage. The use of montage is highly assured throughout, and
the complex pulse of political life in Britain and France is
telescoped efficiently.

After Pitt, Reed expressed his patriotism more directly, in a
series of training films for the British army. His first effort was
The New Lot (1942), a forty-four minute short on the nature of
military life. Initiation into the unfamiliar and unsettling world
of the army was understandably regarded by the English as a
serious challenge, fraught with psychological difficulties, and

Reed was assisted in the production of *The New Lot* by the Department of Army Psychology. The finished product seems to have surpassed everyone's expectation, both as an educational tool and in terms of its intrinsic merit. In the wake of this success, the War Office and the Ministry of Information were in agreement that Reed should be encouraged to create a full-length narrative version of this material for commercial distribution. Additional reinforcement came from Filippo Del Guidice, a producer at Rank's Two Cities Films. Soon Reed was at work on his new project, along with an illustrious screenwriter, the novelist Eric Ambler.

The Way Ahead was completed in time for a dramatic premier date: D-Day. The film received an enthusiastic reception both in England and America, though American critics were more excited about it than American audiences. For some critics, the picture has retained its appeal. Writing in 1974, Voigt felt that it 'looks much better today than other contemporary war films'.[9] Similarly, the author of Reed's obituary in *The Times* hailed its 'warm and sympathetic understanding of human nature'.[10] Lest the effusions seem parochial it should be recorded that the *New York Times* pronounced the film 'much-respected'.[11]

At the time of its release, *The Way Ahead* received equally high praise. C. A. Lejune, in England's *Observer*, called it a 'very fine film . . . the best . . . of the year'.[12] *Variety* described it as a 'stout story' and hailed the 'underlying genuineness of the picture'.[13] *Time* magazine declared that Reed 'Tells with considerable force the real stories of modern war',[14] while *Newsweek* felt that he 'matches the Noel Coward–navy film *In Which We Serve* punch for punch . . .'[15] At the *New York Times* , Crowther was even more elated than the *Time* and *Newsweek* reviewers: 'The authors have beautifully outlined a group of intriguing characters, Mr. Reed has disposed them in credible images and all the actors have played them most trenchantly.'[16]

In truth, however, there is not as much to respect in *The Way Ahead* as one would like. Neither Reed nor Ambler was especially suited to the species of rousing, crudely energetic propaganda that the film required – that is, if it was to survive the turbulence of its time and place. Ambler had shown his skill at murky, velvet-lined intrigue in *Coffin For Dimitrios, Journey Into Fear* and other spy novels, but he could not reach into his accustomed bag of tricks this time, nor could Reed make much use of his elegant style, his wit or his all-important irony. Spiking this last-named gun was the most serious self-limitation Reed had to impose in *The Way Ahead*. Since by design, the film's purpose was to extol Britain's fighting men, Reed's native scepticism had nowhere to express itself. Without it, the flow of artistic energies in the work slowed to a trickle. As the new recruits pass, stage by stage, from softness and immaturity to battle-hardened veteranhood, from resentment of their officers to veneration of them, the feeling one has is, so what?

As usual, Reed's actors are faultlessly selected – David Niven, Stanley Holloway, Leo Genn and James Donald are the principals – a group of civilians whom we are allowed to tag along with from the time they receive their induction notices to their deadly engagement with Rommel's troops in North Africa. Ambler and Reed strive for a representative sampling of infantrymen and so we get a salesman, a fireman, an office worker, etc. The officer class is represented by a debonair Lieutenant Jim Perry (Niven) and a fire-eating Sergeant Fletcher (William Hartnell). On the psychological level, the range of performers extends from an extroverted man's man to a worried young husband to a snob.

A complex and meaningful drama could have been carved out of this subject-matter, but the political requirements of the film were simply too prescriptive. After initial resistance, the new recruits had to adjust definitively to army life, and their new status had to seem not only desirable but merited. Consequently, the movie is left without villains; other than the invisible Germans, there are only heroes and heroes-to-be. As for the movie's conflict, it is as purely synthetic as the dummies the men stab at with their bayonets. Until the battle sequence near the end, the only true objective the trainees face is the tough regimen of the army, particularly as embodied in the despised Sergeant Fletcher. The audience, however, is cued to see him as a model of military excellence from the beginning, and the regimen as salutary for the self-indulgent civilians. The film's *raison d'être* was, after all, an appeal for national unity at a time when England's very survival was at stake. As a consequence, not much reality could be allowed to seep into the narrative, certainly none of the genuine friction, injustice and class-consciousness one might expect to encounter in an English boot camp.

The men's resentment towards their hard-driving sergeant

reaches its peak when one of them, Lloyd (James Donald), complains to Lieutenant Perry. Both Perry and Sergeant Fletcher are exquisitely tolerant of this puerile protest and when the time is right, Perry pillories the company sternly for its failure to perform adequately during war games. This proves to be the turning point, and henceforth the recruits transform themselves into soldiers.

The company is allotted two leaves during the course of the film, the second coming on top of the first in a confusing narrative jumble. The snapshots we get of the men in their home environment should help to round out each of the portraits, but instead each remains flat. The salesman chats convivially with an old coworker in his store, then, implausibly, leaps back into the fray to help sell a bird bath to a woman customer. The fireman, Brewer (Holloway), sinks back into an armchair and sighs contentedly over his peaceful home environment just before his daughter turns some cacophonous music up full blast (the irony is as leaden as it sounds). Worst of all is the sequence with Lloyd, who, in an excruciating variant of the busman's holiday, spends his furlough haranguing his friends – and us – on the indispensability of the British infantryman. As it develops, Reed has saved his few pyrotechnics for the climax. There is a big, fairly compelling scene at the troopship when the men set off for North Africa. Later, when the ship is torpedoed by a U-boat, Reed finally unleashes some of the technical expertise he had manifested in earlier films. The brief disaster scenes hurtle along at a terrific pace, with a lot of quick cutting and unusual camera angles to convey the initial shock and disorder.

Subsequently, following a prolonged period of dusty idleness in a flyblown North African village, the protagonists receive their baptism of fire as the German forces strike suddenly. Reed stages the ensuing battle very confidently, with the big guns booming, planes swooping down like deadly wasps, and buildings crumbling under the barrage. The Germans call for unconditional surrender, but Britons never will be slaves – especially not these paradigmatic Tommies – and they defiantly reject the demand. In our last sight of them, Reed's fondness for indirect perspectives nicely abets the symbolic intentions of the movie: the seven recruits, now hardened fighting men, are led forward by Niven and Hartnell through a protective curtain of smoke into an uncertain future, the 'way ahead'. 'Come on lads', calls out Sergeant Fletcher, 'once more for the day you missed in exercises.'

The women in *The Way Ahead* are as unhappily close to plaster of paris as the men. They are models of patience and understanding as their men march off to battle; they constitute the other side of the recruiting posters, the faithful girls left behind. Marjorie (Renee Asherson), an army clerk, patriotically invites the boys for tea and a real, home-style bath, though she leaves her spry old mother (Mary Jerrold) to play hostess. Some of the men have spouses or lady friends, but the best-looking girl in the film, Mrs Perry (Penelope Ward), belongs to Lieutenant Perry. (Later, of course, she belonged to Reed himself.) A more picture-perfect British wife is hard to imagine and she's egalitarian too. Towards the end of the film, she joins the other women to compare news from the men.

The spirit of absolute democracy that reigns in the gathering of women is indicative of the absence of class prejudice or condescension in *The Way Ahead*, a feature which is generally deemed one of its chief strengths. Although class divisions are clearly discernible in the distinctions of rank, occupation and accent, Reed does nothing to underscore these familiar characteristics of the English caste system. His detached, sharply realistic eye catches numerous reflections of this system, though he neither defends nor attacks it; still less does he smother his 'little people' with patronizing sympathy. The characters are uniformly bland, like a large spread of processed foods, but they are not offensive or bigoted.

One footnote should be appended to our discussion of the film: it provided Peter Ustinov with one of his earliest screen roles. As Rispoli, a sullen Arab cafe owner who speaks only French, Ustinov is converted from Anglophobia to Anglophilia by watching the Tommies play a game of darts! His moderately amusing sequences were presumably his own creation, since he received a credit as coscenarist. His two-tiered participation in the film, coupled with the comically exotic role he played, were a harbinger of the flamboyant, diversified career that lay ahead.

Having filed a minority report on *The Way Ahead*, it is possible wholeheartedly to join the majority view on Reed's next film, *The*

True Glory, a thrilling documentary account of the D-Day land-
ing and the subsequent conquest of Europe. A joint British–
American effort, the movie was the product of a collaboration
between Reed and the American playwright and director Garson
Kanin. The completed film had a prologue by no less than
Dwight Eisenhower himself. Reed and Kanin undertook the
awesome task of distilling a feature-length movie from approximately ten million feet of film, much of it shot in action. These
continents of celluloid came from the archives of a dozen countries and represented the work of 1400 different cameramen, of
whom 130 were killed or wounded.

The True Glory opened in New York only a few months after
The Way Ahead and brought Reed a new shower of accolades from
the critics. In *Cue*, Jesse Zunser spoke of the it as a 'war film
without parallel in history!'[17] Even without an exclamation
point, *Time* was just as exclamatory: 'In a word it is what the
moviemakers strive for and seldom achieve: colossal.'[18] For
Crowther of the *New York Times* the film was marked by 'overwhelming eloquence' and offered a 'brilliantly composed screen
tribute to the courage and perseverance of our fighting men . . .'[19]
Only James Agee in the *The Nation* was somewhat guarded in his
praise: 'Lacks the greatness of the best short war films, but for
the hugely complicated kind of job it is, it could hardly have
been done better.'[20]

Eisenhower's robust preamble sets the tone of the rest of the
film. The movie's high-minded inclusiveness takes some interesting forms. Although a familiar orotund BBC type provides the
main thread of the narrative, hundreds of other voices break in
along the way to supply small, pungent glosses on life at the
front. These personalized vignettes are flavoured with the distinctive speech rhythms of the men and women who recount
them. French, Scottish, Irish and several American dialects
(even Brooklynese) are among the accents that make up the
splendid polyglot. Purportedly the voices of actual Allied servicemen (and numerous civilians) speaking in 'their own words',
these interpolations are lively and pungent. Less successful,
ironically, is the more high-flown commentary of the central
narrator, which the film-makers decided to cast in blank verse.
The result, as Dwight Macdonald remarked in another context,
is more blank than verse.

But on the microcosmic level of the ordinary GI or Tommy,

Reed's film is both true and glorious, a pre-Studs Terkel oral history of the war. The film begins on a note of painful honesty, with an American serviceman confessing that the greeting he and his platoon received in England – a band playing 'White Christmas' – was 'pretty corny', though well-intentioned. An officer in the Royal Navy admits to getting roadsick while towing his craft to the Rhine. A Canadian recounts the bloody fighting at Caen, one of the major battle theatres of the D-Day invasion. Several Frenchmen summarize the miseries of the occupation. An American supply officer complains, with a self-congratulatory tone, that Patton's advance into Germany was so swift that new maps could not be prepared quickly enough. Amidst the torrent of comments, none is more exuberant than the tankman at the banks of the Rhine, where every bridge except the one at Remagen had been destroyed: 'A miracle. The watch on the Rhine was finished . . . washed up . . . or to coin a phrase, "kaput!"' After his words, a sign flashes by briefly: 'Cross the Rhine with dry feet courtesy of the Third Army.'

The superb footage, intercut with maps, makes the Allies' progress fairly easy to follow. The beach-heads at Normandy, the terrible fighting at Caen, the airborne invasion of Holland, the struggle to free the Antwerp estuary in order to maintain the supply lines, Von Runkle's counteroffensive, the Battle of the Bulge and the conquest of Germany itself – each stage in the monumental campaign comes brilliantly to life. In view of his past achievements, there is no reason to minimize Reed's part in telling this collaborative story. The pacing is unfailingly brisk; using quick cuts and sharp transitions, Reed sweeps us forward through the most complex military encounters of the Second World War, cleverly resorting to shorthand to convey bulky information compactly. The panoramic events of warfare are nicely counterpointed with small, personal details – the touches for which Reed was already heralded – such as an old French lady dressed in black near the English naval yards. In one startling leap, the camera moves from the battlefronts to a quiet, orderly London street, where the citizenry is 'doing its bit' by simply carrying on as usual. All the fabled heroism of the stoical Londoners is captured in this single contrast. On a larger scale, Reed balances the euophoria of liberation – thousands of jubilant French cheering the arrival of American troops in Rennes, De Gaulle's triumphant return to Paris – with the barbarism of the concentration camps, where a survivor is seen kissing a soldier's hand.

The same deliberate play of antitheses concludes the film. Fraternizing among British, American and Russian servicemen leads to a young soldier's hopeful prophecy: 'To the victor belongs the spoils. That's what they say. Well, what are the spoils? Only this: a chance to build a free world better than before. Maybe it's the last chance. Remember that.' At the same time, a huge military cemetery, with its vast forest of crosses, haunts the last moments of *The True Glory* and casts a backward shadow over everything that preceded it.

The official record of the collosal effort to free Europe and smash the Third Reich could not be expected to deal dispassionately or charitably with the other side. Captured Germans are displayed in unattractive poses, while a GI's remarks sort them into five or six categories (sullen, defiant, pathetic, etc.). Still, the film avoids outright contempt, crudity or the attribution of diabolism. It is vastly more humane and intelligent than the average American brand of war movie, where the view of our adversaries can usually be summed up by one of Hollywood's most famous lines: 'One fried Jap going down.'

The True Glory closed two phases of Reed's career, war films and documentaries. Other than *The Key*, a wartime romance, he was never again to work in either genre. Between 1942 and 1945, however, he had adapted so successfully to both these forms that he emerged from the war years as the foremost director in England. Assessing the heights Reed had scaled, Sarris observes that his 'prestige' as a national director now enabled him to impose his ironic temperament on themes that did not require patriotic conformity'.[21] Reed himself perceived a humbler benefit in the films he made during the war. In an interview with Ezra Goodman in 1947, he remarked that these movies had 'been of inestimable value . . . in bringing a heightened sense of realism' to his work.[22] His self-evaluation is so soft-spoken, as always, that one has no idea whether he had any inkling of his true potential, for he stood on the threshold of a cinematic accomplishment unequalled by any other British director working on native soil.

6   Reed's Masterpiece: *Odd Man Out*

Happily, Reed's maturation had not completely outstripped that of the film community that spawned him. The English cinema itself had come of age during the Second World War in a scientific and entrepreneurial sense and now boasted not only a legion of proficient editors, cinematographers, set designers and other technically advanced personnel, but also two major film impresarios, J. Arthur Rank and Alexander Korda, who had created solid foundations for themselves in the 1930s and who had the creative and commercial ambition to put all the new British talent to work. The result of these various forces was a surge of activity in the English cinema which at last made it possible for Britain to break out of her cinematic parochialism and capture a place in the world film community, though it was not a place she was able to maintain permanently. Among directors, Reed was unquestionably the principal force in this exciting movement, and his *Odd Man Out* – made for Rank's company, Two Cities, and released in 1947 – provided an especially glowing example of the new maturity of English films.

Seldom in the history of the British movie industry had a director been able to assemble so much first-rate talent. The camerawork was assigned to Robert Krasker, probably the finest cinematographer in England at the time. Fresh from his brilliant work on Laurence Olivier's *Henry V* and David Lean's *Brief Encounter*, Krasker was one of the few men whose patient craftsmanship and innovative ideas matched Reed's. As in Reed's two previous films, William Alwyn composed the score, but here the subject-matter allowed him to explore far more creative avenues than in *The Way Ahead* and *The True Glory*. Unlike most film scores, some of Alwyn's music composed before the film, so that the actions of the characters could be harmonized with it. Occasionally the melodies suggest haunting old Irish airs, but overall it conveys a taut, fragmented manner; at points the delicate patterns of orchestral colouring almost suggest Delius. There are three motifs that serve as labels for characters: a sprightly theme for Shell, the irrespressible little bird-seller; a lyrical flourish for Kathleen, the fervently romantic heroine; and a threnody for Johnny McQueen, the wounded rebel leader. According to Alwyn,[1] part of the preparation undertaken by the film's star, James Mason, consisted of adjusting Johnny's disabled walk to the tragic rhythm of the music. Moreover, sections of the score were sometimes played for the cast as a mood-inducing device before shooting a scene. The composer also carefully synchronized his efforts with not only the intricately told story but the numerous sound effects that Reed interpolated into the film. The two were ably seconded by the sound engineer, Harry Miller, and the editor, Fergus McDonnell.

Odd Man Out was the first of several Reed works that dealt with an outcast, a man on the run. The source of the story was F. L. Green's novel of the same name, a bleak tale about a leader of a revolutionary organization in Northern Ireland who, wounded in a hold-up attempt at a mill, embarks on an extraordinary odyssey as he struggles to find his way to safety. In preparing the screenplay for *Odd Man Out*, Reed had as free a hand as in other aspects of the project. Green was hired to adapt the novel himself, but as a safeguard he was teamed with R. C. Sherriff, author of the famous play *Journey's End* and a scenarist with years of experience. Reed conferred extensively with Green about the screenplay in Belfast and, while there, spent a good deal of time searching out appropriate settings for the narrative. His love of location shooting could now be indulged to the fullest, which in this instance meant a month of filming in Belfast.

Reed also saw to it that his ideas were as effectively implemented in front of the cameras as behind them. The casting of Mason was a particularly brilliant stroke: the leading English matinee idol of the day, he was a superb actor as well, with all the technical resources one could wish for at his disposal, very much a necessity in a part which compelled him to be semi-comatose much of the time. Robert Newton, who had cultivated a special aptitude for portraying rogues, eccentrics and madmen, was a sensible choice for Lukey, the somewhat deranged painter who provides Johnny with a temporary refuge. For the most part, Reed distributed the other roles among the best-known

Irish acting ensemble in the world, the Abbey Players: F. J.
McCormick appeared as Shell, W. G. Fay as Father Tom, Cyril
Cusack as Pat and Dennis O'Dea as the Head Constable.

The exceptional care that went into the creation of *Odd Man
Out* paid off in handsome aesthetic dividends. The film was
clearly Reed's most artistically far-reaching endeavour and contemporary reviewers all treated it with the sobriety it deserved.
Surely Sarris is misleading when he states that *Odd Man Out* had
a 'mixed reception in Europe and America',[2] a summation which
implies that every laudatory notice was counterbalanced by a
pejorative one. Actually there is no major periodical or influen-
tial critic who failed to extol Reed's picture, though the reviewers
qualified their praise.

Naturally the British notices were the most uniformly elated.
With the native cinema just struggling to its feet in the postwar
years, a movie as formidable as *Odd Man Out* was – whatever its
shortcomings – cause for jubilation among English reviewers.
The Times, never much of an outlet for film criticism, mostly
confined itself to an animated plot summary, though it found
time to exult over the ensemble acting and to compare the work
to 'good French films and the best kind of theatrical repertory'.[3]
Vastly more extensive and perceptive was Arthur Vesselo's
critique in *Sight and Sound*, the distinguished British film journal,
which hailed the movie's 'dramatic intensity', deeming it the
'best and most genuine film of the quarter'. Vesselo perceived in
it 'some of the tragic poetry we associate with the Irish
playwrights'.[4] Writing in *The New Statesman and Nation*, William
Whitebait praised Reed for his ability to orchestrate the numerous different moods, styles and settings in *Odd Man Out*, for
having 'grasped all this diverse material and projected it in a
single form'.[5]

In the United States, the founding father of film criticism,
James Agee, reviewed the movie almost two months before its
release and established the basic parameters within which the
movie was to be discussed. For Agee, Reed's new work was a
highly uneven accomplishment in which the first hour had
'excitement enough to oversupply any dozen merely "good"
pictures', but in its latter portion became 'more wildly adventurous, more mystical, more half-baked'. Still, on balance, he found
it a 'reckless, head-on attempt at greatness, and the attempt
frequently succeeds'.[6] John McCarten of the *New Yorker*, at his

lower level of intellect and fervour, was in complete accord with Agee: 'Carol Reed . . . has woven a fine web of melodrama out of the quarry's narrow squeaks with the police and his encounters with people afraid either to help or to hinder him . . . as the picture rolls on, however, Mr. Reed regrettably begins to underline the story's philosophic aspects . . . and the going . . . gets a trifle heavy.'[7] John Mason Brown, normally a theatre critic, was so impressed by *Odd Man Out* that he devoted a lengthy essay to it, 'The Hunted and the Haunted', in *Saturday Review*, in which he compared the movie to John Galsworthy's play *Escape*. Although the movie reaches out for 'philosophical meaning that it never grasps', wrote Brown, it creates its narrative 'stirringly in distinctive movie terms, displays great integrity', is peopled with characters who 'belong to city streets and pubs and tenements rather than to movie lots' and offers 'welcome proofs of what a motion picture can be when it happens to have been made by a man of taste, invention, and imagination . . .'[8] The *New York Times*'s Crowther scorned the film-makers search for 'some vague illumination of the meanings of charity and faith', but was nevertheless excited by it as 'a most intriguing film'.[9] Only Philip Hartung, true to the religious ethos of *Commonweal*, was more exhilarated by the allegorical second half of the movie (it 'gives this picture its meaning and extraordinary dignity')[10] than the more thriller-oriented portion that preceded it.

In the thirty-eight years since its release, *Odd Man Out* has attained the status of a classic and has received far more thoughtful retrospective commentaries than any other Reed film. In their surveys of Reed, Sarris and Voigt devote a sizeable amount of space to the film and there have also been lengthy assessments by Abraham Polonsky,[11] Julia Symmonds[12] and Karel Reisz.[13] By far the most exhaustive examination of *Odd Man Out* is James De Felice's *Filmguide to Odd Man Out*, a model of patient research and sensible analysis.[14]

Among the literary figures whose work Reed transferred to the screen during his long career, F. L. Green is one of the most obscure. During the 1930s and 1940s, Green produced a series of moderately popular novels, but ultimately he suffered the saddest of artistic fates: he is best remembered not for a work of fiction but for its movie version, in which he must share the credit with a coscenarist, a director, a cast of actors and numerous technicians.

An Anglo-Irishman who lived for many years in Belfast, Green was passionately involved in the problems of Ulster, and it is hardly surprising that his novel reflects the raw tensions of that tormented land. At the same time, it is strikingly similar to the fiction of a more renowned namesake, Graham Greene. Like the author of *The Power and the Glory* and *The Heart of the Matter*, Green attempts to fuse psychological realism and religious themes and apply them both to the thriller format. There are, however, important differences between the two writers in style, tone and outlook, as well as in the quality of their work. Greene's headlong narratives speed from incident to incident as tersely as possible, while his gloomy sensibility is specifically and unmistakably Catholic. By contrast, Green's stories lumber a bit, their pace retarded by a highly decorative style and by the constant intrusion of philosophical set pieces, little arias on man's fate that stop the dramatic momentum in its tracks. In addition, Green's religious proclivities, though aggressively Christian, are non-doctrinal; they suggest a rather diffuse, even sickly, evangelicalism. That Reed did so much of his best work with two English novelists whose names differ only in spelling and whose fiction was, all things considered, so closely related, is yet another fascinating oddity in his paradox-laden career.

Since *Odd Man Out* is almost indisputably Reed's masterpiece, the changes it underwent in its transcription from fiction to film become especially pertinent, and it is important to examine his source at length. Published in 1945, the novel drew favourable notices and sold reasonably well. Its subject, the die-hard revolutionary struggle and terrorism in Northern Ireland, seems perennially topical in the United Kingdom. Its timeliness was tragically renewed by the bloody events of the 1970s, as Belfast again became a battleground between Protestants and Catholics. As a consequence, the novel was reissued in 1971, with a still from the movie as its cover. However, those who turn eagerly to the book as a sociopolitical document are likely to put it down just as quickly as they picked it up. Green's anti-revolutionary biases are so ferocious as to preclude any authentic exposition of insurrectionary ideals. The IRA-like organization in *Odd Man Out* is treated with such aversion and contempt that any thorough going or even limited examination of its ideals is impossible. Led by the fanatical Johnny and the even more fanatical Dennis, the gang terrorizes all of Ulster, robbing, murdering, looting and gun-running – all in the name of some poorly defined 'cause'. To

Green, these mad-dog rebels are 'sour idealists' whose rebellion wreaks havoc rather than righting any wrongs.[15] They elicit little or no support from the populace, except when it is coerced at gunpoint, while the police, who never exceed their authority in any fashion, hunt the criminals down with unrelenting determination. Like the movie, the book follows the wounded fugitive Johnny through his last desperate hours, but unlike the film it carefully wrests from him a final, spiritually-charged admission that his rebellion has been futile and meaningless.

If the specific goals of the IRA are ignored, so are the larger issues of Anglo-Irish society. The political injustices that have ignited the unrest in Belfast are bypassed completely. Though the inferior status of Irish Catholics was as evident in 1945 as it is today, Green seems less troubled by this inequality than by attempts to correct it. Indeed, the words 'Catholic' and 'Protestant' hardly appear in the book. No attempt is made to distinguish the social and religious heritage of the revolutionaries, who are presumably Catholics, from Belfast's Anglican majority. Father Tom, a venerable old priest who tries to save Johnny's soul, seems totally unschooled in the rituals and orthodoxies of his own church. Rather feebly, Green tells us that he was 'beyond dogma and creed',[16] but this hardly explains his apparent failure to inform the heroine, Kathleen, that suicide is a cardinal sin and that it is mandated that he perform extreme unction over dying Catholics.

As a political novel, then, *Odd Man Out* is sorely deficient. In a broader sense, it is simply too relentless and undiscriminating in its hatreds to retain a reader's interest. Johnny and his associates are pilloried for their fanaticism, but when it suits Green's purposes the Belfast citizenry is reproached for its callous response to Johnny's plight. With everyone subject to such a jaundiced presentation, no single character can make much of a claim on our sympathies.

Transferring this story to the screen, Reed knew exactly where and when to be unfaithful. In Green's novel, the sum of the parts is exactly equal to the whole, and his unattractive rebels comprise the membership of a brutal and pointless political movement. While some critics have rebuked Reed for submerging the political dimensions of his story, this is a far cry from issuing a fierce indictment of the Irish Catholic cause and villainizing its members. As Reed has said many times, he is not in any sense a polemical – or even a political – director. The dramatic and philosophical aspects of his subject are what interest him. In the interview with Goodman, he pointed out that '*The Stars Look Down* . . . was a coalmining film which argued for the nationalization of the mines' but that he would 'make a picture tomorrow arguing the reverse of nationalization if the story were valid enough'.[17] In the cast of *Odd Man Out*, other than Johnny's incipient revulsion with violence, Reed neither endorses nor rejects the Irish cause. This aloofness is readily justified, since unlike Green, his sympathies are deeply engaged at the human level.

In the novel, the author's disgust with human behaviour is sweeping, and the only note of affirmation he strikes is religious. Contemplating his wasted and worthless life, Johnny realizes how universal his condition is: 'But he knew, too, that he had done only as the rest of mankind had done.'[18] A few seconds later, Johnny soars up to a pinnacle of religious exaltation and it is evident once again that for Green the City of God has a distinctly Protestant caste. In part, Reed's film is also imbued with a Protestant sensibility, but here Christianity is only one aspect of the overall *Weltanschauung*, which is perhaps more accurately described as a type of religious humanism; certainly it is non-doctrinal. Few English language films have ever been conceived with as much premeditation as *Odd Man Out*; frame by frame, it shows the intelligence and fullness of development of which Reed was capable.

This clarity of vision is manifested even before the plot gets underway. Reed opens with a bird's eye view of an unidentified coastal city which we presume to be Belfast and in which we glimpse ships, docks, industrial and residential life. Next the camera guides us down a bell tower to a squalid tenement district in which boisterous children are playing football. The effect is to narrow the movie's focus to Belfast, while suggesting the city's spectrum-like variety and the greater world beyond it at the same time. The introduction of children during this prologue, evidently casual, is actually not random at all; it is a matter of design, since they reappear throughout the story, serving a remarkable number of functions. The poverty we encounter in this initial shot is also informative, a partial explanation for the desperate cause to which Johnny and his companions have bound themselves.

Next we are introduced to Dennis (Robert Beatty), Johnny's

second-in-command, who is idling in a bookstall pretending to peruse a volume when the clock sounds and he departs suddenly. A shot of the clock itself establishes the time as 4 p.m. Time is soon to become a major component in the story, almost a character, and its harbinger-like use at this early juncture is deliberate. The published version of the script provides additional examples of Reed's gift for foreshadowing. Pat (Cyril Cusack), the most trigger-happy of the conspirators, is first introduced to us in a shooting gallery 'shooting at a row of moving ducks'.[19]

From the bookstall, we jump to Kathleen's house, where Dennis joins his comrades in time for the tail-end of the dress rehearsal of the robbery. Through the skilful economy of its dialogue and camerawork, the scene manages to convey a considerable amount of explanation without ever seeming self-consciously expository. We learn that Johnny has escaped from prison after being sentenced to a lengthy term for subversive activities, and has been in hiding with Kathleen (Kathleen Ryan) for months. We are also briefed on the nature and purpose of the robbery and the power structure within the organization. During the planning of the robbery, Reed positions Johnny near an open window; naturally attention is concentrated on him and on the grim sights of Belfast outside. We are thus reminded of the impetus for the robbery at the very moment it is about to be carried out. When Pat, Nolan (Roy Irving) and Murphy (Dan O'Herlihy) have departed, Dennis prepares to broach a difficult subject and the difficulty is underscored for us by the camera angle Reed has chosen. Unable to look Johnny in the eye, Dennis turns his back. The camera isolates him from the waist up, as he tries to dissuade Johnny from leading the raid on the mill, asserting that the months of confinement have left him unfit for a task of this kind. Johnny angrily rejects Dennis's argument, but we are made to feel a gravity in Dennis's words that is portentous. The second-in-command leaves and a subsequent scene between Johnny and Kathleen sketches their relationship briskly. We see that Kathleen is in love with Johnny, but that his own passions are occupied primarily by the 'cause'.

This ominous, downbeat prologue goes far beyond the normal movie exposition. Not only does it propel the story forward and introduce us to the characters, it creates the moral and symbolic framework of the narrative. Here again the gap between the film and its source is instructive. Astutely, De Felice points to the fact that the novel starts with the robbery itself, thus giving us no opportunity to comprehend the motivations of Johnny or anyone else in the revolutionary cadre. The film, on the other hand, carefully indicates that Johnny's thinking has shifted away from violent and illegal rebellion to peaceful, constitutional protest. Hence, as De Felice puts it, 'the opening scene establishes an ethical frame in which Johnny is presented as a moral, sensitive protagonist questioning the values of violent action'.[20] The initial scenes in *Odd Man Out* also construct the clever latticework of themes that underlie the film: the utilization of children as an ironic perspective on adult behaviour; the machinery of classical tragedy, with its unities and its predeterminism; the relentless grip of time; and the use of religious symbolism in the context of a post-industrial society.

Reed's use of children, one of his most heavily discussed attributes, was complex and frequent. Although it can be traced as far back as *The Young Mr Pitt* or even, arguably, to *Midshipman Easy*, no one could have guessed from these early works the extent to which children would figure in the director's work. It is only with *Odd Man Out* that they finally assume a prominent role. Tucked in around the periphery of the action, they serve a number of functions: silent observers of a mysterious and frightening adult world; unknowing mirrors of that world, embodying reflections of it that are sometimes romantic, callous and grotesque; occasional participants in the tangled dramas of their elders, blindly contributing to the flow of events.

The first children we see in *Odd Man Out* are the happy swarm of 'athletes' in the opening sequence that serves as our orientation to Belfast. Though it lasts only a few seconds, this snapshot accomplishes several different ends. The exuberance and joyous abandon of youth is effectively communicated, while at the same time the sooty grimness of their environment is announced by the slum neighbourhood around them. On another level, the fragile eden of childhood, with its harmless recreations, is immediately juxtaposed with the deadly games of the grown-ups, who carry weapons and play for keeps.

As the story proceeds, the principal action in *Odd Man Out* is watched by small spectators that Reed had unobtrusively inserted here and there. One of the most important of these is a diffident little girl who first appears seated before an open fire amidst a field of rubble near the site of the robbery. She is a mute witness of Johnny's flight into the air raid shelter. Further into the film, another little girl becomes a silent witness to Johnny's suffering. As he lies bleeding in the air raid shelter, a children's football game is in progress outside. When the ball bounces away from the players and into the shelter, a girl with a single skate pursues it. Shy and virtually mute, she follows the ball down into the shelter and finds Johnny. The wounded man is delirious, and in an hallucinatory vision sees the sunlight at the entrance of the shelter as prison bars and the little girl as a turnkey. De Felice finds fear and compassion in the little girl's response to Johnny, but it is hard to see more than stunned surprise.[21] What is more noteworthy about the scene is the adroit interplay of youth and adulthood and of illusion and actuality. The children's game continues unbated in the aftermath of Johnny's suffering, their ball constituting an unemphatic parallel to his gun. At the same time, dreams and reality intersect in the person of the imaginary jailor who, in a wonderful touch, grips a real ball firmly under his arm.

At intervals in the film, the camera captures other children peering into the lives of adults. In the bloody, strife-ridden society of Northern Ireland, even children are always in close proximity to violent death. Our first sight of Pat and Nolan after they have been gunned down by the police offscreen, is a speechless boy gazing at their corpses. Later, as Johnny sits catatonically in the snow, waiting for death, two boys stare out the window. In a beautiful stroke of irony, Reed positions Johnny so that he is invisible to the boys, whose rapt fascination with the white landscape contrasts tellingly with Johnny's sense of it as a shroud and a grave.

By their actions, the children in *Odd Man Out* also furnish an unconscious commentary on the bleak activities of the adults. As the policemen assemble at headquarters to coordinate their manhunt, a group of urchins refracts the drama around it through its own naive perspective, dramatizing everything elatedly. 'The mill is going to give a thousand quid to anyone who gets Johnny', says one boy. 'Dead or alive.' Another jeers at a policeman, waving a wooden gun at him, and yells. 'I'm

Johnny McQueen. All the police are looking for me.' But the glamorous shoot-out between Johnny and the police that the boys envision is worlds removed from the slow, passive death that their hero is simultaneously experiencing.

Later in his search for Johnny, Dennis encounters a pack of boys in the vicinity of the air raid shelter who are reenacting the hold-up, displaying significant fidelity to external detail but a mood of shrill, juvenile melodramatics. Their dialogue resounds through the air: 'I'm Johnny McQueen!' As is common among youngsters, they compete for the most histrionic or heroic parts. 'I am hit!' shrieks one boy. 'I am the fellah who was hit!' calls out a second youth. The two leading actors roll down some steps and grapple at the bottom. 'Go, on, Johnny', the onlookers shout. 'Hit him.' Then come the shootings and the getaway. It is all recreated with a self-confidence and ease that contrasts ironically with the actual hold-up we have just seen, in which the desperadoes were more desperate than anything else – frightened, fumbling, hasty and, in the case of Johnny, dazed and physically ill.

In this sequence, Reed also explores dimensions of boyhood that few British and American directors were courageous enough to deal with: the unintended cruelty that often constitutes the darker side of boyhood. In their own ignorant way, the boys mock Johnny's misery. Of course, it must be borne in mind that these are slum kids, and as such, hardened by their impoverished lives. The ragged clothes they wear emphasize their toughness as much as their poverty. When they boldly taunt the police, we are reminded somewhat of Buñuel's street-educated, brutalized urchins in *Los Olvidados*.

As Dennis approaches the boys for information about Johnny's whereabouts, the mood of *Los Olvidados* is upon us again. The boys first practise a kind of youthful sardonicism, answering Dennis's questions with random fictions: that the police are gone from the area around the mill, that Johnny has been found, etc. Then they are openly grasping when Dennis offers to buy the information he needs. Nowhere in the film is Reed's resistance to sentimentality as evident as in the carefully calculated shot of the horde of hardened little gamins hurling their outstretched palms up into Dennis's face and crying, 'Mister! Mister! Give's a

1. *The Stars Look Down* David Fenwick (Michael Redgrave), Jenny Sunley (Margaret Lockwood) and Joe Gowlan (Emlyn Williams) dine out in a restaurant in Tynecastle. Metro Goldwyn Mayer. Still by courtesy of Auerbach Film Enterprises Ltd

2. *The Young Mr Pitt* William Pitt (Robert Donat) and Eleanor Eden (Phyllis Calvert) share a romantic interlude. 20th Century-Fox. Still by courtesy of 20th Century-Fox

3. *The Odd Man Out* Rosie (Fay Compton) comforts wounded Irish Rebel Leader Johnny McQueen (James Mason). Universal Pictures Corporation. Still from the film 'Odd Man Out' by courtesy of The Rank Organisation plc and Janus Films

4. *The Fallen Idol* Felipe (Bobby Henrey), Julie (Michèle Morgan) and Baines (Ralph Richardson) share tea and a pastry in a small café. 20th Century-Fox. Still by courtesy of THORN EMI Screen Entertainment and Janus Films

5. *The Third Man* Holly Martins (Joseph Cotten) roams Vienna in search of an explanation for his friend Harry Lime's mysterious death. 20th Century-Fox. Still by courtesy of THORN EMI Screen Entertainment and Janus Films

6. *Our Man in Havana* James Wormold (Alec Guinness) and Captain Segura (Ernie Kovaks) engage in a bizarre and dangerous form of chess. Columbia Pictures Corporation. Still by courtesy of Columbia Pictures Corporation

7. *Oliver!* Mayfair in the age of Dickens, abloom with splendid song and dance. Columbia Pictures Corporation. Still by courtesy of Columbia Pictures Corporation

8. *The Last Warrior* (*Flap*, USA) Flapping Eagle (Anthony Quinn) cavorts with his girlfriend Dorothy Bluebell (Shelley Winters). Warner Bros Inc.

pahny, mister!' The camera angle deftly underscores their cupidity rather than their impoverishment, showing us a fully erect Dennis from below, with a forest of hands reaching up at the bottom of the frame. This strategy is repeated in a later scene, when Dennis seeks to wheedle information about Johnny from another pack of rambunctious boys in the neighbourhood of the mill. The youngsters recreate the robbery in cops and robbers fashion.

The children in such scenes are presented as a grotesque satire of human failings. The only exception is the girl with the skate, who is subtly distanced from the others, both spatially and morally. Dennis spots her on the other side of the street, and after dispensing with the boys in a quick shower of coins, he approaches her. Everything that transpires between the two is antithetical to the previous scene. Unlike the voluble, obstreperous boys, the girl is quiet, volunteers information only after considerable coaxing and accepts Dennis's money very hesitantly. Even the camerawork is antipodal to the other scene; Dennis stoops down on his haunches to converse with the girl, symbolically joining her on her own level. With the boys, he retained his towering superiority. Here it is not over-ingenious to see a protectiveness, a compassionate quality in the girl's attitude towards Johnny, whose secret she has guarded tenaciously. Here uniqueness is symbolized by her single skate, and we can agree with De Felice's conception of her as a counterpart to Johnny, an 'odd one out'.

With this episode we have moved from the second of the three functions Reed's children perform to the third. The girl is more than simply a distorted mirror of adulthood. She becomes an actor in that world herself and changes its course of events. Up to this point she has performed the purely passive act of guarding the secret of Johnny's hiding place, but now under Dennis's gentle prompting, she leads him to Johnny, thus causing a new and critical turn in the plot. Having brought along a bandage in order to disguise himself as Johnny, Dennis is able to decoy the police while Johnny slips away from the shelter. Here commences the main portion of Johnny's *via dolorosa*.

De Felice refers to the children in *Odd Man Out* as a variant of the Greek chorus and despite the non-Grecian frivolity of their commentary, one can easily see what he has in mind.[22] The

Athenian robes fit the children a little better when one realizes that Reed has deliberately set out to create a classical tragedy. For example, strict adherence to the unities is maintained throughout the movie. Hence, there is a single locale, Belfast, one overriding theme, the need for charity, and a timespan that is less than the maximum which Aristotle mandated. (Often incorrectly identified as twelve hours, the story's time span is actually eight hours.) After the first aerial perspective of Belfast, the perimeters of the city are quickly submerged in its cheerless squalour.

Time is a palpable presence throughout *Odd Man Out*, concretized in the huge, sombre face of a town clock, more than a little reminiscent of Big Ben. Our earliest sight of it comes in the visual prologue to the story. From its towering height, it looms over the bleak, unhappy scene below with the brooding detachment of an Old Testament deity. Periodically, Reed returns to it to remind us that Johnny's progress, even when it brings him to a refuge, is essentially a death march. His agony begins at four in the afternoon, the hour that appears on the clock when we see it for the first time and ends at midnight. We glimpse it again several times, generally in the background, punctuating the sequences as the story evolves. Its chiming recurs ever more often, unobtrusively recording the characters' emotions and the movements of the story. More dramatically, it fills the screen at the end of the film, announcing the hour of Johnny's death, midnight. The clock has a 'voice' too; its stern peals embroider the action throughout the film. When they sound during the planning of the robbery, they only signify that it is tea time, but later, during the hold-up itself, they underscore the crucial role that time has suddenly assumed. At the bloody climax of the scene at Teresa's, the chimes become the death knell of Pat and Nolan, betrayed to the police by their hostess. Elsewhere, the clock sounds eight, while in a juxtaposed sequence, also accompanied by the eight o'clock chimes, Kathleen makes desperate arrangements with a seaman for Johnny's escape. Further along, the relentless tolling of the clock punctuates Shell's search for Johnny in the junkyard and Johnny's arrival at the artist's studio, where it adds special force to the urgency of the moment, since we know that Johnny has only an hour or so to reach the ship.

Reed's goal in all this is, naturally, to achieve a sense of inevitability and hence satisfy another of the requirements of classical tragedy. In much of the action of *Odd Man Out*, fate edges the episodes in black, darkening them with presentiments of ill-fortune. With the movie barely under way, we are made to see that the best laid plans of Johnny and his cohorts are likely to go awry. The trigger-happy Pat responds to Johnny's ban on any violence by declaring cockily, 'Anyone who asks for it can have it.' Afterwards, during the short altercation between Dennis and Johnny, Johnny vehemently insists on his abilities to fulfil his duties, despite his long incarceration, first in prison, then at Kathleen's house. But when he breaks his shoelace a few moments later, it is hard not to see it – outwardly insignificant though it may be – as another bad omen.

Presentiments of disaster continue to accumulate as the revolutionaries proceed to the robbery by car and embark upon their desperate venture. It is here that dialogue is at a minimum and the language of cinematography takes over. With the assistance of Krasker's superb camerawork, Reed is able to convey all the heart-stopping tension and brooding fatefulness of the robbery. Judicious editing and shrewd camera angles tell us everything about the aborted hold-up and Johnny's contribution to its failure. In the car, Reed hurls a quick, rather dizzying succession of images at us, tilting the camera as he does so and interspersing a shot of Johnny passing his hand over his eyes. The effect is to propel us immediately inside Johnny's mind, where we experience the same disorientation he does. Nor does all this end when the car pulls up at the mill. A stage direction in the script calls for the chimney of the mill to be 'shot in such a way to give the impression it is leaning forward over Johnny'.[23] Krasker complied fully, first establishing the perspective as Johnny's and then providing an almost perfectly vertical angle on the chimney. The effect is highly expressionistic, like many of the other touches in *Odd Man Out*; in fact, it is quite reminiscent of the famous shot in Murnau's *The Last Laugh* in which the guilt-ridden Emil Jannings imagines a hotel leaning over him menacingly.

The robbery itself, narrated through an astonishing repertoire of cinematic devices, has received as much critical scrutiny as any sequence in the Reed canon. That De Felice's long monograph should devote a disproportionately large amount of space to the hold-up is hardly surprising. But much attention has also been lavished on this section of *Odd Man Out* by Karel Reisz, the director and former film critic, in *The Technique of Film Editing*. In an ordinary 'heist' or 'caper' film, the only purpose of the nerve-ravaging strategies Reed employs would be to intensify the suspense, as Hitchcock does in film after film and as Reed himself did in *Night Train*. However, the generally fatalistic atmosphere of *Odd Man Out*, established within the first five minutes, casts its shadow over the robbery too. In this way, small sources of tension become gloomy forebodings of disaster.

As noted earlier, Reed was not content to rely exclusively on a conventional movie score, with its facile glossary of terms for the visual narrative; instead, he interspersed natural sounds as a kind of obligatto to Alwyn's music. Sounds at a Belfast mill were recorded for the soundtrack, and the authentic moaning and creaking of the machinery are skilfully interwoven. It creates an aural background for the interior shots, in which we follow Johnny's gang through the different stages of the robbery. As Reisz points out, the monotonous throb of the machinery becomes a measure of the excruciating wait that the robbers must endure while money is stuffed into briefcases. The sound track grows even more subjective when it is deliberately modulated; the noise of the machinery is amplified to simulate the increasing dominance it has over the minds of the revolutionaries. In the same way, the footsteps of Johnny and his confederates – recorded from the sound of men walking on wooden boards – are artificially augmented as they enter and leave the mill. On their way out, the boodle in hand, their 'hurried footsteps are heard over the pulsating beat of the mill...'[24]

As the robbery proceeds at its agonizingly slow pace, Reed interrupts to remind us of the getaway car outside, with its worried driver. Various sounds prey on Pat's mind too – the footsteps of passers-by, the clop of a horse-drawn cart, the motor of his own car (which he has kept running). The ascending pitch and volume of these sounds reaches its shrill apex when at last someone hits the alarm button and the piercing rings follow the frantic robbers to their car.

The remainder of this universally admired segment of the film is a triumph of acting, writing and camerawork. The struggle between Johnny and the clerk is edited so elliptically that its two primary results – the wounding of Johnny and the death of the guard – both happen offscreen, while the camera studies the paralyzed reactions of Johnny's three accomplices. We are then plunged into the flux and turbulence of actual experience, with nothing that has a predigested, rationally ordered look. The blurred effect that these events leave in the mind of the audience is strictly by design. Like Joseph Conrad, whose work Reed was to adapt a few years later, Reed seeks to plunge us completely into the actual experience, without the reassuring benefit of preconception.

Fate has been at work throughout the robbery and now it tightens its grip. The brilliantly edited getaway attempt has Johnny clinging to the running board, as his fearful companions attempt to pull him inside and simultaneously hurtle away from the scene at top speed. The vividness achieved during these critical seconds, like many other moments in *Odd Man Out*, is so successful that one feels Johnny's peril and pain as one's own. At last the car jumps up on the curb briefly and when it returns jarringly to the street, the door strikes Johnny and knocks him off the car onto the road. We get a close-up of Johnny making a 'vain attempt to grasp the hood of the car' and falling backwards. Then with the 'camera shooting from moving car', it 'pans with Johnny as he falls out'.[25] To underscore the anguish of this calamity, a powerful musical chord is sounded, the first music we have heard in the robbery sequence.

As most commentators have observed, the pace of the film diminishes markedly once the hunt for Johnny begins. The adumbrations of tragedy continue to accumulate, however: a white dog pursues the fleeing Johnny, foreshadowing the all-out, city-wide manhunt that is to come; Johnny is 'buried' in a local junkyard by Gin Jimmy (Joseph Tomelty); Granny (Kitty Kirwan) tells a mournful tale of a rebel gunman like Johnny who left on an assignment and never came back; Schubert's 'Unfinished Symphony' quietly accompanies the conversation of Nolan and Pat.

Chance, an inverted form of the cruel predeterminism in *Odd Man Out*, also plays a part in determining events, as in Hardy's novels. It thwarts all of the bravery and resourcefulness of Johnny's second-in-command, Dennis, and the compassion of Rosie (Fay Compton), the 'nurse' who attends to Johnny's wounds. In each case, the bandages prove to be the character's undoing. After a virtuoso display of athletic ability, Dennis is captured when the police find his discarded bandage and trail him to the streetcar. Similarly, Johnny sheds his bandages outside the Four Winds bar and unwittingly provides Shell with the clue to the fugitive's hiding place. A few minutes before this, the selfishness of a young woman in a phone booth has prevented Johnny from making a call that might have allowed him to summon help.

The mood of pessimism in *Odd Man Out* is all-pervasive and in this respect is comparable to Hemingway's work. But where Hemingway's heroes are allowed to attain a certain grandeur before they are destroyed, Johnny is immobilized early in the film, and except for occasional, enfeebled gestures is unable to act. The great-souled, heroic qualities that have traditionally been ascribed to tragic figures remain, at best, an inchoate aspect of Johnny, sketched in roughly during the planning of the robbery and implied by the nobility that Johnny takes on during his ordeal. Furthermore, the crucial flaw that we have come to expect from a tragic hero doesn't assume significant proportions in *Odd Man Out*. The question of Johnny's role in his own downfall is pertinent here. There is a clear element of hubris in Johnny's refusal to let Dennis lead the strike raid on the mill. Unwilling to surrender his primacy as the leader of the organization, even temporarily, he endangers his own life and, by extension, that of his comrades. On the other hand, once he has put himself in harm's way, the brutal machinery of determinism takes over and his suffering seems only dimly related to a 'tragic flaw'. In truth, he is pinioned by fate and, as Sarris and others have observed, his capacity for moral choice is greatly diminished. When Kathleen engineers Johnny's death to save him from capture she 'destroys the last vestige' of this choice.[26] To some degree, one is inclined to view *Odd Man Out* as a tragedy without a tragic hero.

Allied with inexorable time is the deepening gloom of the weather, which, with unmistakable symbolism, slowly metamorphoses from sunlight to rain to snow. The rebels' initial optimism about their 'job' is as sunny as the sky outside the window. After the bungled robbery, however, the thermometer plummets, calibrating not only the deterioration of the weather but the worsening condition of the gang and their wounded leader. The mood of the city becomes black and icy, a dark night of the soul for Johnny. Reed's success with this aspect of *Odd*

Man Out, the atmosphere of the city at night, has attracted a
good deal of critical attention and inspired comparisons with the
American *film noir* school. The slick black streets, the gutters and
pavements, the horse-drawn cabs and scudding cars, the refuse
and litter, the automobile horns and chatter of pedestrians, the
pubs and stores – all these details are caught by Krasker's
camera and become part of the nocturnal frescoes that decorate
the already powerful story. Reassessing the movie for *The Nation*
four months after his notice in *Time*, Agee offers this remarkable
verdict: 'If the world should end tomorrow . . . this film would
furnish one of the more appropriate epitaphs: a sad, magnificent
summing up of a night city. Movies have always been particularly good at appreciating cities at night: but of a night city this
is the best image I have seen.'[27]

As we noted earlier, the characters and events in *Odd Man Out*
move through a Christian framework, and the film has been
studied as a religious work – most extensively by John Hadsell[28]
Religious artefacts are a vital part of the movie's decor; statues of
the saints can be seen in the background of Kathleen's house, for
example, and in the junkyard sequence the semi-conscious
Johnny lies next to a discarded angel. That these were intended
as more than naturalistic decor becomes indisputable in the
allegorical segments which are prominent in the latter portion of
the film. Father Tom is meant as an archetypal clergyman, a
spokesman for the realm of the spirit. His assessment of Johnny
is strictly doctrinal, moral in the narrowest religious sense.
Johnny has committed murder and, whatever the circumstances,
he must face God's judgement. As a consequence, it is only the
rebel leader's soul that matters to Father Tom. He tries to
dissuade Shell from selling Johnny for money, offering him 'faith'
instead. Here the movie becomes so abstract it is didactic and
implausible at the same time. It converts a raffish, seedy bird-
dealer into a truth-seeker, ingenuously questioning Father Tom,
and later Tober (Brook Jones), the medical school drop-out with
whom he and Lukey share a house, about the accessibility of the
higher form of reward that the priest advocates.

In the age-old conflict between church and state, the law and
the commandments, the Head Constable (Dennis O'Dea)
speaks for Caesar. In his inflexibly rule-oriented bureaucratic
world, Johnny must be rendered up to him. The policeman

demands Johnny's body for punishment as Father Tom demands his soul for penance. Their clash of values is encapsulated
in a series of sharp exchanges.

On another plane, it is easy enough to see the whole film as an
elaborate religious allegory. Johnny's suffering, endured first on
behalf of the cause he serves, and then of humanity in general,
makes him a clear candidate for Christ-figure status. His excruciating odyssey becomes the stations of the cross, culminating in
the crucifixion-like posture he assumes at the end of the journey,
leaning against the railing with arms outstretched.

The film veers closest to outright allegory whenever Shell is on
screen. The feisty bird-seller has an obviously emblematic name,
supplied by Green. In McCormick's magnificent portrayal,
Shell's steps are more like hops, and his quick, darting eye
movements and bodily agility seem like appropriate characteristics of a fragile creature who must somehow survive in a world of
larger beings like Tober and Lukey, the flamboyant artist. They
too are symbols, the former signifying the scientific mind and the
latter art.

Shell's theological lessons resume when he explores the subject of religious belief with Tober. 'What is faith?', he inquires.
'It's life', Tober replies, rather unhelpfully, and when Shell
repeats the question, Tober says, 'Only one man had it.' Here
the balance between the real and the symbolic becomes most
precarious. Since, on the whole, Shell is depicted as a crafty
street hustler, with a sharp eye for profit, his round-eyed curiosity over the value of faith has the effect of transforming him from
a person to a figure in a waxen tableaux, a morality play in
which Everyman's search for the mysterious commodity 'faith'
eventually carries him beyond corruption and vice. Consequently, Shell's initially mercenary motives give way to selfless
concern for Johnny's welfare. In the beginning the wounded
man's pride tag is all that interests Shell; in the end, faith is the
reward that he seeks. The vaporous abstractions that Shell
pursues in these scenes – Love, Faith, Life – lift *Odd Man Out* off
its true foundations, which are gritty realism.

Matters are further complicated by the expressionistic sets
Reed has used for these sequences. The old Victorian house in
which Tober, Shell and Lukey live is a study in decayed
nineteenth-century grandeur, with soaring ceilings, a long staircase, ornate decor and sombre lighting; it is a brooding presence

one might expect in a film by Lang or Murnau from the 1920s. This baroque quality reaches a peak in a scene that puts the philosophical Tober in a pensive pose near the stove, while Shell's head emerges behind him through a gap in the door.

At the same time, the film takes its master theme, charity, from the New Testament. As most critics have agreed, *Odd Man Out* deals less with Johnny McQueen than with people's reaction to him. He is an agonized mirror in which people see their own souls flash back at them; they are defined by the cruelty or kindness with which they respond to Johnny's plight. In a sense, it is these responses that give the film its momentum, as Johnny stumbles helplessly from refuge to refuge, and Reed works hard to avoid any sense of monotony, an accomplishment that is crucial to the film's success. With the aid of an exceptionally strong screenplay, Reed is able to create a wide array of permutations in the treatment that Johnny receives from the other characters. His protectors include the mute and mysterious skate girl, a kind of mystical companion of Johnny's but without much practical assistance to offer. Radically different – and yet completely similar – are Rosie and Maudie (Beryl Measor), with their gabby, utterly pragmatic approach. A couple of middle-aged Englishwomen, they epitomize the British temperament at its best, fussy perhaps but indefatigably courteous and decent. (They alone would be enough to convince us that the point of view in *Odd Man Out* is fundamentally English, not Irish.)

At the other end of the spectrum are those who can find no compassion in themselves for Johnny, who have no charity. Alfie (Arthur Hambling), Rosie's husband, is pompously moralistic about Johnny's crime but his hypocrisy is exposed when his wife remarks that 'maybe you will get the big reward'. Jimmy and Fencie (William Hartnell), on the other hand, are callously neutral, each looking out exclusively for 'number one'. Inadvertently, both provide refuges for Johnny but neither is motivated by moral considerations; their announced goal is to avoid *any* involvement in Johnny's fate. Tober's posture toward Johnny is only superficially more humane; he merely thinks of dressing Johnny's wounds in the name of his former calling, though he knows his patient will go to the gallows. Lukey is indifferent to Johnny's suffering and sees him merely as a means of overcoming artistic mediocrity and capturing a genuinely intense vision on canvas.

In a loose sense, virtually all of the characters in *Odd Man Out* can be divided into two groups: those who are searching for Johnny and can't find him and those who don't want to find him but do. Of the key figures in the man-hunt, each has his own distinct motivation. In Voigt's words, Johnny is 'helped or hindered . . . for all sorts of reasons, selfish and unselfish'.[29]

As Johnny careens from shelter to shelter and person to person, his strength continually ebbing, Reed's indictment of human indifference grows with quiet force. His Irish microcosm becomes a world without charity, and it is Johnny's vision of this world that accounts for two of the film's most powerful sequences. Secreted in a crib at Fencie's bar, Johnny, now delirious, stares down at the beer bubbles on the table. Each becomes a hallucinatory cameo of one of his would-be saviours – Father Tom, the Head Constable, etc. – all squabbling furiously over him. He raises his head and opens his mouth to cry out, but before a sound issues from him, Reed cuts instantly to the bar room outside the crib. When Johnny's scream – a massive *cri de coeur* – bursts forth a second later, its effect is immeasurably enhanced by the paralyzed silence it induces in the noisy, crowded bar. That the effect on the patrons lasts only for a second is a moral commentary in itself.

Immediately afterwards, Johnny is 'rescued' by Lukey, who spirits him off to his studio so the dying man can be immortalized on a canvas. In the atelier, Reed gives us the fullest statement of the charity motif. As Lukey and Tober squabble over the final disposition of Johnny McQueen – does he belong to art or science? – the wounded man is seized by another delirium. Again the scene is rendered subjectively. In Johnny's frenzied gaze, Lukey's pictures seem to arrange themselves in rows. The assortment of weird, exaggerated faces become both pews and the parishioners assembled in them. A ghostly Father Tom appears to preside over the congregation, and Johnny appeals to him for the spiritual guidance he provided years before: 'Tell me, Father, the way you used to tell us – ', he says. But Father Tom remains mute, and it is Johnny who proclaims the resounding truth that Reed has been building towards: 'Though I speak with the tongues of men and of angels and have not Charity, I am become as sounding brass or a tinkling cymbal.'

Mason's declamation of the lines captures all the magisterial eloquence of the famous lines from Corinthians. Photographed from a low angle, the actor is given the lofty stature of a Biblical prophet, an Isaiah or Daniel pronouncing judgement not only on the crass individuals around him but on the entire grasping world of mankind, through whose midst he has just passed. The majesty of Mason's declaration stuns the trio of men in the room, but the awed silence here cannot last any longer than the one at Fencie's. The turbulence of human activity must resume, unredeemed by even the faintest comprehension of its headlong corruption. 'He's delirious', says Lukey.

The film's obedience to Aristotelian principles of dramaturgy – discussed above – is enhanced by its sense of restraint; with the exception of the Lukey scenes and some of the allegorizing elsewhere, Reed maintains a tight grip on his materials, avoiding dramatic excesses and transmitting the emotional life of the story through his subdued, ironic temperament. The fact that so much of Johnny's suffering is wordless, a dumb show completely free of histrionics, is in itself indicative of Reed's intentions. This is as true of the movie's small moments as of its grand ones. The foreshadowing implicit in Nolan's remark about the steps at Teresa ('Just like the mill') is just that – implicit, a tacit articulation of an idea that would get a megaphone-like treatment in the films of many other directors.

Violence is also kept at a minimum and dealt with glancingly. Reed's aversion to bloodshed, perhaps an extension of his naturally reticent personality, was noticeable as early as *Night Train*, but here for the first time it becomes a distinctive personal mannerism. In a story that might have liberated the sanguinary impulses of other film-makers, Reed concentrates on people's response to brutality and on its thematic relevance rather than on the gore itself. What a relief, in an era where blood is spilled so readily by respectable directors like Martin Scorsese, Brian DePalma and Francis Coppola.

Restraint is unquestionably a principal asset of *Odd Man Out*, although on another level, much of the spirit behind the film seems comparatively romantic. Sarris calls attention to the film's passionate devotion to the 'fanatical romanticism' of Kathleen, a heroine for whom love and idealism cannot be compromised, even if death is the only alternative.[30] Johnny's immobilizing pain, though it suggests a twentieth-century anti-hero, also has its affinities with an older romantic heritage in which poets glorified their suffering and made it an insignia of greatness. Thus, Byron's Childe Harolde dragged his bleeding heart across Europe, and Shelley's persona in 'Ode to the West Wind' fell eloquently upon the thorns of life. Similarly, Johnny's agony is heroic; it ennobles him, conferring a stature that none of the other characters, including Father Tom, ever attains. Reed's camera angles often remind us of Johnny's stature by making Mason, a relatively short man, seem taller than most of the other actors. In approved romantic fashion, Mason's individuality – his anguished separateness – is looked on more favourably than the fearful conformity of Irish society.

Reed's romanticism shows its most extreme aspects in the Lukey/Tober/Shell sequences, where heightened individualism becomes deliberate exaggeration. Tober, the gifted failure, is a descendant of Sidney Carton and other gifted failures. Like them, his bitterness and disillusionment frequently take the form of gloomy philosophizing about mankind. Shell's simple, literal observation that Johnny is dying is elevated by Tober into a general diagnosis of the human condition: 'We're all dyin'.' Reed has been reproved by various critics for his blunt, unapologetic attempt at universalizing his themes, but it can just as easily be argued that the compulsive attitudinizing of Tober and Lukey are entirely in character. Moreover, in context their sententiousness has a surprising resonance, a soaring quality that recalls the resonant language of Conrad.

Lukey is even more unquestionably drawn from romantic models than Tober. Amplified by Newton, whose acting – contrary to what has been written about it – is no more or less feverish than is suitable for Lukey. In a departure from the general pattern, Reed's view of Lukey is harsher than Green's. In his literary manifestation, Lukey is a crude genius, too far ahead of his time to be appreciated. His portrait of Johnny is too triumphant for its own good; it enrages Johnny so much that he destroys it. The uses of adversity prove to be sweet, however, in that the heartbroken artist emerges from the experience with a sharpened sense of his artistic destiny. In the film, Lukey's roughness receives more emphasis than his artistry. He is as obscure and impoverished as the character in the book, but the paintings we see – Halloween masks – don't seem intended to convince us of Lukey's talent. Nor do any of his companions, with the exception of Shell, treat him with much respect. On the other hand, we are evidently meant to regard his portrait of Johnny, though unfinished, as ablaze with brilliance, an inspired work. Significantly, Shell's enquiry about what Lukey sees in Johnny's eyes elicits a reply that is almost delivered in a trance, so intensely felt is it: 'The truth about us all.'

Of course, what we have labelled romanticism in *Odd Man Out* might just as easily be categorized as theatricality, a trait Reed had indulged with enjoyable results in other films. After Johnny's long, grey, agonized journey through the streets of Belfast, the dramatic colouring that Reed throws over the Lukey scenes is an invigorating change. The basic material is taken fairly directly from Green, but Reed gives it a wholly different spirit. In place of Green's downbeat, lugubrious episodes, the director enlivens the sequences with zest and energy and even humour (of the graveyard variety). What seems stolid on the printed page becomes spirited on the screen. Viewed in this context, the alleged excesses of the Lukey segment of the story – the fantastic setting, the cosmic declarations, the rather extravagant character of Lukey himself, the knockabout byplay between Lukey and Shell, Lukey's megalomania and dark-eyed visions, and other forms of self-dramatization – have a greater artistic validity than has been previously conceded.

Reed's indebtedness to orthodox Christian doctrine notwithstanding, his world view is, finally, not Christian. Outside the briefly reassuring aura of biblical injunctions and cadences, of ecclesiastical symbols and Christ-like gesture, lies the cold, unfeeling embrace of what Hemingway called 'eternity or the lack of it'. There is no true sense of divine order behind *Odd Man Out* and certainly no sense of obtainable grace. Instead, as in the existential universe of Hemingway, Faulkner and numberless other modern writers, men blunder through their existences as victims of circumstance; rewards and punishments are visited randomly on mankind, without evident justification. Murphy, who is as guilty as Pat and Nolan, is not punished. Through a fluke, the courageous Dennis is apprehended by the police, while the treacherous Teresa is left to enjoy the benefits of her betrayal. Johnny, the noblest of the gang and an incipient pacifist, violates the most sacred of religious commandments, but by accident. His subjective 'passion' is never presented as punitive; it is as much a product of fate as the murder he didn't mean to commit. His death does not occur amidst incense, organ music and celestial choirs, the parting of the heavens or any intimations of these things. Life *is* a vale of tears, Reed tells us, but there is no afterlife to redeem it.

The pessimism of *Odd Man Out* has a continental mood that is more commonly encountered in France than England, not a country known for saturnine cinema, especially not in the 1940s. Reed's fascination with other cultures and his desire to achieve a truly international quality became a lynchpin of his work, though here it is expressed far less overtly than in the polyglot casts he was to assemble in later movies. What does emanate from *Odd Man Out* is the influence of Marcel Carné – not the Carné of the incomparable *Les Enfants du Paradis* but the humbler *Quai des Brumes* and *Le Jour se lève*, those overrated excursions into doomed heroism and aborted love. Reed may have signalled his affection for these works when he named Jean Gabin, the star of both, as his favourite actor. Certainly Mason has Gabin-like attributes in *Odd Man Out*, in which he plays a common man's hero, operating outside the law, earning the love of a woman who tries but fails to help him escape from a city where he is a marked man. Reed's rendering of this narrative pattern is far more effective than Carné's, however, by virtue of its greater humanity, warmth, naturalistic detail and technical adventurousness.

Still, Reed is no less unrelentingly bleak about the human condition than Carné. The only redemption available in *Odd Man Out* is fleeting and fragile: the power of love, of loyalty, of compassion. A quiet humanism illumines Reed's film, brightening the darkest sequences, but when the lights go out, it is not God's countenance we see, but a solemn, black-faced clock, impersonal and indifferent. It is the last image we see in this masterpiece.

7 At the Summit: Two with Graham Greene

One would think that the great critical and commercial success of *Odd Man Out* would have made it inevitable that Rank sponsor another project of Reed's. Instead, the two parted professional company forever, and Reed's next five films were made for Alexander Korda's London Films. Even at this juncture in his career, Reed was becoming oriented towards American-scaled budgets, and the Rank organization was simply not geared towards such prodigious expenditures, even for a major director. Reed's next film, *The Fallen Idol*, was a joint British–American production financed by Korda and David Selznick. Based on Graham Greene's short story 'The Basement Room', it had a script by the author himself and a cast that included Ralph Richardson, fresh from his triumph in *The Heiress*, and Michèle Morgan, the popular French beauty. The pivotal role in the story, a seven-year-old boy, was taken by Bobby Henrey, a youth of French–English parentage who had never acted before.

The film was released in Europe in 1948 and created a sensation. The awards it won included the British Film of the Year Award and first prize at the Venice Film Festival. Exported to the US a year later, it inspired elation among the reviewers. 'Most of the uproar . . . was solidly justified', *Time* decided, calling it an 'absorbing drama'.[1] This view was even more heartily articulated by Crowther at the *New York Times*, who found it 'one of the keenest revelations of a child we have ever had on the screen'.[2] *Variety* praised it as a 'fine sensitive story'[3] and John McCarten at the *New Yorker* described it as 'witty and engrossing', with a 'beguiling performance' by its young star, Bobby Henrey.[4] The enthusiasm of the American critics was sufficient to bring Reed his first important American prize – the New York Film Critics award.

According to Greene, 'The Basement Room' was written 'on a

cargo steamer on the way home from Liberia to relieve the tedium of the voyage'. It is a far more melancholy work than the film that was made from it, though the skeleton of the plot is approximately the same, at least up to the point of Mrs Baines's death. Her fatal fall is not an accidental slip as in the film, however, but the consequence of a struggle with her husband, whom she has surprised with his mistress. He is guilty and when the police come, he makes 'dumb, pathetic' appeals to the boy, Phil, to protect him. But Phil has become so horrified by the machinating adult world around him that he remains unresponsive to his old idol and even betrays him to the police. Beneath the melodramatic surface, Greene interpolates a Freudian case history, using the traumatic incidents that are visited on Phil as the explanation for his complete withdrawal into 'deep dilettante selfishness' in later life. At another point, Greene emphasizes the boy's psychic fate: 'Life fell on him with savagery: you couldn't blame him if he never faced it again in sixty years.'

If we are surprised at the thought of a movie adapted from a story as bleak as 'The Basement Room', so was Greene: 'it seemed to me that the subject was unfilmable – a murder committed by the most sympathetic character and an unhappy ending which would certainly have imperilled the £250 000 that films nowadays cost'.[5] But as it developed, Reed had a sunnier, more commercial version of Greene's story in mind. The Baines of *The Fallen Idol* is innocent of any crime and although Phil's ingenuous, unintentionally incriminating remarks to the police keep the butler teetering on the brink of tragedy, he never tumbles in and is finally exonerated. Gone too is the seaminess with which Greene coated 'The Basement Room' and the flash-forwards into the psyche of the elderly Phil. The setting is shifted from a mansion in Belgravia Square to an unspecified foreign embassy. Reed also seized the opportunity to indulge his love of menageries and household pets by inserting a sequence at the zoo and by giving the young hero a pet snake.

As revised under Reed's supervision, Greene's narrative retains most of its wit, intelligence and moral commentary but bears even more of a similarity to a murder mystery than the original, particularly the smooth brand of 'drawing room' crime drama in which the English have specialized for half a century. A romantic triangle, the most immemorial of foundations for such a story, provides most of the key motivations in *Idol*. It leads to a sudden, violent death – apparently murder – and soon we have a nervous suspect and a coolly rational inspector from Scotland Yard. It is his series of probing, unsettling questions that generates much of the sweaty-palmed suspense in the final segment of the film. Within this terribly conventional framework, Reed is wickedly unconventional. His sense of irony plays lightly over the surface of a well-worn genre, giving it unexpected new contours, reshaping it ingeniously. Our great fear isn't that the inspector may fail to find the right man but that he may succeed in finding the wrong one. He is, after all, investigating a murder that never took place. The piercing, criminological flashlight he beams into the events leads in the wrong direction altogether.

The ratio of humour and thrills is another feature we have come to associate with the British thriller. In *Idol*, the ratio is exquisitely preserved throughout. The death of Mrs Baines (Sonia Dresdel), which sends terror-stricken Phil out into the night in his pyjamas, is followed by a whimsical episode at the police station. Rose (Dora Bryan), the breezy gregarious prostitute, uses the language of her trade in attempting to elicit information from the virtually mute boy. Later in the film, just as the inspector's interrogation of the principals seems to be mounting towards an explosion, he is suddenly interrupted by a fussy little clock-setter (Hay Petrie) who bursts officiously in and insists on attending to the embassy's antique grandfather clock. (Greene attributes this inspiration to Reed.)[6]

Reed's film is also related to its genre by the emphasis on the importance of clues and incriminating evidence, of objects in general; a potted palm, a telegram twisted into a glider, a pair of black shoes and other 'props' relate *Idol* to the melodramatic roots of the detective story. Like all melodrama, a measure of contrivance is inevitable, a deliberate manipulation of the incidents into an aesthetically supercharged form so as to produce an exciting, though fairly artificial situation.

If this were all *Idol* had to offer, it would fit nicely on the shelf beside *Night Train*. Unlike the earlier film, however, this is a thriller with an uncommonly high IQ. From the beginning, Reed and Greene place Phil at the centre of the story and the boy's psychology is a powerful determinant in the lurid events in which he becomes involved. His love for Baines is, after all, one of the mainsprings of the plot. It is pursuit of the butler that thrusts him into the midst of Baines's rendezvous with Julie (Morgan); this in turn leads to Mrs Baines's shocked realization that her husband is unfaithful to her and sets in motion the Medea-like revenge plot which ends in her own death. Subsequently, it is Phil's frantic effort to cover up for his beloved Baines that buries the servant in suspicion.

It is easy enough to see Baines as a surrogate father, but also easy to miss the scrupulous devotion to plausibility whereby this relationship is constructed. Much of it is sketched for us in the opening scene or two when we meet Phil's father (Gerald Hinze), the ambassador of a French-speaking country (it is explained that 'Phil' is actually short for 'Felipe'). He is departing for Paris to escort his wife, who has recovered from a serious illness, back home. Relations between the boy and his distinguished father are cold and perfunctory. The ambassador leaves in a flurry of last-minute instructions to his subordinate, paying very little attention to his son, who bids his father farewell from the embassy's sweeping staircase. The emotional distance between father and son is further emphasized when Phil watches from a remote window as the ambassador gets into a waiting limousine. Moreover, we learn shortly afterwards that Phil's mother has been away so long he hardly remembers her. The embassy itself helps reinforce the orphan-like status Phil must endure; despite (or because) of its grandiose and opulent contours, it cannot fulfil Phil's emotional needs. It is a palace rather than a home – intensely formal, glazed, rococo. At many points in the film, we observe the neglected Phil making his desultory way from room to room, or lingering indifferently in his favourite spot, the top of the majestic staircase. An only child surrounded exclusively by busy grown-ups, he has no peer group for diversion and reinforcement.

In this chilly atmosphere, Baines is the one source of consolation and attention for Phil. With more time for the boy than the ambassador and more insight into the boy's needs, he can take him to the zoo or regale him with fantastic tales of extravagant adventure – set in faraway locales. The glamorous past that Baines manufactures for himself in his stories is especially well tailored to Phil's needs, however unconsciously so. Not only do the extraordinary sagas provide near-hypnotic diversion for the boy, they afford him an outlet for the hero-worship that is so characteristic of youth. Juxtaposing the real father with the surrogate, Reed captures the contrast succinctly: finishing his tepid goodby to his natural father, Phil immediately greets the lovable butler with radiant features and a jubilant cry of 'Baines!' Surely it is Reed's voice we are hearing too, the remembered longing of a neglected, never-acknowledged son, and the affective identification is probably what accounts for the piercing authenticity of Phil's elation.

At the other end of the boy's emotional spectrum is Mrs Baines. If Baines has the status of a storybook champion, it is Phil's frantic effort to cover up for his beloved Baines that incriminates the helpless servant. Mrs Baines is cast – with equal vividness – as a witch. Dressed largely in black, she torments Phil with her harsh, puritanical outlook. Serving *in loco parentis* after the ambassador leaves, she is able to give fullest expression to her tyrannical impulses. Behaviour which, under normal circumstances, would be unpleasant and irritating, now becomes pathological, sadistic.

Reed and Greene cast such a malevolent hue over Mrs Baines's temperament – setting it off starkly against the sunny, joyful relationship between Baines and Phil – that the film's moral scheme is frequently in danger of simple-minded polarization. The black and white values that threaten to overtake the movie never quite succeed, however. For one thing, Sonia Dresdel's fervent and technically accomplished acting brings the pulse of life to the wife's villainous hysteria and vengefulness. For another, the symbolism with which Reed has decorated his themes is refreshingly unorthodox and intricate, yet seamlessly integrated into the narrative. Values that would ordinarily be positive are turned inside out, made to trade places with ostensibly negative qualities. For example, Mrs Baines's cleanliness is made to symbolize the basic sterility of her soul. Near the beginning of the film, two gossipy, magpie-like scrubwomen complain that nothing is ever clean enough for Mrs Baines. At other points, she is seen rebuking Baines and Phil for disorder or lack of tidiness. A paradigm of coldness and repression, Mrs Baines is driven to sterilize the world around her so as to bring it into conformity with her own personality.

Baines and Phil, on the other hand, are capable of love and joy and the psychic dislocations this emotion can bring; its fundamental irrationality is reflected by the occasional wayward conduct in their daily lives. Phil cannot clean his room to Mrs

Baines's satisfaction and, from her point of view, risks becoming additionally soiled by spending so much time in the kitchen (the 'basement room' of the story) with Baines. He also violates her strict ban on leaving the house and goes out in search of Baines. With deftly managed parallelism, Reed sends the errant Phil blundering innocently into his equally errant idol in the assignation at the pastry shop. There he is given a furtive sweet, yet another archetypal childhood pleasure that Mrs Baines has sought to proscribe.

The cleanliness motif surfaces again in the cafe scene through an adroit reversal of expectations. When Julie begins to sob, Baines asks Phil for his handkerchief and Phil replies regretfully, 'It's clean', as if this unfortunate symbol of Mrs Baines's world made the article distasteful. Clearly Baines too is thinking of the antiseptic soul of his wife when, earlier in the movie, he exclaims, 'Too much carbolic makes you long for rot.'

Baines's remark is multilayered, illuminating us about another level of his friendship with Phil. The remark may also have been intended as an echo of the tall tales Baines had spun for the boy. With its heat, its wild animals and its primitive cultures, Africa is a continent where 'rot' of one sort or another is prevalent. The recurrent references to Baines's experience in the dark continent are more than just ornamental. These vignettes, however imaginary, conjure up a world that is antithetical to Mrs Baines's. It discards her tiny, scrubbed-down, rule-oriented domain in favour of one that is lushly overgrown, poetically charged, anarchic, tangled and thrilling. In Phil's case, all this is a child's dream of freebooting excitement. It promises a momentary release from the boredom of his cold, affluent prison. The stories seem no less therapeutic for Baines, who is badly in need of escape fantasies himself. Into his wildly fictionalized autobiography he projects his deepest wish fulfilment, freedom from his oppressive, degrading marriage to a dictatorial wife. Too weak to break the shackles Mrs Baines has imposed, he can fantasize about a life without uxoriousness. As he conceives it, the 'heart of darkness' is strictly a man's world, with unlimited outlets for traditional masculine drives and ideals. There Baines is a hunter and a warrior, a man among men who easily establishes his dominance over the natives. 'Never even used a gun', he embroiders in his account to Phil. 'Only a whip.' Significantly, women are largely absent from this society, and there is no one, black or white, male or female, to challege Baines's regime. Occasionally a local chieftain might attempt a feeble uprising, but Baines quickly crushes these rebellions by 'blackie'.

Reality meets fantasy when Baines takes Phil to the zoo, where the representatives of the jungle are rendered harmless by their cages. They seem almost tame and domesticated and serve as an ironic counterpoint to the fearsome beasts that roamed through Baines's fabricated adventure stories. Paradoxically, when the butler has the opportunity to observe the wild animals he has talked about so often, he is too distracted by Julie – a woman! – to pay much attention to them.

Another more important link between real life and the jungle fantasy is created by Phil's pet, a small snake named MacGregor. The reptile, cherished by Phil, is a *bête noir* to Mrs Baines. With its earthly, scaly, sinuous associations, it is clearly the grossest affront to her bleached and sanitized existence. In this sense, it harmonizes nicely with the film's inverted patterns of symbolism, turning our normal feelings about reptiles – malevolent, slimy or whatever – inside out. When Mrs Baines kills MacGregor, then, the murderous act serves a number of functions: fuelling Phil's hatred of her, which contributes to the ominous momentum of the plot; establishing Mrs Baines's total inability to deal with affective relationships; arousing sufficient animosity in the moviegoer that his sympathies are unalterably bound to Baines and Phil and that Mrs Baines's death seems deserved as well as convenient.

Any story that introduces a snake and then sets it in conflict with a woman, is bound to set explicators off in search of Biblical and sexual parallels. Here the scriptural story is reversed: the woman visits evil upon the reptile. For any edenic associations, we must turn to the dream world of African adventure shared by Baines and his young charge. As for sexuality, an unavoidable subject in any treatment of the 'eternal triangle', Mrs Baines's severe appearance – her unflattering hair style, harsh black dress and shoes, etc. – renders her asexual or almost antisexual. In contrast, Michèle Morgan's soft, refined Gallic beauty is accentuated by her silken coiffure and the attractively tailored suits she wears during most of her time on the screen. Her meltingly soft eyes accentuate her femininity. On balance, though, *Idol* is not a film in which Biblical interpretations are especially helpful. The few theological correlations that do appear are too inexact to be worth serious exploration.

As summarized here, Phil's interaction with the adults in *Idol* may make him sound fully integrated into the tissue of adult life, but of course he is not. One of the great paradoxes of Reed's film is that the figure who occupies the very heart of the story is himself barred from full participation. During much of the movie he is outside looking in, a frustrated – sometimes desperate – observer of an adult sphere he only partially comprehends. In his curious comments on *Idol*, Durgnat faults the movie for not creating a 'bridge between the mind of the hero-worshipping child and the adult realm . . .'[7] The criticism seems singularly wrongheaded in view of the fact that Reed's intention was to *stress* the gap between a child's view of the world and an adult's. Phil's inexperience keeps him from understanding the emotional currents that are shooting past him. Not yet corrupted by the deceit and hypocrisy of the grown-ups, he remains an innocent, puzzled by the tangled webs, too pure not to be confused by the perilous contests his elders are playing. One of the earliest manifestations of this purity occurs during Baines's first account of his apocryphal adventures in Africa. A wife was impossible under those circumstances, says Baines, because all the women there were black. 'Does she have to be white?', asks the wide-eyed Phil. His ignorant tolerance contrasts favourably with Baines's mature intolerance.

Thus, Baines's extramarital relationship with Julie is beyond Phil's grasp, as is the deranged jealousy with which Mrs Baines tries to wrest from him the truth about her husband. In the cafe scene, the two lovers converse elliptically, carefully concealing the amorous reality of their meeting from Phil, though not from the audience. Even with two languages at his command, the boy cannot understand why in the zoo sequence Baines and Julie are so much more interested in each other than in the animals; why the comments of the policemen and the prostitute at the station-house, so full of puzzling innuendo, seem so deliberately unintelligible; why Mrs Baines's telegram, with its incriminating information, is so important to Baines and Detective Crower (Dennis O'Dea). At several points, the boy mechanically echoes the sentiments of his elders, but these concurrences are as unwitting, uninformed and ignorant as the reenactments of the hold-up in *Odd Man Out* by the gang of street urchins. Indeed, one cannot help but remember them when Baines observes bitterly, 'What a fool a man is' and Phil responds, 'That's what I think too.' Or when Phil, having watched Baines's fruitless effort at severing the ties with his wife, remarks, 'I'll ask for my freedom too.' In a visual permutation of this contrast, the damning telegram from Mrs Baines becomes a child's paper airplane, a child's toy, gliding down from the top of the staircase towards the police.

Adult life is rendered especially frightening to Phil by its deceit, a quality Reed saw all too much of in his parents. In the cafe, Baines introduces Julie as his 'niece' and the two lovers speak cryptically, masking their true meaning in a code language. Afterwards, Phil is unknowingly implicated in Baines's dishonesty when the butler asks him not to mention Julie to Mrs Baines. 'I don't ask you to say what isn't true', he qualifies with clever casuistry. In a subsequent scene, the ferocious Mrs Baines tricks Phil into divulging the very information he had been pledged to keep. The greatest act of deception in the film is the elaborate trap she then constructs for her unfaithful husband. When chance takes over and sends Mrs Baines tumbling to her untimely death, Baines finds it necessary to lie to the police, even though he is not guilty. By this time, Phils is a fully-fledged participant in the murky, shadow game of prevarication that the adults insist on playing. With his own frantic lies, he strives to shield Baines from the authorities. But he is not as experienced at the game as his elders and hence his attempts at exonerating Baines only implicate the servant further.

The deception in *Idol* begins harmlessly enough with Baines's lively stories about his experiences in Africa; these seem to be remotely related to the glorious fabrications of the artist. Certainly it is difficult to see how they can do any damage. On another plane, Baines seeks to legitimize dishonesty by attributing humanitarian values to it: 'Sometimes lies are a kindness.' However, subsequent events establish that Baines is only rationalizing his own inability to face up to his dictatorial wife. The code word Baines uses for this systematized deceit is 'secrets'. Baines has a secret for Phil, and so does Mrs Baines. When the ordeal is finally over, Phil is so traumatized by what has happened that the inspector's innocuous offer to 'tell you a secret' horrifies the boy. The tempo and volume of the lying in *Idol* accelerate as the plot simmers and moves toward its climax. By the time the postmortem investigation begins casting the gravest suspicions on Baines, fictions are pouring freely – even wildly – from Phil, Julie and of course Baines himself. The semi-hysterical Phil, unconsciously caricaturing the grown-ups, cries out, 'We've got to think of lies to tell them all the time. And then they won't find out the truth.' At another juncture, Baines has a more knowing, rueful comment: 'Trouble is, we've told a fearful lot of lies.'

If Phil's behaviour is an unconscious parody of adults and if Baines's deficiencies are unknowingly indicated through Phil's damaging attempts to help him, then the final blow comes when the desperate butler is compelled to admit that his colourful anecdotes about Africa are counterfeit. When Phil mentions them in front of Detective Crower, Baines responds miserably, 'I've never been to Africa.' Phil looks stunned by this revelation and if his reaction was explored more carefully, the story might indeed have been an analysis of a 'fallen idol.' As it is, Phil's brief disillusionment is quickly submerged in his frantic struggle to help prove Baines's innocence. In any case, a backward gaze at the story indicates that Phil's idolization of Baines extends only to the overblown African tales; for the most part, Baines's role in Phil's life is that of a father figure, an outlet for emotional needs. Moreover the happy ending erases any signs of a 'fall'. Reed and Greene were fully aware of this, and, as Greene tells us, the 'meaningless title . . . was chosen by the distributors'.[8] The title, resonant and dramatic though it is, really doesn't identify the movie properly.

Phil can also be viewed in another context, as one more in Reed's series of essays on the destructiveness of innocence. As far back as *Kipps*, the director had manifested an interest in *naifs*, simple souls whose uncomplicated behaviour proves to be dangerously ill-suited to the complicated world of men. Like Johnny in *Odd Man Out*, Phil's motivations are morally pure, uncontaminated by hypocrisy, self-interest or deviousness. Nevertheless, it is the very purity of these motivations that nearly brings Baines and Julie to grief, since the boy is unable to make sense of the intricacies of adult life, which he so profoundly influences. Well intentioned, he nevertheless brings the people he most cares about to the brink of tragedy. For example, it is his reckless affection for Baines that sends him out in search of the butler, only to discover the assignation in the tea shop. The boy's knowledge further complicates a situation that is already too complicated. His effect on Mrs Baines is probably negligible, though one could argue that his naive attempt to keep everyone's secret is what, inadvertantly, precipitates the final tragedy.

Nowhere is the unstable power of innocence more evident than in the episode of the telegram. Phil wants desperately to help Baines, but the damning information that he has unthinkingly folded up into a paper airplane somehow comes sailing gracefully down from the top of the stairs, in complete disregard of Baines's terrified appeal. The trivializing yet explosive effects of innocence are perfectly melded in the paper plane – a child's toy, after all, yet in Phil's hands a life-and-death document. Baines, whom Phil wants most of all to save, is the one who, through the boy's blundering, comes closest to perishing.

Here is another artistic crossroads at which Reed and Greene go their separate ways. Greene has always been a clever storyteller but just as often an austere moralist, condemning his characters to icy, Catholic purgatories. Reed, with his underlying humanity, conveys more warmth than his collaborator. The affection between Baines and Phil is seldom vitiated by irony. Moreover, the cruelty with which Phil abandons his friend in 'The Basement Room' has no analogue in *Idol*. While Greene's Phil retreats coldly into the sanctuary of childhood, in Reed's treatment the boy becomes more and more frenzied as he tries to save Baines. Unlike his namesake in the story, his revelations before the police are never even remotely deliberate.

But Baines survives, as it happens, and the audience is allowed a soothing denouement in which love prevails, and even the butler's crippled relationship with Phil is restored. Perhaps Reed felt that after the unrelenting tragedy of *Odd Man Out*, he wished to remind moviegoers that he was a popular entertainer as well as a tragedian, that he could send them home happy as well as emotionally drained. Still, nothing that Reed did at this memorable period in his career was quite as simple as it looked. The conventionally happy ending of *Idol* is offset by a secondary theme that is grave and solemn: Phil's initiation into adulthood.

The maturation proceeds in stages. The Phil we first become acquainted with is immersed in the carefree, unsullied joys of boyhood; only the intermittent tyranny of Mrs Baines detracts from the boy's pleasures. Later, as the coils of adult deception tighten about Phil, he is severely traumatized, driven to frenzy by the terrifying realities that replace his playful antics and daydreams of Africa. Out of his psychological ordeal, he emerges into a deeper, fuller – and more cheerless – vision of life. In our last sight of him, Reed adroitly and economically introduces us to the mature Phil. Again, he is at the top of the stairs – in a shot that corresponds ironically to his first appearance – and looks down at his parents, who have just arrived in the entryway. 'Felipe, here is your mother', his father calls out ebulliently. Anything but joyous, Phil displays a sombre visage, a graven mask of lost innocence, as he slowly descends the stairs and vanishes from the frame.

Reed's skill with actors is as unfaltering here as in his previous work, and they gave the polished screenplay an extra sheen. Richardson reveals all of Baines's weakness and irresolution but never loses our sympathy, while Morgan, rarely more than an adequate actress in English language films, achieves a warmth and vulnerability that offsets her glamour. Dresdel is so effective in her portrayal of poisoned love and wounded, overbearing womanhood that she almost converts a caricature into a character. The triumph of the film, however, is young Henrey, an amateur who adapted so naturally to the requirements of his role that he eclipsed most of the child actors of the day. It is difficult to imagine Bobby Driscoll or Roddy McDowell conveying a similar range of moods – affection, alienation, anxiety, terror – in the totally natural, unaffected manner that Reed elicited from his star. Childlike befuddlement in the face of grown-up malice has never been more memorably communicated.

If Reed allowed the sportiveness in his nature to prevail in *The Fallen Idol*, he once again reverted to melancholy in *The Third Man*, his next film. An essay in postwar gloom and cynicism, the movie was a powerful fusion of all the motifs and technical devices in his previous movies. It was his greatest success, both critically and financially, and many film scholars have proclaimed it his masterpiece. One can endorse their enthusiasm without necessarily agreeing to elevate the movie above such brilliant efforts as *Odd Man Out* and *Outcast of the Islands*, which, it could be argued, have an emotional power and an integrity of character and theme that *The Third Man* does not quite attain.

The genesis of the movie was an inspiration of Alexander Korda's to make a movie that exploited the international drama and photogenic face of occupied Vienna. Reed was retained for the project and teamed again with Graham Greene, his favourite scenarist. The germ of the story was a line Greene had jotted down years before: 'I had paid my last farewell to Harry a week ago, when his coffin was lowered into the frozen February ground, so that it was with incredulity that I saw him pass by, without a sign of recognition, among the host of strangers in the Strand.'[9] From this premise, Greene first wrote a short novel, then a screenplay, brewing up a dazzling plot about glamorous racketeers, declassed noblemen and a beautiful refugee that was ideally suited to Reed's talents and temperament. An ample budget made it possible to hire first-rate actors and to shoot on location in Vienna.

It is no surprise, then, that almost everyone in 1949 found *The Third Man* to their taste, even the austere judges of the Cannes Film Festival, who awarded it the golden palm (first prize). The English reviews could scarcely have been more adulatory, and for the third time running Reed won the British Film of the Year Award. In the United States, the movie travelled into movie theatres under a downpour of critical accolades. 'This is a full-blooded, absorbing story . . . which reflects credit on all concerned', said *Variety*.[10] The *Time* reviewer was even more exultant, describing the film as 'crammed with cinematic plums that would do the early Hitchcock proud . . .'[11] The notice in *Newsweek* was also effusive, celebrating Reed's 'remarkable ability to employ imaginative and revealing detail and vivid supplementary characterizations . . .'[12] At the *New York Times*, Crowther pronounced *The Third Man* an 'extraordinarily fascinating picture', though with typical Crowtheresque obtuseness he cautioned his readers to expect merely a 'first-rate contrivance in the way of melodrama'.[13] Over the next twenty-five years, Crowther, the final word on film at the most illustrious newspaper in the country, had been and was to continue to be the Polonius of movie critics, the voice of homiletic, middle-brow, establishmentarian views and, as such, a figure of some derision among film scholars and the more intellectual movie critics.

Greene's gifts as a storyteller were never more brilliantly displayed than in his script for *The Third Man*. It is difficult to think of a thriller whose architecture is so shrewd, whose scenes are so gracefully interlocked, whose action climbs so compellingly yet effortlessly towards its climax. Funerals stand at either end of the story, buttressing it like two bookends, though in each case the obsequies are being performed for the same man, Harry Lime (Orson Welles). In between these two 'deaths' lies one of the classic patterns of the suspense story – a man's quest to penetrate the mystery surrounding a friend's death. We follow Holly Martin's inept but dogged pursuit of the enigmatic 'third man' who supposedly witnessed Lime's death, but who, as it turns out, is actually Lime himself. Along the way, Martins (Joseph Cotten) is assaulted by ever more shocking revelations – that Lime may have been murdered, that Lime is actually alive, that Lime is a racketeer whose watered down penicillin has crippled innumerable children. One of the principal axioms of the thriller is thus observed: the need for a constant series of reverses, twists, surprises.

The narrative fabric from which these surprises emerge is seamless. Martins's desire to resolve the enigma of Harry's death leads him to four friends of Harry's: 'Baron' Kurtz (Ernst Deutsch), an unctuous, preening nobleman; Dr Winkel (Erich Pometo), a white-haired old physician; Mr Popescu (Siegfried Breuer), a Romanian gentleman with refined manners; Anna Schmidt (Alida Valli), Harry's beautiful girlfriend, with whom Holly falls in love and tries to rescue from deportation. Kurtz, Winkel and Popescu are confederates in Lime's smuggling ring and each gives an account of Harry's death which is not quite consistent with the others. As the alarming incongruencies manifest themselves, an atmosphere of peril develops. The conspirators' efforts at deterring Martins can be divided into three stages: (1) lying as persuasively as possible; (2) murdering the porter (Paul Hoerbiger) in order to silence him and to frighten Martins; and (3) attempting to assassinate Martins himself. Thus Greene has given his protagonist two motivations for assisting the police – his love for Anna and his reluctant acceptance of the fact that Harry is a cancer on the society around him, a man who is willing to profit from the death or maiming of small children. Indeed, there is scarcely any action in the film that is not intelligently and thoughtfully motivated. When the film-makers want their characters to steer the plot this way or that, they never fail to supply them with credible behaviour. Unlike so much escape fare, the excitement in *The Third Man* is never arbitrary; the thrilling developments are carefully anchored to basic human drives and impulses.

It is astounding, therefore, to encounter Roy Armes's categorization of the movie as 'typical entertainment',[14] when in fact it could not be more atypical. Still more astonishing is Durgnat's disdainful reference to the 'conventionality of its themes'.[15] More than any film of its kind ever made, *The Third Man* transcends its nominal classification as a thriller, investigating a number of serious themes with potency and intelligence. As in *Idol*, the intellectual focus of the movie is the suffering that innocence can promote. In a rudimentary way, Orson Welles himself had experimented with this theme in his film of Ambler's *Journey Into Fear*, and it is surely no accident that Joseph Cotten, who played the unglamorous, fumbling engineer drawn into foreign intrigue in Welles's movie, was selected for a similar role in *The Third Man*. In *Journey*, however, Cotten was closer to the stereotype of a movie hero; ultimately, his relationship to the villainous secret agents and to the lovely heroine followed traditional Hollywood lines. By contrast, Martins is a clumsy and misguided idealist whose unworldliness has deadly ramifications for other people. Heedless of the warnings of sober, professional Major Calloway (Trevor Howard), Martins insists on meddling quixotically in a situation that is totally outside his range of experience. Directly or indirectly, he is responsible for the deaths of three men – the porter, Sergeant Paine (Bernard Lee) and Harry Lime. The world is better off without Lime, but the other two are innocent victims. Though no less well intentioned than Reed's other simpletons, Martins operates by a standardized morality that is simply too one-eyed for the layered intricacies of real life – especially in the confusing netherworld of Vienna. Everyone in *The Third Man* seems impatient with Martins's incessant over-simplification and no one more so than Anna, who complains, 'For heaven's sake, stop making him in *your* image. Harry was real.'

If Martins's adherence to obsolete Sunday school pieties is a limitation, he is even more severely handicapped by the ragbag of romantic cliches he has accumulated from popular fiction. It is through their rosy adolescent hue that his perception of reality is filtered. Ingeniously, Greene and Reed make Martins a man who writes Westerns for a living, a prisoner of the stale platitudes about the Old West which he propagates freely in his rip-roaring novels. His outlook is modelled as closely as possible on his fictive heroes – e.g. the Lone Rider of Santa Fe – and he strives to make Zane Grey his guide to the Viennese underworld. Portentously announcing his intention to discredit Lieutenant Calloway, he likens his activities to a story of his 'about a rider who hunted down a sheriff who was victimizing his best friend'. Remarks of this sort only provoke such stingingly accurate rebukes from Calloway as 'This isn't Santa Fe, I'm not a sheriff, and you aren't a cowboy.'

In this, as in so many other respects, the scenario benefits from the pungency and literary background that a man of letters like Greene can provide. The literary society at which Martins is invited to speak is characterized with a sureness that makes it a marvellous source of entertainment, while at the same time commenting further on Martins's inadequacy. Forced to deal with the mature wisdom of great artists, such as Joyce, he can only mumble inanities; he is far more comfortable with the shallowness and artificialities of pulp fiction. (On yet another level, Greene may have been indulging in playful self-parody, since his own excursions into popular fiction – his 'entertainments' – are well known. Indeed, the prose version of *The Third Man*, published in 1950, was just such a work.)

Martins is very much an innocent abroad and his creators display little enthusiasm for innocence. The episode at the literary society is one of several examples of the anti-heroic treatment to which Martins is subjected throughout *The Third Man*. Elsewhere we see him put to flight by the slain porter's son, Hansl (Herbert Halbik), a small boy with a ball whose ingenuous remarks arouse the suspicions of onlookers. Following his embarrassing address at the literary society, Martins is pursued by assassins, but the only injury he sustains is a parrot bite on his hand. In a sequence at Anna's apartment immediately afterwards, his affectionate behaviour is rebuffed not only by Anna herself but by her cat. Even his name, Holly Martins, seems to mock his romantic and heroic pretensions.

But Reed and Greene transcend the mere comic deflation of square-jawed innocence, adding a subtext that they had used effectively in *Idol* – the potential destructiveness of innocence. Here the theme receives a far more sombre treatment, as the tragic consequences of Martins's well-meaning incompetence accumulate. Directly or indirectly, he is responsible for the murder of the porter and Sergeant Paine and perhaps even for the deportation of Anna. Sarris goes so far as to arraign Martins for Lime's death, though it is hard to see the justice of consigning him to an 'emotional wasteland created by his inability to feel any guilt for his action'. In Sarris's view, Holly 'first betrays' his old friend 'and then executes him'.[16] One can agree with the general charge – Martins never shows any cognizance of, let alone remorse for, the effects of his actions – without accepting the particular illustration of it. The dramatic logic of the story makes Lime's demise inevitable, even desirable.

Still, as in *Idol* and other Reed films, the chief miseries are created by the collision of a naive soul with a fallen world. The corruption in which Martins finds himself immersed cannot be dispelled by his wide-eyed posture towards it any more than Phil's innocence could save Baines. Innocence is not redemptive in the theology of *The Third Man*; it only complicates an already twisted, sinister universe.

The casting of Joseph Cotten as Martins, though the part was originally written for an Englishman, was a happy choice, and Cotten probes every corner of his character's limited soul. The traces of patrician Virginia in the actor's voice give him a dignity that helps offset his often bumptious behaviour and laughable, semi-literate profession. In the same way, Cotten finds a vulnerability in Martins which softens the impact of his clumsy, insensitive sleuth work. Through the canny shaping of Cotten's performance, Reed prevents his audience from losing all sympathy for Martins, which is the effect of Greene's novel.

The impact of Cotten's character is enhanced by the inclusion of a second *naif*, Hansl. There is a delicious perversity in the way the film-makers deny the boy any traditionally lovable 'movie moppet' characteristics, using him instead as a source of mordant fun. With his pudgy torso and a face as circular as the ball he plays with incessantly, he is reminiscent of a goblin child, someone eerie, disquieting, not quite human. A disembodied, mitten-covered hand is the first glimpse of the boy that we are given, as he toddles around a corner into the room where Martins is talking to the porter. His childlike babble of German, especially the shrill and never-ending cry of 'Papa, papa' fills the audience's ear with reverberations of pathos, fear, affection and irritation. Deliberately and boldly, Reed even allows the boy's squealing to arouse a certain revulsion in the audience, a clever preparation for the outright fear the child generates when he inadvertently throws suspicion for his father's murder on Martins. His infantile chatter, apparently innocuous, has sufficiently ominous overtones for a crowd of adult onlookers to set them in pursuit of Martins with menacing gazes.

For Reed and Greene, then, good deeds do not necessarily shine forth in a naughty world. Similarly, goodness is not automatically armed against the world's wickedness. Indeed, the movie-makers seem convinced of the ineffectuality of goodness, whose pale, limp passivity is contrasted throughout with the striding vigour of evil, at once cunning and robust. Martins is no match for his old friend Lime in the cat and mouse game they engage in; Lime deftly outmanoeuvres him at every point. Although of course Lime is an expert racketeer, well schooled in the talents of the underworld, he seems to have enjoyed this advantage over the more slow-witted Martins even in boyhood. It is an aptitude for survival that is rooted in his innate unscrupulousness, as we learn when Martins gives us a thumbnail sketch of the youthful Lime: 'He could fix anything. How to put your temperature up before an exam . . . the best cribs. How to avoid this and that.' In addition, Martins's relative stolidity and lack of sophistication is contrasted with Lime's suavete and insouciant cosmopolitanism.

Welles's brilliant performance, possibly the finest of his career after *Citizen Kane*, makes Lime every bit as charismatic as he is intended to be. It is certainly one of the extraordinary ironies of Welles's career that when the role of Lime was first offered to him, he turned it down as too small. He did come to Vienna to convey his refusal personally, however, and Reed seized the opportunity to lure the actor into the film by persuading him to appear in a trial run of one scene, the chase through the sewers. Reed later recounted the amusing and illuminating sequence of events which led to Welles's acceptance of the part:

> Reluctantly, he agreed. 'Those sewers will give me pneumonia,' he grumbled, as he descended the iron steps. We shot the scene. Then Orson asked us to shoot it again although I was satisfied with the first take. He had some idea of how to play the scene more dramatically. He talked with the cameraman, made some suggestions, and did the chase again. Then again. The upshot was that Orson did that scene ten times, became enthusiastic about the story – and stayed in Vienna to finish the picture. And, of course, he gave a miraculous performance.[17]

Welles did not actually direct *The Third Man,* or write his own scenes, as some of his followers have claimed, but his contribution as an actor was promethean enough. With his wolfish, amoral charm, he is surely one of the most glamorous villains in the history of the cinema. Yet the film's achievement is all the more remarkable in that Reed and Greene had the daring to make Lime's villainy utterly uncompromising. Unlike the sentimental hoodlums of *Dead End, Manhattan Melodrama* and *The Asphalt Jungle,* his ruthlessness is not redeemed by a 'soft spot' for his mother, for his boyhood buddy, for horses. In fact, he betrays his mistress to the Russian authorities, bringing about her deportation, and is only deterred from slaying Martins when he learns that it will do him no good, since his hoax has already been discovered.

With his mischievous slash of a grin, his devil-may-care black eyes, and his swaggering adventurism, Welles makes Lime practically irresistible – in spite of his crimes and in spite of the fact that he is only on screen for approximately ten minutes. Through Welles's superb realization of his character, Harry easily displaces the film's nominal hero, Martins, though of course this is the film-makers' intention. Where Martins lacks self-control, as exhibited in his excessive drinking and his adolescent passion for Anna, Lime is always cool and self-possessed. Where Martins is obtuse, Lime is shrewd. Predictably, Anna prefers the memory of Harry to the reality of Martins, gently discouraging his attentions. While his ardour for her grows, she continues to see him only as a link to her 'dead' lover, accidentally referring to him as 'Harry' twice in the film.

As a force for good, Anna is no less ineffectual than Martins. Her plight as a displaced person awakens our sympathy, which can only be intensified by her beauty and dignity, but she is guilty of moral blindness that works to Lime's advantage. Far from combatting his depravity, she refuses even to acknowledge it, let alone aid the police in apprehending him. Her romantic fatalism has an integrity of sorts, but it does not protect her from the dangerous vicissitudes of life in postwar Vienna and she suffers accordingly. The screenplay confines Anna's character within a narrow emotional range, but Valli fills every inch of it with unwavering dramatic conviction. Like several of Reed's other heroines, Anna is resigned to romantic frustration, to thwarted passion, and Valli epitomizes sad-eyed, tragic beauty like no one but Garbo.

Major Calloway is the most potent agent of goodness in the film, an exemplar of sturdy Anglo-Saxon values. Bluff and plainspoken to the point of harshness, he is nevertheless always fair, blending a rough-hewn humanity with his departmental responsibilities. As in his commentaries on Martins and Lime, Sarris does violence to the text of the movie when he describes Calloway as an exponent of 'cynical efficiency in his attitude towards the non-political crimes spawned in a world he has helped to create', a man without 'idealism or compassion'.[18] Calloway's exertions on behalf of Anna, whom he temporarily rescues from deportation, are nothing if not compassionate.

Calloway's professional apparatus is tough and efficient, yet he is not able to apprehend Lime on his own. Evil remains more resourceful than goodness throughout most of the film. Lime's downfall occurs only when Martins allows the police to exploit the credibility he still enjoys with his friend. In the final analysis, it is impossible to defeat Lucifer without adopting Lucifer's methods – trickery and deceit. Fair play, however dogged, is not sufficient in itself. At the same time, it must be conceded that Reed and Greene are less successful at developing the notion of an unequal contest between good and evil than they are at demonstrating the potential perils of innocence. Lime's gullibility about the meeting with Martins is not plausible and seems to satisfy the needs of the melodrama in *The Third Man*, creating a standard climax in which the villain is annihilated – rather than sustaining the movie's metaphysical themes.

On another level, though, the famous manhunt in the sewers that ends the film is an exquisitely logical consummation of one of the motifs that Reed and Greene are most obsessed with: the corruption of contemporary Viennese society. In a prologue to the film – spoken by Cotten in the American version and by Reed himself in the English original – we are given a quick, irreverent postmortem on Vienna: 'I never knew the old Vienna before the war, with its Strauss music, its glamour and easy charm . . . I really got to know it in the classic period of the black market. We'd run anything if people wanted it enough and had the money to pay.' As the preamble continues, we are introduced to a city that has succumbed to decay and crime. The stunning montage of shots that illustrates the commentary includes bomb-shattered buildings and shabby streets. The illicit currents of present-day Vienna are summarized by an arm with several watches and a woman handing over money in exchange for boxes of illegal items. When we finally see the famous Danube river, a body is floating in it, and the accompanying narration reminds us, with cruel irony, that amateurs 'can't stay the course like professionals'. The remainder of the film is magnificently keyed to this brisk preface. The war has shattered the codes that the Viennese once lived by, and they have replaced it with a *modus vivendi* that is stripped of ethics or morality. Everyone in Vienna utilizes the black market, Kurtz tells Martins casually: 'We all sell cigarettes and that kind of thing.' Most of the evidence we see bears out his contention. Even Anna offers Holly bootlegged whiskey and is happy when he declines, commenting, 'Good. I hope to sell it.' The uniformity of municipal corruption in Vienna can be seen from the fact that Lime's confederates are not recruited from the underbelly of society but from its elite: Dr Winkel whom we meet carving up a chicken for dinner guests in good bourgeois fashion; Kurtz, the nobleman; Popescu, whose demeanour is civilized and refined, even when he is on the verge of murdering Martins.

The depiction of the conspirators is enriched and complemented by the city around them, whose every shade and reverberation is registered by Reed's cameraman, the invaluable Robert Krasker. Rarely has a locale been used so tellingly. Vienna seems almost sentient, a creature of decayed and ominous beauty, and Reed's use of it to comment on his story has been justly lauded. Rubble and partially demolished buildings fill nearly every frame of the movie, a constant reminder of the devastation of war that has just ended. The narrow streets suggest enclosure rather than quaintness – a prison for lives shattered by the war – while the city's architecture and cultural heritage is made to seem onerous, a source of oppression rather than cultural pride, a mortmain. The elaborate statuary, marble staircases, brooding stone facades, only create a burdensome and fetid atmosphere, the sense of a city smothered in its own past. Dr Winkel's statue-choked house is a case in point.

Decadence, then, is all-pervasive, as typified by the effeminate Kurtz, an aristocrat who has been reduced to a cabaret artiste. His first meeting with Holly occurs at the Cafe Mozart, where nothing resembling Mozart's music is heard. Later, the two encounter one another again at the Cafe Casanova where we learn abruptly that the Baron plays the violin for a living. The name of the establishment is appropriately voluptuous, given the overripe melodies that emerge from Kurtz's instrument. He is a figure of evil, as is his associate Popescu, a man exceptionally well qualified to deliver a portentous warning to Martins: 'Everybody ought to go careful in a city like this.' The dry rot of Vienna, physically and morally, claims numerous victims, and the motif of decay receives a suitably cloacal wrap-up when Reed actually takes us into the sewers for the film's conclusion.

Even the foregoing comments do not do the fullest possible justice to the remarkable texture of *The Third Man*. The movie's themes and characters are further augmented by the clever interpolation of animal imagery, a specialty of Reed's, as we have seen. The feline Harry Lime is associated with Anna's cat, the garrulous and foolish Martins with a parrot, and the effete Kurtz with a lap dog. Elsewhere another dimension, a playful one, is added by Reed's fondness for theatrical flourishes, here indulged extensively. The frivolous operetta in which Anna appears is a frothy contrast to the grim realities of contemporary Vienna. In the scene at the Casanova Club, every saccharine stroke of Kurtz's bow provides an entertaining musical commentary on its surroundings. When the snare is laid for Lime, the tense period of waiting is humorously interrupted by a carnival figure, an obtuse old balloon peddlar who mindlessly repeats, 'Balloon, Mynheer? Balloon?' as Major Calloway impatiently tries to wave him away. Lime is quite a showman himself, and the self-dramatization he displays when he finally steps out and reveals himself to Martins is spectacular. Framed in the doorway of a house and suddenly illuminated by a light from above, he mocks the idea of villainhood, his all-black garb counterpointed by a magnetic, perversely likeable smile.

If the film has a scene that is especially studded with *coups de théâtre*, it is certainly the famed sequence at the Prater ferris wheel. Although Lime may not have anything to do with establishing the point of rendezvous with Martins, it is a perfect expression of the racketeer's prankish, flamboyant, colourful personality. (Fittingly, Anna says of him: 'He never grew up. The world grew up around him.') As the two friends reach the apogee of the ride and the car pauses, Lime pulls the door open and his next theatrical flourish is a wonderfully melodramatic, almost cape-swirling gesture. 'You should be pretty easy to get rid of", he says darkly, examining Martins with the professional detachment of a man who has killed many times. 'Don't think they'd look for a bullet after you hit that ground.' After the ride, Lime's mood of cheerful cynicism is restored and his last flourish is solely verbal, a world-renowed *moi* that Welles wrote himself: 'In Italy for thirty years under the Borgias they had warfare, terror, murder, bloodshed – they produced Michelangelo, Leonardo, and the Renaissance. In Switzerland, they had brotherly love, five hundred years of democracy and peace, and what did that produce? The cuckoo clock.'

The dialogue between Lime and Martins in the ferris wheel car is also intriguing as a highly compressed reprise of the dominant motifs of the movie. The sense of enclosure that is conveyed by the narrow streets and small, overstuffed rooms, by Lime's grave and by the sewers, is also evoked here. The view of Harry as a self-seeking opportunist is confirmed by his menacing gesture towards Martins, by the exposition of his callous treatment of Martins in their boyhood days, and by the revelation that he has betrayed Anna to the Russians. The mood of ruthless, depersonalized internationalism is also recapitulated in Lime's self-justification: 'Governments talk of the people and the proletariat, and I talk of the mugs. They have their five year plans and I have mine.' There is not much about political life in Vienna that fails to corroborate Lime's *Weltanschauung*, though Greene's articulation of it is somewhat flat and perfunctory. (Similar sentiments in *The Quiet American* are presented with more intellectual substance.) He is more effective when he reiterates the film's theological viewpoint, perhaps because religious ideas require less specification than political ones. 'You used to believe in God', Martins tells Lime. 'Oh, I still believe, old man', Lime replies jauntily. 'In God and mercy and all that. The dead are happier dead. They don't miss much.'

The many-sided excellence of *The Third Man* is, of course, not simply the result of a first-rate director working at the top of his powers but of a cinematic team working at the same peak level under that director's supervision. In addition to the contributions of Greene and Krasker, the film benefits enormously from the much acclaimed zither score by Anton Karas, whom Reed discovered in a Viennese nightclub while shooting the movie. So excited was Reed by the *outré* possibilities of the zither that he commissioned Karas to write the entire score. The music that Karas supplied must have exceeded Reed's expectations because he allowed it to seep into every corner of the film. As we move from scene to scene, the tremulous strings supply an auditory transcription for every mood in the movie, and although Karas occasionally overpunctuates the action, he is on the whole smashingly successful. The dominant themes are a lush, mournful lyricism; a slightly dissonant motif that generates suspense (as in the porter's confrontation with his offscreen assailant); a vivacious walking theme (used to convey Lime's impish, if menacing, *joie de vie*); and a poignant little waltz that fills the cafe in which Cotten awaits his last rendezvous with Lime. The distinctly commercial appeal of Karas's music was validated when the 'Harry Lime Theme', a collection of snippets, conquered the hit parade, selling four million copies in England alone, and when the score itself was nominated for an Academy Award. Despite its melodiousness, the score is not without an underlying cynicism, and one can understand Kael's remark that the music brings the 'evil seductively near'.[19] In addition to its other virtues, the unusually pronounced and lingering overtones produced by the zither add tremendously to the suggestiveness of a movie that favours innuendo and implication.

The film's denouement is a breathtaking blend of inspiration, formal perfection and sheer nerve. Harry's second burial is a replica of the first, but Reed nevertheless incorporates some subtle alterations to indicate shifts that have occurred in the main body of the narrative. In the first funeral, Anna declines to sprinkle the token spoonful of earth on her lover's coffin; in the second, knowing for sure that he is gone, she accepts the priest's offer. As the mourners at Lime's grave go their separate ways, Cotten again accepts a lift into town from Major Calloway. Passing Anna on the road, however, he asks to be let out and, after grumbling about the impracticality of the idea, Calloway accedes. A curtain of autumnal leaves is falling over the countryside, creating a last image of the decay that has played such a formidable part in the film's ambiance. The concluding moments display an aesthetic boldness unparalleled in English language films, the gamble of a remarkable artist.

The camera doesn't move an inch, as Reed isolates Martins,

smoking a cigarette by the side of the road, in a long shot. From the distant background, Anna emerges slowly into the frame, sombre, walking at an even clip. Not only does she deny us the easy gratification of a happy ending, she doesn't even cast a glance in Martins's direction. As the camera remains stationary, she walks towards us and disappears from sight. The hopelessness of Martins's love could not be more starkly portrayed.

Ironically, it was Reed, the popular entertainer, and not Greene, the serious novelist, who insisted on an unhappy ending and on the devastatingly bleak, idiosyncratic conclusion that was used. Greene felt that 'an entertainment of this kind was too light . . . to carry the weight of an unhappy ending . . . I was afraid few people would wait in their seats during the girl's long walk from the graveside . . .' It was, he tells us, one of 'the very few major disputes between Carol Reed and myself . . . and he has been proved triumphantly right'.[20] Triumphantly: the ending is mesmeric.

The last moments of the film are courageously true to the intellectual and emotional logic of the story, which is anti-romantic, anti-heroic and (some would say) anti-humanistic. To the extent that the movie is illustrative of this last-named quality, however, it would probably be more accurate to trace it to Greene rather than Reed. The ennobling quest of Johnny McQueen for charity, a search for which Reed obviously felt profound sympathy, has no equivalent in Greene's universe of doomed, erring, sinful mortals, the universe of Scobie (*Heart of the Matter*), Andrews (*The Man Within*) and Pinky (*The Power and the Glory*). The religious scepticism of Greene's novels, the sense of the frailty of human nature, dominates *The Third Man* and its kinship to Greene's novels is hard to miss. Perhaps Greene's sense of involvement in the theological dimension of his story was heightened by its being set in a Catholic country. In the book Lime is explicitly identified as a Catholic; in the film he is only someone who 'used to believe in God', as Martins reminds him. His funeral appears to be Catholic, however, and we hear the priest intoning in Latin.

That the sacrament is being performed for a dead criminal tells us a good deal about Greene's theology. In his inexorably Catholic outlook, the human condition is always corrupt, a rigged game in which even the best-intentioned of us merely choose between alternate roads to damnation; in this case, the choice is between double-crossing your best friend or allowing him to continue flooding the hospitals with watered-down penicillin and crippling children. As in so much of the work of Reed and Greene, both together and apart, betrayal is an important dramatic component. Unlike Reed, however, Greene allows scepticism to devolve easily into pessimism and pessimism into morbidity. For him, there is no salvation this side of the grave. Small wonder that Greene's most often-quoted remark is 'Life is not a choice between black and white but black and gray.'[21]

Similarly, Reed's oblique approach to death and suffering – a distinctive directorial trait from his fledgling days onward – is never as sadistic as what we encounter in Greene's novels. Of the three deaths in *The Third Man*, only Paine's occurs onscreen. By the same token, the mangled children are withheld from our gaze, as Reed's camera whisks us through the hospital in a stunning montage; a discarded teddy bear, poignant and isolated, is the sole visual evidence of the fate of the children.

Among the many other trademarks that Reed had cultivated by 1949 was an intense internationalism, a blend of different cultures and languages that was unique in the otherwise homogeneous British cinema. The cultural pluralism of *Night Train*, shallowly handled though it was, nevertheless presaged the cosmopolitan milieu of the foreign embassy in *The Fallen Idol*. In *The Third Man*, the mood of multinationalism is greater still, since five different national groups are represented, though only two languages – English and German – are actually spoken on the screen.

None of Reed's films prior to *The Third Man*, technically polished though they are, reveals quite the same mastery of the cinematic alphabet. The lighting achieves chiaroscuro effects that depict the gloomy, sinister quality of Vienna concisely and graphically. Frequently Reed and Krasker, who won a much-deserved Oscar for his work, isolate the characters amidst this gloom, positioning them in empty streets or under shuttered windows. The expressionistic techniques which Voigt thought were incongruous in *The Stars Look Down* are unquestionably appropriate here. The same is true of the tilted camera angles, used to intensify the feeling of deviousness that the story ascribes to Vienna in general and to Lime and his companions in particular. The same cinematic adventurousness marks almost every shot in the film, from the elliptically edited sequence in the hospital to the long takes, like the beautiful tracking shot that leads us out of Anna's windows and down to a shadowy figure in a doorway, to the daringly stationary view of Anna walking past Holly at the end. Only Reed could have achieved the brilliant paradox of a technically static sequence that is dramatically dynamic, as gripping and unforgettable as the movie that preceded it.

When Reed gathered up the accolades that *The Third Man* earned him, he occupied a pinnacle that no English director other than Hitchcock had attained. Others had had isolated successes – Reed's own mentor, Alexander Korda, had directed a memorable hit in 1933, *The Private Life of Henry VIII* but only Reed and Hitchcock could look back over a sustained series of triumphs. With *Odd Man Out*, Reed reached the apex of his powers and in his two subsequent films he tested the range and the depth of those powers, exploring fresh subject-matter while maintaining a distinct cinematic personality. Here the fascination he had always displayed in the purely cinematographic side of film-making flowers into deft camera angles, which provide such expert visual italics for the story and characters; the superb editing, which maximizes every moment of drama; and the aural ingenuity, which almost equals the concerto of sound effects in *Odd Man Out*.

Thematically, Reed's 'figure in the carpet' may have stayed the same, but the fabric and design from which it emerged changed in subtle, intriguing ways. In *Odd Man Out*, the Johnny McQueen character embodied innocence as a Christ figure stumbling through a world of human frailty, while in *Fallen Idol*, the *naif* was a boy too young to understand the fateful impact his well-intentioned actions could have on corrupt adults, and in *The Third Man* there was yet another clever permutation: innocence in the form of adult folly, specifically a rash bumbler trying to do good for people who are, each for his own reason, beyond redemption. The auteur theory notwithstanding, the importance of Graham Greene's contribution to these themes, and to most of the other dimensions of the films, should not be overlooked. The creative partnership with Greene was easily Reed's most fruitful collaboration and it is not difficult to see why. The disparities in temperament and artistic preference between the two men have been duly noted, but the parallels are far more compelling: each had a proclivity for thrillers, each liked to release the tensions of melodrama with humour, each favoured a dry wit over broader forms of comedy, each used irony almost reflexively as a surgical instrument for probing the human condition. With what exquisite coordination do the two men exercise these talents in *Fallen Idol* and *The Third Man*!

8 Experimentation and Retreat

The success of *The Third Man* propelled Reed to the peak of his career, making him a director of international importance whose movies accomplished the rare merger of commerce and art; they earned praise from the reviewers and sold plenty of tickets as well. The 1940s had been a triumphant decade for Reed and from the pinnacle of *The Third Man*, he surveyed a future of expanding opportunities. His decision to strike off in a new artistic direction rather than cautiously husbanding the profitable aptitude for thrillers he had displayed was courageous. Weighing a number of different potential film assignments, he at last settled on an adaptation of Joseph Conrad's second novel, *An Outcast of the Islands* (1896), a work which Korda – a Conrad enthusiast – had been urging him to film. Korda's enthusiasm was a *sine qua non*, since the endeavour would have been self-defeating otherwise; a good cinematic likeness of Conrad's tale required a large and convincing cast and a Far Eastern locale. Most of the movie was shot on location in the region where the story was actually set: Ceylon, Borneo and the Malayas. In a story with few of the narrative surprises of *The Third Man*, topnotch acting was also crucial, and Reed enjoyed the luxury of picking performers who fitted their roles as snugly as possible: Trevor Howard as Willems; Robert Morley as Almayer; Ralph Richardson as Captain Lingard; Wendy Hiller as Mrs Almayer; the beautiful Pakistani actress Kerima as Aîssa.

Yet despite all these advantages, *Outcast* received comparatively unfavourable reviews. *Time* was virtually the only important periodical that gave the film a strong endorsement, lauding it for a 'story that surges and eddies', 'a superb cast' and a drama 'played out among a group of characters whose violent passions spend themselves like a tropical downpour'.[1] In an infrequent parting of the ways, *Newsweek* differed from its arch-rival because the 'pictorial treat' that Reed supplied in *Outcast* was all a matter of surface; the drama did not 'live up to its investiture'.[2] *Variety*, unable to perceive a known commercial formula in the movie, flailed away at it uncomprehendingly, calling the plot 'loosely constructed' and accusing Reed of an inability to 'capture the authentic atmosphere of the Far East', an incredible charge in the light of the film's astonishing anthropological accuracy.[3] Crowther found some aesthetic satisfaction in the acting and in the movie's evocation of 'elemental drives', but his overall judgement was that *Outcast* was 'neither arresting nor profound'.[4]

Audiences were equally unhappy with *Outcast*, making it the first real setback Reed had sustained in a decade or more. The movie received comparatively little distribution and is rarely seen today, either in theatres or on television. In 1957, Sarris was impressed by the film, but in 1968 he found little to recommend in it other than the actors' readings of Conrad's 'heroic rhetoric'.[5] Among other major film critics, only Kael has extolled *Outcast* consistently and emphatically, calling it one of the 'most underrated and unattended of important modern films'.[6]

'Underrated' is certainly the word for it. Contrary to *Variety*'s declarations, the atmosphere of Malaya is potently captured. The sweltering humidity, the rank lushness of the jungle, the exoticism, colour and brutality of native life – all are spread across Reed's canvas like expertly applied impasto. With the exception of a few professional actors, each of the natives in *Outcast* is exactly what he seems: a local tribesman of the areas in which the movie was made. The remote Asian locales – characterized by sluggish, brown waters; luxuriant, tropical jungles; and bamboo and thatched roof architecture – have none of the synthetic exoticism that bedizens most Hollywood excursions into the South Seas. The river village in which the story takes place is a brilliant replica of a hamlet in Borneo which set designer Vincent Korda reproduced for the shooting in Ceylon. The sampans and outriggers that surge through the waters are real native craft. Had Conrad lived to see *Outcast*, it's hard to imagine what he could have objected to in its visualization of his East Indian setting.

Crowther refers to *Outcast* as a 'rather free adaptation',[7] though it's hard to tell whether he had read the book or not. If he had, he would have found only a few significant alterations in the narrative. Compression was unavoidable in translating Conrad's textual complexity, psychological density and richness of incident to the screen. The book is divided into five parts, and Reed and his scenarist, William Fairchild, jettisoned the final segment altogether. Fundamentally, however, Reed engages the extraordinarily difficult novel with impassioned fidelity to its gloomy subject-matter and corrosive scepticism about human nature. Like many reviewers, Crowther insisted that Reed's movie sat comfortably on the shelf next to *White Cargo* and other tales of white men going to pieces in the tropics. This point of view could not be more intellectually purblind, even semiliterate (an affliction of much film criticism, unfortunately), since Conrad was one of the seminal figures in the tradition Crowther describes. Other than Kipling, who preceded him by a decade or so, Conrad was the first English writer to use the Far East as the locale for modern psychological dramas. Maugham followed Conrad's lead, coarsening his material and belabouring his ironies, and Leon Gordon's *White Cargo* was a further cheapening of the original ambiance created by the great Anglo-Polish master. In contrast to Gordon, Conrad never sentimentalizes his narrative and neither does Reed's adaptation. For Willems, there is no redemption from the consequences of his base passions once he succumbs to them. His dismissal from Hudig's establishment in Macassar leaves him *in extremis*, but Lingard gives him a second chance by taking him to Sambir, a remote village and trading post which only Lingard can navigate his way into; in this tropical purgatory, Willems will, ostensibly, be removed from the temptation he has faced heretofore. But instead of redeeming himself, as the protaganist of a more conventional Far Eastern adventure would, he descends even deeper into the pit, and Reed records his degradation with an uncompromising detachment that Conrad would have admired. The codes that governed the white man's civilization were, for Conrad, a crucial bulwark against what he called the 'immense indifference of things',[8] and indifference that could destroy men psychologically as easily as it annihilated them physically. The bodily death of Kurtz in *Heart of Darkness* comes long after the depravities of the jungle have eroded his soul. For Conrad, who, in his seafaring days, had seen the Congo and all points east at their most savage and uninhibited, restraint and self-discipline were quintessential virtues, and if they could not be coerced from mankind through societal mores, then some devotion to honest toil was a necessary form of protection; certainly it is what saves Marlow in *Heart of Darkness*. Given the English devotion to self-control, it was logical that Conrad became a fervent Anglophile, and no one is better suited to convey the horrifying loss of self-restraint that an Englishman like Carol Reed.

The plot of *Outcast* is soundly constructed, yet the story is largely psychological in emphasis, and it is the passions of the characters which determine the events rather than the other way around. The boredom and restlessness from which Willems suffers in Sambir leaves him vulnerable to temptation and, since there is no money to steal, lust replaces greed, insatiable lust for Aîssa (Kerima), the beautiful daughter of the blind chieftain Badavi (A. V. Bramble). The girl's tribesmen, allies of Lingard's rival Ali (Dharma Emmanuel), are thus able to blackmail Willems into revealing the treacherous route into Sambir, which the old captain has incautiously shown his young protégé. The act of betrayal, often pivotal to Conrad's fiction, was one that also obsessed Reed, as we have seen.

From Willems' first sight of the hypnotic Aîssa to his final realization that she is his doom, Reed's camera follows the course of his swelling passion with silent eloquence and almost no dialogue. His initial glimpse of her is not especially underscored, as it would be in an American film, and later when he watches her move about the native community we are made to feel his desires as part of the general pattern of life in Sambir and of the heated emotions that prevail in the tropics. Although Kerima has no dialogue, she is all that one could hope for in an Aîssa – a dark-eyed beauty who moves about with regal but savage pride and communicates great emotional intensity. As the agent of Willems' downfall, she is completely persuasive.

In comparing the Willems of the novel with same character in the film, Voigt argues that 'Conrad's tale makes Willems a victim of circumstances and his own folly, but the film suggests a more deliberate calculation on his part from the very beginning.' It is undeniable that Conrad's Willems is less uniformly devious than Reed's, but without generating any additional sympathy. In the novel, Willems' suicide attempt following the loss of his job with Hudig is legitimate, whereas in the film it is feigned; it is a ploy designed to penetrate Lingard's seething anger over the scandal and awaken his pity and protectiveness. Some critics have castigated Reed for this change, but the discrepancy they point to is actually too slight to warrant much criticism. In both versions, Willems is essentially a rotter, a monster of egotism and vanity whose every word and deed proclaims his want of moral fibre. Voigt speaks of the 'conflict in Willems' character' as the fulcrum of the novel,[9] yet Conrad never releases the luckless wastrel from the crushing vice of his irony. Indeed, Willems is not allowed a single impulse that is untainted by self-deception or ulterior motives. Reed at least permits Willems an honest psychological struggle over whether to divulge the secret course into Sambir or not. 'Do you think I'm a black-guard?', he replies angrily to Ali when the latter demands the information, and Reed, unlike Conrad, does nothing to undercut these sentiments. Similarly, the movie includes a quiet scene between Willems and Mrs Almayer in which Willems discloses his infatuation with Aîssa in a tone of helpless entrapment that awakens some sympathy in us. Conrad, on the other hand, imposes such a crushing burden of scepticism on Willems – and all the other characters, apart from Lingard – that at times they seem overly manipulated. Conrad's obsessively bleak view of people creates an atmosphere of special pleading, despite his obvious genius.

In the case of Almayer, Reed is entirely faithful to Conrad's depiction of the trader as a self-important prig. The epitome of a respectable burgher, Almayer has felt compelled to transport his stuffy bourgeois life all the way to Malaya, with every bit of pietism, hypocrisy and smugness intact. His cosy domestic environment is made to seem airless and numbing, a miniature Kensington inhabited by his well-corsetted, tea-bearing wife and his shrill daughter Nina (Annabel Morley, Robert Morley's daughter). The scapegrace Willems is repelled by the pompous proprieties of Almayer's home – having abandoned his own in Singapore – and the rancorous scenes between the two men, which are among the strongest in the movie, leave the audience more sympathetic to the sneering Willems. As in the book, Almayer's love for his daughter is depicted as a form of senti-mental egoism. So completely does he identify with her that he converts his own birthday celebration into a kiddie affair, with little paper hats and a big birthday cake with a forest of candles. He seems to have regressed into infantilism, and when Willems shows up – late, of course – we are meant to share his disdain for the proceedings. Nothing could convey this contempt more than the exquisite moment when he lights his cigar in a candle on the cake.

Reed follows Conrad in establishing Almayer's stance towards Willems as one of outraged respectability throughout and in unmasking Almayer as the embodiment of self-interest and heartlessness. His loathing for Willems is fuelled more by anxious fears that Willems may supplant him with Lingard and become a partner than by disgust over Willems' deterioration. Our loyalties gravitate decisively towards Willems when the latter comes to Almayer to beg for a chance to set up his own trading post (presumably as an alternative to betraying Lingard). His physical and emotional condition is pitiable, but Almayer turns him away ruthlessly. When the vengeful Willems returns at the head of the Badavi tribe – following the safe passage into the lagoon – we are not unhappy to see Almayer sewn up in his hammock and swung to and fro over a fire by the sadistic natives.

On the other hand, Lingard has been significantly redrawn from the character who originally came off Conrad's easel. Although the old captain, a recurrent figure in Conrad's fiction, has heroic attributes, there is a *naïveté* to his nature and an egotism as well. He is one of Conrad's 'big children of the sea',[10] men whose unreflective, duty-oriented approach to life protects them from the corruption – be it corporeal or emotional – to which man is so susceptible. Conrad categorizes his subject emphatically: 'To Lingard – simple himself – all things were simple. He seldom read. Books were not much in his way, and he had to work hard navigating, trading . . .' In addition, Lingard has an unwavering conviction of the rectitude of his actions, regarding himself as an unimpeachable lawgiver: 'His deep-seated and immovable conviction that only he – he, Lingard – knew what was good for them [the natives] was characteristic of him . . .' Lingard is viewed through the same scrims of ironic detachment as all the other characters, but unlike Willems, Almayer and the rest of the *Narrenschiff* in *Outcast*, in his case the irony is never scornful. Indeed, Conrad's critique of Lingard is affectionate and approving. The old captain is praised for 'his benevolent instincts', and his assumption that he knows best for the natives is 'not so very far wrong'.[11]

In this regard Conrad's many-sided creation is not reproduced in the movie version, and this is perhaps the most damning discrepancy between the book and the film. It may be the flaw Kael had in mind when she wrote that the Lingard character was a mistake.[12] Reed and Fairchild replace the simplistic, iron-fisted hero of Conrad's intricate imagination with a benign, saintly creature who is a good deal less interesting. We must bear in mind that the decision to adapt *Outcast* was daring to begin with, since the work lacks a traditional hero or even a close approximation of one, as in *Lord Jim* or *Heart of Darkness*. No doubt Reed was hedging his bets somewhat by elevating Lingard to a quasi-heroic stature so that, despite his advanced years and comparatively limited participation in the story, he could be looked on as a surrogate hero whom audiences might venerate. One's disappointment at meeting this altogether stalwart, orthodox Lingard is reduced substantially by the high calibre of Richardson's performance, which satisfies the modest dramatic requirements of the part beautifully. Moreover, Lingard can be seen as another variant of the misguided idealist or simple-souled figure who so commonly inhabits a Reed film. It is his reflexive act of charity which places Willems in the position of temptation that ultimately brings grief to all.

The other important changes that Reed made in Conrad's material were largely matters of omission. No film director could hope to reproduce the fine tissue of psychological analysis that envelops each of the people in the novel. Moreover, even the outward details of their lives had to be concentrated. Gone is the splendidly realized history of the Badavi tribe, about whom swirl the wars, intrigues and jealousies of the various Malay peoples and whose vividly portrayed cast of warriors, chieftains and counsellors occupy fascinating subplots in the novel. Of these figures only Badavi and his adviser Babalatchi (George Coulouris) survive, and only vestigially at that. Still, the outcast of the islands, Conrad's titular hero, is Willems and his story comes triumphantly to life.

Although Conrad's carefully interpolated tales of tribal conflict have been shrunken to a few lines of dialogue, the Malays are nevertheless a palpable presence in *Outcast*. The teeming native life that fills the peripheries of the passionate dramas of the white man are marvellously contrapuntal. Far more than mere local colour, the Malay villagers constitute a culture that is radically different from the English traders. Since the tribesmen are not Sam Jaffees or Eduardo Ciannellis or any of the other ruck of Hollywood character actors in heavy make-up, their cultural distinctness has impact and immediacy. The simple, primitive values of the Malays – martial valour, fealty to parents and tribal elders, etc. – cannot be explored as exhaustively as in the book, but Reed does a good job of sketching them in briskly. Above all, the omnipresent mass of brown-skinned people serves as a constant reminder to us that the white men are an alien presence in Southeast Asia. The natives are onlookers throughout the movie, a silent and sullen audience for the sordid interaction of their great white fathers.

Much of the strength of the movie lies in Reed's ability to reproduce a powerful literary work on the screen, yet the director leaves his own signature on the film as well, both in the elements of *Outcast* he chooses to emphasize and in the new features he introduces. While Lingard is an unequivocally more noble figure in the movie than in the novel, Reed has retained the old captain's *naïveté*, and at times his behaviour calls to mind Reed's other essays in guilelessness and the damage it can cause. Voigt even goes so far as to describe Lingard as one of 'Reed's simple-minded fools who wreaks destruction because he cannot come to terms with the reality around him'.[13] Conrad's conception of this kindly indulgence as a major theme in Lingard's life is foreshortened in the movie, but it is underscored nevertheless. Almayer, who has been humiliated, injured and financially ruined by Willems, rebukes his partner bitterly for earlier instances of magnanimity: 'a mangy dog who bit people and the Chinaman, rescued at sea, who killed half of the crew'.

Another of Reed's trademarks is the inclusion of children as unwitting commentators on adult folly. Transcribing straight from Conrad, Reed and Fairchild lovingly reproduce the sequence of the torment of Almayer in his hammock, accompanied by the merry cries of Nina, who thinks she is at a party. Having previously been taught playfully to denounce Willems as a 'pig', she squeals the same epithet at her father, wholly ignorant of what is actually happening. Reed's own contribution to this aspect of the film, the shocking innocence of a child's perspective on the world of adults, is the 'river boy', an orphan who paddles about in a tiny boat searching for a father. Attaching himself to the unwilling Willems, he trails after the miserable white man, smiling and giggling as Willems plunges further into his self-destructive vortex, a voice of unintended mockery. During the erotically charged, feverish scene in which Willems and Aïssa at last consummate their love, the river boy's lone laughter expands into a chorus of derision as dozens of children cackle in the background, a most ironic accompaniment for the lovers.

Reed's cinematic effects never seemed more brilliant than in *Outcast*. Working with John Wilcox rather than Robert Krasker this time, Reed was able to dazzle the eye just as faultlessly as he had in previous movies. The early scenes are cut with such speed and exactitude that the details of Willems' downfall – the mere prologue for what follows – are thoroughly engrossing themselves and Reed almost makes us wish that the film had lingered over these events a little longer. In every sequence, the camera angles are wonderfully varied, and deep focus is used to good effect to suggest the bas-relief of tribal life behind the white man's tawdry agonies. In one graphic, beautifully composed shot, Reed positions Willems in the foreground, and in the background, Aïssa, the scheming Babalatchi, the aged Badavi and the devious Arab Ali. Only the two scenes in which a ship is guided past treacherous rocks into the lagoon are unsatisfactory, the result of inferior matting techniques.

To see Reed's film after reading Conrad's book is to meet every character perfectly incarnated. And no choice was wiser than casting Morley as Almayer; he inhabits the part with a noisy, self-satisfied officiousness that could scarcely be improved on. So fascinatingly loathsome does Morley make his character that when Willems leads the natives in the vengeful pillage of Almayer's house, we enjoy his humiliation in the hammock. With his weak chin and bulging eyes, he looks like an astonished, terrified guppy.

Trevor Howard, an actor of such consummate professionalism that he may never have given a less than competent performance, is at the top of his form in *Outcast*, which may be his best work as a film actor. It is most striking for the variety and intensity of passion that Howard was able to exhibit, a rare accomplishment from an actor whose countrymen are so noted for their *sangfroid* and emotional reserve. The spectrum of feelings through which Willems passes includes haughty smugness, disdain, ennui, cackling triumph, feverish love, rage, frenzy and morbid despair. His realization of these emotions never misses by a flicker.

The Lingard character has been criticized for its godlike dimension, as we have seen. Richardson has since said that he was not happy with *Outcast* or his performance in it. Still, while the dramatic conception is not as complex as it might have been, Richardson's proud and dignified bearing and sonorous readings animate the old captain quite commendably. Becapped, striding about majestically in his blue and white officer's uniform, Richardson is irresistible.

Outcast is easily the least appreciated of Reed's major movies. Yet the Far Eastern milieu is as lush and reverberant as we could possibly have hoped it would be, and the story is almost never vitiated or debased by commercialism. Other than the softening of Lingard, there is not a single artistic compromise of significance in the movie. Beyond its other laudable attributes, it stands as one of the most powerful evocations of human degradation ever to reach an audience through a commercial medium like film. Its moods are all potent because Reed's direction and Wilcox's camerawork are supplemented by Conrad's dialogue, which Fairchild sensibly and skilfully interpolated into his script. When Willems asks to borrow Almayer's gun before setting off to find Aîssa, Almayer replies venemously: 'Bosh! Hunt deer! It's a gazelle you are after . . . You want gold anklets and silk sarongs for that game – my mighty hunter.' In a scene in which Babalatchi tries to coax the secret of the channel passageway from Willems, he brushes aside the white man's protestations about the insuperable difficulties of the voyage, playing on Willems' vanity with cunning understatement: 'A man like you never says more than he can do.'

By transcribing Conrad's dialogue so faithfully, Reed and Fairchild have also preserved the distinctive rhythms and intonations of each player in the drama. Babalatchi sustains the same key throughout – a low murmur of deviousness – while Almayer is a consistent boom of pomposity and Willems alternates between passionate outpourings over Aîssa and the dagger-like scorn with which he habitually punctures Almayer. The only character who achieves true nobility of languages is, of course, the Olympian Lingard. After the catastrophe that Willems brings down on Sambir, the seaman philosophizes in dour, appropriately nautical metaphors: 'Fouled like a tangled rigging on a dirty night, yet one must see it clear for running before going below for good.' The vigour of Lingard's dialogue culminates in his spell-binding denunciation of Willems, a rush of soaring poetry that leaves us as stunned as its victim:

> No promise of yours is any good to me . . . I'm going to take your future into my own hands. You shall stay here. You are not fit to go among people. Who could suspect, who could guess, who could imagine what is in you? I couldn't. You are my mistake. I shall hide you here. If I let you out, you will go among unsuspecting men and lie and cheat and steal for some money or for some woman. I don't choose to shoot you. It would be the safest way. But I won't. Do not expect me to forgive you. To forgive one must first have been angry and then contemptuous. There's nothing in me now – no anger, no disappointment. To me you are not Willems, the man I thought much of and helped, the man who was my friend. You are not a human being to be forgiven or destroyed. You're a bitter thought, something without bodily shape. You are my shame.

In his next film, *The Man Between* (1953), Reed seemed to be trying to pull in his horns. The brilliant, creative boldness of *Outcast* had not paid off critically or financially, and his own unhappy verdict on the movie was that the story material was essentially 'intractable'.[14] In *The Man Between*, he retreated to his biggest hit, *The Third Man*, to rummage about for new ideas, to see what could be recycled. Some scholars characterize the script as an original screenplay (by Walter Ebert and Harry Kurnitz), others as Kurnitz's adaptation of a novel by Ebert, *Susanne in Berlin*. (The book is unobtainable in the US.) Whatever the case, neither man could be expected to equal Greene's achievement. Reed's attempt at creative backtracking led him to a setting – ravaged postwar Berlin – that unmistakably paralleled the decadent Viennese locale of *The Third Man*. Like so many of Reed's movies, the exteriors for *The Man Between* were shot on location. A meticulously realistic backdrop was always one of Reed's goals, and he filmed some scenes a mere ten minutes from the East German Volkspolizei, who constitute an important feature of the movie. Interviewed during the shooting of the film,

Reed explained that he was filming in such close proximity to the tension-frought checkpoint because he hoped to 'convey something that was not visual – the jittery feeling that pervades the area'.[15] In addition, the demolished buildings that he wanted to use as a symbol of German devastation in the aftermath of the war were primarily located in the Russian sector.

To reviewers in 1953, Reed's attempt at making another *Third Man* was more mechanical than inspired. Crowther accused the film of being 'unmercifully tangled in melodramatic cliches', though he conceded that it did create a 'feeling of tenseness'.[16] *Cue* reproved Reed for the 'pat pattern of the story',[17] Alpert of *Saturday Review* thought the film was 'less satisfactory' than the director's other movies,[18] while, mysteriously enough, *Variety* was aggravated because of an 'unduly imaginative plot', and predicted that the presence of three name players – James Mason, Claire Bloom and Hildegarde Neff – might generate popular interest in the film.[19] *Variety*'s prophecy was incorrect.

As in *The Third Man*, the city is an integral part of the drama, a recognizable force, as well as a symbol of the lives it encapsulates. The demoralization of life in a defeated and pillaged nation is suggested vividly by Desmond Dickinson's camera, which dispassionately surveys the decay of bombed-out buildings, the vacant lots and the omnipresent rubble of Berlin. The citizens are a desperate breed, with moods ranging from desolate to cynical to agitated. Naturally corruption is as intrinsic a feature of life in Berlin as in Vienna. The plot deals with political factions who traffic in human life, which is presented as one manifestation of the frenzied intrigues between East and West, whose trench-coated agents kidnap people from one another's zones. The point of view through which all this is perceived is that of Suzanne (Bloom), an impulsive but demure English girl whose arrival in Britain to visit her brother Martin (Geoffrey Toone) and his German wife Bettina (Neff) sets the story in motion. Through her eyes we see the squalor of the city, as the camera, casually inspecting the airport on Suzanne's arrival, discovers a boy picking through garbage and a malevolent-looking clown. The heroine is picked up by Bettina, who soon establishes herself as another victim of the city; she alternates between states of depression and nervousness, though we aren't told why. Perhaps the teenage boy (Dieter Kraus) whom Suzanne notices spying on her house has something to do with it. Reed scatters such details here and there in his film.

On the movie's melodramatic level, all these displays of tension and decay function as portents, informing the moviegoer that something is up. Berlin, like Vienna, is too dangerous a city to be merely a giant municipal ward for battle-scarred Germans. As *The Third Man* had its enigmatic Harry Lime, so *The Man Between* has a shadowy figure named Ivo (Mason, with a not terribly convincing German accent). He is acquainted with Bettina, who is afraid of him for reasons that are not explained for quite some time, and he is highly attentive to Suzanne, again for reasons that are unclear. In *The Third Man*, Lime had three sinister confederates; here they are compressed into one bulky Berliner, Halendar (Aribert Waescher), who typifies the sleaziness of his city as much as Kurtz and Winkel typified theirs. Like them, he also is involved in racketeering, though the nature of the crimes is withheld much longer than in *The Third Man*. Eventually we learn that Halendar is blackmailing Ivo, who has a criminal past, and is forcing him to aid in a kidnapping attempt on Kastner (Ernest Schroeder), whose success at spiriting refugees out of East Berlin has outraged the Communist authorities. To do his part, Ivo has his own blackmail victim, Bettina, who was once Ivo's wife and is legally still married to him.

As in earlier Reed films, there is a *naif* at the centre, or near the centre, of the action in *The Man Between* – Suzanne, whose ingenuous, school-girl approach to misery and evil seems incongruous in postwar Berlin. She is attracted to the suave, cosmopolitan Ivo and the two engage in a number of dialogues in which youthful idealism, on the one side, and mature scepticism on the other clash again and again. Suzanne is the product of a victorious nation, one that was not even invaded, while Ivo, a former lawyer who is now a minor criminal, is the disenchanted son of a brutally defeated people.

In other hands, the conflict between Suzanne and Ivo might have had the throb of true drama, but Reed doesn't ever give it much energy or passion. What intellectual and dramatic excitement does exist is dissipated by Ivo's conversion to goodness. Where Lime sacrifices a woman to save himself, Ivo does just the reverse. At great personal risk, he helps Suzanne escape from Halendar's lair after she has been mistaken for Bettina and kidnapped. The latter part of the film is a familiar drama of flight as the two – now lovers, more or less – try frantically to avoid capture by the East Germans as they slip in and out of a number of grimy refuges on their way to West Berlin and freedom. In a very uncharacteristic moment of sentimentality, Reed turns his hero inside out in order to have him lay down his life to save Suzanne. It is an act of stock heroism, the synthetic movie-style salvation attained by scoundrels like Johnny Eager in the film of the same name and by the John Garfield character in *Castle on the Hudson*. It is illuminating, in an oblique way, to note that whereas betrayal was a crucial factor in the psychological and narrative framework of each Reed film from *Odd Man Out* onward, here it is replaced by self-sacrifice, which sugars and softens the dramatic impact.

This failure of nerve and imagination in the handling of Ivo is all too typical of *The Man Between*, which seems like a sketch for a good movie, a decent first draft. Unhappily, the scenario mainly serves to reveal the extent to which Reed was dependent on the quality of the script he was given, regardless of his own sometimes enormous creative input. In this respect, he was no different than most other directors; yet after a decade or so of increasingly impressive films, movies that displayed a skilful entertainer as well as a man of great sensibility, Reed had directed a film in which, despite creative control, he had delivered an unfulfilling work. Kurnitz simply did not have the sensitivity, the flair and the sneaky wit of Graham Greene. A screenwriter with twenty years' experience, he had also written detective novels under the name Marco Page. As a scenarist, however, his talent was most abundant in comedy (*See Here, Private Hargrove, Once More With Feeling*) and mystery-comedy (*The Shadow of the Thin Man*), not in the sort of hard-nosed thrillers which depend on firmness of construction and a powerful sense of ambiance. Moreover, a philosophical thriller such as Reed conceived required a poetry of despair that was more indigenous to the war-weary European imagination than the buoyant, well-paid *volksgeist* of Hollywood.

The Man Between is partially redeemed by a handful of Reed-isms here and there. One of the scenes between Suzanne and Ivo occurs in an ice-skating rink and is cleverly staged. The bicycle spy, an adolescent creeping through the web of adult treachery, was by this time a commonly observed trademark of the director's work. Reed's theatrical side is reflected in an operatic sequence, an excerpt from Strauss's opera *Salome*. The scene is important to the plot, and at the same time subtly juxtaposes the biblical decadence of the opera with contemporary German seaminess. Reed even tries for a distant echo of Lime's watered-down penicillin and the hospital sequence in *The Third Man*: Martin is a doctor who treats East German refugees who, presumably through the callous behaviour of the Communists, are suffering from tuberculosis. By general agreement, the best effect in the movie is the villain's snow-encrusted car, which, like some frightening primordial monster, stalks the unsuspecting Suzanne and finally swallows her up.

After *The Man Between*, Reed shot off in yet another direction with *A Kid For Two Farthings*, an adaptation of Wolf Manko-witz's novel of English ghetto life. A whimsical and poetic fable with an overlay of Jewish folklore, *Kid* has struck many critics as an odd choice for Reed, who had made his reputation with thrillers and films of social consciousness. Still, the story's hero is a six-year-old boy with an absent father; it is told from his point of view and contains yet another pet. Furthermore, Reed's work had always been suffused with the ideals of cultural pluralism, a cosmopolitanism that transcended the petty hates and parochialism that characterize most European nations. As he narrowed his focus to Northern Irish Catholic society in *Odd Man Out*, he turned his gaze inward at another English subculture in *Kid*. Then, too, the climax of the movie is a wrestling sequence that Reed treats with the showmanly orientation that was often one of his central virtues.

Exteriors for *Kid* were shot in London's Petticoat Lane, a bustling East End marketplace comparable to New York's Lower Eastside. The scenes that required controlled studio conditions were shot on an excellent reconstruction of an East End street at Shepperton Studios. *Kid* was Reed's first colour film and his choice, he said, was strictly aesthetic. The East End, he commented, 'was not a good setting in black and white for what is really a gay sensitive story'.[20] The quality of Wilfred Shingleton's colour, like many strictly technical aspects of European cinema, was not up to American standards, but a more serious problem in *Kid* is that Reed cast his movie with a somewhat reckless abandon that is quite uncharacteristic of him; it's almost as if the bazaar atmosphere of Petticoat Lane had inebriated him and set him rushing from shop to stall to booth in his collection of performers. The leading role, a boy named Joe, went to a young unknown, Jonathan Ashmore. Other parts were filled by accomplished British character actors, including David Kossoff as Kandinsky, a tailor; Celia Johnson as Joanna, Joe's mother; Lou Jacobi as Blackie Isaacs, a fight manager; Brenda de Banzie as 'Lady Ruby', a store manager. Unfortunately, Mankowitz's story called for a wrestler, Shmule, which presented problems in a nation with a notable paucity of brawn. Reed's solution was to hire Joe Robinson, a former heavyweight wrestling champ with some modest show business experience. Shmule girlfriend Sonia was no more dispensable than he, and whether through commercial pressure or a seizure of poor judgement, Reed gave this role to Diana Dors, a junior edition of Marilyn Monroe and one of the lesser sex goddesses of the 1950s.

Released in England in 1955 and in the United States in 1956, *Kid* was greeted with mixed notices. Alpert thought the film was 'warm, mellow, sentimental'.[21] *Variety* pronounced the picture 'off-beat entertainment, rich in color and atmosphere'.[22] Crowther, on the other hand, had some praise for Reed's 'compassion for children', but felt that the director's 'sweet conceit cannot stand the stickiness of Sam's and Sonia's romance . . .'[23] In the *New Yorker*, McCarten decided that the movie wasn't 'up to the standard Mr. Reed set in his previous exercise in juvenilia',[24] and *Time* found the film's 'flavor too sweet'.[25] The public was lukewarm in both England and America. Although *Kid* is a thoroughly obscure movie today, it does have one formidable advocate, Pauline Kael, who has termed it a film that 'achieves enough small miracles to lift it to an unfamiliar realm . . .'[26]

It is easy to understand the visual potential that Reed perceived in *Kid*. The East End setting offered a teaming, bursting little universe of colour, drama and bizarre sights and faces. Thus the director had another outlet for his naturalistic impulses, and he and his cameraman, Edward Scaife this time, stuffed every frame with lusty, Hogarthian fullness and ethnic vitality. The street cries are heard over the credits and almost immediately we are submerged in the throngs of pedestrians who surge through the streets, amidst pushcarts, open air markets, bellowing peddlars and shopkeepers. An old Jewish man whom Reed noticed one day while scouting locations, Meier Leibovitch, is inserted as Reb Mendel Gramophone, a character who sits reading a book in front of his 'record store'. Meanwhile, 'Ice' Berg (Sidney James) peddles jewellery and an Indian fortune teller (Derek Sidney) plies his oracular craft. And so on.

Once the action starts, Reed sees to it that the background of most of the scenes is enriched by local colour set down in strokes like the opening sequence. Much of the time, however, the backdrop seems more absorbing than the plot, which despite all the strenuous good efforts of Mankowitz and Reed usually suggests more will than imagination, more creative intentions than actual accomplishment. Singer or Malamud might have been able to do something memorable with the story's premise – under the influence of a philosophical tailor, a boy imagines his goat is a unicorn who can grant any wish – but Mankowitz is unable to summon up the haunting power that such a tale requires. From Disraeli on, Anglo-Jewish writers have never had the same success with ethnic subject-matter as American Jews, perhaps because their roots in Jewish history and culture aren't strong enough or because an overpoweringly homogeneous national culture like England's prevents such roots.

Whatever the explanation, Mankowitz's novel, in which he had complete command of his material, lacks the enchantment he strove for. The title, which derives from a Jewish song ('One kid, one kid, which my father bought for two farthings') is intriguing and fittingly authentic, and the accumulation of sociological detail is certainly effective. ('He watched people eating eels and shaking vinegar on them, and then looked back at the large wide slices of red melon with glossy black seeds bursting from them.'[27]) Disappointingly, though, the bittersweet folktale that is summoned out of this *mise-en-scène* is too anaemic to take hold of our imagination. This deficiency is compounded in the film by the unhappy decision to convert the almost exclusively Jewish characters in the novel into Gentiles. Thus the wrestler, Shmule, is baptized Sam and Joe's mother Rebecca becomes Joanna; Sonia is allowed to retain her name, but no hint of Judaism is attached to the character. Of the principal players, only Kossoff remains Jewish. The effect is to strip the Petticoat Lane ambiance of much of its colour and energy and to impair the ethnic credibility of the drama. The scenes between little Joe and Kandinsky (another of Reed's substitute fathers) are the most engaging, attaining a wistful, poignant mood as the old man schools the boy with a mixture of realism and shrewdly knowing fantasy. The boy's unhappy relationship with his pets, which always die, is touching in an idiosyncratic way, as is his delusion that the 'unicorn' can perform miracles.

The fantasy element in *Kid* is supposed to be preserved through a delicate balance between the reality of the boy's current pet – not only not a unicorn but an enfeebled goat at that – and the prayers that seem to be answered through the boy's invocation of the unicorn's powers. In time-honoured tradition, the magic always has a naturalistic explanation, but we never really know if supernatural forces have been at work or only the vicissitudes of human fate. In the case of *Kid*, there is insufficient ingenuity in the balance between the magical and the realistic developments. (Example: Kandinsky longs for an automatic steam press, and, after Joe wishes for one, someone recalls that a nearby company may have a used press to sell.) The climactic sequence is a wrestling match between Sam and the sadistic giant Python (Primo Carnera) in which Sam takes a terrible battering for half the contest and then, infused with power by the unicorn, demolishes his mountain-sized adversary easily. The novel simply gives him the victory through superior skill and speed, but evidently something more spectacular was needed for a major action sequence in a movie. Naturalistically, the course that the fight takes in the film seems illogical, while the exhibition of supernaturalism is conveyed flatly, without poetry or dark power of any kind. Behind the myth that *Kid* dramatizes lies the simple but meaningful notion that boyhood is a time when mythical beasts seem possible but that growing up means surrendering the glorious hallucinations of youth. Hence, the death of the unicorn at the end of *Kid*, though saddening, is thematically justified. To grow up is to enter the imperfect world of adulthood, where everyone has feet of clay. In the rough and tumble realities of Petticoat Lane, fragile creatures like unicorns cannot survive. 'Unicorns can't grow in Fashion Street', says Kandinsky, 'but boys have to.'

The portions of *Kid* that spring to life do so only briefly, like an unconscious patient coming around occasionally. The rest of the time we have to contend with comatose performances like those of Robinson and Dors, two of the least endearing lovers in the history of the screen. Their personalities can be summed up anatomically: she in her peroxided hair and buxom figure and he in his biceps. In the novel Shmule and Sonia are prudently subordinated to Joe's story, but Reed allows them to usurp the latter segments of the movie. As for Carnera, he is a better actor than Robinson, yet Reed seems to have had difficulty adjusting the tone of his performance, and it veers uncertainly between villainy and buffoonery. Celia Johnson, whom Reed had introduced to the screen in *A Letter From Home* and who had made such an impact in *Brief Encounter*, is wasted in the lacklustre part of Joanna, a woman waiting for her husband to summon her and their son to join him in South Africa. Neither she nor the Etonian-sounding Ashmore have accents that are appropriate to their milieu. Kossoff, who had enjoyed a number of successes in Jewish parts before *Kid*, gives the one exemplary performance in *Kid* among the leading actors. Sensibly, he underplays his warm-hearted, wise old codger, giving it dramatic cogency that could not otherwise have been extracted from Mankowitz's thin conceptions. Kossoff's work is all the more remarkable for the fact that he was only in his mid-thirties when he played the part. When we look beyond Kossoff, however, *Kid* is certainly the low point in Reed's long string of flawlessly acted films. The deterioration in the calibre of performance that he was able to elicit from his cast is sudden and terribly wrenching.

In the three films that followed *The Third Man*, Reed set out to explore further the boundaries of his capacity as a film-maker. The results were uneven. *Outcast of the Islands* is an achievement of a high order – and in many ways a different achievement from the works that went before – but it reveals a rupture between the artist and the showman which had never before been discernible in Reed's work. He had always inhabited a cinematic region in which intelligence and imagination could exist alongside popular appeal. With *Outcast* he allowed his enthusiasm for the material to carry him beyond the perimeters of mass appeal; the story was simply too downbeat and its main characters too unsympathetic (at least in conventional movie terms) to attract a large audience. An artist working in a popular medium like film, especially a devastatingly expensive one, simply cannot allow his box office performance to sag; however he might wish it otherwise, these are the realities of his profession. No doubt it was Reed's awareness of these realities that prompted him to backpeddle from the boldness of *Outcast* to the apparent security of *The Man Between* (even the title declares the work's indebtedness to the director's greatest hit). In his next project, *A Kid For Two Farthings*, he attempted to compromise between the

new and the old, the experimental and the time-honoured. The
result was decidedly muddled. He selected a wonderfully fresh
subject, Anglo-Jewish life, one which heretofore had completely
eluded the camera's eye; but unhappily, his rendering of it
seemed largely counterfeit, particularly in the light of his normal
obsession with social authenticity. The attempt at a rich narrative merger of folk poetry, realism, fantasy and old-fashioned
movie ingredients failed and the decision to put two singularly
unappetizing lovers at the centre of the story was disastrous. By
1955, Reed's art was beginning to look as palsied as the baby
goat in his film, and he desperately needed a method of resusci-
tating it.

9   Working in Hollywood

The death of Alexander Korda in January 1956 deprived Reed of
a valuable patron as well as a dear friend. Nevertheless, with his
still lofty reputation, he could presumably have gone on working
in England, though opportunities would have been far rarer, as
we can readily deduce from the slim *oeuvres* of most British
directors who did remain at home. Like most of his contemporaries, Reed saw that, with Alex gone, the prospects for regular
employment on adequately financed movies were far better in
America than in Britain.

Although it is a critical commonplace that Reed's work took
an abrupt nosedive as soon as his 'American period' began, it is
possible, without being at all perverse, to argue just the opposite.
That Reed might rehabilitate himself in Hollywood, a zone in
which atrophy is thought to be the normal process for a distinguished European director, would probably not have occurred to
anyone in the 1950s, yet this is what happened. Since Reed
confided so little in his interviews, we can only speculate as
to his motivations when he signed to direct *Trapeze* for Hecht–
Lancaster in 1956. With two flops in a row, neither offset by
emphatic critical praise, perhaps he was eager for a gilt-edged
property, a film with as high a guarantee of success as possible.
Trapeze was a big-budget Hollywood film set in one of show
business's favourite milieus – the circus – shot in colour and
Cinemascope and ornamented with two of the major American
stars of the day, Burt Lancaster and Tony Curtis, plus a sexy
European star (Gina Lollobrigida), making her American debut.
Whatever Reed was thinking when he accepted the offer, the
decision seems to have been pivotal to his career; from 1956 on,
he worked exclusively on American or American-financed movies – to the detriment of his art, in the opinion of some.

With a $4 million budget, *Trapeze* was one of the most expen-
sive films of the year and was shot on location at the Cirque d'
Hiver in Paris. For added verisimilitude, a number of celebrated

European circus performers of the day were incorporated into the backdrop of the story. In archetypally sumptuous Hollywood fashion, it was found necessary to hire a whole circus troupe in order to be certain of obtaining the services of three of its acts. In circus-crazy Paris, it was even possible to attract 900 000 Frenchmen to watch the stars of *Trapeze* wafted through the streets on a float.

The reviews of the film were mixed, though even the friendliest critics, explicitly or implicitly, labelled the movie a big commercial extravaganza, enjoyable but empty. In England, the *Manchester Weekly* commented that 'Sir Carol's work comes alive', despite the fact that the story 'is too simple, silly and melodramatic'.[1] *Variety* hailed the movie's 'honest sawdust flavor' and 'high-flying screen entertainment',[2] while *Look*[3] and *Life*[4] devoted major picture-spreads to the film. According to *Time*, there were 'plenty of exciting sideshows'[5] in Reed's picture, but its script was a 'barrel of soggy tanbark'. Crowther was the harshest of the major critics, condemning the movie for a 'dismally obvious and monotonous story' and its 'bleakly two-dimensional characters . . .'[6]

Moviegoers were generally entranced and when the cash registers stopped ringing, *Trapeze* showed a profit of $8 million, a figure which emerged when the scenarist and novelist Daniel Fuchs sued the producers for allegedly plagiarizing their script from his short story, 'The Daring Young Man on the Flying Trapeze'. Hecht, Hill and Lancaster settled out of court for $50 000, though insisting to the end that their source was Max Catto's novel *The Killing Frost*.

Even if *Trapeze* is indebted to the Fuchs story, its major source is certainly *The Killing Frost*, a sprawling potboiler by the once-popular Catto, an English writer whose real name was Max Finkell. A steamy, old-fashioned melodrama in six parts, the novel relates the tragic history of Tino Orsini, from his youth in New York City to his career as a flyer in a European circus to his trial and execution for the murder of his estranged lover, Sarah Linden. The last fifth of the book is devoted to the sleuthwork of one Father Francis, a latter-day Father Brown, who exonerates Tino by locating the real killer, Mike Ribble, a fellow aerialist for whom Sarah abandoned Tino. In an interesting twist, it was Tino whom Ribble actually wanted, though the homosexuality motif remains submerged. When he is exposed at last, Ribble commits suicide and, in a fatigued attempt at a drumroll of pulp tragedy, Catto writes about the end of the 'crazy, meaningless dance' of the three lives that have been extinguished.[7]

Reed and his screenwriters transformed the English Sarah into an Italian named Lola so as to accomodate Lollobrigida and abbreviated the bulky tale considerably, dramatizing only the circus episodes (about one-third of the novel) and lightening its morbid tone. Though the stormy love triangle is presented almost verbatim, it does not end in grief; rather Ribble (Lancaster) and Lola are united in the end, and Tino (Curtis) achieves an unparalleled professional triumph on the high wire and a contract from John Ringling North with which to console himself.

The public's enthusiasm for *Trapeze* is a tribute to the professionalism that went into the movie, an expertly manufactured entertainment which is also tinted here and there by Reed's sensibility and artistry. The screenplay, by James R. Webb (with uncredited assistance from Wolf Mankowitz), orchestrates a number of different elements – romance and adventurous displays of acrobatic brilliance; a father–son relationship; a brooding hero, a sleek-skinned juvenile and a sumptuous leading lady; a do-or-die climax in the main ring under a crowd-packed big top. Reed and his screenwriters steer the plot through its tangles, its rising and falling action, its complications, with unfailing attention to plausibility. One can reject a supercharged, gussied up vehicle like *Trapeze*, but having once accepted it on its own terms, the movie is hard to fault. Much of the story turns on self-serving intrigues – the efforts of Lola to infiltrate the aerial act of Mike Ribble and Tino Orsini; Ribble's attempt to manipulate Lola's feelings for him in such a way as to free Tino from her clutches and ensure that he will be a great trapeze artist; the plan of the circus owner, Bouglione (Thomas Gomez), to replace Ribble with another catcher. The welter of passions, intrigues and jealousies of the three aerialists lead inexorably to the final episode in which Tino performs a 'triple somersault' under the most hair-raising conditions. The rivalry over Lola's affections that erupts between the two men is standard-issue hokum, yet it cleverly invests the sequence with an extra layer of emotionalism which is much needed. For one thing, it permits a suspense-building delay while Ribble tries to argue Tino into attempting the deadly stunt, highly desirable in view of the swiftness with which the test will be over once undertaken. The feat also presents Curtis with the opportunity to eclipse the now-hated Ribble, whose own try at executing a triple years before left him maimed. Down below, another turn of the screw is administered by Bouglione, the circus owner, who orders that the safety net be removed on the assumption – incorrect but credible – that this will dissuade Ribble and Tino. Thus does Reed's film, in its commercial fashion, mesh character and action beautifully in every segment.

Although *Trapeze* cannot be excavated too much for the buried gold that lay beneath the surface of Reed's other films, it has intriguing dimensions to it. As movie heroes go, Ribble is compelling, the most interesting person in *Trapeze*. There is an inherent dramatic loss in the scrapping of the homosexual theme (it was unavoidable, given the era), as in the smoothing out of the rough edges that Catto gave his character, a fairly insensitive brute. Still, there are compensating gains. Whereas the Ribble of the novel was crippled in a meaningless accident involving a circus animal, Lancaster's Ribble suffered his injury in the pursuit of his art. Maimed during an attempt to execute a triple, he becomes a pop version of that venerable archetype, the crippled artist; the tradition extends all the way back to the mythological figure, Hephaestus, the limping god and patron of the decorative arts. In Ribble's case, his injury excludes him from his own art. Naturally his damaged leg is emblematic of an inner wound. 'Here is where he's smashed', say Max the Dwarf (Max Puleo), tapping his chest. The internal laceration is more serious than his physical ailment, since it cuts him off from human communion.

There is nothing new in this conception of course – Mel Ferrer, the crippled dancer in *Lili*, had embodied it only a few years before – but Reed sees to it that the device is played for all its worth. Lancaster, a former circus performer, had longed to make a circus film for years and was able to achieve a conviction that lifts the role above its pedestrian foundations. Reed directs him with complete commitment to the material, the only way *Trapeze* could succeed. Lancaster's athletic, muscular appearance – his intense physicality – and his lame, halting movements create an effective tension. In the same way, Reed gets double duty out of Lancaster's cane, an obvious symbol of his deformity but also a tool for adventure in the incident-oriented plot.

Following an episode in which Lancaster courageously coaxes an escaped lion back in its cage, losing his cane in the process, Curtis tails an old lady who is returning the cane to Ribble and learns the truth about Ribble's relationship with Lola, a revelation that is crucial to the movie's climax.

There are other levels to Ribble as well. His bitterness is not only personal but aesthetic as well. He is enraged by the debasement of his former profession, which is now bedizened with gimmickry, such as the floridly costumed sexuality that Lola forces him to introduce into his flying act. 'When the circus was real, flying was a religion', he says broodingly. 'Now what have you got? Pink lights and ballet girls . . . and blue sawdust.' The money-minded Bouglione is singled out as a representative culprit. There is an unmistakably anti-feminine bias to Lancaster's philosophy, and in the end, when he has his way finally, there are only daring young men on the flying trapeze; Lola watches anxiously from below.

Lurking behind the Ribble character is the old notion of artists as residents of their own private universe, gifted freaks who are a world unto themselves. Reed never strives for more than a Hollywood-pop exposition of this theme, but on that plane he handles the motif well. The circus people frequent a bistro significantly named the Cafe Des Artistes, where even the lights over the bar sway like a trapeze. Shortly after a dialogue between Curtis and Lancaster in the cafe, they walk away down the street on their hands, talking away animatedly. This simple allegory of the artistic life is given its fullest expression in the endless schooling to which Lancaster subjects Curtis when he finally agrees to teach him a triple. The self-discipline and struggle, the tireless effort that go into mastering any art form, is exultantly conveyed in those training sessions. Reed helps us take the dream of a triple seriously by communicating the anguish that accompanies this conquest of space and gravity and by letting his performers speak in an aerialist's argot that achieves authenticity without thickening into an opaque jargon. 'Swingbar hit your shins, didn't it?', Ribble calls out to Tino after a mishap. 'Always happens when you break too late.' At another point in the long, intense training sessions, he delivers stern, urgent instructions: 'Don't bend your knees. Now break – let your feet come up! Don't force it. Take a natural set!'

Reed is also adept at suggesting mild analogies between the

aerialists' performance and their private lives. In life, as on the high wire, Lola's strength is her sexuality, and her relationship to the two men is devious and problem-ridden; she is a *femme fatale* playing the two off against each other. She insinuates herself into their psyches as she did into their act. Ribble, the sturdy catcher, and Curtis, the talented but untried flyer, play out similar roles as men.

The inherent theatricality of his subject-matter seems to have excited Reed's sensibility. Here, after all, was the greatest show on earth. Apart from this feature of the movie, however, there are not many of Reed's characteristic flourishes in *Trapeze*. Children do not figure in the story, nor is there a true *naif* like Holly Martins, unless a vestige of one can be perceived in Tino, whose gullibility towards Lola causes difficulties for himself and Ribble. Reed's imagination seems to have been exceptionally stirred by the possible combination of circus colourfulness and naturalism. The *mise-en-scène* in *Trapeze* is as thick as sawdust: in the background of the story, Max the Dwarf plays his harmonica and tells anxious jokes about gaining height; workers are glimpsed feeding the seals; a clown performs on a saxophone; the owner wanders about with a chimp in tow. But one of Reed's best touches in *Trapeze* isn't even concerned with the circus but with a withered old lady who merely harmonizes with the grotesque atmosphere under the Big Top. Enquiring about Ribble's whereabouts, Tino is told, 'Follow the old woman.' Subsequently, in a small bar, having delivered the cane to Ribble, the woman passes Tino idling in front of a portrait of a girl and says, 'She is very beautiful, is she not? That was me and not so long ago.' The line, which is completely unexpected, pronounces judgement on the vanity of human wishes and the transcience of the beauty Ribble and Tino are so ardently pursuing. That the remark is delivered in French, a throwaway, is in itself evidence of what an idiosyncratic talent Reed was.

In the other artistic departments, Reed was ably served by art director Rino Mondellini and cinematographer Robert Krasker, with whom the director had been reunited after an hiatus of several films. Initially Krasker had a problem with double images created by the high velocity of the trapeze artists, but having solved that, he achieved a fluid series of images, photographing the aerialists from every conceivable angle, his lens pursuing them with properly vertiginous results. With Krasker's help, Reed had found a way to make the vast empty spaces of Cinemascope visually arresting. Malcolm Arnold's score is undistinguished, but fortunately he had help from Johann Strauss, whose 'Blue Danube', with its swooping, graceful melodies, is the only musical equivalent one can imagine for the high wire artists the film celebrates.

The popularity of *Trapeze*, one of the major commercial successes of Reed's career, lifted his credibility in the dollar-conscious eyes of American film executives to whom he had been forced to mortgage his talents. He was now in a position to promote himself for ambitious projects, projects that ideally would balance commercial appeal with artistry at least as well as *Trapeze* had. In 1958, Reed had optioned Graham Greene's new novel, *Our Man in Havana*, a property with which he felt an understandable affinity and which, in view of his previous collaborations with Greene, obviously held great promise. Before *Havana* could be launched, however, Reed accepted an offer to direct a film over which he was unlikely to be able to exert the kind of creative control he had in his best work.

In the mid 1950s, the American screenwriter Carl Foreman, whose credits included *High Noon* and *Champion*, found himself blacklisted and had to earn his living by writing anonymously. In the late 1950s, he was at last able to persuade Columbia Pictures to finance film properties which he would not only write under his own name but also produce. Foreman, who fancied himself a highbrow, wanted to christen his resurrected career with a blue ribbon production rather than the standard escape fare which, for the most part, had been his forte. His choice was *The Key*, adapted from *Stella*, Jan De Hartog's Second World War novella about the extraordinarily courageous tugboats that went to the aid of stricken cargo ships. (Paired with another De Hartog novella, *Stella* was published in the United States as *The Distant Shore*.) The story appealed to Foreman for a number of reasons. As a Second World War veteran himself, he could readily identify with the subject-matter. Moreover, De Hartog's novel offered an attractive symmetry between crowd-pleasing action sequences and a spectrum of eerie, allegorical features. The Dutch hero would, of course, be converted to an American and the part would go to a major star, so as to satisfy the

domestic audiences; but at the same time, the story's European
flavour, and its rousing testimonial to the naval heroism of the
British and the Dutch, would make the film appealing to Euro-
peans. The final insurance policy for *The Key* would be to hire a
distinguished European director, though not an overly arty one,
someone, who could add the cachet of his name to the film
without diminishing its box office potential. In short, someone
like Sir Carol Reed.

Completed for an autumn release, *The Key* was a major production and promoted with appropriate care. Because of the
film's international quality, Foreman persuaded Columbia to
open it around the world simultaneously rather than following
the accepted practice of exploiting the American market first.
The American premier came a month afterwards, and if the
reviews had been an index of the movie's probable popularity, it
should have been a blockbuster. *Variety* anticipated another 'b.o.'
winner for Reed and Foreman and characterized it as 'very
nearly a great film'.[8] For Crowther, it was a 'good film but not
the great one it might have been'[9] and for *Saturday Review*'s John
Carden a movie with 'impressive visual counterpoint . . .'[10] *Time*
peered into the film's subconscious, to detect the 'glinting corpus
of a hero myth – the story of the fight with a dragon, the release
of a captive, the awakening of a sleeping beauty', making it 'one
of the year's most strongly affecting pictures'.[11] The frivolous
McCarten led the tiny group of dissenting critics, chastising
Reed and Foreman for being superficial and noting that it was
'at its best when it takes us out upon the troubled briny . . .'[12]
Despite the generally warm notices, however, America did not
take to *The Key*. Its domestic gross was a feeble $2.2 million, and
only the handsome European return, $7 million, allowed the
movie to turn a slight profit. Today it is yet another forgotten
film of Reed's.

Looking back to 1958, it is easier to comprehend the indifference of American audiences than the enthusiasm of the Euro-
peans. The film's components fail to cohere, though individually
some are praiseworthy. Much of the difficulty lies in the original
material, which simply resists even the best efforts of a Carol
Reed. The core of De Hartog's story is the surreal tragedy of
Stella, an English girl whose lover, a tugboat captain, perished
in a rescue attempt. After his death, another seaman shows up at
Stella's apartment and, instead of sending him away, she elects

to replace her dead lover with this newcomer. Since the mortality rate of tugboat captains is extremely high, Stella's apartment is soon a revolving door of lovers. Although warm and animated towards each of these men, she clearly sees them uniformly, as symbols of something abstract, not personal. The love story alternates with thrilling, authoritatively detailed accounts of naval rescue operations, and at last one of these brings the hero to a fateful reckoning. Attacked by a Nazi submarine, the hero rams into it and somehow survives. Realizing that it was the 'innocence' of the rescue-oriented tugboat commanders that made Stella 'love us all as if we were one' and that he has now 'joined the murderers', he reluctantly surrenders his key to another man.[13] Later he has a change of heart and rushes to Stella's apartment, where his terrifying presence – he is now an agent of the reality from which Stella is protecting herself – induces hysteria. She leaves for London and the hero's final, crushing disillusionment comes when he learns that the woman he loved, apparently restored to sanity, is calmly writing to a boyfriend back home.

The novel suffers from misdirection, drifting moorlessly between fantasy and reality. The realistic setting, with its meticulously specific wartime trappings, makes the wispy tale of Stella seem implausible instead of poetically charged and cloud-borne as intended. The notion of a sensitive woman escaping from the ravages of war into a dream world of interchangeable lovers has the rather airless quality of a literary conceit, and it would need a very different context to be even minimally satisfying.

In the film version, the soft edges of the story have been lathed and planed into a more naturalistic, less symbolic shape, but other than altering the nationalities of some of the characters and revising the ending, the basic contours remain unchanged. Foreman's screenplay hews pretty closely to the novel and is flat-footed throughout, achieving a measure of evocativeness only where there are nuances to be seized from the original text. In other films, Reed had made a specialty of unusual, captivating prologues, cinematically swift introductions that presented theme and subject as atmospherically as possible. Consider *Odd Man Out, The Third Man, Trapeze*. It's impossible to know whether he had something better in mind than what Foreman's script calls for – a shot of Holden (David Ross), newly arrived in England to assist the British rescue teams, walking through the

local shipyards. The contrast in scale between the immensity of
the shipyards and the minuteness of a single man is pointless
since there is no thematic use for it in the movie, which deals
with the crew and commanders of very *small* boats. Immediately
afterwards, Ross encounters an old friend, Captain Chris Ford
(Trevor Howard), and Foreman lamely funnels as much exposition through the scene as he can. We learn that the tugs are
considered the Red Cross of the sea, that their work is fraught
with danger, that Ross is an American serving with the Canadian forces because the United States has not yet entered the
war. And so it goes for the remainder of Foreman's scenario as
the characters meet, celebrate Christmas, part company, love
and fight and die. At the heart of the tale is the enigmatic Stella
(Sophia Loren), the dark lady of the sea, whose lovers all
experience an intuition of their coming demise and pass the key
to her apartment along to another man. At the beginning of the
movie, she is Chris's fiancée, but a few scenes later he is dead
and Ross has inherited the key and the woman who goes with it.
The psychological tension in the movie stems from the battle
between Ross's fearful suspicion that Stella has no loyalty to
anyone and his growing love for her. Embarking on an especially
perilous assignment, he commits a terrible breach of faith by
giving Stella's key to a fellow seaman (Kieron Moore). The
subsequent action sequence, in which Ross rams the submarine
and escapes destruction himself, is as thrilling – and far-fetched
– as it was in the book.

    In the film's denouement, with Ross trying desperately to
recapture his now-alienated beloved, Foreman goes deep into
the Hollywood ragbag for a scene of Stella's train pulling out of
the station, headed for London, with Ross making a frantic
sprint to overtake it. The film was originally released in America
with an ending poised somewhere between ambiguity and sorrow: failing to catch up with the train, Ross vows to find Stella in
London. This is the conclusion that European audiences saw. In
the United States, however, a happy ending was inserted after
the first week or so, and the hero and heroine are reunited.

    There's not much Reed could do with such material except
execute it with more authority than it deserved, add a few
graceful touches here and there and try to get the best work
possible from the actors. The action sequences are well managed, even stirring, as in the series of manoeuvres – photo-

graphed from above – which Ross puts his new ship through as a test, wheeling the craft sharply this way and that. On a grimmer plane, we watch the gallant tugs fight a pathetically uneven contest against the rough seas and Nazi submarines to answer the harried Maydays from Allied freighters. Reed had a generous budget and made exemplary use of it. The climax of the sea battles, Ross's kamikaze effort against the U-boat, is the sort of derring-do that only movie heroes are capable of, yet Reed stages the sequence so dynamically that all the intended excitement is achieved.

Alas, the bulk of the film does not generate the same kind of electricity. Howard is sturdy and reliable as always, every inch the tough old salt which the script asks him to be. Unhappily, the script doesn't require him to be a particular salt, with individual pains, predilections, tics and obsessions. Nor does Foreman equip Holden with anything resembling a distinctive personality. The blandness of the names are all too emblematic of the characters. In addition, Holden, like most Hollywood leading men, gives no sign of an inner life and experiences no problems except those which are externally imposed by war, privation and the exigencies of his romantic situation. He is as reliable as his tug and even less interesting.

Between Foreman's lacklustre screenplay and Holden's deficiency of personality, Reed was left with a denatured hero at the centre of his story. His heroine is, by design, equally colourless, since Stella's only trait is her mysteriousness, and the mystery, once explained, seems shallow and artificial. She's less a creature of flesh and blood than a symbol of the sufferings of womanhood in wartime. Voigt points to another problem: 'since the girl is always presented in a sympathetic light . . . we are not faced with any real conflict.'[14] Loren's reputation as a glamour girl graduated to competent actress is based on her few Italian movies; she has usually been mediocre in English-language films and *The Key* is no exception. Reed was a fine director of actors, but he was not Pygmalion. The only character in *The Key* with even the remotest intensity is Captain Van Dam, a hymn-singing Protestant zealot who seems derived from the Somerset Maugham character Kosti in *The Razor's Edge* out of Dostoevsky. He is the butt of too much humour in the film, especially in view of the fact that the last grisly joke comes when he and his crew are killed in the chapel on their ship. Homolka, who may never have given a bad performance in a forty-year film career, squeezes out every last tormented, twitching, harshly pious inch of his character, grunting and struggling to expand Foreman's stereotypical religious fanatic.

Reed seems considerably more interested in Van Dam than in the other characters who have been placed under his supervision, perhaps because the religious fervour reminded him of *Odd Man Out*. In any case, he seems to have encouraged Homolka to exert his energies in trying to expand Foreman's stereotypical fanatic into something Dostoevskian. It's a good try.

Apart from its scenes of victory – and defeat – at sea, the most vital and absorbing aspects of *The Key* are the carefully modulated intimations of doom that Reed is sometimes able to generate. The hangers rattle in Stella's closet, as if the ghosts of her deceased officers were putting their coats away. Equally spectral is the gigantic shadow cast by her phone, over which so many fateful messages have come. In the film's most creepily suggestive scene, and one of the few to convey the dark poetry that Foreman and Reed strove for, Stella follows Ross to the docks when he is leaving on an especially dangerous mission, although he has ordered her not to. As he sees it, she will be repeating the actions that preceded Ford's death, and he has grown acutely sensitive to omens. Stella follows him anyway, and Reed's camera catches haunting glimpses of her through Ross's terrified eyes, as she glides along a railing above him, a black-clad figure, resonantly ambiguous, combining messages of love with omens of death, a perfect personification of *Liebesrod*. If only Reed could have injected more imagery like this into Foreman's flat uninflected screenplay.

Like *The Third Man*, *Our Man in Havana* was an 'entertainment', consisting of Greene's familiar casserole of sly wit, intricately plotted melodrama and social squalor – all of it lightly topped with a sprinkling of holy water. In this case, the story's Cuban locale pointed to another of Greene's predilections: tropical settings. *The Power and the Glory* takes place in Mexico, *The Quiet American* in Vietnam, *The Comedians* in Haiti. A snug arrangement between Columbia and Kingsmead, a company Reed had formed himself, provided for financing and distribution. An international cast was assembled, including Alec Guinness, Maureen O'Hara, Noel Coward and Burl Ives. Still, Havana remained problematical for a time due to the political instability of Cuba. The fall of the Batista government in 1959 proved to be a blessing for Reed and his associates, who, with little difficulty, were able to secure permission from the victorious rebels to shoot their movie in Havana with little difficulty.

In exchange for their 'green card', the film-makers were required to add over fifty Cubans to the cast and crew and submit to regular visits by a government committee which sought to determine that nothing derogatory to the new government was slipped into the film – despite the fact that the screenplay is a condemnation of the *ancien régime* by a leftist writer. The movie's exterior shots were completed over a five-week period, with Cubans gawping raptly at the famous Anglo faces and Ernie Kovacs reportedly smoking twenty-five Cuban cigars everyday. Back in England, at Shepperton Studios, about eleven weeks went into interior shots.

On the whole, *Havana*, which premiered in late 1959, was cordially received on both sides of the Atlantic. *The Times* called the film 'masterly in accomplishment and richly human'.[15] The *Observer* considered it 'Reed's best film since *The Third Man*',[16] and Penelope Houston, in *Sight and Sound*, said it 'wins on points'.[17] In the United States, *Variety* described it as 'polished and diverting entertainment',[18] Crowther took pleasure in the film's 'urbane and delicious comedy', while expressing a thorough mystification about its deeper implications.[19] *Time* had doubts about *Havana*'s blend of 'mayhem and heehaw', but hailed 'Funnyman Guinness' and 'Funnyman Kovacs'.[20] On the other hand, John McCarten at *The New Yorker* was as cranky about *Havana* as he had been over many other Reed films, accusing Reed of 'stretching one comic idea into a full-length movie'.[21] The public seems to have inclined more towards McCarten's view that the rest of the critical establishment, for the movie, budgeted at $2 million, was only a modest success.

Greene had originally conceived the plot of *Havana* for the Anglo-Brazilian director Alberto Cavalcanti, working up a one-page synopsis for a tale about an English secret agent in Estonia during the Second World War who was selling his government false information out of a desperate need to keep up with the expenses of his spendthrift wife. But Cavalcanti rejected the treatment and Greene eventually switched the story to Havana in the late 1950s because, as he has explained, 'the reader could feel no sympathy for a man who was cheating his country in

Hitler's day . . . However in fantastic Havana, among the absur-
dities of the Cold War . . . there was a situation allowably
comic . . .'[22]

Even without this footnote, most readers could probably
deduce that *Havana*, with its knowing recipe of intrigue, comedy
and romantic interest and its picturesque setting was intended
for the screen. Apart from the greater degree of luridness in the
book (and a few additional episodes), the plot does not undergo
any unusual sea changes in its movie version. James Wormold
(Alec Guinness), an unassuming vacuum cleaner salesman in
Havana with an expensive daughter, is recruited by Hawthorne
(Noel Coward), a British spy, to collect information of political
or military importance in Havana and pass it along for British
intelligence. The spoof of cloak-and-daggering is lovingly realized in Reed's film, though the humour may have been a little
sedate and overrefined for American audiences. In Greene's droll
conceit, the umbrella-toting Hawthorne is the antithesis of an
unobtrusive secret agent. When we first encounter him, shortly
after the film begins, he is striding forcefully through the langor-
ous Latin streets with a small band of musicians trailing along
behind him. He is impeccably overdressed in a black suit that
couldn't be less appropriate for the Cuban climate. In a later
scene, he forces Wormold into a rendezvous in the men's room at
the local country club and camouflages their dialogue by turning
all the faucets on. The scene's Freudian subtext of 'unnatural
acts' is exceptionally bold for a film made under the old Production Code, although Coward's well-known homosexuality may
arouse a queasy sensation that undermines the comic ingenuity
of Greene's conception.

From this witty opening, Reed and Greene continue to direct
their rapiers at the vaunted English spy system, pinking it
exquisitely throughout the film. Its obsession with secrecy is
chaffed not only through the flamboyantly obtrusive Coward,
but also in the cumbersome use of code names like '59200 stroke
5', the appellation which Hawthorne assigns Wormold and by
which he is invariably identified. In a witty visual thrust at the
same circumlocutions, Hawthorne carefully closes a gate with a
few insignificant slats as a preface to disclosing some top secret
information. Perceiving an opportunity to shore up his meagre
income, Wormold recruits imaginary sub-agents, choosing the
names at random from members of the local country club, and

pockets the salaries which London compliantly issues. To earn his pay, he simply files reports from government documents. Coward and his superior, 'C' (Ralph Richardson) are intoxicated by these 'vital revelations' and congratulate one another about their 'man in Havana'. Encouraged by this response, Wormold informs his superiors that he has discovered a gigantic military installation in the mountains, enclosing a blueprint of this ominous construction, which is nothing more than a Brobdingnagian version of one of his vacuum cleaners. Coward and Richardson react with hilarious consternation, assuming that they are gazing at a super-weapon of some kind. Two additional agents, a radio operator and a secretary (O'Hara), are dispatched to assist Wormold in this delicate operation. The mood darkens, however, when Wormold becomes the target for an authentic espionage ring, and, after two murders and two additional attempts, the protagonist must become a hero. Greene has made his name an obvious composite of 'worm' and 'mold', and, one might say, the Wormold turns: he guns down an enemy agent. In the end, though, back in England the film's whimsical spirit returns; when the would-be spy has disclosed his duplicity, the agency is too frightened by the prospect of public embarrassment to prosecute him and offers him an OBE a job instead.

In the espionage parody (the most consistently engaging dimension of *Havana*), Greene's comic inventiveness is superbly incarnated by the actors, from whom Reed elicits performances of seemingly effortless perfection. Coward, who was comparatively waxen and nondescript in his own films, emerges here as the debonair, devilishly clever Coward of theatrical legend, the epitome of brillantined, irresistible sophistication. Whether portraying the bemused Englishman in the tropics or the concerned official of Her Majesty's government, Coward achieves just the right aura: glacéed imperturbability, unwavering propriety and, of course, hereditary understatement. With a few of the same strings to play on in his small supporting role, Richardson is almost a match for Coward.

Reed gets less uniform results from the other characters, subplots and themes in *Havana*, though the movie is so artistically ambitious, sometimes in subterranean ways, that it is always intriguing. There are very few Reed films without a police inspector or detective, if only because he made so many thrillers, and *Havana* is no exception. Here the constabulary role is fulfilled by Captain Segura (Ernie Kovacs), a cigar-puffing officer who suspects Wormold of espionage activity and harasses him throughout the movie in one fashion or another. Kovacs, one of the top comedians of the era until his premature death in 1962, surprised everyone with his masterly performance, disappearing so completely into Segura that only his immortal cigar still protrudes. It is another tribute to Reed's direction that the humour with which Kovacs invests the Segura character is an array of muted Latinisms but with none of the heavy-duty, moustache-preening exaggerations one would expect from a Kovacs TV sketch. Thus, Captain Segura is intelligent and crafty and his comedic moments seem intentional. To be sure, Segura fits the corrupt/tyrannical stereotype of a Caribbean strongman ('There are two classes of people: those who can be tortured and those who can't', he announces), yet he displays other personae too. Enamoured of Wormold's daughter Milly (Jo Morrow), he courts her in gentlemanly fashion. In an effort to coax or trick Wormold away from the British side in the spy game, he accepts the latter's guileful challenge to play checkers with tiny liquor bottles as pieces and a rule that when a player seizes his opponent's piece, he must drink the bottle. The bibulous results of this game are both funny and essential to the machinery of the plot.

The uniformed Segura keeps one boot in the film's comedic regions and the other in its dramatic territory. His love for Milly is contrasted pointedly with Guinness's own ardour for his daughter, but unfortunately, neither actor is convincingly tender or affecting. For all his justly celebrated, multifaceted genius, Guinness has rarely conveyed passion towards other human beings adequately. (In *The Bridge Over the River Kwai*, he loved his construction; in *Tunes of Glory* he had to become deranged to care about the John Mills character.) His principal motivation for plunging into the deceit and danger of his espionage scam is to provide his daughter with a horse and a prestige education in private schools. Yet his love for her is very tepidly displayed; it is stated, not felt. Perhaps part of the problem is that Milly is played by Jo Morrow, a soon-to-be-forgotten starlet of 1960. Morrow is nothing more than a perky pin-up girl; there's nothing about her to love except her looks.

In the casting of an over-homogenized ingenue like Morrow, Reed seems to have been sabotaged by Hollywood's weakness for bathing beauties, stars and familiar faces, regardless of their suitability for the parts assigned them. As the secretary, Beatrice, O'Hara is quite decorative and turns in a more or less acceptable performance – certainly in comparison to Morrow – though her contribution to the movie is actually quite negligible, and the flow of feeling one is supposed to observe between her and Wormold is pallid and thin. Guinness, a towering figure in comic and dramatic roles, is ineffectual as a romantic lead. In *Havana*, which is ably directed in so many ways, the emotional temperature of Guinness's ardour remains low, and one wonders if Reed made much effort to raise it. Despite the virtuosity and expertise of his direction, he seems unexcited by the task of developing a love story. His best scenes are among the men. Even O'Hara, so fiery and tempestuously Irish in movies like *The Quiet Man*, is relatively bland in *Havana*.

Yet, curiously enough, sexuality is an essential motive force in the film, as in the behaviour of Captain Segura, and is even used symbolically at several points. In the novel, Greene indulged his thirst for seedy, decadent milieus extensively, spiking the dry rot with licentiousness. In the movie such sequences are exploited for sociological as well as purely atmospheric purposes. Indeed, the first minute or so of the film is starkly sensual; we watch an attractive, elegant Latin woman swimming across a luxurious pool in the moonlight, as Segura watches. The camera cuts to a lovestruck young Cuban working-man gazing at a steamy proletarian vamp in a low balcony; suddenly and provocatively she throws him an apple she has been eating. Eroticism links all levels of this culture. Since one of the running gags in the film is the self-appointed, frustrating efforts of an employee of Wormold's, Lopez (Jose Prieto), to pimp for him, we can assume that Reed and Greene are promulgating a sexual commentary on pre-revolutionary Cuban society. For the most part, the creators reveal a typically English restraint in such matters, but near the climax of the film there is a puzzling scene in which Wormold and an agent named Carter (Paul Rogers) who has been sent to assassinate him go to the once-renowned Shanghai Theatre. Invited by one of the girls to unbutton her top, Carter is paralyzed with inhibition, while Wormold, who has urged him to cooperate, looks on with an aura of masculine superiority. Shortly after this exposé of Carter's sexual inadequacy, he is shot dead by Wormold during an attempt on the latter's life. The notion of paralleling sexual potency with strength in other areas is thematically provocative, but unhappily Reed and Greene never get beyond tantalising us with this concept. In general, the treatment of sex in *Havana* is fascinating but inconsistent and underdeveloped.

Crowther tells his readers he found the film 'a little hard to grasp'.[23] Had he been more perceptive, he might have detected a few of the movie's less visible concerns. As other reviewers observed, the Catholic sensibility that lies behind most of Greene's stories surfaces quite overtly in *Havana*. Wormold's dead wife, we are told, was a Catholic who made him promise to raise Milly in her faith, an injunction he has followed determinedly. However, at the convent school which Milly attends, her 'high marks' in dogma and morals are clearly intended to contrast with her self-indulgent, spoiled and worldly conduct. (In Greene's work only non-believers and false Catholics are happy; true votaries of Rome are tormented.) She may be the apple of her father's eye, but she is not a good Catholic. References to praying and to religious articles abound in the film, and Wormold, though presumably a Protestant, pours out the truth of his deception to Beatrice in a thoroughly confessional manner. What is more pertinent to the film's intellectual pretensions, however, is that the corrupt world Greene and Reed portray, though lightened by laughter and playfulness, is very much the vale of tears we encountered in *The Third Man*. This theology seems to have held great appeal for Reed. Again, the hero sins for well-intentioned motives and is punished nevertheless, for his encounter with evil can only taint him. Wormold's lucrative deception is undertaken to improve his daughter's prospects, but life retaliates all the same: his best friend, Dr Hasselbacher (Ives), is coerced into working against him and is eventually murdered. His choices are so restrictive they do not seem to permit a happy outcome; he can either forsake his one opportunity to aid his daughter or enter the diseased world of espionage. For Greene's characters, there is no salvation this side of the grave – unless of course it can be found in a Hollywood-style happy ending, which the author provides in his novel as well as the screenplay.

Any students of Reed's work should be able immediately to tag and label Wormold quite easily: he is another of the guileless beings who so fascinated the director. Wormold's frolicksome and profitable traffic in home-made espionage begins to have seriously unanticipated consequences when the people whose names he has borrowed to use as confederates become the victims of the rival spy organization. Threats, beatings and murder are the outcome of Wormold's deception, the awful culmination being the death of Dr Hasselbacher. The sobering awareness of what he has done drives Wormold to confess at last to Hawthorne. But since *Havana* was intended to amuse more than to thrill or edify, Reed and Greene leave the psychological stratum of their story only lightly excavated. Instead, the film gives way ultimately to such traditional movie constituents as Wormold's revenge on Carter and the happy ending, which neatly wraps up all the problems and brings Wormold home to England safely.

The character who comments most articulately on the depravity of the modern world is Dr Hasselbacher, who sounds like something of a spokesman for Reed and Greene. Elderly, corpulent and embittered, Hasselbacher has withdrawn as much as possible from Vanity Fair. Alcohol keeps him fairly detached from worldly degradation, and he replaces it with his dreamy, poetic experiments and recollections of the glory he once knew as a soldier under the Kaiser. In a critical sequence shortly before his murder, he dresses in his First World War uniform and guiltily admits to Wormold that he has been forced to betray him to the 'other side'. The unwitting or involuntary abandonment of one human being by another is one of the most powerful themes in Greene's and Reed's work, yet its effectiveness is undermined here by the staginess of the Hasselbacher character. Reed was occasionally successful with strutting, attention-grabbing theatrical types – such as Lukey in *Odd Man Out* and Chitterlow in *Kipps* – but when Greene tries to deploy them, they emerge as enervated grotesques to whom the crepe paper of make-believe clings hopelessly. Hasselbacher is simply not credible as written, either in the novel or the film. Ives, the folk singer whom some directors had used skilfully in the past, was not a flexible or experienced enough actor to bring vitality to the character Greene had conceived or even to approximate a German accent. But he was another 'star' that the movie was saddled with.

As virtually all commentators agree, the alloy of comedy and serious drama in *Havana* is not terribly successful. We simply aren't prepared for the sudden shift in tone when the movie transmutes itself from a light-fingered spoof into a tragedy – not just a melodrama but an actual tragedy with the most melancholy philosophical reverberations. One has to respect the doggedness and acumen Reed exhibited in trying to pull off this act of cinematic alchemy. In an interview with Robert Emmett Ginna during the shooting of *Havana*, he said:

> At the beginning I feel we should light our sets for comedy. That is, rather brightly for catching the beauty of the streets too. Then as the picture moves toward melodrama, we will shoot with a wide angle, getting the effects of the walls closing in. We will use . . . hard lights in the night exteriors, making the streets . . . shiny, getting a brittle black-and-white feeling.[21]

All this is achieved in the completed film, but it isn't enough to disguise the clash of moods that was inherent in Greene's screenplay. Still, *Havana* remains an enjoyable film and even where it goes awry it errs in the direction of thematic complexity and challenging ideas.

Reed's direction and Greene's screenplay merge so smoothly that the film's motifs and assumptions seem fully shared by both men, though we know each leaned in his own creative direction. There are noteworthy elements in *Havana* for which Reed is obviously – or at least arguably – the likely source. The off-angle camera shots, one of his lynchpins, are used to good effect, as when they call attention to a boy listening outside the door of Wormold's store or to isolate Wormold himself in an odd, unsettling pose while seated at a luncheon of European traders as he nervously awaits an attempt on his life which Hawthorne has warned him about. The composition of many of Reed's shots again refutes Sarris's allegation that he lacked 'visual complexity'.[25] Indeed, there is so much unusual and unrelated activity in the background of some of Reed's scenes that we grow curious about these stories too. Such was his declard intention, particularly in the case of the young Cuban swain mentioned earlier; his liaison with the woman he has been watching is carefully but unobtrusively interpolated into the background of the action. Cynically, she is later one of the women offered to Wormold!

One or two reviewers in 1960 commented on the parallels between *Havana* and *The Third Man*, and though the former film is not as good, the correspondences are worth mentioning: an exotic city with narrow streets, a main character who brings about the death of his closest friend, a relentless policeman who beleaguers the hero. The music too is a haunting local creation, the plangent melodies of the Hermanos Deniz Cuban Rhythm Band. As in all good art, the parallels suggest an artist with a unified style and temperament who is applying them to fresh subject-matter, supplying new aesthetic rewards rather than tilling the same old fields again.

Reed's decision to become, in effect, an employee of the American film industry from 1956 on has been decried by many film critics and is frequently adduced as the reason for an alleged decline in the calibre of his work after the mid-1950s. Actually, as we have seen, there is good reason for concluding that Reed's career received plenty of adrenalin when he offered his services to Hollywood. The British film world had been briefly energized by Rank and Korda, but in the 1950s even these titans had encountered increasing difficulties in distributing their films to the all-important US market, which the troubled American studios wanted to maintain as their own preserve. Fiscal melancholia settled over the English cinema, and fewer and fewer opportunities were available for its directors; as a consequence, Reed was certainly not alone in seeking American projects.

As for the quality of his work, it seems to have suffered less from the transition from London to Hollywood than from the fact that he could not sustain the exceptionally high creative level he had reached in the period 1945–52. Still, of the movies he made for Hollywood there are several of considerable merit. Certainly the best of them eclipse his last two European efforts, *The Man Between* and *A Kid for Two Farthings*. It is in this context that the critical discussion in the preceding chapter should be viewed; for while *The Key* cannot be counted a success, *Trapeze* and *Our Man in Havana* certainly can. *Trapeze* gives us only glimpses of the Reed who made *The Fallen Idol* and *The Third Man*, but, reunited with Greene in *Havana*, he makes a striking reemergence, deploying all his favourite characters, devices, situations, motifs.

10 Autumn and Winter of a Director's Career

It is inconceivable that Reed could have done much more with the MGM remake of *Mutiny on the Bounty*, his next undertaking, than anyone else. The project could not have been more jinxed if a school of albatrosses had alighted on Marlon Brando's contract in January 1960, when he signed to do the picture. Reed's first meeting with the star in California ought to have been an ill omen of the first order. Brando, then one of the top box office attractions in Hollywood and an indispensable component of the picture, spent two hours trying to convince Reed and the producer, Aaron Rosenberg, to scrap the whole idea of doing *Mutiny* and develop a movie about Caryl Chessman, a recently executed rapist, instead.

On the other hand, Reed also had good reason to feel optimistic, even though he was commencing a mammoth production that was far removed from the tight, controlled, personal dramas with which he was most comfortable. Of the two leading roles in the movie after Brando's, one had gone to an exciting young Irish actor, Richard Harris, and the other to Trevor Howard, with whom Reed had, of course, enjoyed an immensely fruitful and harmonious relationship on previous films. In addition, the script was being written by Eric Ambler, a specialist in the type of entertainment Reed understood best.

But a hale of calamities struck in swift order. A full-scale replica of the *Bounty*, constructed in Nova Scotia at a cost of $750 000, encountered various delays – one nearly fatal – on its passage to Tahiti, where the bulk of the movie was to be shot. Production was scheduled to begin 15 October, but it was 4 December before the ship finally groaned into port. Other disasters included three deaths among the film's personnel, the abrupt departure of a key Tahitian actress midway through filming, and the onset of the devastating Tahitian rainy season.

The movie's biggest catastrophes were man-made, however – the costly and demoralizing eruptions of Brando's ego. Dissatisfied with Ambler's screenplay, he insisted that the concluding episode on Pitcairn Island be shot so as to incorporate his ideas about 'man's inhumanity to man'. Before shooting was completed, five more writers would arrive and depart in the attempt to create a script that had the philosophical thrust Brando envisioned. When he did not get what he wanted, he subjected his coworkers to displays of petulance and self-indulgence that slowed the rate of production to a crawl and sent the film millions of dollars over budget. Meanwhile, he lived in splendor in a Tahitian villa and sampled the local night life extensively. Tempers boiled over on the set, as actors found it impossible to work with Brando and stalked off the set.

We have no explicit record of Reed's reaction to all this, but, as Korda says, it is not hard to imagine the despair of a 'gentle soul' (and, one might add, a disciplined professional) at being confronted by so much stormy chaos. 'I think he quit at the point when he was literally waist deep in water waiting for the script to be sent to him by telegram from whoever was writing it at that point', says Birkin. Actually, he seems to have resigned rather less dramatically, back in Hollywood where the entire cast and crew retreated for several weeks until the weather in Tahiti improved. Reed was replaced by Lewis Milestone, a rigorous, no-nonsense veteran who collided with Brando head-on, causing even more friction, expense and collective trauma. When the $27 million fiasco was finally launched, in the autumn of 1962, it was a critical and commercial failure and had the gloomy side-effect of ending Milestone's career.

The following year Reed turned to a work with which he had a much greater affinity than the Nordoff–Hall warhorse, Shelley Smith's crime novel *The Ballad of the Running Man*, the title of which was shortened to *The Running Man*. Two cherished members of Reed's professional family were with him again, Krasker and Alwyn. John Mortimer, a respected novelist and playwright with a flair for well-made courtroom stories, was hired to write the screenplay. An established star, Laurence Harvey, and two performers whose careers were quickly ascending, Alan Bates and Lee Remick, were hired for the lead roles, and Columbia provided a large enough budget for location shooting in Spain, where most of the story is set. With a crew of 150 English,

Spanish and American personnel, Reed wisely took advantage of
the boisterous merriment of *feria* in Malaga as background. To
reduce expense, the interiors were shot at Ardmore Studios in
Ireland.

On the whole, *The Running Man* received complimentary notices. With its customary buoyant illiteracy, *Variety* announced
that Reed knew how to give a 'yarn a lift and make it holding
entertainment'.[1] *Time* lauded the film unequivocally: 'The tension builds nicely . . . the last reel combines irony, scenery and
the internal combustion engine in a getaway with get up and
get.'[2] *Newsweek*, however, had the opposite point of view, finding
little of merit in the plot, a poor engine 'clanking away . . . in
need of oil'.[3] Judith Crist in the *Herald Tribune* also expressed
disappointment, describing the movie as 'long on excited detail
and short on the detailed excitement we have come to expect
from Carol Reed'.[4] Crowther agreed: 'this Carol Reed film . . .
makes no real dramatic progress . . .'[5]

Published in 1960, *The Running Man* drew perfunctory compli-
ments from critics and did not attract a sufficiently sizeable
readership to warrant a second edition. Although the novel is
stylistically and narratively poised throughout, a crime drama
turned out by a knowing hand, there is little inspiration and no
depth whatsoever. Smith's plot deals with a dashing English
insurance swindler named Rex Buchanan who, with the coerced
assistance of his wife Paula, bilks two or three insurance companies by taking out policies under false identities and faking his
own death. Rex's schemes, though meticulously planned and
quite elaborate, fall short of plausibility, as does the sudden
appearance – possibly coincidental, possibly not – of an insurance investigator, Stephen Maddox, who had interviewed Paula
after her husband's first 'death'. Maddox's motives are unclear
and his actions ambivalent. Growing increasingly panicked, Rex
eventually murders Stephen, then kills Paula accidentally. The
novel leaves him a wreck of a man, bereft of his stolen money,
gutted by anxiety and remorse, virtually certain of punishment.

The screenplay that Reed and Mortimer distilled from this
lurid tale changes names and locations and simplifies the story
line, with a net gain that is small but significant. Rex and Paula
Buchanan become Rex and Stella Black and their principal
sphere of activities is shifted from Switzerland and France to
southern Spain. The film-makers compressed Smith's series of

intricately plotted scams into one comparatively simple swindle that is a shade or two more believable than what we are given in the book. The story's central contrivance, Stephen's turning up 'on holiday' in Spain is presented without alteration and it represents a slackening of artistic rigour that Reed would not have permitted earlier in his career. (Mortimer could not be counted on for much help in strengthening credibility, judging by his work in other mediums; in his novel, *Like Men Betrayed*, for instance, the course of the plot is determined by the wrong character receiving a phone call.)

The film's plot is set in motion when Black (Harvey) crashes his plane in the ocean and dissembles his own death so as to be able to collect the insurance. After first adopting the mask of Charles Erskine, a shoe salesman, he heads quickly for Malaga; there he soon finds himself at a bar with a drunken Australian named Jim Jerome (John Meillon), who conveniently forgets his passport. Presto! Rex has a new identity. After his wife Stella (Remick) joins him, the two are agitated by the appearance of Stephen Maddox. 'What a coincidence', he remarks. The rest of the movie is built on the razor-edge quandary of whether he is telling the truth or is spying on the guilty couple for the insurance company. Having thus wrenched the course of events in an improbable direction to create suspense, the film-makers use equally contrived situations to create an ironic conclusion. Fleeing the Spanish police after an unsuccessful attempt at killing Stephen, Rex happens to pass an airport, finds an idle plane with the keys in it and takes it aloft. Short of gas, he goes down over the ocean and dies muttering about life insurance policies. Since the film began with Rex's 'funeral' after faking his death in the first accident, his ultimate fate has the look of a contrived framing device. Still, if one can accept the awkward scaffolding of *The Running Man*, there is a good deal of fine detail and workmanship to admire in the plot; an ingratiating mix of wit, suspense and pungent dialogue; and several piquant surprises.

Voigt reports that Reed's stated objective in *The Running Man* was to show 'the effects of a guilty conscience on a man who in reality has nothing to fear'.[6] The motif resembles many a crime drama, but Reed's work here is far short of the intense, seedy, Dantean atmosphere of mutual punishment in, say, *Double Indemnity*, although it never drops below a level of smooth professionalism and sometimes rises a good deal above it. Flamboyant and self-possessed, Rex is the dominant partner in the marriage. His wife offers little, if any, resistance to his illicit scheme, and guides the bogus funeral through to its apparently successful conclusion, collects the money and then heads for a rendezvous with Rex in Spain, in accordance with his instructions. Almost immediately, however, she is alarmed by the changes in his personality. Overbearing and ostentatious, he yells at unoffending waiters and drives a huge white convertible down the narrow European streets, honking the horn aggressively. But far more disturbing to Stella is that he now plans additional insurance swindles. His mind has become inebriated by the life of crime, by the thought of himself as a master criminal. His new flamboyance is symbolized by his car, his died blond hair and his occasional adoption of an exaggerated Australian accent.

To Rex's disappointment, however, Stella does not fancy the role of international thief. Nervous and fearful, she desires only a return to normalcy. Rex's new persona is distressing to her, but she is bound to him by legal and emotional bonds and is unable to do anything but watch herself helplessly swept along at his side. Even when his felonious plans for a life of happy swindles emerge, she cannot break free. Nevertheless, the marriage goes sour, rotting away little by little. From the beginning, Rex's corruption comes between them. When he returns after the funeral, he is eager to make love, but Stella, in keeping with her bereaved widowhood, has allowed a doctor to give her a sedative and falls asleep while Rex is shaking her shoulders in frustration. Later, in Malaga, they must keep up appearances, which means maintaining separate residences. As they bicker over Rex's outrageous behaviour, their sexual relationship decays, until, we learn, Stella is completely unresponsive to Rex's attentions. The erosion of the marriage is further mirrored in Rex's cynical remarks about a couple of young Spanish newlyweds; he sneeringly compares the bride and her matronly mother and gazing in the direction of the bridegroom, pronounces a harsh verdict: 'He never should have married her. She'll turn into Mum in no time.'

Finally, the crime exacts an even greater toll when Stella's efforts at determining whether or not Stephen is spreading a net for them drive her to infidelity. Stephen discovers her searching his room, and she has no choice but to pretend she has come for a tryst. The marital discord reaches a peak with Rex's hands around Stella's throat, as his jealous rage over her disclosure of this incident almost drives him to murder. That he does not actually kill her is one of the many respects in which the film is superior to the novel.

To Stella, the Rex who nearly kills her is a barely recognizable degeneration of her husband. She points out that he first meta-morphosed into Charles Erskine, shoe salesman, and then Jim Jerome, the rancher. 'I don't know who I'm married to', she cries. The shifts in identity that Rex undergoes, coupled with his swaggering personality, make him the centre of dramatic gravity in *Running Man*, the most engrossing and complex character. A more mundane artist than Reed would have been content to shove Rex arbitrarily from one mask to the next, offering some fashionable existential rationale, but Reed, old-fashioned in the best sense of the term, is careful to give us an early x-ray of Rex's psyche that makes his eventual overweening self-destructiveness understandable. At his mock funeral, the local pastor (Felix Aylmer) allows unflattering glimpses of Rex's life to seep into his lukewarm eulogy, disclosing that the dead man drove too fast. In a subsequent flashback, we see Rex undertaking a mission which requires him to fly a cargo of bras into Germany under question-able circumstances. The plane crashes and when the Blacks go to their insurance company to collect, Rex is rather obnoxious about the £20 000 he anticipates. But the insurance agent refuses to pay, on legitimate grounds, and Rex grows intemperate, blurting out defiant plans to achieve his goal of acquiring a new plane. In short, Reed and Mortimer see to it that the villainous Rex grows logically out of his predecessors.

The sequence between the Blacks and Maddox are typically Reedian, built with fine strokes of irony, wit and carefully preserved ambiguity. When Rex and Stella commit slips, Stephen never fails to react, but does he perceive the duplicity? His own dialogue is adroitly flecked with apparently harmless, unin-tended references to Rex's swindle. Or are they deliberate? Some of Mortimer's best work has gone into these exchanges. Observing Rex's behemoth of an automobile, Stephen rejects it as 'too much like a getaway car'. When he and the Blacks go swimming and Rex, disappearing for a while, returns suddenly, Stephen laughingly expresses his fears: 'Stella and I thought you drowned.' Later in a restaurant, Rex half-consciously arranges a bunch of matchsticks in the shape of an airplane. 'Do you fly?',

Stephen inquires, as Rex and Stella display flickers of guilt. Such responses are marvellously underplayed. Reed permits no heavy strokes of the bow, insisting on finely nuanced, chamber-music effects.

There are many other ways in which the director has left his signature on *The Running Man*, however faintly. The Spanish setting spreads some lovely scenery behind the action. Never content with mere *mise-en-scène*, Reed crowds as much life into the backdrop as possible, though in a more pedestrian manner than we are used to from him. There is a measure of truth to Voigt's assertion that 'much of the film' looks like a 'glossy travelogue'.[7] Yet some of the Spanish subject-matter transcends this classification, particularly the wedding that blooms joyously in the interstices of the plot, providing a thematic commentary on it. We see a festive gathering outside the church and later, even more jubilantly, the celebration at the restaurant where the Blacks are dining with Stephen. The members of the wedding party, forming a merry contrast to the bleak conubial disintegration of Rex and Stella, are oblivious to the three Anglos.

Far more hawk-eyed are the impecunious, playful Spanish children who swarm through several scenes, constituting yet another Reedian antithesis between adult ignominy and youthful innocence. A small boy attaches himself to Rex, shining his shoes and washing his car. He is another version of the river boy who 'adopted' Willems in *Outcast of the Islands* and the girl who watched the wounded Johnny McQueen in *Odd Man Out*. In one especially piquant moment, as Rex wheels his huge car around to drive to Malaga, we see the boy seated in the back, his face covered with glee. Returning from Malaga, Rex parts with his silent, pint-sized companion, pouring coins into his hands. One brief scene is actually set in a deserted bullring where a group of children pretend to be 'el torro' to Rex's matador, charging delightedly at the red garment he holds out. The encounter is wonderfully in character for him too, since it is emblematic of his reckless, devil-may-care manner. After all, he is, as Stella says, a man who likes to 'take risks'.

Nevertheless, children do not really influence the action in *The Running Man*, anymore than they do in *Outcast*. They merely serve a decorative and symbolic function. The embodiment of innocence in *The Running Man* is, paradoxically, the ex-insurance investigator Maddox, who has nothing of the tough, aggressive detective about him. Even at the beginning of the movie, when he visits Stella to question her about her 'deceased' husband, he has an unsuspecting, wide-eyed quality to him. Later in Spain, having shucked off his former investigatory garb, he becomes so enamoured of Stella that even when we think he might be there to trap her, his sense of duty appears to fade under the spell she casts over him. When at last he reveals that he is just what he seems, an innocuous vacationer, and has no ulterior motive, it becomes clear that Reed has yet again seized the opportunity to depict the lethal effects that innocence can have on the world. The ever more desperate manoeuvres that Rex and Stella make as they plunge further towards disaster are inadvertently set in motion by Stephen. His apparent guilelessness is fully consonant with the motifs and dramatic conflicts of the movie.

As a crime drama, the triangular relationship in *The Running Man* is to some degree blighted by the improbable events commented on earlier. On its more romantic plane, though, it has a purity of execution that Reed had achieved only intermittently since *Outcast*. He is careful to establish Rex and Stephen as antipodal figures – one dark, one fair, one diffident and sensitive, the other boisterous and overbearing; one benevolent, one corrupt. The contrast even extends to hair styles: Bates's hair is matted down in a humdrum, unstylish fashion, while Harvey has his usual silken, beautifully coiffured mane. (In one of Reed's few lapses into over-obviousness, Rex, labelled all too clearly by his name, generally wears black and Stephen white.)

Reworking the Harry–Holly–Anna triangle of *The Third Man*, Reed again evinces his peculiarly unsentimental brand of romanticism. Evil achieves a glamour and potency that goodness cannot attain and exerts a hypnotic appeal, particularly on women. As Holly could not break Lime's hold on Anna, so Stephen cannot woo Stella away from Rex, even when she grows disenchanted with her husband. Anna and Stella are sisters in their preference for doom and defeat with an exciting scoundrel over tame felicity with a less colourful alternative. Anna's rejection of Holly was easier to understand because Reed and Greene deflated him so often, slyly nudging him into one folly or another. Stephen, however, is written to be appealing – sweet-tempered, decent and loyal – and Bates gives flesh to these virtues through a gentle, winning performance. We like him from the first and hope Stella will too. But his somewhat moonstruck disposition towards her is ineffective; she likes the more casual treatment she gets from Rex. Harvey imbues Rex with a rough-edged, petulant quality that sets him apart from the uniformly urbane (if menacing) Harry Lime; yet he has enough high-stepping suaveness and gaudy sex appeal to make his hold over Stella immediately intelligible to us. Harvey, who had inherited most of the roles for attractive English cads when George Sanders grew too old for them, is sheer perfection as the buccaneering Rex. From aggressive charm to unruffled complacency to peevish rages, there is not a mood that fails to register in Harvey's quicksilver performance.

Like Holly, Stephen is a romantic and in Reed's rather mysoginistic view, it is not romanticism that attracts women but self-absorbed worldliness and off-handed sophistication. Stella never sees Stephen as more than a 'nice man' and even her sexual interlude with him occurs only through force of circumstance. (Again, Reed is aesthetically sounder than Smith, who makes Paula fall for Stephen, in violation of the emotional logic of the story and the characterizations.) Even after her alienation from Rex, she shows no interest in Stephen. His dreams of sharing his modest London flat with her are unalluring.

Stephen has come to Spain for a 'big adventure', just as Holly perceives melodramatic potential in every turn of events in Vienna. Both men see their hope realized, but neither comes away with the woman he loves. The loss seems more tragic in Holly's case, since Valli, aided by the greater depth of Greene's screenplay, makes a vastly more magnetic screen presence than Remick, whose cover-girl prettiness lacks the contours of true beauty and who had not yet learned to transcend humdrum competence as an actress. Her performance is so devoid of resonance or shading that it's hard to see what could hold a man's interest. Mortimer and Reed give her a simulacrum of a character, pale and ghostly, and she does nothing to animate it. Bates also has an underwritten part, but through sheer acting talent he does the screenwriter's work for him. As always, Reed exacts the maximum from each of his performers: it's just that there was more to be had from Harvey and Bates than Remick.

A creative gulf as vast as the Gobi Desert separates the relatively suave *The Running Man* from Reed's subsequent endeavour, *The*

Agony and the Ecstasy, an adaptation of Irving Stone's best seller with Charlton Heston as Michelangelo. It's much easier to understand why Reed would accept the assignment than to comprehend 20th Century-Fox's reasons for offering it to him. After *Havana*, Reed had become involved in the *Mutiny on the Bounty* fiasco at MGM but left before the taint of its failure – the film eventually lost millions – could attach itself to his name. Still, it had been years since he had enjoyed a significant commercial success, and he was not in great demand in Hollywood. No doubt a big budget spectacle with a major star seemed like the vehicle that would restore him to credibility with the American studios. But he had never before directed a film that depended on panoramic scope and gargantuan production values for its appeal; indeed, his grandest accomplishments occurred at the other end of the artistic spectrum, with small-scale, fine-grained dramas of social realism or hand-tooled thrillers. One would expect Fox to feel more secure with a latter-day Cecil B. DeMille like Anthony Mann. Perhaps the lofty cultural background of the film seemed to call for a European 'art director' or possibly the handsome financial returns on *Trapeze* suggested the right kind of adaptability in Reed.

Whatever corporate cogitation was involved, Reed fell heir to one of the most expensive, elaborately planned movies of the year. The bulk of the film was shot on location in Italy, some of it in the Tuscan countryside between Florence and Milan, some of it in Rome. In the imperial Hollywood manner, about $10 million was sunk in the project, 4000 extras were used, and the costumes, architecture and decor of sixteenth-century Italy were recreated down to the last metope. As for the artistic masterpiece at the centre of the story, it was discovered that the original Sistine Chapel could not be translated effectively through the chosen cinematic medium, Todd A-O, so a replica was constructed in the De Laurentiis studios in Rome. Like the facsimile of Versailles in *Marie Antoinette*, it was actually larger than the original. Scenarist Philip Dunne, who had shown a command of historical/religious drama in *The Robe* that paid off lavishly, was hired to write the screenplay.

The film's premier was designated a benefit for New York's Metropolitan Museum, but neither this gesture nor the movie itself won much favour from the critics, who subjected Reed's work to merciless critical fire. Writing for the New York *Herald*

Tribune, Crist pronounced the picture 'dull, dull, dull and un-spectacular'.[8] This view was shared by Dorothy Seiberling in *Life*, who complained of 'phony situations, stereotyped characters, tawdry spectacles and . . . two hours and twenty minutes of boredom'.[9] *Newsweek* decried a 'cruelly deceptive promise that is never realized',[10] and Crowther called the movie no more than 'an illustrated lecture on a slow artist at work'.[11] The wittiest critique came from Brendon Gill in *The New Yorker*, who noted that the movie included an intermission 'during which sleeping patrons can be roused with little or no inconvenience to the rest of the audience'.[12] Among better-known newspapers and magazines, *Variety* was the only complimentary voice: 'Tastefully mounted by producer–director Carol Reed, the Fox release has a wide sales appeal . . .'[13]

That the movie's cold treatment by reviewers was matched by a poor showing at the box office is all too easy to comprehend. Every ingredient in *Agony* seems on an epic scale except its level of imagination and intelligence. Synthetic as it is, Stone's book has historical and biographical sweep covering Michelangelo's life from the age of thirteen to his death at eighty-eight and conjuring up the tangled, faraway universe of sixteenth-century Italian life with precision and density. The movie turns Stone's wideangle lens into a zoom and concentrates exclusively on the four-and-a-half year period in which Michelangelo brought his immortal frescoes into being. Perversely, the film refuses to take the giant steps that seem natural to the epic, selecting instead an essentially static subject – the creative process – as its core. One has the sense of a mincing Cyclops, as the movie attempts to brood over and exult in Michelangelo's artistic struggle. Reed had made memorable use of artists in *Odd Man Out* and *Trapeze*, but an element of showmanship and theatricality was inherent to each, and this playfulness seems to have been an important catalyst for his own creative process. Confronted with the masterpiece of the millennium and one of the greatest artistic geniuses of all time (and encumbered by Dunne's numbingly solemn screenplay), there was not much Reed could do but try to keep the topheavy story lumbering along, much as the workers we see in the Carrara Hills sequences lug huge chunks of the celebrated marble out of the quarry.

To offset the lack of dynamism in the story, the film-makers pack as much pomp and spectacle around the edges as they can.

Pope Julius II (Rex Harrison), a warrior pontiff trying to unite Italy under the aegis of the Vatican and drive out the French, is seen leading his troops off to battle and returning at night (one of the better sequences in the movie); the hypnotic white expanse of the renowned quarry is the background for a scene in which workers who are trying to divert the Pope's soldiers so that Michelangelo can escape allow a 150-ton block of marble to tumble down a hillside; the Pope conducts mass in the newly-completed chapel of St Peter's for a large, resplendently attired collection of worshippers. Elsewhere there is even an anemic love interest interpolated: after a fall from the scaffolding, Michelangelo is nursed back to health by the ravishing Contessina de Medici (Diane Cilento), who harbours an unreciprocated passion for the great sculptor.

None of these episodes, however, is much more than a temporary distraction from the crucial drama, the titanic and tiresome conflicts between Julius, who wants his chapel completed as quickly and inexpensively as possible, and Michelangelo, whose progress can only be determined by his genius. Evidently audiences were supposed to be entertained and engrossed by the contrast of worldly, urbane Harrison in his lavish papal vestments confronting intense, single-minded Heston in his drab, unwashed rags. The two even have a running gag that could almost be a textbook example of tautology. 'When will you make an end of it?', asks the Pope. 'When I have finished', the artist replies firmly. Dunne must have been influenced by the so-let-it-be-written-so-let-it-be-done routine from *The Ten Commandments*.

The historical inaccuracies in the movie are abundant. There is no record of Michelangelo's having been ministered to in times of illness by any contessinas, beautiful or otherwise, and most Renaissance historians agree that the real Michelangelo would have probably been more interested in a male nurse anyway. On the homosexual issue, the movie is aggressively dishonest, compelling its Michelangelo to disavow any sexual interest in men. Other fanciful or fraudulent moments in *Agony* include Michelangelo's angry destruction of his first attempt at the chapel and his vision of what the true completion of his work should look like, which is glimpsed one morning in a gloriously arranged mural of cloud banks. The military engagements which thunder dimly in the interstices of the movie are historically accurate, though curiously enough, Reed, who did such a good job of recounting the Second World War in *The True Glory*, appears unable to enlighten us about why – for instance – the French are invading Lombardy or the Germans are massing at the Brenner Pass or Milan is under siege.

The dour Pope Julius of Stone's novel had been brightened up to suit Harrison's gifts, and there was not much Reed needed to coax a gay, high-stepping performance out of him. On the other hand, it was hard to coax anything out of Heston, an actor who has always seemed as if he would be very much at home on Easter Island. With his strapping, barrel-chested good looks and stolid personality, Heston is surely the antithesis of Michelangelo, or any other artist. As the sculptor's would-be mistress, Cilento makes an inappropriately slatternly noblewoman. A comparison of these performances is persuasive evidence of how much of Reed's famous skill with actors was dependent on having good ones to begin with, performers who were at least halfway suitable to their parts. When a lump of marble like Heston was thrust on him, he could not sculpt any better a performance than Heston's other directors.

Three years went by before Reed secured another assignment. The failure of *Agony and the Ecstasy* was costly and Reed bore the stigma, in spite of the fact that it is hard to imagine another director giving satisfying shape to such intractably mediocre material. But in Hollywood, where the director is always to blame – never the star, the property or the studio – Reed was widely regarded as a talent in irreversible deline. Few offers came his way, and when at last, after three years, he was hired again, it was by Romulus, an English house which had acquired the rights to Lionel Bart's *Oliver!*, one of the few English musicals ever to find favour with American audiences. The cleverly titled production firm – its founders were the brothers John and James Woolf (sons of C. M. Woolf) – sought American funding for *Oliver!*, but the money was hard to come by in an era when Hindenburg-scaled disasters like *Dr Doolittle* and *Hello, Dolly* seemed to represent the likely fate of a film musical. Even with Peter Sellers committed to the Fagin role, American producers balked. At last Columbia agreed to gamble on the project, and regardless of the fact that Reed had only directed a few musicals

– and those inconsequential juvenilia thirty years before – he was left at the helm of a risky, $8 million venture.

Curiously enough in semi-literate Hollywood, it was Dickens's name, not Reed's or Lionel Bart's, that convinced Columbia to go forward with the project. Dickens, probably the most popular English novelist who ever lived, had been adapted to the screen with a high rate of success. On the surface, his art derived from elements as reliable as the binomial theorem – chiefly sentimentality and melodrama – while his pages bustled with brilliant caricatures, figures so graphically drawn that even the most unrefined sensibility could respond to them. Whatever bulging warehouses of social criticism or Freudianism graduate students and scholars might find in Dickens's work, he was, on a more elementary level, a great popular entertainer, conceivably the greatest in the history of the English speaking literature. The executives at Columbia must have also calmed their nerves with the thought that, as an English director stewarding a new version of an English classic, to be filmed on English soil, Reed would presumably feel a special affinity for the property and that under his touch it would quicken into life.

To most critics and the vast majority of filmgoers, this presumption proved correct. Sensibly, Columbia opened the film for the Christmas season and promoted it as a family movie. Reviewers, who are often only slightly less influenced by a movie's advertising campaign than the public, are usually contemptuous of a film with the packaging that *Oliver!* received; indeed, they often use the picture for target practice, perfecting their command of invective. But Reed had turned in such a superior effort that only a few critics were dissatisfied. Vincent Canby, who inherited Crowther's post at the *New York Times* that year, reviled the movie as bulky and turgid: 'The focus of the movie is so wide . . . and the logistics of the production so heavy, that Oliver himself . . . gets flattened out, almost lost . . .'[14] In the *New Republic*, Stanley Kauffmann complained that although the direction was not a 'disgrace', the film 'isn't worth much'.[15] Among the yeas were Crist, who had moved from the defunct *Herald Tribune* to *New York Magazine* and who recommended *Oliver!* as a show with 'some sparkle and some wit' that was 'nowhere an insult to your intelligence';[16] *Variety*, which concluded that 'there's plenty of mileage left in the famous story';[17]

and Richard Schickel, then with *Life*, who called Reed's film an 'impeccable musical'.[18] The most extended rave came from Kael, who had begun reviewing for *The New Yorker* in 1967. In a graceful, 2000-word essay entitled 'The Concealed Art of Carol Reed', she garlanded the movie with discerning praise, interpolating as well a capsulization of Reed's whole career to date and some pertinent commentary on Dickens's novel. 'I . . . applaud the commercial heroism of a director who can steer a huge production and keep his sanity and perspective and decent human feelings as beautifully intact as they are in *Oliver!*'[19]

Unlike *The Agony and Ecstasy*, this was not a film in which Reed was straitened by the requirements of the star system and his carefully selected players, many of them veterans of the stage production, are perfectly matched with their roles. Sellers had long since moved on to more secure offers, so the role of Fagin went to the man who originated it on the stage, Ron Moody, a gifted performer who was equally adept at singing, dancing and acting. From this dextrous blend emerges a thoroughly infectious music-hall permutation of the famous villain. Softened considerably from the Fagin of Dickens's novel, Moody's rendering leaves the old man's feloniousness, cunning and unction intact, adding as well a colourful, roguish quality. This Fagin is a lovable scalliwag. Under Reed's expert supervision, Moody consistently maintains a perfect harmony among the various traits of his characterization.

Since Reed had an extensive background as an interpreter of children's problems, it is less surprising that he handled the children in the show as well as Fagin. Eight-year-old Mark Lester, who had impressed critics in Jack Clayton's *Our Father's House* (and those few patrons who saw this intriguing and neglected thriller) was chosen as Oliver. Like Joe in *A Kid for Two Farthings*, Lester's accent is improbably upper class, but in most other respects he gives Reed all that any director could hope for – sweetness without glucose; pathos without mawkishness; spirit without heroics. Everything about him is unforced and natural; in neither his acting nor his song and dance numbers is there anything of the fabricated prodigyhood that makes so many child stars in America quite insufferable. His dramatic sense always attuned to complements, Reed shapes this performance as a foil for Jack Dawkins, the Artful Dodger (Jack Wild), a wised-up street kid whose premature shrewdness is contrasted

with Oliver's innocence and expressed in the Dodger's polished
performing skills as well as his acting.

The radiant, boisterous work of Lester, Wild and the other
child actors in *Oliver!* is splendid proof that Reed had not lost his
empathy for children, that he was still a magician with them.
Indeed, during the shooting he craftily derived professional
advantage from the most immemorial of all acts of conjury.
Birkin recalls the stunt with zest:

> There's a moment when Fagin opened up his box of treasures
> for Oliver, and Carol wanted a reaction shot from Mark, his
> face lighting up with wonder. But he couldn't get it. Mark
> couldn't do it; it just looked phoney. Carol went home that
> night quite bothered about the matter. Then he contacted a
> friend of his who owned a pet shop and went and collected a
> white rabbit. Next day he got together with the cameraman
> and the other crew members so they could have the cameras
> and the lights all set up when Mark came on the set. When he
> did, Carol said, 'Oh Mark, I think I've got something that
> might rather amuse you', and produced from his jacket a
> white rabbit. Mark's face lit up and Carol got his shot. It's just
> the sort of thing he would dream up.

In a happy moment of nepotism, Reed's nephew, Oliver Reed,
was cast as Bill Sikes, and the younger Reed gave his uncle
exactly the right degree of slouching, scowling villainy. If this
Bill Sikes is less menacing than Robert Newton's in the David
Lean version of *Oliver Twist*, it is surely attributable to the
discrepancy between a straight drama and a musical. Sikes is
partnered with an admirable Nancy, Shani Wallis, who is as
good in her ballads as in her up-tempo numbers. (Reed's first
choice for this part was Shirley Bassey, but Columbia vetoed her
because it was felt a black Nancy would alienate filmgoers in the
American South.)

To insure a Hollywood-calibre gloss on the songs, songwriter-
arranger Johnny Green was hired as musical director. With his
assistance, Reed was able to package the songs with maximum
dramatic impact. 'As Long As He Needs Me', Nancy's ode to
Sikes, her lover, is the exception; a less pile-driving, dead-on
presentation of this inane ballad would have served it better. But
in his two big music-hall turns, 'You've Got to Pick a Pocket Or

Two' and 'Considering the Situation', Moody is properly sly, exuberant and comically contemptuous, with a fine portfolio of raffish mannerisms and inflections. The major production numbers in the first half of the film, 'Food, Glorious Food' and 'Consider Yourself at Home' are choreographed with abundant, old-fashioned Broadway-style energy by Oona White. Here, as in all the musical interludes, Reed's fusion of song and story is peerless, the transition from dialogue to words and music, plus dancing, could not be smoother. By almost universal agreement, the high point of *Oliver!* is 'Who Will Buy?' the beautiful motley of street songs that opens the second half of the film. From the first *a cappella*, pure-soprano statement of the man theme by the flower girl in the deserted Bloomsbury Square, the music builds gracefully into an oratorio of the ordinary. The other peddlars arrive gradually, sounding the variations and secondary motifs, and are eventually joined by policemen, maids, lords and ladies. Finally the now-sunlit square is flooded with a river of humanity. There is no denying that the song itself is a derivative of Gershwin's street songs from *Porgy and Bess* and the treatment is hardly original. But originality isn't the only virtue in art. Bart's imitation is an excellent one, while the tried-and-true staging is superbly suited to the material.

Kael also commends Reed for his appropriately stylized approach to the property and for his conversion of Dickens's classic to the requirements of contemporary musical comedy.[20] The inherent artificiality of the musical form makes it the wrong medium for extreme realism, grim social critiques or philosophical commentary. The songs and production numbers automatically distance us from the real world and make the characters' problems a matter of artifice. Understandably, Reed keeps the energy level of his show as high as he can, but never allows more than an engagingly synthetic form of reality to break through; even the slum settings, which Dickens conceived as a conscience-rousing appeal for economic and social reform, have a story-book ambiance. Although the novel achieves a weight and power that is, of course, missing from *Oliver!*, the maudlin melodrama that runs through the centre of the work is vastly more palatable in Reed's stylized interpretation. Moreover, two-thirds of the story – the worst two-thirds, one might add – have been scrapped, as in the David Lean film, and the masonry of what remains has been reconstituted to eliminate Dickens's excruciating implausibilities and coincidences.

Since Reed's work provides us with opportunities to see a distinctive sensibility and style at work, we are naturally tempted to look for other thematic preoccupations of his in *Oliver!*, such as the turmoil that is caused when innocence is unleashed on the world. This aspect of *Oliver!* may have helped engage Reed's creative powers more fully, but it is really only a dim echo of the theme he had explored in his masterpieces. After all, no blame is ever attributed to Oliver for the problems he inadvertently causes; his nobility is a shining contrast to the squalid schemers who surround him. On the other hand, the film gave Reed yet another orphan boy to embrace, and the opportunity to incorporate some of the animal symbolism with which Dickens had embroidered his book. As Reed linked people to cats and birds in *The Third Man*, here he finds correspondences between the mastiff-like Bill Sikes and his pet bulldog, Bulls-Eye.

Reed's work on *Oliver!* is splendidly seconded at the technical end by the extraordinarily sumptuous, painterly effects of Oswald Morris's photography, Terence Marsh's art direction and John Box's sets, which spread before us the full, bursting microcosm of nineteenth-century London. Naturalistically detailed, yet bathed in a romantic aura, the sets give us the smokey and decrepit atmosphere of the pickpockets' lair, the quaint Victorian bookshops and stores, the thronging, carriage-crowded streets, the patrician reserve of semicircular Bloomsbury Square. With effects like these, enriching every level of *Oliver!*, Reed and his marvellous team of craftsman leave the audience in a mood to ask, 'Please sir, can I have some more.'

Reed appeared to have regained his cinematic footing decisively with *Oliver!*, but the impression was misleading – as his subsequent films demonstrated. The critical and popular success of the film greatly strengthened Reed's hand in Hollywood. Unfortunately, he exercised astonishingly poor judgement in taking advantage of his opportunity. While his passion for experimenting with new material had been one of his principal strengths in the past, his instincts betrayed him here; the property he chose to develop next was Claire Huffaker's humorous Western novel

Nobody Loves a Drunken Indian, a crudely pro-Indian, sentimental comedy about a rebellious Paiute named Flapping Eagle. What appeal this novel could have had for Reed has mystified almost everyone who has ever had anything to say about the film. Where Reed's humour is refined, Huffaker's is coarse; where Reed's subject-matter is cosmopolitan, Huffaker's is regional; where Reed's irony is nimble, Huffaker's is cumbersome. What he liked about the novel, Reed told Thomas of the *Los Angeles Times*, 'was that it was a minority film'. 'These Indians', he said, 'fought for what they believed they should fight for – not knowing how to do it . . . What appealed to me was to get in a different setting. I don't like to stay in a certain type of picture.'[21] Perhaps the director heard a dim echo of his inarticulate, badly oppressed mining folk in the chants of the Indians. As for Reed's hunger for fresh subjects, this normally healthy appetite proved to be self-defeating. For whatever reason, he chose to subordinate himself to the flimsy material Huffaker gave him, and the film he made keeps its nose glued to the well-worn path of the original plot.

Examined in retrospect, *Flap* seems wholly a product of the 1960s. Theoretically, the moviegoers of 1970, many of whom were fresh from civil rights marches, could respond with indignation to the predicament of the Indians. After *Easy Rider*, unhappy endings had become a more or less accepted (or at least tolerated) way of expressing the nation's self-loathing. The humour, although it has the subtlety of a tommyhawk, does take direct aim at the lowest common denominator, a philosophy which has worked often enough. Moreover, with superstar Anthony Quinn turning in one of his exuberant, roistering hero–peasant roles, the box office insurance must have looked decent.

In the aftermath of *Oliver!*, a sizeable investment in a Reed film clearly made economic sense to American studios, and Warners put up $6 million, a significant bankroll for 1970. The critics were quick to advise the company on what a poor investment it had made. For *Variety*, the film was an 'over-produced American Indian comedy' with 'dim B.O.'[22] At the other end of the intellectual spectrum, Kauffmann of the *New Republic* denounced the work as a 'corny, ill-made picture full of tedious movie brawls'.[23] *Saturday Review*'s Arthur Knight (by this time alternating with Hollis Alpert) was somewhat gentler, suggesting that the film 'deserves far better than the second class treatment Warners has been giving it', though there is not much in his generally pejorative remarks about the picture to substantiate his claim.[24] The movie's one true defender was Howard Thompson in the *New York Times*, who described it as a film about the 'bleak plight of today's American Indian, a movie that is as funny as it is moving'.[25] American filmgoers clearly agreed with the majority critical view on *Flap*, and, after a brief flurry of bookings, the picture was withdrawn from circulation.

The movie's early scenes strive to establish the miserable, degrading conditions under which the Indians are compelled to live. Yet Reed, who had compressed the sufferings of Welsh coal miners and Irish revolutionaries into a dignified and affecting shorthand, here renders every feature of social oppression in heavy black lacquer. Apparently Reed's characteristic restraint could not be exported to an Indian reservation in Santa Clara, New Mexico, where the picture was shot. There we meet demoralized Indians caught helplessly between two cultures. Broke, underemployed, disparaged, socially adrift, they console themselves with firewater. Irony is also a form of solace, though their minor acts of deception against their tormentors seem trivial. Their chief commercial outlet is the Silver Dollar Trading Post, where the shelves and racks are choked with Indian knicknacks. A condescending white woman coos over a doll and, as we learn, gets just what she deserves: something 'made in Japan'. Most of the whites are strictly effigies of middle America, as sneering and mean-spirited as their counterparts in blaxploitation movies, but the true villain of the piece is Officer Rafferty (Victor French), a local policeman. Rafferty treats all Indians with the same impartial contempt and sadism, the only exception being Flapping Eagle (Quinn) or 'Flap', a disgruntled war hero for whom he reserves a special loathing. Flap is a natural leader, the most potentially subversive Indian around, and hence the biggest threat to a cop's sense of social order.

The suffering of the Indians is demographically uniform, cutting across all ages, sexes and levels of education. Eleven Snowflake (Tony Bill), an articulate, educated young buck and Wounded Bear (Victor Jory), a leathery old sage with a diploma-mill law degree, fare no better in the local society than the misfit Flap. Nor are the tribal elders any help: the nominal heads of the reservation are supinely obedient to the white authority figures from nearby Phoenix.

Despite this melancholy subject-matter, the style and tone of *Flap* is predominantly comic. Reed and Huffaker may have hoped to create the same unusual creative tension Reed had achieved in his many earlier attempts at the seriocomic, but whatever the director's motivation, he encourages the worst excesses in his players. Quinn is drunk and disorderly all over the neighbourhood, but particularly at his favourite spot, a brothel run by his girlfriend, coyly named Dorothy Bluebell (Shelley Winters). His loud, inebriated speeches about the mistreatment of the Indians are supposed to be warm and winning, but they merely seem flatulent. Winters is as egregiously colourful, foul-mouthed and boisterous as ever, a grotesque tornado of a woman, the Earth Mother from Forty-Second Street. Her shrill, Amazon-sized jealousy over Quinn's infidelity is one of the played-out comic veins from which Reed tries to quarry a few laughs. She knocks Quinn down at one point, and when he points to her own sexual conduct and complains of her hypocrisy ('But you do it every night'), she thunders back, 'Yes, but I'm a professional.' Other similarly misbegotten attempts at humour include the sight of Quinn emerging from a bathroom buttoning up his pants and a trick horse who throws riders on cue and surreptitiously drinks Flap's whisky when the Indian isn't looking.

The dramatic and comic spine of the story is the discovery by Wounded Bear of two arcane government treaties which finally allow Flap and his followers to convert their festering discontent into insurrectionary energies. Their first major counterattack is to halt a nearby construction crew, which is disturbing the reservation, by pretending the crew is desecrating an Indian burial ground. A clause in one of the treaties provides that Indians can claim any object left unattended on the reservation. After a railroad car they have furtively released one night rolls onto the reservation, the Indians jubilantly proclaim it theirs and transform it into a 'long, thin apartment'. We are meant to experience merry exultation in the Indians' pranks, which baffle and thwart the establishment.

Reed gets no better results when he shifts abruptly from comedy to melodrama two-thirds of the way through his film. After an epic fist fight between Flap and Rafferty (bedecked with such subtleties as Flap enveloping his antagonist in an Indian blanket), Flap flees on horseback. The chase climaxes in a duel between Flap and a pursuing helicopter, an episode that seems pilfered from the Kirk Douglas film *Lonely Are the Brave*. At its climax, *Flap* doesn't even have a flicker of a smile on its face. One of Laughing Bear's treaties reveals that Phoenix is actually Indian property, and Flap leads his people into the city to assert their rights. The townspeople are incredulous and unreceptive until the charismatic Flap conquers them with a display of oratorical eloquence that creates a reverential, almost mesmerized silence that William Jennings Bryan would have envied. But causes need a martyr – so goes the eternal left-wing credo – and Flap is assassinated by Rafferty. (At least we are spared the leaden irony of the novel, in which both Flap and his horse are slain, symbolically gunned down on the courthouse steps.) As in so much proletarian literature of the 1930s, hope and courage survive in the fallen leader's lieutenant – in this case, Eleven Snowflake – who tells the chastened white people that the Vanishing American won't vanish until justice has been done. Like his name, Flapping Eagle remains a true and irrepressible insignia of his country.

Quinn's performance is as expansive, as Homerically scaled as ever, a robust, hearty, life-affirming fusion of Zorba the Greek and Bombalino, the hero of *The Secret of Santa Vittoria*. From a strictly naturalistic viewpoint, the star's acting is counterfeit, yet what else could be done with the role except pump all the star juice into it that was possible? As Kauffmann, who annihilated the movie, wrote of Quinn: 'Anthony Quinn ought to be just a big bore by now . . . But damn it, he's good. He not only has the technique and power to sustain the big moments, he has the intensity of imagination to root the character in quiet reality.'[26] Everybody around the star seems tedious and phony, but even at his most excessive he retains his magnetism.

Regardless of its deficiencies, even *Flap* was superior to Reed's last film, *The Public Eye*, a lifeless comic soufflé lacking even the coarse energy and vigorous sentimentalizing of the Quinn vehicle. No doubt Reed viewed the endeavour as a wise retreat to creative territory where he was more at home. He was dealing with an urbane English comedy in which his light-fingered ironies could flourish and his rapport with the setting, London, would allow him to bathe the story in atmosphere. The project had the additional virtues of pretested material – *The Public Eye* had been well received as a one-act play, first performed in 1964 – and an ideal collaborator, the author of the original work, Peter Shaffer. Initially intended for Julie Andrews and Peter Ustinov, the leading roles went to Mia Farrow, a major American star, and Topol, the Israeli actor who a year before had carried off one of the plum movie roles of the decade, Tevye in *Fiddler on the Roof*.

But the movie that was created from these components amused very few critics and almost none of the filmgoing public. A stillborn enterprise that received as little distribution as *Flap*, the movie's winding sheets were comments like 'rubbish' (Penelope Gilliatt in *The New Yorker*);[27] 'bound to suffer stiff competition from more exhilarating cinematic brews' (*Variety*);[28] 'unbelievably boring' (Canby, the *New York Times*).[29] Among the better-known critics, Crist was a minority of one, praising *The Public Eye* for its 'mellow touch' and 'high-style tendresse'.[30]

Many reviewers diagnosed the ailment in *Public Eye* as an over-enlarged script, since Shaffer had to expand a half-hour flight of fancy into a full-length movie. There is no question that the play Shaffer wrote was artistically superior to the screenplay he adapted from it; yet apart from the attenuation, *The Public Eye*'s inherent premises seem fatally artificial and its dialogue deficient in the crispness and elegance that are the key requisites of a divertissement like this. Consider Shaffer's wobbly *donné*: a flamboyant detective, Christoforou (Topol), is hired by a jealous husband, Charles Sidley (Michael Jayston), to tail his flakey wife, Belinda (Farrow); ironically, the detective becomes the wife's closest confidant and engineers a reconciliation between the alienated couple. The situation is too arch to be conducive to good drama. The potential contrivance and coyness outweigh the comedic possibilities.

Structurally, the film functions by counterpointing the stuffy, overstarched world of Sidley, a rich accountant, and the more spontaneous, exploratory approach to life favoured by Belinda. They 'meet cute' when she is working as a waitress in a London restaurant and expresses her artless charm by spilling food all over Charles. Naturally, it's love at first sight. Unhappily, the headlong courtship and marriage gradually begin to leave Belinda feeling caged up with a coldly correct, unfeeling spouse. His fine old Tudor home is contrasted with Belinda's rootlessness, his taste for Mahler and Aldous Huxley with her enthusiasm for rock music, his buttoned-down, soulless profession with her catch-as-catch-can approach to employment. A 1960s flower child whose petals are miraculously intact, Belinda is a dreamy innocent whose last thought is unfaithfulness. Reading *Madam Bovary* has not, as her husband fears, driven her to seek a lover but rather to seek emotional sustenance that is unavailable at home. For her there is nourishment in watching the dolphins in the park, the fountains and formal gardens at Syon House, and even gorging herself on ice cream and old Peter Cushing/ Christopher Lee horror movies.

In the movie's only stirring of creative life – a faint one at that – Christoforou determines the truth about Belinda's 'assignations' and becomes her silent and acknowledged admirer, a wordless companion who is never far away. With a more imaginative character than the detective and a better actor to play him than Topol, this aspect of the film might have cast a spell. Instead, Reed and Shaffer, mistaking mere theatricality for dynamism, trick their creation out in attention-grabbing appurtenances and mannerisms. A variant of the clumsy but warm-hearted private eye (see Walter Matthau's early films for the genuine article), Christoforou stuffs his disorderly briefcase with dossiers while removing endless quantities of food – yogurt, grapefruit, etc. Naturally the joke is not just that he is a seemingly incompetent detective but also obtrusive; dressed in a blinding white coat and a peaked cap, he shoots about town on a motor scooter. No brainless gumshoe, he is an ex-philosophy student; his intellectual capacities are displayed not only in his professional aptitudes as marriage counsellor and all-around wise man, but in his command of old eastern proverbs ('He who follows in the flesh often leads in the spirit'). In conception and execution, Christoforou is a tiresomely busy creature.

As with *Flap*, the reviewers detected a creative exhaustion hovering over Reed's efforts. Thematically, there is very little in the film to convey a distinctive directorial personality – Reed's or anyone else's – and there's no sense of his uncanny skill in handling actors. Still, it may be unfair to blame him for being unequal to the task of getting better work out of the likes of Jayston, Topol and Farrow, particularly in view of the lacklustre script they were asked to play from. Jayston makes a drab role seem even drabber by his pedestrian, humorless rendering; he's stuffily British as required, but he communicates none of the potential fire and romance that would presumably have attracted Belinda to begin with and that would make him capable of redemption from the corporate dullness which he serves. Farrow is her usual nasal-voiced, forlorn, bird-like self, hopping feebly from branch to branch on life's boughs, so devoid of sensuality or vivacity (traits of the Belinda in the play) that we would expect her to go on spilling food on male customers for all eternity without attracting one of them. Topol is an actor of great exuberance, aggressively personable, with gestures so outsized they seem to belong on Mount Rushmore.

The scorecard on Reed's last five films, while definitely not outstanding, is by no means an unrelieved disappointment either. *The Running Man* may pale by comparison to Reed's best work, but it doesn't look nearly as anemic next to the thrillers of cruder, less inventive directors than Reed such as Anthony Mann and Sidney Furie. With all its shortcomings, it remains suave and ingratiating and its strong family resemblance to Reed's other thrillers makes it an absorbing study for any student of the director's *oeuvre*. The minuet of scoundrel, *naif* and irresistible beauty may recall *The Third Man*, but the steps are far from identical. Apart from the film's other virtues, it is fascinating to see Reed – in the tradition of all great creators, regardless of the art form – working yet another clever, fully individualized variation on his most cherished material.

The pleasures one derives from *Oliver!* are different, of course, since the director had vastly less opportunity to tamper with the subject-matter, which was predetermined by Dickens and Lionel Bart. With *Flap* and *The Public Eye*, however, he ought to have felt restored to the creative process which had always been most fruitful for him – adapting a minor play or work of fiction and giving it the shape and flavour with which he was most comfortable. That he had lost his touch seems the sad, inevitable conclusion of these misbegotten endeavours. The younger Reed would have transformed the dreary originals into something remarkable; the older Reed simply let them remain dreary.

But most directors who continue to work beyond their prime leave us a final legacy of unsatisfactory work, proof that they are as human as we are. How much praise can one honestly assign to

Griffith's *The Struggle*, Chaplin's *A King in New York*, Ford's *Seven Women* or Hitchcock's *The Family Plot?* One's mind skips back almost automatically to the director's masterpieces or even to works that are merely beguiling, works such as the stylish *Running Man* and the exhilarating *Oliver!*

11 Reed: A Final Assessment

If one's only familiarity with Reed's work were his aesthetic proclamations, he would sound more like a journeyman director than the genius he actually was. In his simple, plain-spoken aesthetic, the emphasis was always on patient craftsmanship and careful preparation. During the ten- or fifteen-year period in which his reputation was at its apogee, he chose each subject with the greatest care and dove into it completely. Between 1945 and 1953, the span in which his most revered work appeared, he made only five films, an average of one every fifteen months. What a contrast to American directors of similar standing in the 1940s and 1950s, who turned out as many as two or three pictures a year.

Like many film-makers, Reed was more comfortable with adaptations of novels and plays than with original screenplays. Given the time-consuming, costly business of making a movie, Reed preferred to work with a narrative that had been 'pre-tested'. He liked to start with a foundation already solidly in place. Between *The True Glory* and *The Public Eye*, Reed directed only two original screenplays (if we count *The Man Between*), and on one of them, *The Third Man*, he had, in a sense, safeguarded himself by collaborating with a scenarist who liked to warm up for his screenplays by writing a novel first. As an experienced novelist and screenwriter, Greene was Reed's paradigm of a partner. In the director's many adaptations of other men's plays and fiction he sought to duplicate the high quality of his films with Greene by hiring the author of the original wherever possible, even if the writer had had no experience in the film medium. 'It's talent that counts, not technique', he told Lejeune in the *New York Times* interview. The article went on to describe Reed's desire 'to have a creative writer on the job with freshness and freedom from formula . . . rather than sign up the usual army of professional scenarists.'[1] He himself was an uncredited collaborator on most of his films, supervising the creative process closely. Rejecting the strategies of more intuitive, improvisatory film-makers, Reed perfected his scripts ahead of time, combing out every burr before putting them in front of the cameras. This period of gestation usually took at least three months.

Reed applied the same painstaking care and devotion to every aspect of his films, superintending the design of costumes and sets, the placement of cameras, the choice of extras, the lighting and a thousand other ingredients that are part of the elaborate machinery of film-making. Discussing the all-encompassing command that Reed had to assume to get the results he did, Ginna gives a most graphic description of the multitudinous details that were involved in shooting one scene of *Our Man in Havana* and concludes: 'Scene 46 had taken two days to shoot, had involved 350 people, and had cost $48 000 . . .' Nor did Reed feel that his stewardship of a movie was completed when the cameras stopped turning:

> Following the picture through to the last detail is critical . . . You know, not enough directors are willing to do this. They are too eager to run off and play in the south of France – they want their money fast and easy. As soon as shooting is over, they're thinking of their next picture and are willing to turn the current one over to the studio to cut . . . To make a good film you've got to sit down at the moviola day after day – all day – running the footage over and over, trying combinations.[2]

An early devotee of realistic settings, Reed was hamstrung in his apprentice years by the economic pressures of film-making in Britain, where he was compelled to shoot all or most of a given film on the studio lot. If he could manage it, he incorporated a few days of location-shooting into his movies, and when his first major opportunity arrived, the coal-mining drama *The Stars Look Down*, he was passionately committed to using real collieries as much as possible. In the 1940s and 1950s, when he commanded generous budgets, he invested a month or more in scouting for the best possible locales for his movies. In the case of *Outcast of the Islands*, Reed and his associates toured Borneo, Ceylon and the Malayas in their search for an authentic South Seas ambiance. Although, with the exception of *The Third Man*, Reed filmed most of his interiors in studios, where sets could be

constructed to exact specifications and conditions could be carefully controlled, he did not make a single movie after the war
that did not include extensive location work, often in foreign
locales like Paris, Havana and Rome.

Much has been written about Reed's remarkable ability to
communicate with actors. No other major director in Europe or
America cast his films as intelligently as Reed or achieved as
consistently high a level of acting (though in fairness it must be
pointed out that many directors, especially in Hollywood, had to
contend with stars who were thrust on them by the studio,
regardless of their suitability for a particular role). A former
actor himself, Reed was praised by no less than Sir Michael
Redgrave for his empathy with performers: 'he understands the
actor's temperament perhaps as well as any director alive.'[3]
Reed was the polar opposite of the self-proclaimed prometheuses
of later years like Stanley Kubrick, who deliberately keep the
actors in the dark, while shaping their movies to an undisclosed
vision of their own. With Reed, the vision had at least been spelt
out in script form in advance. In addition to his many other
preparations for shooting, Reed required extensive rehearsals,
during which he did everything in his power to relax his actors.
In the interview with Lejeune, he commented on the problem of
agitated performers: 'all actors, particularly men, are nervous in
the first weeks of shooting. Either they overact or underact in
their anxiety to show they can really do it. It comes out first in
the hands – nervous movements and fiddling with their fingers. I
always give them something to hold – a book to turn over,
furniture to push about or lean against – until they've got the feel
of the thing.'[4] And it was a rare case indeed when a performer
did not get 'the feel of the thing' under Reed's tutelage. Among
their other accomplishments, his films offer an omnibus of fine
characterizations, including drolly rendered London bobbies
and their country cousins (the local constabulary in *The Fallen
Idol*, the Wilfred Lawson character in *Bank Holiday*), idealistic
reformers (Michael Redgrave in *The Stars Look Down*), stiff-
upper-lip army officers (David Niven in *The Way Ahead*), doomed
archangels (James Mason in *Odd Man Out*), pompous Colonel
Blimps (Robert Morley in *Outcast of the Islands*), coolly imperturb-
able secret agents (Noel Coward and Ralph Richardson in *Our
Man in Havana*), tragic beauties with haunting eyes (Kerima,

Valli), slouching villains (Oliver Reed in *Oliver!*) and, of course, scores of bewildered children and engaging rogues.

To aid the actors in getting under the skin of their characters, Reed tried to shoot his films in sequence, contrary to the usual practice of film-making. 'After a few weeks', he said, 'the actors know where they are, and what the parts mean, and you can afford to dodge about a bit.'[5] Throughout a production, he sought to coax the best possible performance from each of his players by maintaining an adroit balance between diplomacy and firmness. He elicited contributions and suggestions from the performers – 'bits of business' – and generated a 'warm and friendly feeling' on the set, where, said Redgrave, the 'actor is encouraged to feel that he has also assisted in the preparation of the film'.[6] Reed always stressed the critical importance of coop-eration in creating a film, a lesson he said he had learned while working for the Hollywood director Jack Ruben on *Java Head* in 1934. None the less Reed remained the prime mover behind his films, a force that never vacillated in achieving its design.

In terms of film technique, Reed belonged to no recognizable school, nor did he found one himself (one of the reasons why his achievement is so undervalued today). He was certainly not a pioneering force in world cinema, but rather an eclectic talent who drew on every cinematic style which he deemed useful to him. 'I . . . prefer moving shots to cutting', he once said, 'be-cause I am not awfully keen on the single close shot on the screen, particularly when reactions have to be shown between two or more people . . .'[7] Indeed, a considerable amount of his work displays a far greater proclivity for the German express-ionist methods than the montage effects encountered in other important national film cultures. His pictures abound in odd camera angles – generating psychological tension – and floods of bleak, joyless lighting, with sharp clashes of black and white and patchworks of jagged, menacing shadows. These are devices he absorbed from Murnau, Lang, Pabst and other eminent alum-nae of the pre-Hitler cinema. The cinematography in a Reed film is apt to rely on the 'long take', on tracking shots and other manifestations of the mobile camera rather than on the elaborate cutting that characterizes montage. Yet, when it suited him, Reed used montage as memorably as any follower of Eisenstein or Griffith. Consider the renowned robbery sequence in *Odd Man*

Out and what Andrew Sarris called the 'urgent cross-cutting' of
The Fallen Idol.[8]

Moreover, Reed was just as varied and technically adventurous with his aural effects as he was with his camera, augmenting
the sound in his movies to italicize the drama and mixing music
and sound with some of the experimental fervour of the young
René Clair. The scores of his films were ambitious and unpredictable, though he was hampered by the relative lack of musical
talent in his homeland, a nation that has produced few, if any,
major composers since Purcell. Often his own instincts were
better than those of the composers he hired. The farrago of zither
motifs in *The Third Man*, coaxed from Karas during a period of
several intense weeks at the director's home, were Reed's idea,
and represent a bold departure from conventional movie music.

Yet despite the vast machinery Reed deployed, his technique
remained essentially unobtrusive, even invisible. His favourite
director was William Wyler, and he was fond of pointing out
that 'the brilliance of Wyler's technique lies in its concealment'.
With few exceptions (such as the score in *The Third Man*), none of
the components in Reed's films calls attention to itself or juts out
of the fabric of the story. He denied that he ever used film as a
vehicle for his own political or philosophical ideas, and while
this is emphatically untrue, no one could challenge his assertion
that, for him, the narrative and its characters were the *sine qua
non*: 'I believe in the story itself, in sincerity and in transmitting a
feeling about people.'[9] As Redgrave put it, 'Sometimes the best
originality is the originality that conceals itself.'[10]

As germane as this 'concealed art' is to Reed's work, it is
misleading to call him an impersonal director, as several critics
have. Seldom in the history of English language films has there
been a director who gave his work a more fully individualized
stamp. Reed left his signature on almost every aspect of his
pictures – camerawork, sets, plot, acting, point of view. In this
century the urge to identify all important art as, in some sense, a
'portrait of the artist' has been nearly irresistible and though the
formula seldom applies as well to a collaborative medium like
film as to other art forms, overtly autobiographical films have
been made at least since *8½*; in addition, it is possible to argue
that in works as diverse as *Modern Times* and *Citizen Kane*, one can
detect not only the maker's hand but his psyche and personal
history as well. So it is with Reed perhaps, who, says Michael

Korda, was a man in search of a father, a replacement for Beerbohm Tree. The quest seems to lie half-submerged in his accounts of rejected, alienated or parentless children (most of them boys), the surrogate fathers they cherish and the glimpses of adult depravity that are forced on them. It is especially hard to miss the autobiographical motivation behind Reed's curious decision to film 'The Basement Room,' a story in which a child's natural father is as remote as a deity, while his substitute father, although less majestic, is far more supportive and close at hand.

In a more general sense, we can perceive Reed's personal qualities of compassion and humanity (attested to by both Korda and Greene) suffusing his films like a beautiful dye. This humanistic colouring helps balance the dark effect of his irony and keeps it from ever coarsening into cynicism. Reed's tact and self-restraint are also mirrored in the countless scenes of melodrama from which he has so strenuously excluded any brutality, sensationalism or vulgarity. It is the welter of human passions, beating away beneath the famous British reserve (or bursting through it in *Outcast of the Islands*) that occupies Reed, the dramatic chemistry that Faulkner summed up simply as 'the human heart in conflict with itself'. His subject is nothing more than that – and, in his best work, never less. How incredible, therefore to encounter the judgement of critics like Gerald Mast, who categorizes Reed as an 'escapist' director.[11]

As a British film-maker, Reed is something of a collosus without a pedestal. It would appear that *Sight and Sound*, while regularly composing odes to the least of Hollywood directors, has never devoted more than a few paragraphs to Reed. This neglect seems mystifying in view of the international recognition Reed achieved for a national cinema which, apart from Hitchcock, was not only provincial but so lacklustre that theatre owners had to be compelled to display its wares by an Act of Parliament. Beginning as an assembly-line director like so many British film-makers, manufacturing ready-made stories on short shooting schedules and pinchpenny budgets, Reed would have surely passed into the same shadowy limbo as most of his contemporaries (names like Brian Desmond Hurst, Adrian Brunel and Walter Forde), were it not for a singular combination of ability and opportunity. His intellectual roots were sunk deep in the empirical, anti-metaphysical tradition that has been a preeminent strain in English cultural life for centuries. Locke and Hume created the foundations of English philosophy, stressing the primacy of sensory data over mystical and *a priori* illuminations, and the country's greatest man of letters, Dr Johnson, angrily kicked a rock to refute Bishop Berkeley's notion that the existence of a material world was unprovable. The English have always been in love with the real world, and with this background it is only logical that most great British novels and plays should be constructed from the brick and mortar of facts; that the realistic movement in England should have eclipsed that of most other nations; that sociology should have become such a critical tool to English writers. From Jane Austen to Anthony Powell and Angus Wilson, British fiction has usually been most comfortable when viewing man amidst the fine mesh of his social world.

In the cinema, however, most English directors were indifferent or even averse to stories cut from the rough, prosaic fabric of contemporary British life. Almost instinctively they turned to the colourful, bewigged past, to heroic war dramas, to works blatantly synthesized from Hollywood ingredients, to adaptations of the more superficial West End dramas or literary masterpieces that were safely remote from the current scene or popular novels in which a faded Victorian sensibility throbbed pathetically. Not so Reed, who showed himself to be a true-blooded heir of England's most vital heritage by striving for scrupulously accurate textures of realism wherever he could. The minor sociologizing of early films such as *Laburnum Grove* and *Bank Holiday* were practice sessions for the all-out attempts at verisimilitude in *Stars*, *Odd Man Out* and later Reed works.

A champion of realism, Reed was also a formalist who had no intention of allowing naturalistic detail to spill out incontinently; rather he channelled it carefully into pools and streams that fit the overall landscaping of his stories. The narrative shape of Reed's best work suggests a gifted story-teller with an almost intuitive grasp of his calling, of how and when to present dramatic conflict, generate suspense, build climaxes and win an audience's sympathy or reverse its expectations. The style in which these elements are managed seems to appear effortlessly on the director's easel, a series of smooth, patient strokes of the sort associated with well-made British plays of the pre-John Osborne era. Reed eschews the rough edges that later English film-makers like Lindsay Anderson, John Schlesinger and Kenneth Loach, the cinematic progeny of Osborne, were to permit – even cultivate – but his love of baroque effects keeps the drawing-room refinement of his drama from succumbing to the complacencies and *longeurs* that can often afflict British films, particularly in the era when the works of Terence Rattigan and Noel Coward, rather than those of Osborne and the 'angry young men', were the paradigms of good dramatic form. Further proof against blandness is found in Reed's irony, a marvellously protean entity which could take the form of gentle social satire (*Bank Holiday*), quietly impassioned moral indictments (*Odd Man Out*), rococo playfulness (*Laburnum Grove*), simple parody (*Our Man in Havana*), and melodramatic legerdemain (*The Running Man*).

Yet unlike the later Welles, in whose work stylistics becomes an end in itself (the ominous shadows, Grand Guignol characters, gothic settings and other theatrical trappings are largely devoid of content), Reed uses his technique as a medium for mature ideas. The collision of innocent beings with an imperfect, even corrupt humanity – bringing pain and annihilation rather than redemption – is obviously Reed's most pervasive and profoundly ironic theme, but there are other arresting motifs that he examined over the years: the magnetism of evil and the comparative pallor of goodness; the terrified loneliness and incomprehension with which children are doomed to watch the sphere of adulthood; the roots of betrayal and its consequences; the metabolism of the artistic process, especially in the performing arts.

The greatness of Reed's work lies in his ability to give graceful dramatic form to these ideas, to convey them with wit and insight and, above all, restraint. Sarris sentences Reed to a category called 'Less Than Meets the Eye',[12] but actually there is more; the director frequently manages to suggest a cache of additional drama and unspoken thoughts and revelations glimmering beneath the surface of the tale. Since he was English, we can look on his constitutional understatement as a national trait, as common in Albion as fish and chips or an Oxonian accent, but to be an effective director it is not enough merely to possess reserve; one must have something *in* reserve, and Reed most emphatically did. Indeed, in this context it is instructive to recall

Outcast; with its most un-British overflow of volcanic passions, its overheated tropical emotions, Reed is still in complete control of the tone: he keeps the lid on.

With his elaborate repertoire of talents, Reed brought a cosmopolitanism to English films that surely must have inspired his great contemporary David Lean as well as other rising young directors – Jack Clayton, Tony Richardson, Schlesinger, Anderson, *et al*. Rough working-class dramas like *Saturday Night and Sunday Morning*, *This Sporting Life* and *The Loneliness of the Long Distance Runner* seem worlds removed from Reed's work, of course, though his steadfast insistence on social realism over the artificialities that once prevailed in the English cinema is a significant bridge. It is also important not to overlook Reed's impact in the United States, where his sophisticated films brought the intellect and mature artistry of Europe to American audiences without the language barrier that severely limited the distribution of major continental works.

Locked out of the pantheon, Reed is not the subject of much scholarship, and in the United States revivals of his work are limited to an occasional resurrection of *Odd Man Out* or *The Third Man*; even they pop in and out of the film vaults all too briefly and all too rarely. A wholesale retrospective of his work might help to rectify the situation by forcing film students, movie critics and the general public to confront the varied and abundant body of Reed's work: the headlong charms of *A Girl Must Live*; the faultless comedy of manners of *Kipps*; the documentary power of *The True Glory*; the poetic tragedy of *Odd Man Out*; the wit and elegantly shaped melodrama of *The Fallen Idol* and *The Third Man*; the raw, unequivocal miseries of *An Outcast of the Islands*; the glossily entertaining commercial pleasures of *Trapeze*; the urbane thrills of *The Running Man*; the beautifully cadenced, high-stepping exuberance of *Oliver!* In the aftermath of this tide of evidence, an advocate for Carol Reed could confidently rest his case.

Notes and References

CHAPTER 1

To provide an intellectual and cultural framework for examining Carol
Reed's films, a history of the British cinema from its origins through to
the Second World War is offered in this chapter. Although Reed began
directing in 1935, 1939 seemed a tidier, more logical cut-off point for
the survey. All the information in the chapter is synthesized from
several excellent works on the subject: Roy Armes's *A Critical History of
the British Cinema*, Ernest Betts' *The Film Business*, Ivan Butler's *Cinema
in Britain*, Denis Gifford's *British Film Catalogue*, Rachel Low's *History of
the British Film*, and George Perry's *The Great British Picture Show*.

CHAPTER 2

1. Michael Korda, *Charmed Lives* (New York, 1979) p. 229; Madeleine
   Bingham, *The Great Lover* (London, 1978).
2. Frances Donaldson, *The Actor-Managers* (London, 1970) p. 165.
3. Interview with the author. Unless otherwise identified, all quota-
   tions in this study from Max Reed, Michael Korda and Andrew
   Birkin derive from interviews.
4. C. A. Lejeune, 'Portrait of England's No. 1 Director', *New York
   Times*, 7 September 1941, p. 3.
5. Harvey Breit, ' "I Give the Public What I Like" ', *New York Times
   Magazine*, 15 January 1950, pp. 18-19.
6. Korda, *Charmed Lives*, p. 244.
7. Kevin Thomas, 'Director of "Eagle" Stays Unflappable', *The Los
   Angeles Times*, 24 August 1969.

CHAPTER 3

1. Michael Voigt, 'Pictures of Innocence: Sir Carol Reed', *Focus on
   Film*, no. 17 (Spring 1974) 34.
2. '*Midshipman Easy*', *The Times*, 23 December 1935.

3. Graham Greene, *The Pleasure Dome* (London, 1927) p. 42 (Greene's collected film criticism from *The Spectator*).
4. Voigt, 'Pictures of Innocence', p. 18.
5. Frederick Marryat, *Mr. Midshipman Easy* (New York, 1866) p. 127.
6. Ibid., p. 132.
7. Greene, *The Pleasure Dome*, p. 91.
8. Andrew Sarris, 'Carol Reed in the Context of His Time', *Film Culture*, 2, 4 (1956) 15.
9. Basil Wright, 'The Director: Carol Reed', in *The Year's Work in Film*, ed. by Roger Manvell (London, 1950) p. 11
10. Frank S. Nugent, '*Talk of the Devil*', *New York Times*, 15 May 1937, p. 23.
11. 'Three on a Weekend', *Variety*, 9 February 1938, p. 15.
12. Otis Ferguson, 'Pictures From England', *The New Republic*, 146 (14 September 1938) 160.
13. 'Three on a Weekend', *New York Times*, 2 June 1938, p. 19.
14. Wright, 'The Director', p. 11.
15. '*Climbing High*', *New York Times*, 5 June 1939, p. 20.
16. '*Climbing High*',*Variety*, 14 December 1938, p. 12.
17. Archer Winston, '*Climbing High*', *New York Post*, 5 June 1939.
18. Wanda Hale, '*Climbing High*', *New York Daily News*, 4 June 1939.
19. '*Climbing High*', *New York Morning Telegraph*, 4 June 1939.
20. Bosley Crowther, '*A Girl Must Live*', *New York Times*, 24 March 1942. p. 25.
21. Winston, *New York Post*, 24 May 1942.
22. '*A Girl Must Live*', *Variety* 10 May 1939.

CHAPTER 4

1. Pauline Kael, *Kiss Kiss Bang Bang* (New York, 1969) pp. 439–41.
2. Richard Whitehall, '*The Stars Look Down*', *Films and Filming*, 4 (January 1962) pp. 22–3, 45–6.
3. '*The Stars Look Down*', *The Times*, 22 January 1940.
4. Aubrey Flanagan, '*The Stars Look Down*', *Motion Picture Herald*, 27 January 1940.
5. Graham Greene, *The Pleasure Dome*, (London, 1972) p. 265.
6. Paul Rotha, '*The Stars Look Down*', *Documentary News Letter*, no. 3 (March 1940) p. 12.
7. '*The Stars Look Down*', *Variety*, 15 July 1941.
8. '*The Stars Look Down*', *New York Times*, 24 July 1941, p. 15.
9. '*The Stars Look Down*', *Newsweek*, 18 (28 July 1941) 53.
10. Archer Winston, '*The Stars Look Down*', *New York Post*, 24 July 1941.
11. Kael, *Kiss Kiss Bang Bang*, p. 441.

12. Crowther, '*The Stars Look Down*', p. 15.
13. Andrew Sarris, 'Carol Reed in the Context of His Time', *Film Culture*, 2, 4 (1956) 15.
14. Michael Redgrave, *Mask or Face* (New York, 1958) p. 135.
15. Michael Voigt, 'Pictures of Innocence: Sir Carol Reed', *Focus on Films*, no. 17 (Spring 1974) 21.
16. Rudyard Kipling, *Something of Myself* (London, 1937) p. 225.
17. '*Night Train*', *Time*, 37 (13 January 1941) 73.
18. '*Night Train*', *New York Times*, 30 November 1940, p. 21.
19. Otis Ferguson, 'A Hit and a Miss', *The New Republic*, 124 (13 January 1941) 54.
20. Basil Wright, 'The Director: Carol Reed', in *The Year's Work in Film*, ed. by Roger Manvell (London, 1950) p. 11.
21. Sarris, 'Carol Reed in the Context of His Time', p. 15.
22. Voight, 'Pictures of Innocence', p. 21.
23. Bosley Crowther, '*The Girl in the News*', *New York Times*, 5 May 1941, p. 13.
24. Sarris, 'Carol Reed in the Context of His Time', p. 15.
25. '*Kipps*', *Variety*, 1 April 1941.
26. Robert W. Dana, '*Kipps*', *New York Herald Tribune*, 5 May 1942.
27. Irene Thirer, '*Kipps*', *New York Post*, 25 May 1942.
28. '*Kipps*', *New York Times*, 25 May 1942, p.11.
29. Milton Meltzer, '*Kipps*', *The Daily Worker*, 25 May 1942.
30. Sarris, 'Carol Reed in the Context of His Time', p. 15.

CHAPTER 5

1. Arthur Winston, '*Young Mr. Pitt*', *New York Post*, 11 March 1943.
2. Kate Cameron, '*Young Mr. Pitt*', *New York Daily News*, 11 March 1943.
3. '*Young Mr. Pitt*', *Variety*, 1 July 1942.
4. Philip T. Hartung, 'Milton! Thou Shouldst Be', *Commonweal*, 37 (26 March 1943), 568.
5. Bosley Crowther, '*Young Mr. Pitt*', *New York Times*, 11 March 1943, p. 17.
6. Basil Wright, 'The Director: Carol Reed', in *The Year's Work in Film*, ed. Roger Manvell (London, 1950) pp. 11–12.
7. Raymond Durgnat, *A Mirror for England: British Movies from Austerity to Affluence* (London, 1970) p. 106.
8. Andrew Sarris, 'Carol Reed in the Context of His Time', *Film Culture*, 2, 4 (1956) 16.
9. Michael Voigt, 'Pictures of Innocence: Sir Carol Reed', *Focus on Films*, no. 17 (Spring 1974) 22.
10. Reed obituary, *The Times*, 27 April 1976.

11. Reed obituary, *New York Times*, 27 April 1976, p. 38.
12. C. A. Lejeune, '*The Way Ahead*', *Observer*, 9 July 1944.
13. '*The Way Ahead*', *Variety*, 21 June 1944.
14. '*The Way Ahead*', *Time*, 45 (28 May 1945) 56.
15. 'England Expects', *Newsweek*, 25 (28 May 1945) 114.
16. Crowther, '*The Way Ahead*', *New York Times*, 4 June 1945, p. 22.
17. Jesse Zunser, '*The True Glory*', *Cue*, 3 (8 September 1945) 11.
18. '*The True Glory*', *Time*, 46 (17 September 1945) 95.
19. Crowther, '*The True Glory*', *New York Times*, 7 September 1945.
20. James Agee, '*The True Glory*', *The Nation*, 161 (29 September 1945) 321
21. Sarris, 'Carol Reed in the Context of His Time', p. 16.
22. Ezra Goodman, 'Carol Reed', *Theatre Arts*, 5 (May 1947) 57.

CHAPTER 6

1. John Huntley, 'Film Music in Britain, 1947–48' in *British Film Yearbook*, ed. Peter Noble (London, 1948) p. 39.
2. Andrew Sarris, 'Carol Reed in the Context of His Time', *Film Culture*, 2, 4 (1956) 17.
3. '*Odd Man Out*', *The Times*, 31 January 1947, 4.
4. Arthur Vesselo, *Odd Man Out*', *Sight and Sound*, 61 (Spring 1947) 39.
5. William Whitebait, '*Odd Man Out*', *The New Statesman and Nation* (8 February 1947), 13.
6. James Agee, '*Odd Man Out*', *Time*, 49 (3 March 1947) 81.
7. John McCarten, 'A Man Hunt', *The New Yorker*, 23 (3 May 1947) 94.
8. John Mason Brown, '*The Hunt and the Hunted*', *Saturday Review*, 30 (24 May 1947) 25.
9. Bosley Crowther, '*Odd Man Out*', *New York Times*, 24 April 1947, p. 30.
10. Philip T. Hartung, 'No Tinkling Cymbal', *Commonweal*, 46 (9 May 1947) 94.
11. Abraham Polonsky, '*Odd Man Out* and *Monsieur Verdoux*', *Hollywood Quarterly*, 4 (July 1947).
12. Julia Symmonds, 'Reflections on *Odd Man Out*', *Film Quarterly* (Summer 1947) 52–6.
13. Karel Reisz, *The Technique of Film Editing* (New York, 1953) pp. 261–71.
14. James De Felice, *Filmguide to Odd Man Out* (Bloomington, 1975).
15. F. L. Green, *Odd Man Out* (London, 1947) p. 36.
16. Ibid., p. 103.

17. Ezra Goodman, 'Carol Reed', *Theatre Arts*, 5 (May 1947) 57.
18. Green, *Odd Man Out*, p. 82.
19. Roger Manvell, *Three British Screen Plays* (London, 1950) p. 85.
20. De Felice, *Filmguide*, p. 26.
21. Ibid., p. 30.
22. Ibid., p. 29.
23. Manvell, *Three British Screen Plays*, p. 95.
24. Reisz, *Film Editing*, p. 263.
25. Ibid., p. 264.
26. Sarris, 'Carol Reed in the Context of His Time', p. 17.
27. Agee, '*Odd Man Out*', *The Nation*, 165 (19 July 1947) 81.
28. John Hadsell, '*Odd Man Out*', *Classics of Film*, ed. by Arthur Lenning (Madison, 1965) pp. 179–87.
29. Michael Voigt, 'Pictures of Innocence: Sir Carol Reed', *Focus on Films*, no. 17 (Spring, 1974) 24.
30. Sarris, 'Carol Reed in the Context of His Time', p. 17.

CHAPTER 7

1. '*The Fallen Idol*', *Time*, 53 (4 April 1949) 98.
2. Bosley Crowther, '*The Fallen Idol*', *New York Times*, 16 November 1949, p. 39.
3. '*The Fallen Idol*',*Variety*, 16 November 1949).
4. John McCarten, 'Good Boy', *The New Yorker*, 25 (19 November 1949) 110.
5. Graham Greene, *The Third Man and The Fallen Idol* (London, 1974) pp. 151, 193, 183, 180, 151.
6. Ibid., p. 152.
7. Raymond Durgnat, *A Mirror for England: British Movies from Austerity to Affluence* (London, 1970) p. 167.
8. Greene, *The Third Man*, p. 151.
9. Ibid., p. 3.
10. '*The Third Man*', *Variety*, 7 September 1949.
11. '*The Third Man*', *Time*, 55 (6 February 1950) 82.
12. '*The Third Man*', *Newsweek*, 35 (13 February 1950) 89.
13. Crowther, '*The Third Man*', *New York Times*, 3 February 1950, p. 29.
14. Roy Armes, *A Critical History of the British Cinema* (New York, 1978) p. 207.
15. Durgnat, *Mirror for England*, p. 167.
16. Andrew Sarris, 'Carol Reed in the Context of His Time', *Film Culture*, 2, 4 (1956) 12.
17. David Zinman, *Fifty Classic Motion Pictures* (New York, 1970) p. 294.

18. Sarris, 'Carol Reed in the Context of His Time', p. 12.
19. Pauline Kael, *Kiss Kiss Bang Bang* (New York, 1969) p. 452.
20. Greene, *The Third Man*, p. 6.
21. Greene, 'The Lost Childhood', in *Collected Essays* (London, 1969) p. 18.

CHAPTER 8

1. '*Outcast of the Islands*', *Time*, 59 (28 April 1952) 98.
2. '*Outcast of the Islands*', *Newsweek*, 39 (26 May 1952) 91.
3. '*Outcast of the Islands*', *Variety*, 15 January 1952.
4. Bosley Crowther, '*Outcast of the Islands*', *New York Times*, 16 May 1952, p. 19.
5. Andrew Sarris, *The American Cinema* (New York 1968) p. 164.
6. Pauline Kael, *Kiss Kiss Bang Bang* (New York, 1969) p. 410.
7. Crowther, '*Outcast*', p. 19.
8. Joseph Conrad, *Nostromo* (London, 1963) p. 501.
9. Michael Voigt, 'Pictures of Innocence: Sir Carol Reed', *Focus on Films*, no. 17 (Spring 1974) 29.
10. Conrad, *The Nigger of the Narcissus* in *The Portable Conrad* (New York, 1966) p. 313.
11. Conrad, *An Outcast of the Islands* (Harmondsworth, 1975) pp. 165, 167.
12. Kael, *Kiss Kiss Bang Bang*, p. 411.
13. Voigt, 'Pictures of Innocence', p. 30.
14. Ibid., p. 28.
15. Louis Berg, 'The Day Berlin Starred', *This Week*, 28 June 1953.
16. Crowther, '*The Man Between*', *New York Times*, 19 November 1953, p. 41.
17. 'Fourteenth Century Italy and 20th Century Berlin', *Cue*, 21 November 1953.
18. Hollis Alpert, '*The Man Between*', *Saturday Review*, 36 (28 November 1953) 31.
19. '*The Man Between*', *Variety*, 30 September 1953.
20. Voigt, 'Pictures of Innocence', p. 30.
21. Alpert, '*A Kid For Two Farthings*', *Saturday Review*, 39 (14 April 1956) 35.
22. '*A Kid For Two Farthings*', *Variety*, 18 May 1955.
23. Crowther, '*A Kid For Two Farthings*', *New York Times*, 18 April 1956, p. 25.
24. John McCarten, 'Two Tots and a Lot of Girls', *The New Yorker*, 32 (28 April 1956) 89.
25. '*A Kid For Two Farthings*', *Time*, 66 (7 May 1956) 108.

26. Kael, *Kiss Kiss Bang Bang*, p. 362.
27. Wolf Mankowitz, *A Kid For Two Farthings* (London, 1953) pp. 24, 31.

CHAPTER 9

1. 'Lollobrigida on a Trapeze', *Manchester Weekly*, 5 June 1956.
2. '*Trapeze*', *Variety*, 30 May 1956.
3. 'Gina Joins the Circus', *Look*, 40 (15 May 1956) 56.
4. 'A Netful at the Circus', *Life*, 40 (4 June 1956) 75.
5. '*Trapeze*', *Time*, 67 (8 June 1956) 102.
6. Bosley Crowther, '*Trapeze*', *New York Times*, 5 June 1956, p. 39.
7. Max Catto, *The Killing Frost* (London, 1950) p. 298.
8. '*The Key*', *Variety*, 11 June 1958.
9. Crowther, '*The Key*', *New York Times*, 2 July 1958, p. 23.
10. John Carden, 'An Essay in Fear', *Saturday Review*, 41 (5 July 1958) 22.
11. '*The Key*', *Time*, 72 (14 July 1958) 72.
12. John McCarten, 'War and Love', *The New Yorker*, 34 (12 July 1958) 98.
13. Jan De Hartog, *The Distant Shore* (New York, 1952) pp. 118–19.
14. Michael Voigt, 'Pictures of Innocence: Sir Carol Reed', *Focus on Films*, no. 17 (Spring 1974) 31.
15. 'Spying for the Connoisseur', *The Times*, 30 December 1959, 9.
16. C. A. Lejeune, 'Cuban Coup', *Observer*, 3 January 1960.
17. '*Our Man in Havana*', *Sight and Sound*, 29, 1 (Winter 1959–60) 35.
18. '*Our Man in Havana*', *Variety*, 13 January 1960.
19. Crowther, '*Our Man in Havana*', *New York Times*, 28 January 1960, p. 26.
20. '*Our Man in Havana*', *Time*, 75 (8 February 1960) 92.
21. John McCarten, 'All Quiet in Havana', *The New Yorker*, 35 (6 February 1960) 104.
22. Graham Greene, *Ways of Escape* (New York, 1980) p. 248.
23. Crowther, '*Our Man in Havana*', p. 26.
24. Robert Emmett Gina, '*Our Man in Havana*', *Horizon* II (November 1959) 27.
25. Andrew Sarris, *The American Cinema* (New York, 1968) p. 163.

CHAPTER 10

1. '*The Running Man*', *Variety*, 24 September 1963.
2. 'The Insuranceman Cometh', *Time*, 82 (7 October 1963) 111.

3. '*The Running Man*', *Newsweek*, 62 (7 October 1963) 111.
4. Judith Crist, '*The Running Man*', *New York Herald Tribune*, 3 October 1963.
5. Bosley Crowther, '*The Running Man*', *New York Times*, 3 October 1963, p. 31.
6. Michael Voigt, 'Pictures of Innocence: Sir Carol Reed', *Focus on Films*, no. 17 (Spring 1974) 31.
7. Ibid., p. 31.
8. Crist, *New York Herald Tribune*, 8 October 1965.
9. Dorothy Seiberling, 'There I Was Flat on My Back Trying to Be a Genius', *Life*, 59 (12 December 1965) 75.
10. 'Fig Leaf', *Newsweek*, 41 (16 October 1965) 121.
11. Crowther, '*The Agony and the Ecstasy*', *New York Times*, 9 October 1965, p. 5.
12. Brendon Gill, 'The Renaissance and After', *The New Yorker*, 41 (16 October 1965) 228.
13. '*The Agony and the Ecstacy*', *Variety*, 15 September 1965.
14. Vincent Canby, '*Oliver!*', *New York Times*, 12 December 1968, p. 62.
15. Stanley Kauffmann, 'Greetings and Groans', *The New Republic*, 160 (18 January 1969) 23.
16. Judith Crist, 'Losing Nothing in Translation', *New York*, 1 (16 December 1968) 54.
17. '*Oliver!*', *Variety*, 2 October 1968.
18. Richard Schickel, 'How About an Oscar for *Oliver!?*', *Life*, 66 (4 April 1969) 16.
19. Pauline Kael, 'The Concealed Art of Carol Reed', *The New Yorker*, 44 (14 December 1968) 193–6.
20. Ibid., p. 194.
21. Kevin Thomas, 'Director of *Eagle* Stays Unflappable', *Los Angeles Times*, 24 August 1969.
22. '*Flap*', *Variety*, 28 October 1970.
23. Stanley Kauffmann, '*Flap*', *The New Republic*, 164 (23 January 1971) 22.
24. Arthur Knight, 'Flashes in a Pan', *Saturday Review*, 53 (19 December 1970) 38.
25. Howard Thompson, '*Flap*', *New York Times*, 1 January 1971, p. 17.
26. Kauffmann, '*Flap*', p. 22.
27. Penelope Gilliatt, '*The Public Eye*', *The New Yorker*, 48 (29 July 1972) 54.
28. '*The Public Eye*', *Variety*, 5 May 1972.
29. Vincent Canby, '*The Public Eye*', *New York Times*, 19 July 1972, p. 22.
30. Judith Crist, 'It's Still the Same Old Story, But You'd Never Know', *New York*, 5 (17 July 1972) 50.

CHAPTER 11

1. C. A. Lejeune, 'Portrait of England's No. 1 Film Director', *New York Times*, 7 September 1941, p. 3.
2. Robert Emmett Ginna, '*Our Man in Havana*', *Horizon*, II (November 1959) 125, 31, 122.
3. Michael Redgrave, *Mask or Face* (New York, 1958) p. 135.
4. Lejeune, 'Portrait', p. 3.
5. Ibid., p. 3.
6. Redgrave, *Mask or Face*, p. 135.
7. Ezra Goodman, 'Carol Reed', *Theatre Arts*, 5 (May 1947) 57.
8. Andrew Sarris, 'Carol Reed in the Context of His Time', *Film Culture*, 1 (1956) 11.
9. Goodman, 'Carol Reed', p. 57.
10. Redgrave, *Mask or Face*, p. 136.
11. Gerald Mast, *A Short History of the Movies* (Indianapolis, 1976) p. 414.
12. Sarris, *The American Cinema* (New York, 1968) p. 163.

Selected Bibliography

BOOKS

Armes, Roy. *A Critical History of the British Cinema* (New York: Oxford University Press, 1978).

Betts, Ernest. *The Film Business: A History of British Cinema, 1896–1972* (London: George Allen & Unwin, 1973).

Butler, Ivan. *Cinema in Britain* (London: Tantivy Press, 1973).

Catto, Max. *The Killing Frost* (London: Methuen, 1950).

Conrad, Joseph. *An Outcast of the Islands* (Harmondsworth: Penguin Books, 1975).

Cronin, A. J. *The Stars Look Down* (New York: Simon & Schuster, 1935).

De Felice, James. *Filmguide to Odd Man Out* (Bloomington: Indiana University Press, 1975).

Dickens, Charles. *Oliver Twist* (New York: New American Library, 1962).

Dickens, Charles. *Oliver Twist* (New York: New American Library, 1962).

Donaldson, Frances. *The Actor-Managers*

Durgnat, Raymond. *A Mirror for England: British Movies from Austerity to Affluence* (New York: Praeger, 1971).

Gifford, Denis. *British Film Catalogue* (New York: McGraw-Hill, 1973).

Green, F. L. *Odd Man Out* (London: Michael Joseph, 1947).

Greene, Graham. *The Third Man and The Fallen Idol* (London: Heinemann, 1974).

———. *Our Man in Havana* Harmondsworth: Penguin Books, 1970).

Henrey, Robert. *A Film Star in Belgrave Square* (London: Peter Davis, 1949).

Huffaker, Claire. *Nobody Loves a Drunken Indian* (New York: McKay, 1967).

Low, Rachel. *A History of the British Film*, vols 2, 3 and 4 (London: George Allen & Unwin, 1949, 1950, 1971).

Low, Rachel and Roger Manvell. *A History of the British Film*, vol. 1 (London: George Allen & Unwin, 1948).

Mankowitz, Wolf. *A Kid For Two Farthings* (London: André Deutsch, 1953).

Marryatt, Frederick. *Mr. Midshipman Easy* (New York: D. Appleton & Co., 1866).
Mast, Gerald. *A Short History of the Movies* (Indianapolis: Bobbs-Merrill, 1976).
Perry, George. *The Great British Picture Show* (London: Hart-Davis MacGibbon, 1974).
Shaffer, Peter. *The Public Eye and the Private Ear* (London: Secker & Warburg, 1972).
Smith, Shelley. *The Ballad of the Running Man* (New York: Harper & Brothers, 1961).
Stone, Irving. *The Agony and the Ecstacy* (New York: New American Library, 1961).
Wells, H. G. *Kipps* (New York: Charles Scribner's Sons, 1905).

EXTRACTS

Bingham, Madeleine. *The Great Lover* (London: Hamisch Hamilton, 1978). Provides valuable information on Reed's parentage.
De Hartog, Jan. *The Distant Shore* (New York: Harper & Row, 1952).
Forman, Denis. *Films, 1945–1950* (London: Longman, Green, 1951). Useful summary of Reed's career.
Greene, Graham. *The Pleasure Dome* (London: Secker & Warburg, 1972). Includes perceptive reviews of *Midshipman Easy*, *Laburnum Grove* and *The Stars Look Down*, accurately forecasting Reed's later contributions.
_____. *Collected Essays* (London: Bodley Head, 1969).
_____. *Ways of Escape* (New York: Simon & Schuster, 1980). Contains valuable information on the genesis of the three Reed–Greene collaborations.
Hadsell, John. '*Odd Man Out*' in *Classics of the Film*, ed. Arthur Lenning (Madison: Wisconsin Film Society Press, 1965). A critique of *Odd Man Out* which concentrates on the film's Christian themes and imagery.
Huntley, John. 'Film Music in Britain, 1947–48', in *British Film Yearbook*, ed. Peter Noble. (London: Skelton Robinson, 1948). Offers detailed analysis of William Alwyn's score for *Odd Man Out*.
Huntley, John and Roger Manvell. *The Technique of Film Music* (London: Focal Press, 1957). The introduction is by Alwyn, who explains his approach to composing for the screen, illustrating some of his points with references to the final scene in *Odd Man Out*.
Kael, Pauline. *Kiss Kiss Bang Bang* (New York: Bantam Books, 1969). Kael offers brief but incisive discussions of several Reed films.

Korda, Michael. *Charmed Lives* (New York: Random House, 1979). Virtually the only biographical portrait of Reed by someone who knew him.

Manvell, Roger. *A Seat at the Cinema* (London: Evans Brothers, 1951). A sensible, laudatory essay on *Odd Man Out*.

———. *Three British Screen Plays* (London: Methuen, 1950). Contains the screenplays of *Brief Encounter*, *Scott of the Antarctic* and *Odd Man Out*. The Reed work includes material not used in the actual film.

Philips, Gene D., S.J. *Graham Greene: The Films of His Fiction* (New York: Teachers College, Columbia University, 1974). Chapter-length critiques of *The Fallen Idol*, *The Third Man* and *Our Man in Havana*, incorporating all available information on the Reed–Greene partnership.

Redgrave, Michael. *Mask or Face* (New York: Theatre Arts Books, 1958). The great actor contributes a few observations about his experiences working with Reed.

Reisz, Karel. *The Technique of Film Editing* (New York: Communication Arts Books, 1953). Provides a lengthy discussion of the technique behind the hold-up sequence in *Odd Man Out*.

Rothe, Anna (ed). 'Carol Reed', in *Current Biography* (New York: H. W. Wilson, 1950). Meagre though it is, this sketch is as good a compilation of facts about Reed's life and career as one can find.

Sarris, Andrew. *The American Cinema* (New York: Dutton, 1968). A short, highly sophisticated attack on Reed's work.

Wilson, Harry. 'Seven Directors', in *British Film Yearbook*, ed. Peter Noble (London: Skelton Robinson, 1949). A summary of Reed's work up to *Odd Man Out*.

Wright, Basil. 'The Director: Carol Reed', in *The Year's Work in Film*, ed. Roger Manvell (London: Longman, Green, 1950). A sympathetic, thoughtful evaluation of Reed's *oeuvre* by a noted British documentarian and critic who was something of an influence on Reed.

Zinman, David. *Fifty Classic Motion Pictures* (New York: Crown Publishers, 1970). Intellectually superficial chapter on *The Third Man* but incorporating a good deal of fresh information about the making of the film.

ARTICLES

Agee, James. '*Odd Man Out*', *Time* (3 March 1947) 81. In a short typically jazzed-up review for *Time*, Agee nevertheless examines *Odd Man Out* perceptively, establishing the basic framework within which the picture will be discussed.

———. '*Odd Man Out*', *The Nation*, 165 (19 July 1947) 79–81. A later, more reflective piece offering additional insights into the film – and additional criticisms.

Breit, Harvey. ' "I Give the Public What *I* Like" ', *New York Times Magazine*, 15 January 1950, 18–19. A minimally helpful assessment of Reed and his work just prior to the American release of *The Third Man*.

Brown, John Mason. 'The Hunt and the Hunted', *Saturday Review*, 30 (24 May 1947) 22–25. A long essay hailing *Odd Man Out* for its artistic integrity, though pointing out the film's weaknesses as well.

Ferguson, Otis. 'Pictures From England', *The New Republic*, 146 (14 September 1938) 160. In what is the first critique of a Reed film by an important American reviewer, Ferguson recognizes the director's refreshing gift for realistic social detail.

Ginna, Robert Emmett. '*Our Man in Havana*', *Horizon*, II (November 1959) 26–31, 122–26. Intelligent, extensive and very illuminating article on the filming of *Havana*, with much information about the production itself and one of the fullest statements of his artistic principles Reed ever made.

Goodman, Ezra. 'Carol Reed', *Theatre Arts*, 5 (May 1947) 57–9. Plodding interview with Reed at the time of the American release of *Odd Man Out*; somewhat redeemed by useful comments of Reed's about his craft.

Kael, Pauline. 'The Concealed Art of Carol Reed', *The New Yorker*, 44 (14 December 1968) 193–6.
Outstanding essay on Reed, incorporated into review of *Oliver!*

Kennedy, Paul P. 'The Carol Reed Formula', *New York Times*, 30 November 1947. A biography of Reed with comments about his approach to film-making.

Lejeune, C. A. 'Portrait of England's No. 1 Director', *New York Times*, 7 September 1941, p. 3. One of the few truly revelatory interviews with Reed, including a précis of his aesthetics and working methods and a thoroughgoing attempt to capture his appearance and elusive personality on paper.

Sarris, Andrew. 'Carol Reed in the Context of His Time', *Film Culture*, 2, 4 (1956) 14–17 and 1 (1957) 11–14. Probably the best of all attempts at a comprehensive critique of Reed's *oeuvre* (up to 1956), an erudite and discerning treatment that appraises Reed's place in film history as well as his significance to the British cinema.

Vesselo, Arthur. '*Odd Man Out*', *Sight and Sound*, 61 (Spring 1947) 39–40. An enthusiastic and probing review of the film in the leading British film journal; destined to be one of the few instances in which *S&S* devoted any space to a premier English director.

Voigt, Michael. 'Pictures of Innocence: Sir Carol Reed', *Focus on Films*, no. 17 (Spring 1974) 17–38. Excellent survey of Reed's career with an intelligent evaluation of his artistic development all the way from *Midshipman Easy* to *The Public Eye*.

Whitehall, Richard. '*The Stars Look Down*', *Films and Filming*, 4 (January 1962) 22–3, 45–6. A fascinating, heavily detailed account of the filming of *Stars*, filled with particulars about every aspect of the production, almost none of which has ever appeared anywhere else.

Filmography

In a few instances, complete credits for Reed's early films were impossible to obtain – hence the gaps in this compilation.

It Happened in Paris (Associated Talking Pictures, 1935)
Producer: Bray Wyndham
Codirector: Robert Wyler
Screenplay: John Huston and H. F. Maltby, from Yves Mirande's play *L'Arpete*
Cast: John Loder (Paul), Nancy Burne (Jacqueline), Edward H. Robins (Knight), Dorothy Boyd (Patricia), Esme Percy (Pommier), Minnie Rayner (Concierge), Laurence Grossmith (Bernard), Paul Sheridan (Baptiste), Billy Shine (Albert), Warren Jenkins (Raymond), Val Norton (Roger), Kyrle Bellew (Elvira), Nancy Pawley (Ernestine)

Midshipman Easy (Associated Talking Pictures, 1935); US: *Men of the Sea*
Producer: Basil Dean, Thorold Dickinson
Screenplay: Anthony Kimmins, from Captain Frederick Marryat's novel *Mr Midshipman Easy*
Cinematographer: John W. Boyle
Editor: Sidney Cole
Cast: Hughie Green (Midshipman Easy), Margaret Lockwood (Donna Agnes), Roger Livesey (Captain Wilson), Robert Adams (Mesty), Harry Tate (Mr Biggs), Dennis Wyndham (Don Silvio), Tom Gill (Gascoigne), Lewis Casson (Mr Easy), Dorothy Holmes-Gore (Mrs Easy), Frederick Burtwell (Mr Easthupp), Arnold Lucy (John Rebiera), Esme Church (Donna Rebiera)

Laburnum Grove (Associated Talking Pictures, 1936)
Producer: Basil Dean
Screenplay: Anthony Kimmins, from J. B. Priestley's play *Laburnum Grove*
Cinematographer: John W. Boyle
Art Director: Edward Carrick, Denis Wreford
Music: Ernest Irving
Editor: Jack Kitchin

Cast: Edmund Gwenn (Mr Redfern), Cedric Hardwicke (Mr Baxley), Victoria Hopper (Elsie), Ethel Coleridge (Mrs Baxley), Katie Johnson (Mrs Redfern), Francis James (Harold Russ), James Harcourt (Joe Fletten), Norman Walker (Man With Glasses), David Hawthorne (Inspector Stack), Frederick Burtwell (Simpson), Terence Conlin (Police Sergeant)

Talk of the Devil (British & Dominions, 1936)
Producer: Jack Raymond
Story: Carol Reed, Anthony Kimmins
Screenplay: Reed, Kimmins and George Barraud
Cinematographer: Francis Carver
Art Director: Wilfred Arnold
Music: Percival Mackey
Editor: Helen Lewis, Merrill White Ltd, John Morris
Cast: Ricardo Cortez (Ray Allen), Sally Eilers (Ann), Randle Ayrton (John Findlay), Basil Sydney (Stephen Findlay), Fred Culley (Alderson), Charles Carson (Lord Dymchurch), Gordon McLeod (Inspector), Margaret Rutherford (Stephen's Housekeeper)

Who's Your Lady Friend? (Dorian, 1937)
Producer: Martin Sabine
Screenplay: Anthony Kimmins and Julius Hoest, from the play *Der Herr Ohne Wohnung*, by Oesterreicher and Jenbach
Cinematographer: Jan Stallach
Art Director: Erwin Scharf
Music: Richard Stolz, Ernest Irving, Vivian Ellis
Editor: Ernest Aldridge
Cast: Frances Day (Lulu), Vic Oliver (Dr Mangold), Betty Stockfeld (Mrs Mangold), Romney Brent (Fred), Margaret Lockwood (Mimi), Frederick Ranalow (The Cabby), Sarah Churchill (The Maid)

Bank Holiday (Gainsborough, 1938); US *Three on a Weekend*
Producer: Edward Black
Story: Rodney Ackland, Hans Wilhelm
Screenplay: Ackland, Wilhelm, Roger Burford
Cinematographer: Arthur Crabtree
Art Director: Vetchinsky
Music: Louis Levy
Editor: R. E. Dearing
Cast: John Lodge (Stephen Howard), Margaret Lockwood (Catherine), Hugh Williams (Geoffrey), Rene Ray (Doreen), Merle Tottenham (Milly), Linden Travers (Ann Howard), Wally Patch (Arthur), Kathleen Harrison (May), Garry Marsh ('Follies' Manager),

Jeanne Stuart (Miss Mayfair), Wilfrid Lawson (Police Sergeant),
Felix Aylmer (Surgeon), Michael Rennie (Guardsman)

Penny Paradise (Associated Talking Pictures, 1938)
Producer: Basil Dean
Story: Basil Dean
Cinematographer: Ronald Neame, Gordon Dines
Art Director: Wilfred Shingleton
Editor: Ernest Aldridge
Cast: Edmund Gwenn (Joe), Jimmy O'Dea (Pat), Betty Driver
(Betty), Ethel Coleridge (Aunt Agnes), Syd Crossley (Uncle Lance-
lot), James Harcourt (Amos Cook), Jack Livesey (Bert), Maire
O'Neil (Widow Clegg)

Climbing High (Gaumont–British, 1938)
Story: Lesser Samuels, Marian Dix
Screenplay: Stephen Clarkson
Cinematographer: Mutz Greenbaum
Art Director: H. Murton, Alfred Junge
Music: Louis Levy
Editor: Michael Gordon, A. Barnes
Cast: Jessie Matthews (Diana), Michael Redgrave (Nicky), Noel Ma-
dison (Gibson), Alastair Sim (Max), Margaret Vyner (Lady Con-
stance), Mary Clare (Lady Emily), Francis L. Sullivan (Madman),
Enid Stamp-Taylor (Winnie), Basil Radford (Reggie)

A Girl Must Live (Gainsborough, 1939)
Producer: Edward Black
Story: Emery Bonnet
Screenplay: Frank Launder, Austin Melford
Cinematographer: Jack Cox
Art Director: Vetchinsky
Music: Louis Levy
Editor: R. E. Dearing
Cast: Margaret Lockwood (Leslie James), Renée Houston (Gloria
Lind), Lilli Palmer (Clytie Devine), George Robey (Horace Blount),
Hugh Sinclair (Earl of Pangborough), Naunton Wayne (Hugo
Smythe-Parkinson), David Burns (Joe Gold), Mary Clare (Mrs
Wallis), Kathleen Harrison (Penelope), Drusilla Wills (Miss Polk-
inghorn), Wilson Coleman (Mr Jolliffe), Kathleen Boutall (Mrs
Blount), Muriel Aked and Martita Hunt (Mesdames Dupont)

The Stars Look Down (Grafton, 1940)
Producer: Issidore Goldsmith
Screenplay: J. B. Williams, from A. J. Cronin's novel *The Stars Look
Down*

Cinematographer: Mutz Greenbaum, Henry Harris
Art Director: James Carter
Music: Hans May
Editor: Reginald Beck
Cast: Michael Redgrave (David Fenwick), Margaret Lockwood (Jenny Sunley), Emlyn Williams (Joe Gowlan), Nancy Price (Martha Fenwick), Edward Rigby (Robert Fenwick), Allan Jeayes (Richard Barras), Cecil Parker (Stanley Millington), Milton Rosmer (Harry Nugent, MP), Olga Lindo (Mrs Sunley), Desmond Tester (Hughie Fenwick, David Markham (Arthur Barras), Frederick Burtwell (Heddon), Edmund Willard (Ramage)

Night Train to Munich (20th Century-Fox, 1940); US: *Night Train*
Producer: Edward Black
Story: Gordon Wellesley
Screenplay: Frank Launder, Sidney Gilliat
Cinematographer: Otto Kanturek
Art Director: Vetchinsky
Music: Louis Levy
Editor: R. E. Dearing
Cast: Rex Harrison (Gus Bennett), Margaret Lockwood (Anna Bomasch), Paul Henreid (Karl Marsen), Basil Radford (Charters), Naunton Wayne (Caldicott), James Harcourt (Axel Bomasch), Felix Aylmer (Dr Fredericks), Roland Culver (Roberts), Eliot Makeham (Schwab), Raymond Huntley (Kampenfeldt)

The Girl in the News (20th Century-Fox, 1941)
Producer: Edward Black
Screenplay: Sidney Gilliat, From Roy Vickers's novel *The Girl in the News*
Cinematographer: Otto Kanturek
Art Director: Vetchinsky
Music: Louis Levy
Editor: R. E. Dearing
Cast: Margaret Lockwood (Anne Graham), Barry K. Barnes (Stephen Farrington), Emlyn Williams (Tracy), Roger Livesey (Bill Mather), Margaretta Scott (Judith Bentley), Basil Radford (Dr Treadgrave), Irene Handl (Miss Blaker), Mervyn Johns (James Fetherwood), Betty Jardine (Elsie), Felix Aylmer (Prosecuting Counsel)

Kipps (20th Century-Fox, 1941); US: *The Remarkable Mr. Kipps*
Producer: Edward Black
Screenplay: Sidney Gilliat, from H. G. Wells's novel *Kipps*
Cinematographer: Arthur Crabtree
Art Director: Vetchinsky

Music: Louis Levy
Editor: Alfred Roome
Cast: Michael Redgrave (Kipps), Diana Wynyard (Helen Walshing-
ham), Arthur Riscoe (Chitterlow), Phyllis Calvert (Ann Pornick),
Max Adrian (Chester Coote), Helen Haye (Mrs Walshingham),
Lloyd Pearson (Shalford), Michael Wilding (Ronnie Walshingham),
Edward Rigby (Buggins), Mackenzie Ward (Pearce), Hermione
Baddeley (Miss Mergle), Betty Ann Davies (Flo Bates), Irene
Browne (Mrs Bindon–Botting)

A Letter from Home (20th Century-Fox, 1941)
Producer: Edward Black
Screenplay: Rodney Ackland and Arthur Boys
Cinematographer: Jack Cox
Cast: Celia Johnson

The Young Mr Pitt (20th Century-Fox, 1942)
Producer: Edward Black
Story: Viscount Castlerosse
Screenplay: Frank Launder, Sidney Gilliat
Cinematographer: Frederick Young
Art Director: Vetchinsky
Music: Louis Levy
Editor: R. E. Dearing
Cast: Robert Donat (William Pitt), Robert Morley (Charles James
Fox), Phyllis Calvert (Eleanor Eden), John Mills (William Wilber-
force), Raymond Lovell (George III), Max Adrian (Sheridan), Felix
Aylmer (Lord North), Albert Lieven (Talleyrand), Stephen Hag-
gard (Lord Nelson), Geoffrey Atkins (Pitt as a boy), Jean Cadell
(Mrs Sperry), Henry Hewitt (Addington), Herbert Lom (Napoleon)

The New Lot (Army Kinematographic Service, 1942)
The Way Ahead (Two Cities, 1944)
Producer: Norman Walker, John Sutro
Story: Eric Ambler
Screenplay: Eric Ambler, Peter Ustinov
Cinematographer: Guy Green
Art Director: David Rawnsley
Music: William Alwyn
Editor: Fergus McDonell
Cast: David Niven (Jim Perry), Raymond Huntley (Davenport), Bill
Hartnell (Sergeant Fletcher), Stanley Holloway (Brewer), James
Donald (Lloyd), John Laurie (Luke), Leslie Dwyer (Beck), Peter
Ustinov (Rispoli), Leo Genn (Company Commander), Renée Asher-

son (Marjorie Gillingham), Mary Jerrold (Mrs Gillingham), Penelope Ward (Mrs Perry)

The True Glory (Ministry of Information, Britain; Office of War Information, US, 1945)
Co-director: Garson Kanin
Screenplay: Private Harry Brown, Staff Sergeant Guy Trosper, Sergeant Saul Levitt, Major Eric Maschwitz, Captain Frank Harvey, Flight Lieutenant Arthur Macrae, Flight Officer Jenny Nicholson, Private Peter Ustinov, Gerald Kersh ·
Cinematographer: Army Film Unit, American Army Pictorial Service, cameramen of Britain, US, Canada, France, Belgium, Poland, Netherlands, Czechoslovakia, Norway
Music: William Alwyn
Editor: Lt Robert Verrell, Sgt Leiberwitz, Sgt Bob Farrell, Sgt Jerry Cowen, Sgt Bob Carrick, Sgt Bob Clark

Odd Man Out (Two Cities, 1947)
Producer: Carol Reed
Screenplay: F. L. Green, R. C. Sherriff, from Green's novel *Odd Man Out*
Cinematographer: Robert Krasker
Art Director: Ralph Brinton
Music: William Alwyn
Editor: Fergus McDonell
Cast: James Mason (Johnny), Robert Newton (Lukey), Robert Beatty (Dennis), F. J. McCormick (Shell), Fay Compton (Rosie), Beryl Measor (Maudie), Cyril Cusack (Pat), Dan O'Herlihy (Nolan), Roy Irving (Murphy), Kathleen Ryan (Kathleen), Denis O'Dea (Head Constable), Maureen Delany (Theresa), Kitty Kirwan (Granny), Elwyn Brook Jones (Tober), W. G. Fay (Father Tom), Joseph Tomelty (Cabby), Arthur Hambling (Alfie), William Hartnell (Fencie)

The Fallen Idol (London Films, 1948)
Producer: Carol Reed
Screenplay: Graham Greene, from his story 'The Basement Room'
Cinematographer: Georges Perinal
Art Director: Vincent Korda, James Sawyer
Music: William Alwyn
Editor: Oswald Hafenrichter
Cast: Ralph Richardson (Baines), Michèle Morgan (Julie), Bobby Henrey (Felipe), Sonia Dresdel (Mrs Baines), Dennis O'Dea (Detective Inspector Crower), Walter Fitzgerald (Dr Fenton), Karel Ste-

panek (First Secretary), Joan Young (Mrs Barrow), Dandy Nichols (Mrs Patterson), Bernard Lee (Det. Hart), Jack Hawkins (Det. Lake), Geoffrey Keen (Det. Davis), Torin Thatcher (Policeman 'A'), George Woodbridge (Policeman), Dora Bryan (Rose), Hay Petrie (Clockwinder), Gerald Hinze (Ambassador)

The Third Man (London Films, 1949)
Producer: Carol Reed
Screenplay: Graham Greene
Cinematographer: Robert Krasker
Art Director: Vincent Korda
Music: Anton Karas
Editor: Oswald Hafenrichter
Cast: Joseph Cotten (Holly Martins), Trevor Howard (Major Calloway), Valli (Anna Schmidt), Orson Welles (Harry Lime), Bernard Lee (Sergeant Paine), Ernst Deutsch ('Baron' Kurtz), Paul Hoerbiger (Harry's Porter), Siegfried Beuer (Popescu), Erich Pomto (Dr Winkel), Wilfrid Hyde-White (Crabbin), Herbert Halbik (Hansl)

Outcast of the Islands (London Films, 1952)
Producer: Carol Reed
Screenplay: William Fairchild, from Joseph Conrad's Novel *An Outcast of the Islands*
Cinematographer: John Wilcox
Art Director: Vincent Korda
Music: Brian Easdale
Editor: Bert Bates
Cast: Trevor Howard (Willems), Ralph Richardson (Captain Lingard), Robert Morley (Almayer), Wendy Hiller (Mrs Almayer), Kerima (Aîssa), George Coulouris (Babalatchi), A. V. Bramble (Badavi), Wilfrid Hyde-White (Vinck), Dharma Emmanuel (Ali), Annabel Morley (Nina Almayer), Betty Ann Davies (Mrs Willems)

The Man Between (London Films, 1953)
Producer: Carol Reed
Screenplay: Harry Kurnitz, from Walter Ebert's novel *Susanne in Berlin*
Cinematographer: Desmond Dickinson
Art Director: Andre Andrejew
Music: John Addison
Editor: A. S. Bates
Cast: James Mason (Ivo), Claire Bloom (Susanne), Hildegarde Neff (Bettina), Geoffrey Toone (Martin), Aribert Waescher (Halendar), Ernest Schroeder (Kastner), Dieter Krause (Horst), Hilde Sessak (Lizzi), Karl John (Inspector Kleiber)

A Kid for Two Farthings (London Films, 1955)
Producer: Carol Reed
Screenplay: Wolf Mankowitz, from his novel *A Kid For Two Farthings*
Cinematographer: Edward Scaife
Art Director: Wilfred Shingleton
Music: Benjamin Frankel
Editor: A. S. Bates
Cast: Celia Johnson (Joanna), Diana Dors (Sonia), David Kossoff
    (Kandinsky), Brenda De Banzie ('Lady' Ruby), Joe Robinson
    (Sam), Jonathan Ashmore (Joe), Sydney Tafler ('Madame' Rita),
    Primo Carnera (Python), Lou Jacobi (Blackie Isaacs), Sidney James
    ('Ice' Berg), Meier Leibovitch (Mendel), Irene Handl (Mrs
    Abramowitz)

Trapeze (Hecht–Lancaster/Susan, 1956)
Producer: James Hill
Screenplay: James R. Webb, Liam O'Brien; from Max Catto's novel
    The Killing Frost
Cinematographer: Robert Krasker
Art Director: Rino Mondellini
Music: Malcolm Arnold
Editor: Bert Bates
Cast: Burt Lancaster (Mike Ribble), Gina Lollobrigida (Lola), Tony
    Curtis (Tino Orsini), Katy Jurado (Rosa), Thomas Gomez (Bou-
    glione), Johnny Puleo (Max the Dwarf), Minor Watson (John
    Ringling North), Gerard Landry (Chikki), J. P. Kerrien (Otto),
    Gabrielle Fontan (Old Woman)

The Key (Open Road, 1958)
Producer: Carl Foreman
Screenplay: Carl Foreman, from Jan De Hartog's novella *Stella*
Cinematographer: Oswald Morris
Art Director: Geoffrey Drake
Music: Malcolm Arnold
Editor: Bert Bates
Cast: William Holden (David Ross), Sophia Loren (Stella), Trevor
    Howard (Chris Ford), Oscar Homolka (Van Dam), Kieron Moore
    (Kane), Bernard Lee (Wadlow), Beatrix Lehmann (Housekeeper),
    Noel Purcell (Hotel Porter), Bryan Forbes (Weaver), Russell Waters
    (Sparks)

Our Man in Havana (Columbia, 1959)
Producer: Carol Reed
Screenplay: Graham Greene, from his novel *Our Man in Havana*
Cinematographer: Oswald Morris

Art Director: John Box
Music: Hermanos Deniz Cuban Rhythm Band
Editor: Bert Bates
Cast: Alec Guinness (Jim Wormold), Maureen O'Hara (Beatrice), Burl Ives (Dr Hasselbacher), Ernie Kovacs (Segura), Noel Coward (Hawthorne), Ralph Richardson ('C'), Jo Morrow (Milly), Paul Rogers (Carter), Gregoire Aslan (Cifuentes), Jose Prieto (Lopez), Timothy Bateson (Rudy), Duncan MacRae (MacDougal)

The Running Man (Columbia, 1963)
Producer: Carol Reed
Screenplay: John Mortimer, from Shelley Smith's novel *The Ballad of the Running Man*
Cinematographer: Robert Krasker
Art Director: John Stoll
Music: William Alwyn
Editor: Bert Bates
Cast: Laurence Harvey (Rex Black), Lee Remick (Stella), Alan Bates (Stephen), Felix Aylmer (Parson), Eleanor Summerfield (Hilda Tanner), Allan Cuthbertson (Jerkins), Harold Goldblatt (Tom Webster), Noel Purcell (Miles Bleeker), John Meillon (Jim Jerome)

The Agony and the Ecstasy (20th Century-Fox, 1965)
Producer: Carol Reed
Screenplay: Philip Dunne, from Irving Stone's novel *The Agony and the Ecstacy*
Cinematographer: Leon Shamroy
Art Director: Jack Martin Smith
Music: Alex North
Editor: Samuel E. Beetley
Cast: Charlton Heston (Michelangelo), Rex Harrison (Pope Julius II), Diane Cilento (Contessina de Medici), Harry Andrews (Bramante), Alberto Lupo (Duke of Urbino), Adolfo Celi (Giovanni de Medici), Venantino Venantini (Paris De Grassis), John Stacey (Sangallo), Fausto Tozzi (Foreman), Tomas Milian (Raphael), Alec McCowen (Cardinal)

Oliver! (Romulus/Warwick/Columbia, 1968)
Producer: John Woolf
Screenplay: Vernon Harris, from the musical *Oliver!* by Lionel Bart
Cinematographer: Oswald Morris
Art Director: Terence Marsh
Music and Lyrics: Lionel Bart
Editor: Ralph Kemplen

Cast: Ron Moody (Fagin), Shani Wallis (Nancy), Oliver Reed (Bill Sikes), Harry Secombe (Mr Bumble), Hugh Griffith (The Magistrate), Jack Wild (Jack Dawkins), Clive Moss (Charlie Bates), Peggy Mount (Widow Corney), Leonard Rossiter (Mr Sowerberry)

The Last Warrior (Warner Brothers, 1970); US: *Flap*
Producer: Jerry Adler
Screenplay: Clair Huffaker, from his novel *Nobody Loves a Drunken Indian*
Cinematographer: Fred J. Koenekamp
Art Director: Mort Rabinowitz
Music: Marvin Hamlisch
Editor: Frank Bracht
Cast: Anthony Quinn (Flapping Eagle), Shelley Winters (Dorothy Bluebell), Tony Bill (Eleven Snowflake), Claude Akins (Lobo Jackson), Victor Jory (Wounded Bear), Victor French (Rafferty), Rodolfo Acosta (Storekeeper), Don Collier (Mike Lyons), Susana Miranda (Ann Looking Deer), Anthony Caruso (Silver Dollar)

Follow Me (Universal, 1971); US: *The Public Eye*
Producer: Hal B. Wallis
Screenplay: Peter Shaffer, from his play *The Public Eye*
Cinematographer: Christopher Challis
Art Director: Robert Cartwright
Music: John Barry
Editor: Anne Coates
Cast: Mia Farrow (Belinda), Topol (Julian Christoforou), Michael Jayston (Charles Sidley), Margaret Rawlings (Mrs Sidley), Annette Crosbie (Miss Framer), Dudley Foster (Mr Mayhew), Michael Aldridge (Sir Philip Crouch), Gabrielle Brune (Lady Crouch), Michael Barrington (Mr Scrampton), Neil McCarthy (Parkinson)

Index